9-20-60   54-12171   Mc Gee

POLITICS IN AMERICA

Books by D. W. Brogan

GOVERNMENT OF THE PEOPLE

ABRAHAM LINCOLN

FRANCE UNDER THE REPUBLIC

POLITICS AND LAW IN THE UNITED STATES

THE ENGLISH PEOPLE

THE AMERICAN CHARACTER

THE FREE STATE

FRENCH PERSONALITIES AND PROBLEMS

AMERICAN THEMES

THE PRICE OF REVOLUTION

POLITICS IN AMERICA

POLITICS
IN
AMERICA

by
D. W. Brogan

HARPER & BROTHERS, PUBLISHERS
New York

POLITICS IN AMERICA

Copyright, 1954, by D. W. Brogan
Printed in the United States of America

All rights in this book are reserved.
No part of the book may be used or reproduced
in any manner whatsoever without written permission except in the case of brief quotations
embodied in critical articles and reviews. For
information address Harper & Brothers
49 East 33rd Street, New York 16, N. Y.

For permission to reprint, the following acknowledgments are
made to

The Macmillan Company (New York) for "Bryan, Bryan,
Bryan, Bryan" from *The Collected Poems* of Vachel Lindsay,
Copyright, 1948, by The Macmillan Company

Sheed & Ward, Inc., for a verse from *Sonnets and Verse* by
Hilaire Belloc.

This book is published in England
under the title of *An Introduction to American Politics*

Library of Congress catalog card number: 54-12171

To
THEODORA HILL

CONTENTS

PREFACE

THE purpose of this book is simply to make the American political system intelligible. It has no thesis except that the system has its own logic, its own justification and is, in general, a success. It cannot be easily altered (despite the adoption since the end of the first world war of five constitutional amendments). This system, too, should be studied in its own terms; its successes and failures seen in their American context.

The system, too, is studied in its national or federal aspects; state and local politics are only dealt with as far as they affect national politics. Of course, a dispute in Dogpatch may affect Congress and even the presidency but I have not tried to describe the politics even of a state like New York or California. Nor have I dealt with American institutions in a rigidly systematic way. Some institutions have more than one kind of importance; I have tried to deal with each type of importance. I have tried to describe institutions and practices as soon as they appear but, in some cases, I have postponed a fuller discussion to a later section of the book, when the fuller account is made more intelligible by what has gone before.

I owe warm thanks not only to the authors who have allowed me to quote from them but to the scores, hundreds of Americans from whom I have learned so much.

D. W. BROGAN

Washington's Birthday, 1954

Chapter One

THE CHARACTER OF THE AMERICAN POLITY

I

THE American Constitution is the oldest written constitution in existence. It can claim, indeed, to be the first constitution in the modern world, and that it has survived so long is a tribute to the sagacity, moderation, and sense of the possible shown by its makers. When it went into effect in 1789, the French monarchy still stood; there was a Holy Roman Emperor, a Venetian Republic and a Dutch Republic, an Autocrat in St. Petersburg, a Sultan-Caliph in Constantinople, an Emperor vested with the 'mandate of Heaven' in Pekin and a Shogun ruling the hermit empire of Japan in the name of a secluded, impotent and almost unknown Mikado.

Even in countries where formal political continuity has been preserved, it can plausibly be maintained that far greater changes have taken place in the political realities, if not in the forms, than have taken place in the United States. Queen Elizabeth II and King Gustaf Adolf VI hold offices far less like those of their predecessors of 1789, than the office held by General Eisenhower is like the office held by General Washington. Forms and realities have changed less in the United States than in any other political organization, even than in Tibet.[1]

Duration is not the only political virtue, but it is a virtue. Constitutions, by their name and function, can be deemed successes

[1] General Eisenhower took, in 1953, exactly the same oath as did General Washington in 1789.

only if they last long enough to give stability to the political life of the society they are supposed to serve. The American Constitution passes that test. But a constitution can survive in a form that makes it less and less adequate for the needs of the society it purports to serve, and either that society is cribbed, cabined and confined, held within an armour that forbids adaptation or growth, or the constitution is disregarded and the true political forces grow up beside it, paying only lip service to the antique and obsolete forms, as Prussia grew up in the carapace of the constitution of the Holy Roman Empire of the German People. That has not happened in the United States. The Constitution is still at the centre of American government and politics. It must be reckoned with every day by the President, by the Congress, by the Courts, by labour, by business. It has proved sufficiently adaptable to permit the expansion of the thin line of newly emancipated colonies along the Atlantic seaboard to the Pacific, the multiplication of the population fifty-fold and the extension of the armed power of the United States almost round the globe. It has permitted the growth of these remote and, in 1789, impoverished colonies to an economic power and a material wealth unprecedented in human history. And it has done all this without distorting its fundamental character or denying the political theories and system of values on which it was based.

The American Constitution has been a success; so Americans think, so the reflective portion of non-American mankind must concede. But because that Constitution has been a success, it has acquired in the eyes of those who have best reason to know how successful it has been, 'The People of the United States', a claim to reverence, to uncritical acceptance, that has no parallel in the world. For it should be remembered that the United States is based on this written document, that the shrine in which it and the Declaration of Independence are housed, has the same claim on American religious awe as Westminster Abbey and the Stone of Destiny have for the English, that the sacred *ampoule* of Reims had for the French before the cutting of the thread of French history in 1789.[1]

[1] Until 1952, these two documents were kept in an illuminated shrine in the Library of Congress. They are now housed in the National Archives building in a stronghold believed adequate to protect not only against the moth, the rust, the thieves, but the atom bomb.

There are other constitutions and other constitutional documents. But they are not foundation documents as is the Constitution of the United States. Magna Charta is not the birth certificate of England. The British North America Act is not the birth certificate of Canada; it is the record of the terms on which other colonies joined themselves to Canada. The name of Australia, to some degree the fact of Australia, existed before the Commonwealth of Australia was called into existence by an act of the British Parliament. But 'We the People of the United States' came into existence either in 1776 or 1789, not before and not otherwise than in these two documents.[1]

The consequences of an identifiable birth of the United States not merely certified by, but caused by, the issuance and acceptance of these documents are great and permanent. Even if the Declaration of Independence has no legal effect in America, its declaration of truths held to be self-evident—'That all men are created equal, that they are endowed by their Creator with certain unalienable rights, that among these are Life, Liberty and the Pursuit of Happiness' has been and is of incalculable importance. It is this declaration of purposes and principles that creates what Gunnar Myrdal has called 'the American dilemma', the contrast between promise and performance. That contrast, in the American political religion, as in the religion of St. Paul, produces tensions, repentance and better performance. The preamble to the Constitution has no legal force either. Yet the phrases 'We the People of the United States, in order to form a more perfect Union, establish Justice, insure domestic

[1] It has been plausibly held that the phrase with which the Constitution opens, 'We the People of the United States' did not describe and was not meant to describe any 'people' existing in 1787 when the Constitution was drafted, but was shorthand for the names of the peoples of the states then existing who might, by accepting the Constitution, create 'The People of the United States'. It might be held by the pedantic that the Articles of Confederation in 1781 are the first constitution, the present operative document being an elaborate amendment of the earlier. That, if true, would merely show that there were three, not two, fundamental documents to consider. But the Articles of Confederation, in life or in death, never evoked any of the admiration or adoration given, after a time, to the Constitution, and that is the political fact which we are considering.

Tranquility, provide for the common Defence, promote the general Welfare, and secure the Blessings of Liberty to ourselves and our Posterity, do ordain and establish this Constitution for the United States of America', have made history and effective law. 'The People of the United States,' in part at least, exists because it was so named in the bond. The Union is more perfect because the People was called on to form a more perfect Union and the general welfare has been sought and in great degree promoted, because that was laid down in 1787 as one main duty of the new polity.[1]

One result of this concentration of attention and of reverence on a document which is a formal law has been to give to the political life of 'the People of the United States' a peculiarly legal, often a pedantically legal character. There, in this known document, is the sole source of the power of the government of the United States. Behind that document may lie the unlimited power of 'the People of the United States', but since 1789, that People has seen itself embodied, has seen its will expressed only through this document.

The importance of this legal way of looking at political problems was never made more manifest than in the period when the Constitution was most manifestly failing to promote or preserve a 'more perfect Union'. For both sides in the Civil War appealed to the Constitution. Jefferson Davis did not claim to act on the unalienable right of 'the People to alter or abolish . . . any government destructive of the ends for which it was formed', which the Declaration of Independence had declared to be one of the bases of free government. He claimed to be acting on a true interpretation of the Constitution of the United States and on the authority of its makers, the Peoples of the States. And Lincoln did not retort, even after the Emancipation Proclamation, that he was waging war for the establishment of the unalienable rights of man, of which liberty was

[1] The 'general Welfare' referred to in the preamble is often confused by the man in the street (and by at least one President, Franklin D. Roosevelt) with the 'general Welfare' referred to in Article I, Section 8 of the Constitution. 'The Congress shall have power to lay and collect, Taxes, Duties, Imposts and Excises, to pay the Debts and provide for the common Defence and general Welfare of the United States.' Courts and most lawyers distinguish between the pious aspiration of the Preamble and the specific and more limited power granted in this section, but the average American has confused the two, with important political consequences.

one. He, too, was concerned with the rights and duties given him and imposed on him by the Constitution which he had sworn 'faithfully [to] execute'. He might, in the Second Inaugural, when both slavery and secession were visibly doomed, see in this terrible war the due punishment of national sin. But divine vengeance on national sin is not a doctrine to be found in the Constitution of the United States, nor, we may assume, did many Americans, North or South, accept it even as a religious doctrine, as Lincoln well knew.

More instances could be given to show the permanence of this legal-constitutional approach and more will be given in their proper place. All that it is needful to insist on here, is that the American people, after more than a century and a half of experience, is as much as ever convinced that, within the framework of that Constitution and in no other way, lies political salvation for them. This may be a foolish doctrine but it is the doctrine, the living political faith of the American people. That faith is shown in another way, in the acceptance of the idea that the normal extension of the territorial authority of the United States is by the accession or creation of new states, with the same powers, the same duties, the same general political character as the original thirteen founders. There was no absolute necessity for the application of this doctrine. The remoter territories could have been kept in a tutelary condition for long periods. They could have been admitted on inferior terms; discrimination could have been made between state and state (and more power or less accorded to the various states in consequence). But with a deep and justified confidence in the adequacy and powers of expansion of the American system, the thirteen states have been increased to forty-eight, despite the fears and ambitions of spokesmen for states and sections. The system is not yet complete; outlying territories like Alaska, Hawaii and Puerto Rico are not yet admitted to the sisterhood, but if they remain in the Union, their day will come and come soon, for the system has its own logic and its own power of compelling action.[1] This unity has been dearly

---

[1] There is a marked difference in British and American 'imperial' theory. British theory accepts, even rejoices in, differences, in anomalies, in the tax autonomy of the Isle of Man, in the indescribable relation to the Commonwealth, of the Republic of India (or the even more indescribable relationship of the Republic of Ireland to Great Britain). American

bought and has, in its practical effects, often been resented. Even in a small, homogeneous, easily defined society, there are local interests and there are stresses and strains arising from them. How much more is this true of a country the size of all Europe (including European Russia), with a population of 160,000,000 scattered, in very differing degrees of density, over 3,000,000 square miles, over an area with climate and resources ranging from those of Finland to those of Andalusia, even of Egypt! It is not surprising that the Union still needs perfecting; what is surprising is the degree of union attained. And the great emotional tragedy of American history, the war that stirs the deepest emotions, is still the Civil War that came when other ends than unity were preferred.

The memory of the breakdown of political sagacity and political discipline that resulted in the Civil War is not the only reason for the formal conservatism of much of American political life, for an antiquarianism which may be harmless, but often is not. Like all great political peoples, like the Romans and the English, the Americans understand the need for maintaining forms. The political augurs may smile as they meet each other in the cloakrooms of Congress or in hotel rooms at national conventions, but it is a rash man who abolishes a ritual merely because it is obsolete and serves no immediately visible 'practical' function (as if the maintenance of political habits of loyalty and cooperation were not practical in the highest degree).

The phrase 'the People of the United States' is a phrase that, at any given moment, is not free from ambiguity. The Constitution was framed, among other reasons, to 'secure the Blessings of Liberty to ourselves and our Posterity', but it has extended these blessings to many millions who are not the posterity of the Founders or of their contemporaries. Probably more than half of the American people, in 1954, are descended from immigrants who have entered the United States since 1789. Nearly a tenth of the present inhabitants of the United States were born outside its boundaries (in the not remote past, the proportion was higher); nearly a third of the

---

theory and practice, like French imperial theory, prefer assimilation, uniformity of powers and institutions. Of course there is a further difference between the French and American theories of expansion; the French is mainly theory, the American is a theory put into practice.

present population are only one or, at most, two generations deep in the United States.

It is natural and right, then, that such a political society should rely on verbal affirmations, on formal organization of loyalty, of national feeling, should see allegiance, not as an accident of birth, but as an exercise of will, should preach, out of necessity as well as taste, a political religion, set up a political church outside which there is, in America, no salvation. The United States did not just come into existence over a long period of time. It was made in what is, historically, a brief period of time and by conscious will. The Americans (even before they existed as a body politic) willed to exist as an independent group of republics, of 'cities' in the antique sense, before becoming the United States created by the Constitution.[1]

And not only is there present the element of will, there is absent the element of the traditional, the time-hallowed, the charismatic. The United States has a birthday, so there is a pre-United States yet American past. But 1776 is a very different date from 1066 or 1789. King Alfred and St. Joan both antedate the two great years of English and French history. A society expanding so rapidly in area and in numbers, accepting new states and new peoples, was and is in danger of internal dissolution, as the Roman Republic and the Roman hegemony in Italy were weakened and finally destroyed. Yet more strange streams have flowed into the Hudson and Mississippi, from Europe, from Africa, from other parts of America, than ever flowed from Orontes into Tiber. The making of Americans has been a continuous task. And as Augustus tried to give the deliquescent Roman society of his time a basis in the habits and traditions of an older and healthier age, so the Americans have continually borne in mind the precept of Ennius, given long before Augustus:

Moribus antiquis res stat Romana virisque.

Yet the maintenance of the ancient ways is attempted under special difficulties. There is no hereditary monarchy to canalize emotion, especially female emotion; there is no established church; there is no naturally accepted hierarchy; there is no real national capital,

[1] The Latin title of the United States brings out this antique view of the constituting states, 'Civitates Americae Foederatae.'

concentrating within itself the leaders in politics, the arts, business, conspicuous consumption. Although, as will be shown, the American people are today far more 'religious' than are most of the peoples of western Europe, their government is formally 'Godless'.[1] Nor has the United States, until very recent times, known the solidifying pressure of outside danger or rivalry. Its exterior history has been a series of happy solutions (from the American point of view) of exterior problems, none of them, except the acquisition of both sides of the Mississippi by the Louisiana Purchase and the extension to the Pacific by the Mexican War and the Oregon settlement with Britain, of any great importance. No amount of patriotic oratory about the iniquities of Britain, Germany or, today, Russia, has ever been as effectual, politically speaking, as the evocation of the memories of the Civil War, the 'waving of the bloody shirt' in the North and in the South alike. And that evocation of the past made for disunity, not unity.

Moreover, the United States was founded by a Revolution and based on a revolutionary theory. It is easy to forget that today, when the word 'revolution' is no longer blessed like Mesopotamia, or has been taken over by revolutionaries who dismiss the principles of the Declaration of Independence and the practices of the Constitution as bourgeois confidence tricks played on a gullible proletariat. So much that was new, daring, and dangerous in 1776 is commonplace or repudiated today. But the fact remains that it was new then.[2] That 'all Governments derive their just powers from the

[1] The inscription 'In God We Trust' was put on the coins during the Civil War by the Secretary of the Treasury, that eminent Episcopalian layman, Salmon P. Chase. Before the Civil War and after there were many attempts to 'put God into the Constitution', but they have all failed. The United States in theory is 'laïc'. It might be noted that in the Constitution of the Confederate States, one of the few changes made on the original constitution was the insertion of the name of God. In that preamble 'the People of the Confederate States, each State acting in its sovereign and independent character' invoked 'the favor and guidance of Almighty God'. This was not accorded.

[2] 'The story of the revolted colonies impresses us first and most distinctly as the supreme manifestation of the law of resistance, as the abstract revolution in its purest and most perfect shape. No people was so free as the insurgents; no government less oppressive than the government which they overthrew. Those who deem Washington and Hamil-

consent of the governed' is not, in 1954, a self-evident truth. But old-fashioned Americans like Senator Hoar who held to the Jeffersonian dogma against innovators like Senator Beveridge, knew the temper of the American people better than did the imperialists who found 'manifest destiny' in the Philippines. The ancestral voices (and other causes) were enough, in the not very long run, to end the American dream of empire. Nor has the basic premise of the equality of man been ineffectual in the long run. It was the Jeffersonian dogma that Lincoln appealed to, at Gettysburg, when he asked himself and the world whether a 'nation conceived in liberty and dedicated to the proposition that all men are created equal . . . could long endure'. It did endure, but at a terrible cost, and the equality dogma of the Declaration is still (like the more perfect Union) in the making, not made. Americans know that their freedom was brought at a great price, even though they were formally born free and equal. They still think, with Emerson, that it was not mere provincial vanity to elevate the skirmish at Concord bridge in 1775 to one of the great events of human history.[1] They think

---

ton honest can apply the term to few European statesmen. Their example presents a thorn, not a cushion, and threatens all existing political forms, with the doubtful exception of the federal constitution of 1787. It teaches that men ought to be in arms even against a remote and constructive danger to their freedom; that even if the cloud is no bigger than a man's hand, it is their right and duty to stake the national existence, to sacrifice lives and fortunes, to cover the country with a lake of blood, to shatter crowns and sceptres and fling parliaments into the sea. On this principle of subversion they erected their commonwealth, and by its virtue lifted the world out of its orbit and assigned a new course to history. Here or nowhere we have the broken chain, the rejected past, precedent and statute superseded by unwritten law, sons wiser than their fathers, ideas rooted in the future, reason cutting as clean as Atropos.' Lord Acton's review, in 1889, of Bryce's *American Commonwealth,* reprinted in *Bryce's American Commonwealth Fiftieth Anniversary* (1939), edited by Robert C. Brooks, p. 201. These are not the views of all Americans today about their Revolution, but Jefferson, even Washington, would be as much out of place at a meeting of the 'Daughters of the American Revolution' as any accidentally surviving old Bolshevik in the Kremlin of 1954.

[1] By the rude bridge that arched the flood,
Their flag to April's breeze unfurled,
Here once the embattled farmers stood,
And fired the shot heard round the world.

that the July days of 1776, like the July days of 1789 and the
October days of 1917, are 'days that shook the world'. They are
conscious that their history, their destiny, has set them a little apart
from the rest of the world, even from that part of it with which they
have the closest spiritual and blood ties. They are unmoved, then,
when it is pointed out to them that much of their life, much of
their attitude to social and political problems, is different from that
of Europe. They remember, emotionally, if not intellectually, that
the Founders chose as a motto for the new political society, 'novus
ordo seclorum', a new order of the ages. They are not surprised that
this vaulting ambition should have been justified, creating a new
political order, not to be judged by some ideal pattern laid up in
Heaven or Westminster. 1776 was a new order and, inevitably, it
had new and original political consequences.[1]

It follows from this, that the study of American political organization and method imposes on the European student a humility
before the facts that may not come easily. Even if his admiration
for the British Constitution is as warm and uncritical as that of
Burke, Macaulay or Woodrow Wilson, he must remember that he
is inspecting a system based on different principles and formed by a
different experience. He must be willing to learn, to assess, to judge,
by human standards, indeed, but human standards that have a new
embodiment. He must be willing to notice the extraordinary
phenomena he is studying, without reacting like the farmer who
saw the giraffe and said 'impossible'. *Sic fortis Etruria crevit.* Thus
and not otherwise did America grow. No one can deny the growth
or should refuse to the study of the political conditions of that
growth at least the courtesy of a suspended judgment.

II

Every nation, every lasting political movement, needs its legends;
its Romulus and Remus, its Alfred and the cakes, its Washington

---

[1] Anticipating the first French Republic and outdaring the Bolsheviks,
the Americans date all important official documents by the 'Year of Our
Lord and of the Independence of the United States'. (Thus 1954 A.D. 'and
of the Independence of the United States, the one hundred and seventy-
seventh'.)

and the cherry tree. The United States, in addition to the personal legends, improbable or unproven, the common change of patriotic fiction, has also the legend of the Constitution. And at no time since the adoption of the Constitution has the legend lacked enthusiastic and uncritical believers until, today, only a dissident and mainly academic minority doubt that, this Constitution supplies the ideal solution of the American political problem whose basic rightness is not to be questioned—and a solution that would equally well serve the rest of the world had they the wisdom and virtue to adopt it.[1]

That after more than a hundred and fifty years of experience of the instrument of government drafted in 1787 and put into effect in 1789, the American people should still hold these views of its merits, hold them more firmly and universally, indeed, in the first term of General Eisenhower than in the first term of General Washington, is a tribute to the merits of the Constitution. The proof of the pudding is in the eating.

But the universal loyalty of the American people to the Constitution is not due solely to the experience of its merits. It is due also to an historical version of its origin that, despite acute historical criticism, remains part of the political religion of all sensible American political men and women. In that historical tradition, the Constitution was the culmination of a beneficent process of which the independence of the United States was the first stage. By the Declaration of Independence, the United States cut itself off from the old, tyrannical, decadent society of Europe. By the Constitution, it secured the fruits of the Declaration for the makers of the Revolution and for their posterity. For the Constitution was represented by its makers at the time of its presentation to the people (or peoples) of the thirteen independent states, and has been seen ever since, not merely as a frame of government, but as a means of social and political salvation. It is not a mere 'lay-out' of political powers like the constitutions of France, Ireland, Canada. It has been in the past and is now the means of salvation for 'The

---

[1] This conviction is so deep rooted that far more Americans than it is easy to realize, still believe that South American states with formal constitutions modelled on that of the United States are more 'free' than Canada and that the political institutions of the 'Republic' of Liberia are more advanced than those of the 'colony' of the Gold Coast.

People of the United States'. And its adoption is seen not only as a successful political manoeuvre, but as a great battle gained in a moment of great danger. The Constitution is a combination of Magna Charta and the Battle of Britain. Were it not seen in this light, it would be more critically regarded.

This view generally held in 1953 was not quite so generally held in 1787 when the text was produced, nor in 1788 when eleven states adopted it as the fundamental law of the United States. But the American Revolution is seen quite as much as a 'bloc' as Clemenceau saw the French Revolution, and the Constitution is both corner-stone and coping-stone.

To understand this attitude, it is necessary to grasp, from the beginning, that the American Revolution was a real revolution, not only in its doctrinal bases, as Acton pointed out, but in its conduct and social and economic results. It is peculiarly difficult for Englishmen to accept this fact since they think (and are taught at school to think) of the American Revolution as the 'War of American Independence', a war lost simply, as the authors of *1066 and All That* put it, because 'the allies were on the other side'. Nor is this all, for it has been convenient for a great political and historical party to make the breach between the Mother Country and the colonies an incident in a struggle common to both 'English-speaking' countries. On this theory, Fox and Washington were fight-ing the same battle, each wearing the 'buff and blue' of the common cause. The methods were a little different. Throwing the tea into Boston Harbour was not quite the same thing as the Middlesex election, but each was an episode in the same general movement of events. The Americans might call their share in these events a 'revolution', but it was a safe, controlled, political adjustment re-calling more the sagacious methods of the English Revolution of 1688 than the 'red, fool, furies of the Seine' of 1789. It was, too, in a sense, an accidental revolution. With more sagacity on one side and a little more restraint on the other, it might have been avoided altogether and what is now the United States be what India was once called, 'the brightest jewel in the crown'.[1]

[1] I am not asserting that there was no revolutionary crisis in the Eng-land of George III, merely pointing out that there was an actual revolu-tion in America.

It is certain that some of the makers of the American Revolution were concerned at first with the control and only later resolved on the overthrow of imperial power, whether that power was parliamentary or royal. It is certain that some were not even then concerned with the overthrow of British power and were less leaders than led. But even if these conservatives had been the only leaders—and they were not—even if there had not been root-and-branch men, determined to cut the imperial painter long before they avowed their intentions, the inner logic of all revolutions was at work. Once the idea of the solution by violence, the resolve to break the most powerful ally of any government, the mere habit of obedience, became first prevalent and then triumphant, the Revolution was out of hand. It was no longer a matter of redressing specific grievances, but of recasting a society.[1] That such an upheaval was not foreseen or wanted by most of the leaders of the Revolution is likely. But one thing they could not foresee or control was the duration of the war. It is only in a farce that men set out, knowingly, for the Hundred Years War. None of the 'embattled farmers' of 1775, nor any of the members of the Boston Caucus Club can have foreseen that the war then begun would last for more than seven years. That, alone, accounted in great part for

---

[1] This point has been most admirably put by a great American scholar. 'It is indeed true that our Revolution was strikingly unlike that of France, and that most of those who originated it had no other than a political programme, and would have considered its work done when political independence of Great Britain had been secured. But who can say to the waves of revolution: Thus far shall we go and no farther? The various fibres of a nation's life are knit together in great complexity. It is impossible to sever some without also loosening others, and setting them free to combine anew in widely different forms. The Americans were much more conservative than the French. But their political and social systems, though both were, as the great orator said, still in the gristle and not yet hardened into the bone of manhood, were too intimately connected to permit that one should remain unchanged while the other was radically altered. The stream of revolution, once started, could not be confined within narrow banks, but spread abroad upon the land. Many economic desires, many social aspirations were set free by the political struggle, many aspects of colonial society profoundly altered by the forces thus let loose.' J. Franklin Jameson, *The American Revolution Considered as a Social Movement* (1926), pp. 10–11.

the dissolution of the old order. That alone accounted in great part for the character of the internal revolution. The war had to be financed and it was financed by ruinous inflation, with its usual results, the destruction of the old settled economic order. In all wars some men do well and some do ill. The Tories who were expelled to Canada or England were replaced by men and families no more radical or revolutionary than the Tories were, but luckier in their choice of side or of no side.[1]

The Virginian planters who escaped paying their debts to the Scottish factors, the new owners of Tory lands, the holders of State and 'Continental' i.e. United States' securities and paper, the heroes and profiteers of the Revolution had much to gain by stabilizing the new *status quo*. Not all of the beneficiaries of the Revolution were 'big men'. But even where there was a great redistribution of land, it was found, as it was to be found in France a few years later, that those already well off did better than those starting from scratch and some of the latter did worse than they would have done had there been no revolution. The De Lancey estate was forfeited, but of the 175 odd purchasers of the West Farm sixty-nine 'gentlemen', 'esquires' and the like bought seventy-five per cent of the land.[2]

Yet however adroit the great beneficiaries of the overthrow of the old order were, the fact that there *had* been an overthrow had

[1] An admirable example of the impact of the Revolution on the social structure of Massachusetts is furnished by the complaints of the exiled Richard Lechmere of Cambridge (Mass.). His 'real estate at Cambridge was sold to Mr. Cabot'; his 'attorney, Mr. Lowell', through Chambers Russell, told him, in 1787, just before the meeting of the Constitutional Convention, that 'his confiscated lands cannot be restored to him'. E. Alfred Jones, *The Loyalists of Massachusetts, Their Memorials, Petitions and Claims* (1930), p. 190.

[2] 'Isaac Roosevelt, one of the most noted Whigs of the time, . . . purchased over 140 lots, Nicholas Gouverneur . . . bought in with Lewis Ogden and Peter Hill, 204 lots. . . . John Delafield, who came to the United States after the Revolution, . . . acquired 50 lots'. Harry B. Yoshpe, *The Disposition of Loyalist Estates in the Southern District of New York* (1939), p. 31. As Dr. Yoshpe points out: 'De Lancey's tenants were not even given the benefit of purchase extended to tenant-farmers by the confiscatory legislation. Forced into competition with wealthy merchants and land-jobbers, many were stripped of their holdings'. *Ibid* p. 33.

obvious and dangerous possibilities. Royal authority in the colonies had been based in great part on mere habit, mere tradition. That habit, that tradition had been broken. The authority of colonial governments had been barely adequate for the simple tasks they set themselves. The authority of their revolutionary successors was not any greater, at any rate after the first few, enthusiastic months of optimistic discounting of the triumphs of Lexington and Bunker Hill. The 'Continental Congress' was no national legislature; it was a mere party committee and the new State governments were, in their turn, committees of the Revolutionary party. Their authority was contested not only by the numerous Tories who did not emigrate, but, in effect, by the passive majority that was neither for King George nor for the United States. It was not merely a matter of States ignoring or only slackly answering the appeals for men, money, supplies that poured out from the perambulating Congress.[1] Only French aid, first covert, then open, kept the patriots or rebels in the field. The British army had, for most of the war, the support of a British fleet in local command of the sea. Thus all the coastal areas were open to raids and to invasion and this would have been a menace to the authority of a much better established government than that which had declared its independence in 1776.[2]

---

[1] Congress was often on the move, sometimes chivied by British troops, sometimes looking for hospitality. It should be remembered that every large American city, at some time or other in the Revolutionary War, fell into British hands. Boston, New York, Philadelphia, Charleston, Savannah were all under King George's authority for greater or longer periods while the new Revolutionary governments were barred from the capitals of the colonies or states they professed to rule. Jefferson, as Governor of Virginia, was not only chased out of the new capital of Richmond, but driven to hasty flight from his own home of Monticello. New York was in British hands from 1776 till 1783. The State government of New York was lodged in rural villages, exercising authority limited in space and depth.

[2] It should be remembered that the much better-established government of President Madison, under the Constitution of 1789, ran into many of the difficulties of the government of the Continental Congress. Indeed, the rout at Bladensburg in 1814 which delivered Washington over to the victorious army of General Ross, was far more disgraceful than the battles unavailingly fought, in 1776, to save New York and, in 1777, to save Philadelphia.

Not until the French fleet established a temporary command of the sea could the war be ended and the new states get breathing time. It is not merely because of formal British recognition of independence that 1783 is one of the decisive dates in American history, but because it marked the beginning of a period of recuperation from the inevitable and not totally destructive disorder of the Revolution and the inevitable and totally destructive disorder of the Revolutionary War.

Like many other peoples, before and since, the Americans, in 1783, identified victory and peace with Utopia. They had, to the surprise of the world and, for many Americans, of themselves, defied Britain successfully. They saw the world open to them for trade, for since they had come to believe that the old colonial system was totally to their disadvantage, they naturally assumed that its destruction would be totally to their advantage. They soon discovered that they were wrong. After some hesitation, the British government refused to admit the successful rebels to the benefits of imperial preference. Their trade with the West Indies was harassed by zealous young officers like Horatio Nelson; their shipping lost its privileged position. The old imperial order was destroyed; Glasgow was temporarily ruined; but this was inadequate compensation for the economic difficulties of Virginia and Massachusetts.

Again, behaving like other people, the Americans impoverished by the war, cut off from their normal sources of supply, went on a buying spree. They, like Samuel Johnson's young man, 'showed the spirit of an heir'. They bought more than they could pay for and a sterling gap soon developed. But there was now no generous ally to extend a precursor of Marshall aid. The French king did make one last gesture; the Dutch hazarded a loan; but the main creditor was England who apparently suffered less from her defeat than France and the United States did from their victory. By 1785, disillusion was general. The credit of the Confederacy was almost nil; the credit of most States and most individuals was no better.

It is obvious, today, that the United States was suffering from causes that no simple political remedy could have cured. The impoverishment wrought by the war was real. The difficulties caused by the unkind conduct of the quondam mother country were real. The trade cycle was at work after the triumphant

Revolutionary War, as it had been after the triumphant end of the 'French and Indian War'.[1]

But the responsibility for these distresses was not imputed by those who suffered from them, to the nature of things. It was imputed, with more and more emphasis, to the form of government that the insurgent States had given themselves as the war drew to an end.

This first constitution of the United States has had, almost from its adoption, a bad press. Finally accepted by the Congress at the end of 1777, it was not adopted by all the states till 1781 when, in February, the long-reluctant state of Maryland at last ratified the 'Articles of Confederation'. Had they been ratified in 1778, they might have been amended as their undoubted inadequacy, for war if not for peace, was made evident. But by 1781, the prestige of Congress had evaporated and it was to Congress that the Articles gave what federal power there was. But by 1781, all real prestige and almost all real power was in the army and in its head, General Washington, if only because of the trust reposed in him by the agents of the French king whose subsidies, not to speak of his fleet and army, alone kept the American enterprise from collapsing. Had the Articles gone into effect before this transfer of real authority, service in Congress might have been more attractive. As it was, it had become almost impossible to persuade citizens of weight in their respective States to serve. And, as the history of the new government under the Constitution of 1787 was to show, the presence of most of the accepted leaders of the States in various branches of the new government was of fundamental importance. Their absence in 1781 was equally important, the other way round.

The coming of peace brought no new accession of strength to the federal 'government'. The necessities of winning the war did impose a minimum of unity on the States and so gave some support to the body that formally represented their common interests. But the coming of peace removed the sense of danger and the only active pressure towards unity.

Again, the Congress under the Articles was faced with a task, political as well as economic, that might have wrecked any government. For example, the Congress could legislate about the organi-

[1] Called in Britain and Europe 'The Seven Years War'.

zation of the western lands transferred to the United States by those
States with rights or claims to the trans-Alleghany regions. But the
settlement, the protection, the development of those lands had
been a problem taxing the resources and wisdom of the imperial
government and its attempts to deal with the problem had been
one of the causes of the Revolution. British power was still
represented in the West, at Detroit and at other forts held in
defiance of the Peace Treaty. With the visible weakness of the
'United States' to encourage them, the British government was in
no mood or need to make concessions, or even accord rights, and
this failure alienated both the pioneer on the frontier and the
speculator in western lands in Philadelphia or New York or Mount
Vernon. The first efforts of the government under *the* Constitution
to deal with the Indians met with military disaster and disgrace.
Not until 1795 did Anthony Wayne undo the errors of St. Clair
and not, indeed, till the war of 1812, did Harrison and Jackson
finally destroy Indian military power. And it was not till 1795, that
the new government under President Washington, was able, by
making what many Americans thought, then and since, a very
poor bargain, to get the British out of Detroit, although Britain
was now desperately engaged with a far more formidable France
than that of the Most Christian King. Again, it can be argued that
not until the Peace of Ghent in 1815, was the problem of British
intervention among the Northwest Indians settled at last.

Another problem that bedevilled the peace and reputation of the
Confederacy was the American claim to free navigation of the Mississippi. This claim was hardly less of a nuisance to the governments
of the first two Presidents and, if it was solved by the purchase of
'Louisiana' by the third, that solution was as much due to the needs
of the First Consul, General Bonaparte, as to the diplomatic and,
possibly, unconstitutional boldness of the third President, Mr.
Jefferson. The examples could be multiplied. The Confederation
was faced with a series of external problems that were, almost
certainly, given the balance of forces at that time, insoluble by any
conceivable American government.

The same can be said of the main charge against the governmental
system of the Congress. It did not collect taxes directly; it had to
assess the States and ask, then beg, then grovel to get the assessments

met. But, again, it may be doubted whether the power to levy direct taxes would have been highly fruitful in the war years and in the immediate post-war years. For the States, which *had* direct taxing powers, were often unable to use them. The correspondence of Jefferson as Governor of Virginia shows him as much plagued by county rights as Congress was by States' rights. New York, ravaged by British troops and partisans, was in no better case.[1]

Since it was by stressing and, indeed, exaggerating the weaknesses of the government of the United States under the Articles that it was possible to induce Congress to sanction the Constitutional Convention of 1787; since it was by continuing that campaign inside the secret deliberations of the Convention that something like unity was achieved; and, lastly, since it was by making the flesh creep after the Convention had called on conventions of the States to ratify, that, narrowly, the victory for the New Constitution was won; it was natural that the real merits of the Articles should have been hidden from subsequent generations.

That the opposition to the new Constitution was widespread was indeed admitted but explained away.[2] That the ratification was secured by something like sharp practice, as well as by promising to rectify an omission, the failure to provide a 'Bill of Rights', was also admitted. But the peccadillos of the Fathers were as nothing in comparison with the dangers from which they saved the United States. This, it was asserted, was 'the Critical Period' of American history. 'Thomas Paine was sadly mistaken when, in the moment of exultation over the peace, he declared that the trying time was ended. The most trying time of all was just beginning. It is not too much to say that the period of five years following the peace of

[1] ' After thus reviewing the history of these six years we see that the real cause of financial impotency in New York was not the unwillingness of the Legislators to vote taxes or turn the proceeds over to Congress, but the inability of the county officers to get the money. It forms a striking example of the weakness of the *State* governmental machinery during the Revolution, a point often overlooked because of the more obvious weakness of Congress. It leads us to some rather interesting speculations as to whether Congress might not have been able to govern tolerably well had the States been able to perform their part equally well'. Thomas C. Cochran, *New York in the Confederation* (1932), p. 55–6.

[2] See pp. 21 *et seqq.*

1783 was the most critical moment in all the history of the American people. The dangers from which we were saved in 1788 were even greater than the dangers from which we were saved in 1865.'[1] It is, in fact, much too much to say anything of the kind and it is worth noting one reason for its being said. The parallel with the Civil War was deliberately drawn by Fiske to accentuate the importance of the tradition of Union, then feeble, now so over-whelmingly strong. The Union, indeed, was now possibly too strong, as it had been too weak a century before, but the lesson taught by the years that followed the Peace of Versailles (1783) must never be forgotten.[2]

[1] John Fiske, *The Critical Period of American History*, p. 55. This famous piece of 'high vulgarization' of history was published in 1888, a hundred years after the ratification of the Constitution, when a certain amount of patriotic excess was permissible. But the phrase, and its implications, stuck for a long time and, to some degree, stick still.

[2] Fiske was, by 1888, if not quite a Mugwump, at any rate enough above party feeling to admire a Democratic President, Grover Cleveland. But the emphasis on the enduring achievement of the framers of the Constitution, on the prophetic souls who saw a nation where others saw only an assemblage of sovereign states, had party advantages for partisan scholars like Henry Cabot Lodge. His preface to his edition of Hamilton's *Works* is significant and representative. 'Two schools of political thought have existed in the United States, and their struggle for supremacy has made the history of the country. One was the national school, the other was the school of States'-Rights. . . . One was founded by Alexander Hamilton, the other by Thomas Jefferson. On the one side, it was maintained that the United States ought to be and were a nation; on the other, that the Union was a confederacy. The conflict between these opposing forces began at the close of the revolution, was ardent in the convention which framed the constitution, continued with ever-increasing intensity for seventy years, and then culminated in the civil war. In that fierce battle the national principle, which had strengthened with every year from the time of the formation of the government, triumphed, and it is now supreme'. *The Works of Alexander Hamilton,* (1885) vol. I, p. V. The implication was plain. Jefferson was the begetter of treason, as the founder of the Democratic party, the party of 'rum, Romanism and rebellion,' as another Republican leader put it at that time. Grant, Sherman, Sheridan had carried on the great work begun by the framers of the Constitution. It was the duty of the Republican party to save their and Hamilton's work. This simple view of American political history and the doctrines about the Union held by various

Despite this over-emphasis on *the* 'critical period', the years that followed the peace were troubled enough. There were grievances in plenty, many of them more keenly felt than those that had provoked the rebellion against British authority. Every section, every class had some ground of complaint, but often enough those complaints differed and the remedies were inconsistent. States with few or poor ports had an interest in an effective federal system that would enable them to share in a general customs revenue. North Carolina and New Jersey had different interests from South Carolina and New York. The war had, in its course, tended to accumulate paper assets in the North and, in its last years, to impose severe material losses on the South. Virginians who feared that an effective federal government and a consequent enforcement of the peace treaty would make it possible to enforce the claims of the Fairfax Family on the 'Northern Neck' had a different attitude to an increase of federal authority from that which came naturally to dwellers on the ill-protected western frontier. The New England states were willing to sacrifice the claim to free navigation of the Mississippi to improve their trading position with Spain. States that needed slaves for the expansion of their economy, like South Carolina and Georgia, took a different attitude to the slave trade from that of Virginia which had more slaves than she could easily support. Populous states had more confidence in a strengthened federation that they could hope to control than had states like Rhode Island or Maryland whose chances of expansion were limited.

But the clash of interests was not only one of sections, it was one of classes. The debtors had not the same interest in federal solvency as had the creditors. The small farmer had little reason to expect much immediate profit from foreign trade and the merchants and

sections is particularly pleasing coming from a descendant of George Cabot. For, in 1804, the year Hamilton died, Cabot wrote to Timothy Pickering that 'a separation now is not desirable, because we should not remedy the evil. . . . But, if a separation should by and by be produced by suffering, I think it might be accompanied by important ameliorations'. Henry Adams, *Documents Relating to New England Federalism, 1800–1815*, p. 349. The first edition was published in 1877. I quote from the edition of 1905.

shopowners of the growing cities could count on the support of their employees in all measures that seemed to promise a restoration of the old prosperity. The veterans (as Americans would call them today) had good reason to want their pay and land warrants honoured, but the interests of the officers who founded the 'Society of the Cincinnati' were not identical with those of the rank and file who had no claim to half-pay for life and had, many of them, been forced to alienate their claims on the rewards promised them by a moderately grateful country. Even the curse of inflation was seen as a blessing by many who were able, notably in Rhode Island, to infuriate the rich by making depreciated paper legal tender.

In the tangle of great and small grievances and conflicting interests, the various attempts to reform, in minor detail, the Articles of Confederation came to naught. Above all the attempts to give the United States a customs revenue and so, a source of income more reliable than that provided by state requisitions, failed. There was no policy on which all or most Americans could agree and unless the United States was to be left to drift along without an effective federal government, the task of reform must be undertaken by a united, minority group that knew what it wanted. By 1785, that group was forming. It was a group of men who wanted a stronger government or, as they would have said, a *government*, for they regarded the Confederation as not being a government in any real sense of the term. It included the public creditors. It included all the possessors of titles to money threatened by the new plague of paper money. It included men who had titles to western lands which were nearly worthless as long as there was no effective government in the western territories. It included merchants and shipbuilders who, as good mercantilists, thought that only a strong federal government could, by navigation acts and commercial treaties, break into the European and Caribbean markets. These were the classes that induced the Congress to call for a Convention of all the States. These were the interests represented when that Convention met in Philadelphia in 1787.

The story of that Convention need not be told. It was presided over, sagaciously, by George Washington, and the fact that he condescended to attend at all gave the Convention a dignity and a hope of success it otherwise would not have had. It was attended by the venerable Franklin. It was attended by one of its chief begetters, the young Alexander Hamilton, whose extreme views as to the amount of unity that was called for diminished his weight, almost as much as did his admiration for the English constitution, which he adored with an uncritical fervour that would have astounded Burke.[1] There was James Wilson, the learned and acute if repetitive Scot. And there was, above all, the learned young Mr. Madison, the Virginia planter, friend and confidant of Washington and also of the very important Mr. Jefferson, absent as Minister in France, but already looming up as the natural leader of the radicals in Virginia and, perhaps, elsewhere.

The history of the Convention, as it sat in the hot Philadelphia summer, is not a matter for a book of this kind. There were deep divisions between States and sections. The great compromise, the giving of representation to the States in the lower house in proportion to population and in the Senate on terms of absolute equality, saved the Convention from collapse. The records of the Convention show how many devices, even such important ones as the method of electing the President and the existence, character, and powers of the office were debated and settled, not in accordance with deep, prearranged schemes or doctrines, but as a result of give and take— and sometimes of last-minute changes in sentiment. The Convention wisely sat in secret, so that when it finally produced its proposed Constitution, the whole document could be given an appearance of symmetry by its public defenders that a day-to-day report of the debates would have made impossible of credence.

The Fathers of the Constitution would have been astonished, in 1787, at the reverence their handiwork was soon to evoke. But if they had wrought better than they knew, they knew that they had wrought well.[2] But (and this was a question put, at once, by the

[1] It is often forgotten that Hamilton left the Convention in pessimistic anger and that, in *The Federalist,* he was defending an instrument of government in which he had little belief and in whose framing he had played a minor role.

[2] 'Permit me to add, in this place, that the science even of government itself seems to be yet almost in its state of infancy. Governments, in general, have been the result of force, fraud, and of accident. After a period of six thousand years has elapsed since the creation, the United States exhibit to the world the first instance, as far as we can learn, of a

opponents of the new Constitution) wrought well for whom? Well for the interests that had organized the campaign for the revision of the Articles, that had provided almost all the delegates and were now to provide the effective means of inducing an apathetic or hostile people to ratify the new system of federal power. By the 'contract' clause; by the prohibition of the issue of paper money by the states; by the implied power of the new federal courts to invalidate legislation setting these prohibitions at naught; by the conferring of powers of effective taxation; by giving the possibility of an aggressive commercial policy to the new government; by creating a government that had at least the possibility of impressing Britain, France and Spain; the framers of the Constitution 'had wrought upon the plan that pleased their private thought', to amend Wordsworth.

Nor was the thought wholly private. The man who was rightly to be called 'the Father of the Constitution', James Madison, was frank enough in the most remarkable of the essays he wrote in the collection designed to win over the hostile Convention of New York. The Constitution was designed to deal with, to temper and control, the most potent cause of political mischief, 'factions'. And the most potent cause of factions was clearly described. 'The most common and durable source of factions has been the various and unequal distribution of property. Those who hold, and those who are without property, have ever formed distinct interests in society. Those who are creditors, and those who are debtors, fall under a like discrimination. A landed interest, a manufacturing interest, a mercantile interest, with many lesser interests, grow up of necessity in civilized nations, and divide them into different classes, actuated by different sentiments and views.'[1] What factions based on varying economic interests could do had been displayed in the recent past. There had been open attempts to defraud creditors and an open

---

nation, unattacked by external force, unconvulsed by domestic insurrections, assembling voluntarily, deliberating fully, and deciding calmly, concerning that system of government, under which they would wish that they and their posterity should live.' James Wilson, *Speech in Pennsylvania Convention, on 24th November, 1787* (*Selected Political Essays of James Wilson,* edited by Randolph G. Adams, (1930) p. 167-8.

[1] *The Federalist,* X, p. 43, edited by Max Beloff (1948).

rebellion, in Massachusetts, against the enforcement of the law. In Daniel Shays, the nervous saw the image of the armed demagogue, a type of which their knowledge of ancient history furnished them with many alarming examples. It was time to call a halt, to put a hook in the nose of the great Leviathan, the people. 'Your people', Hamilton was to say, 'is a great beast'.

The framers of the Constitution were carrying out, with skill, tact and energy, that apparently necessary stage in all revolutions that was to get its name a few years later, Thermidor. But the American Thermidor was orderly, bloodless, and long lasting. It was not followed by Vendémiaire, Brumaire and a royal restoration. The framers of the Constitution were attempting the delicate task of stopping a revolution from running its full course and they were to succeed.[1]

What was clear to Madison was clear to his opponents, too. What had the farmer, completely or nearly self-subsisting, to gain from tariffs and treaties? What had he to gain from the creation of a fleet that would be strong enough to tip the scales in favour of one or other of the great maritime powers and so induce better commercial treatment?[2] What had he and other debtors to gain by the establishment of a government created by creditors for creditors?

[1] The great pioneer in the realistic study of the origins of the Constitution put it admirably. 'If we examine carefully the delicate instrument by which the framers sought to check certain kinds of positive action that might be advocated to the detriment of established and acquired rights, we cannot help marvelling at their skill. Their leading idea was to break up the attacking forces at the starting point: the source of political authority for the several branches of government. This disintegration of positive action at the source was further facilitated by the differentiation in the terms given to the respective departments of the government. And the crowning counterweight to "an interested and over-bearing majority", as Madison phrased it, was secured in the peculiar position assigned to the judiciary, and the use of the sanctity and mystery of the law as a foil to democratic attacks.' Charles A. Beard, *An Economic Interpretation of the Constitution of the United States,* p. 161. These views, almost undisputed now, were, it should be remembered, novel, even iconoclastic, in 1913.

[2] It is, perhaps, worth noting that the candid assumption that American naval power, once created, would be used this way, conflicted with the existing obligations of the United States which was an ally of France bound by a treaty that would have made such an open huckstering policy, a gross breach of public faith.

What had they, the plain people, to gain from the establishment of a government designed by men terrified of democratic licence and majority rule? These were reasonable grounds of opposition and no more selfish, if more short-sighted, than the views of the promoters of the new venture. But they opposed what was to become a great success and they have often been condemned unheard.

Victrix causa Deis placuit sed victa Catoni.

It was long before American historians began to wonder what could be said for Cato and against the party the Gods had favoured.

Nothing shows more clearly the assumptions of American official historiography than the way in which the opposition to the Constitution was for long dismissed as the work of fools, knaves or men misled by local and unpatriotic ambition. There was, in some narrators and commentators, a firm refusal to notice that the conflict was not over abstract political doctrine nor even over the fairly abstract question of states' rights, but over very tangible interests and economic and social rivalries. Thus even so learned and wise a commentator as Bryce could write: 'There were no reactionary conspirators to be feared, for every one prized liberty and equality. There were no questions between classes, no animosities against rank and wealth, for rank and wealth did not exist.'[1] Yet nothing was more clearly stated in the classic exposition of the new constitution, *The Federalist*, than that hostility to wealth was one of the great evils the new Constitution was designed to minimize. It was to redress the errors of majority rule, to put obstacles in the way of the spoliation of the rich minority by the poor and greedy majority that the Constitution took the form it did.[2]

[1] Bryce, *The American Commonwealth* (1888), vol. I. p. 30.
[2] 'There is no maxim, in my opinion, which is more liable to be misapplied, and which therefore needs more elucidation than the current one, that the interest of the majority is the political standard of right and wrong. . . . But taking it in the popular sense, as referring to the immediate augmentation of property and wealth, nothing can be more false. In the latter sense it would be the interest of the majority, in every community, to despoil and enslave the minority of individuals.' James Madison to James Monroe, 5 October 1786. Quoted by Max Beloff in his edition of *The Federalist*, p. xvii.

True, Madison was here writing a private letter. But *The Federalist*, which states the same doctrine in more than one place, was intended to be very public. And one need only open Elliott's Debates[1] almost at random, to find adequately candid expressions of class conflict. Historians near the event were not so coy as some of their successors. The motives of the friends of the Constitution were put by Richard Hildreth with his usual dry lucidity,[2] and John Marshall, as Chief Justice, only repeated in a new form what he had written as the biographer of Washington. To sanction release by a bankruptcy act from the constitutional prohibition to pass legislation invalidating a contract was to make void a provision of the Constitution 'on which the good and wise reposed confidently for securing the prosperity and harmony of our citizens'.[3]

But even if the class conflict was admitted, the possibility that the defenders of one set of class interests, those represented by the opponents of the new Constitution, might have had something to say for themselves other than the mere assertion of blind and selfish interest, was seldom allowed for. Hildreth, though a Benthamite, rather evaded the problem of the identification of interests when he noted that the members of the Convention, 'had seemed to look upon property not so much as one right, to be secured like the rest, but as the great and chief right, of more importance than all others'. But he does not doubt that there rallied to the side of the Constitution, not only those who had palpable interests to serve by its adoption, but many of those who 'had no by-ends to

[1] *The Debates in the Several State Conventions on the Adoption of the Federal Constitution* . . . collected and revised by Jonathan Elliott. The first edition appeared in 1830, so there was plenty of time for Americans to study the candid politics of their ancestors.

[2] 'The Convention as a whole, represented in a marked manner, the talent, intelligence, and especially the conservative sentiment of the country. . . . The public creditors, especially, demanded some authority able to make the people pay.' Hildreth, *The History of the United States* (1849), revised edition, Vol. III, p. 484.

[3] *Ogden v. Saunders,* 1827. Marshall did not base his dissent wholly on the alleged intent of the framers of the Constitution, but he thought their intent would strengthen his argument on the intrinsically binding force of contract *and* that his attribution of intent would be plausible. See Benjamin Fletcher Wright, *The Contract Clause of the Constitution* (1938), pp. 51–2.

serve, and whose interest was identical with the public welfare'. They were opposed by the local politicians, by the less educated and less wealthy portion of the community and by 'all those whose ruined and desperate circumstances led them to prefer disturbance and revolution to the preservation of social order'.[1]

That the opposition to the Constitution, though it had leaders of the popularity and historical eminence of Richard Henry Lee and Patrick Henry, was morally and intellectually negligible, became almost an article of faith. The 'good and wise' were on one side, the foolish and flagitious on the other.[2] In a world in which

[1] Hildreth, op. cit., vol. III, pp. 534–5. It is not, as is sometimes implied, only since the Civil War and the rise of Big Business that the doctrine of property as the primary right protected by political society has been advanced and believed in, in America.

[2] For the unreflecting von Holst, all was simple. 'The most fanatical assumed the lead; men for whom no weapon was too blunt or brutal so long as they could use it. Their argument bordered on the extremest absurdity and their assumptions might have excited the loudest merriment, were it not that the question was one of life or death to the nation.' H. von Holst, *The Constitutional History of the United States,* vol. I. This volume was first published in 1876. I cite from the edition of 1889. Even so scholarly an historian as S. B. Harding attributes the opposition to the Constitution in the traditionally intelligent commonwealth of Massachusetts not only to economic differences of interest, but to democratic vanity, to 'the exaggerated sense of political capacity which has been named as one of the most marked characteristics of the men of this period'. And the Antifederalist leaders were 'a half-dozen obscure men', though they did represent, probably, more than half the men of Massachusetts. S. B. Harding, *The Contest Over the Ratification of the Federal Constitution in the State of Massachusetts* (1896), pp. 2, 63. Professor Trenholme notes that the same charge was made against the leaders of the successful opposition in North Carolina, though their chief spokesman, Willie Jones, was an old Etonian. His name, we learn, was pronounced 'Wylie', not like the plebeian 'Willie'. Louise Irby Trenholme, *The Ratification of the Federal Constitution in North Carolina* (1932), p. 127. Schouler, in 1880, was even more scornful of the opposition in Massachusetts than Harding was to be. 'Nowhere did Anti-Federalism appear so ludicrous in convention, if we may trust the authentic report, as in this State. Long-haired folks, bumpkins, green radicals, and training-day generals came up to Boston from their rural constituencies to cut their awkward antics, and then vanish like Ariel's shapes.' James Schouler, *History of the United States of America Under the Constitution,* vol. I, pp. 59–60. Schouler does admit that our account of the Massachusetts

inflation has been the common remedy of all governments, and of few more than the government of the United States, Constitution or no Constitution, the hankering after paper money of its opponents does not seem so automatically heinous as it did to indignant commentators even a generation ago.[1] Nor was the suspicion that some of the makers of the new Constitution had a direct and, if not a corrupt, at least what the French call an indelicate interest in its success, unjustified. Charles Beard showed that many had such an interest.[2] Even with all the apparatus of historical criticism that is now available, even with the acceptance of the view that not all virtue was on the side of the framers, that indeed, they were 'essentially hard-headed men of affairs . . .' [who] 'came to Philadelphia with their tongues somewhat in their cheeks',[3] it does not follow that their handiwork did not deserve the encomiums that it soon began to get, encomiums that grew in warmth and emotional intensity as the realities of the Revolution and its aftermath were gilded by myth. They had, on the whole, more foresight, more sense of realities than had their opponents; that their foresight and their sense of realities were both sharpened by their

---

Convention comes from a Federalist reporter who may have been as anxious as was Dr. Johnson to see that the Whig dogs did not get the best of it.

[1] Perhaps the oddest example of this intolerance is furnished by the comment of E. Benjamin Andrews on 'the paper money fanaticism' of Rhode Island which kept the smallest state out of the new Union until 1790. For Andrews, at the moment of writing this, 1895, was President of Rhode Island's most famous institution of higher learning, Brown University, and was, two years later, to be squeezed out of the presidency for expressing heretical doubts about the gold standard, so recently under attack by the demagogue, William Jennings Bryan. (See E. Benjamin Andrews, *History of the United States*, vol. I, p. 240.) The opponents of the Constitution were 'the ignorant masses', ibid, p. 255.

[2] Not all supporters had such an interest. Madison, notably, had not and was disgusted with the stock-jobbery that followed the victory of his party. And Robert Lansing of New York, who left the Convention rather than sign the new Constitution, did very well out of speculation in the new bull market in federal securities.

[3] Fred Rodell, *Fifty-Five Men* (1936), p. 22. The innocent remark of President Eisenhower's nominee for the Defence Department that 'what is good for General Motors is good for the United States' was in the spirit of 1787 if not of 1776.

keen personal interest in the success of the Convention is a matter for the moralist rather than for the historian.

But it will not do to put down all the zeal, ingenuity, learning, industry displayed by the leaders of the Convention to nothing but a high sense of personal profit. Some of them, at any rate, believed that only by making it 'a more perfect Union' could the Union survive and that if it did not survive, the American Revolution that they had helped to make, might prove a disastrous mistake. They believed that this was a turning point in world history, that as Lincoln was to say, the United States and its novel experiment in freedom was 'the last, best hope of earth'. They hoped to save the Union and to inspire the friends of liberty everywhere. The wise and worldly-wise Ulysses of the Revolution. Benjamin Franklin, sent the text to a French friend. 'If it succeeds, I do not see why you might not in Europe carry the project of good Henry the 4th into Execution by forming a Federal Union and One Grand Republic of all its different States and Kingdoms.'[1] Three generations later, a great popular leader was to express his, possibly unhistorical, admiration for the work of the Convention, 'As the British Constitution is the most subtle organism which has proceeded from progressive history, so the American Constitution is the most wonderful work ever struck off at a given time by the brain and purpose of man.'[2] And the great historical panegyrist of American democracy, George Bancroft, saw in the framing of the Constitution 'the most cheering act in the political history of mankind', an answer to the question 'Do nations float darkling down the stream of the ages without hope or consolation, swaying with every wind and ignorant whither they are drifting? or, is there a superior power of intelligence and love which is moved by justice and shapes their course?'[3]

But more important than the praise lavished by Gladstone and Bancroft, so long after, was the fact that, almost at once, the text of the Constitution was accepted and, indeed, idolized. 'Before a

[1] Quoted by Carl Van Doren, *The Great Rehearsal: The Story of the Making and Ratifying of the Constitution of the United States* (1948), p. 164.

[2] W. E. Gladstone, 1878. There are at least two versions of this judgment. I have chosen the earlier as given in *Familiar Quotations . . .* by John Bartlett, Twelfth Edition, editor Christopher Morley, p. 450.

[3] George Bancroft, *History of the Formation of the Constitution of the United States of America* 1882, vol. I, p. 3, and vol. II, p. 3.

decade had passed, the Constitution, from being an object of partisan contention, became one of veneration. The new political parties, Federalists and Jeffersonians, which rose in the early years of the Republic, vied with one another in their expressions of respect for the supreme law. Men might differ as to the true meaning of the basic document; they might even come to blows over the nature of the government it erected; but the Constitution itself in time became sacrosanct. . . . The Constitution, it may be said, is America's uncrowned king. It is above party, a common object of veneration, a living symbol of national unity.'[1] And the Constitution is not a king who reigns but does not govern, for to the average American, the sacred text is an oracle that, properly consulted, give an infallible answer and if the answer given by the priests of the oracle is displeasing, the explanation must lie in the intellectual or moral faults of the priesthood, not in the work of the men of 1787.

III

The Constitution of the United States is a model of draftsmanship, of linguistic elegance, of brevity and of apparent clarity. When it is compared with other federal constitutions, like that of Canada, or with the botched, long-winded accumulations of petty legislation that make up the 'constitutions' of so many states of the Union, it is hard to be moderate in admiration for its chief makers James Madison and James Wilson and its chief draftsman Gouverneur Morris. The brevity makes it possible for the average citizen of the United States to read the fundamental law quickly; the elegance makes the reading agreeable and the apparent lucidity makes the reader feel that he has mastered the contents, although the notorious fact that so much time, money and blood has been spent in interpreting this superficially clear document ought to raise more doubts than, apparently, it does. Some of the obscurity that is visible in the Constitution is due to causes that we cannot now determine. Thus it declares that the 'privilege of the writ of *habeas corpus* shall not be suspended, unless when in cases of rebellion or invasion the public

[1] Alfred H. Kelly and Winifred A. Harbison, *The American Constitution* (1948), p. 162–3.

safety may require it'. But who is to determine the fact that there is an invasion or rebellion that requires the suspension? The Constitution does not say and Lincoln, in 1861, assumed that the power lay with him, at any rate when Congress was not sitting.

To repeat, even the fateful and fruitful phrase 'We, the People of the United States', has an uncertain origin. It may have had, from the beginning, in the minds of its authors, a great deal of the weight which Americans came to attribute to it. But it may have been adopted merely to get round the difficulty that no one knew, when the Constitution was proposed in its original form, what states would first adopt it.[1] More serious is the quite erratic prominence given in the text to unimportant provisions that have become obsolete or meaningless and the inadequate stress laid on some basic provisions, not to speak of the ignoring by the Constitution of some powers and allocations of powers of the highest importance. As has been admirably said by a great authority on the historical Constitution, 'A stranger to our institutions would, in fact, obtain only an incorrect and artificial conception of our government if he confined his attention to the Constitution itself. He would have to be told that certain features of the Constitution are never carried out in practice, while some of the most fundamental powers of our government are exercised without any definite constitutional authorization. He would have to learn that the President is not in reality chosen by the electoral college;[2] that his power to adjourn Congress has never been exercised; that taxes have rarely been apportioned according to population, and that certain reconstruction amendments have not been enforced.'[3]

Other sections of the Constitution to which the framers attached great importance, like the reservation to the House of Representatives of the sole right to initiate money bills, have proved a good

[1] 'How far this was the controlling factor and what other motives may have been at work we have no record. The simple fact remains that committee of style cleverly avoided the difficulty before them by phrasing the preamble:—"We, the People of the United States".' Max Farrand, *The Framing of the Constitution* (1913), p. 190-1.

[2] He would also have to learn that there is no one 'electoral college', that 'the Electors shall meet in their respective States' (Article II Section I).

[3] James G. Randall, *Constitutional Problems Under Lincoln* (1926), p. 6-7.

THE CHARACTER OF THE AMERICAN POLITY

deal less effective than was foreseen. Others, like the exclusion of federal office holders from membership in Congress, have been far more important than the Founding Fathers (to borrow an expressive phrase from President Warren Gamaliel Harding) anticipated. And although both provisions owed their origin to British practice, they have had very different results in the American system.

Again, the brevity and occasional vagueness of the sacred text have made it possible (as the integration of American society and the progress of technology have made it desirable) to deem that a power granted to a part of the federal government now enables the present day American government to meet problems, unforeseen and undreamed of in 1787. Thus under the taxing power given to Congress in the Constitution, Congress has regulated business. 'Furthermore, there are some businesses which Congress may tax so heavily as to drive them out of existence, one example being the production of white sulphur matches, another the sale of oleomargarine coloured to look like butter, another the dealing in sawed-off shotguns.'[1] Obviously, the only item listed whose nefarious character can have been foreseen by the framers of the Constitution is the sawed-off shotgun.

The whole mechanism of government set up in 1789 has been kept running only by an extremely elaborate and ingenious party system for which the Constitution makes no provision. Yet that party system owes much of its peculiar character to the necessity of adjusting it to the Constitution and the party system has profoundly altered the Constitution, above all in the way it has altered the method of choosing the President, the relations between the President and Congress and the relations between the two houses.

The great American political invention, 'judicial review', the power of courts to annul state and federal legislation may have been given in the Constitution but, if so, it was not given in so many words.

The customs of the political Constitution have amended and expanded the text. Thus the Constitution provides that senators and representatives shall be residents of the states they represent, but custom, having almost the force of law, has made this restriction

[1] Edward S. Corwin, *The Constitution and What It Means Today* (eighth edition 1946), p. 26.

more restrictive, so that by the 'locality rule' representatives must be residents of the district they represent.

The 'Constitution,' that is to say, is not, today, merely the sacred text, it is the text as it has been lived. And it is other texts as well. It is not the six thousand words of the text that is the 'Constitution' as lawyers know it. Statutes, opinions of the Attorney-General, presidential executive orders, presidential actions setting precedents, above all the decisions, not only of the Supreme Court, but of lower federal courts and of state courts are now part of the Constitution'.[1]

Thus the Constitution is being continually expanded, altered, interpreted. But of course some periods are more fertile in constitutional innovation than others and there is an ebb and flow in the division of power between President and Congress, between the Supreme Court and Congress, and between the Union and the States. The most fertile period of all was between 1789 and 1792, the period of Washington's first term, of the first two Congresses, the brief period of peace, internal and external, before the storms of the French Revolution threatened both. The presidency, the Congress, the federal cabinet, the federal administrative machine, acquired their main characteristics in these four years. In these four years, it was decided, not only that the new Constitution would work, but how it would work. It was decided that the new government had powers of growth only to be inferred from the text, no to be read in it in black and white. It was decided that the Senate would be a different and, in possibilities at any rate, a more important body than had been anticipated.[2] It was de-

---

[1] 'In the "material" sense a constitution is a body of rules in accordance with which a government is organized and operates; and in this sense "the Constitution of the United States" comprises a vastly extended system of legislation, customs and adjudications, of which the constitutional document is, as it were, but the nucleus and into which it tends ever to be absorbed.' Corwin, op. cit, pp. 86–7.

[2] This was so little foreseen that it was seriously argued that senators should be paid more than representatives because while there would be no difficulty in getting first-rate men to serve in the House of Representatives where the power and prestige were bound to lie, it would be hard to get first-rate men to serve in the Senate unless they were rewarded in other ways.

cided that the President would be the direct, effective head of all the executive officers of the Union and that parliamentary government, even in a modified form, would not be grafted on to the text. It was shown that federal authority could act directly on citizens of states, could impose taxes, repress sedition, punish and reward. Indeed, there is hardly an aspect of American institutions that is peculiarly American which cannot be seen in existence in, roughly, its modern form by 1792, with two exceptions. The party system existed in embryo, but only in embryo, and the Supreme Court was as yet unconscious of its powers and, with the whole federal judicial system, existed but hardly operated.

The framers of the Constitution knew that much would depend on the operation of the new Constitution in its first years. A failure of the new instrument of government would be more serious than a failure of the old and might well bring about a complete dissolution of the Union. It was well, then, for the future of the experiment that the Congress that took office in 1789 was, in the main, filled with well-wishers of the Constitution and with many of its actual makers. Important as it had been that Washington had agreed to preside over the Convention, it was even more important that he agreed to be the first President. Had this not been expected, there might have been no office like the presidency in the constitutional draft; had Washington refused to accept office, the first President might have been prevented from giving to the new and untried office the strength and dignity it so quickly acquired. Indeed, had Washington refused to serve, the electoral colleges might well have functioned in those early days before the party system had organized the electorate. A presidency that was really filled by the choice of scattered groups of local politicians, instead of being filled by the direct choice of 'the People of the United States', would have been incapable of playing the role the presidency did play in creating 'the People of the United States'.

In other and important ways, the early days of the presidency gained from Washington's great personal prestige. Had another been President there might have been some case for dignifying the office with imitations of British verbal forms as John Adams the Vice-President, and so, *ex-officio*, presiding officer of the Senate, wished. But Washington did not need such additions to his dignity as honorific titles.[1]

More important was the decision that the executive offices of the new United States should be executed by individuals, not by boards or committees as had been, at times, the practice of the Continental Congress. It was over the Treasury that the battle was fought. For a time, the Continental Congress had concentrated financial power in the hands of one man, the Superintendent, or, as he was often called, 'the Financier' Robert Morris.[2] But such a concentration of power in the hands of one man made many enemies who were reinforced by those who disliked the concentration of such power in the hands of Robert Morris. The Continental Congress went back to the board system and there was nothing in the new Constitution to give a decisive lead. Elbridge Gerry, the old enemy of Morris, was again an enemy of any single head for the Treasury. There was a danger of too much concentration of power, there was a danger of corruption, corruption of Congress in the English manner, corruption of the federal officers themselves.[3]

[1] Adams was stubborn on this point. 'You are against titles. But there are no people in the world so much in favor of titles as the people of America; and the Government will never be properly administered until they are adopted in the fullest manner.' Quoted in James Hart, *The American Presidency in Action, 1789* (1948), p. 39. As American social life shows, Adams was not totally wrong, but again it is a sign of the unique position that the presidency quickly acquired, that 'Mr. President' became a form of address as solemn as any in the world and 'the President' an officer, if not a man, to whom universal respect and precedence is due. (In certain circles, in and around Boston, 'the President', unless the phrase is modified, means the President of Harvard.)

[2] The office was created in 1781 and the title may have been a deliberate imitation of French nomenclature. French finances were then going through one of their periodic periods of 'reform' under Necker as *Surintendant*. One delegate was conscious of the parallel. 'Joseph Jones representing a different point of view, wrote to Washington that the finances needed a Necker to reform them.' Jennings B. Sanders, *Evolution of the Executive Departments of the Continental Congress* (1935), p. 130.

[3] There was more than mere republican suspicion in this attitude. William Duer who was one of the chief agents of Morris and then of Hamilton, before he went bankrupt in a lavish way, may not have been formally corrupt, but he certainly 'cut his ethical corners fine', as Americans are supposed to say.

But the views that Hamilton had expressed in earlier days pre-vailed.[1] The executive departments of the new government would each be headed by one man appointed by the President and *removable by him.*

This most important gloss on the text of the Constitution was not made until after a bitter congressional battle. The Constitution provided that the President 'shall have power . . . by and with the Advice and Consent of the Senate' to 'appoint Ambassadors, other public Ministers and Consuls, Judges of the Supreme Court, and all other Officers of the United States, whose Appointments are not herein otherwise provided for'. Did the power to appoint imply the power to remove and if it did not, was it proper that the power should be given by Congress? It is still a matter of historical speculation whether the First Congress decided for an inherent power of removal, but the power of removal was established and it was and is a power of vast importance, for the power to remove is the necessary support of the power to command, as many Presidents were later to demonstrate.[2]

Not all the decisions made and precedents established by the First Congress were ratified in later practice. The head of the Treasury was given a special relationship to Congress. The Secre-

[1] 'Boards partake of a part of the inconveniences of larger assemblies. Their decisions are slower, their energy less, their responsibility more diffused. . . . Men of the first pretensions will not so readily engage in them, because they will be less conspicuous, of less importance, have less opportunity of distinguishing themselves. The members of Boards will take less pains to inform themselves and arrive to eminence, because they have fewer motives to do it. All these reasons conspire to give a prefer-ence to the plan of vesting the great executive departments of the State in the hands of individuals.' Quoted in Lynton K. Caldwell, *The Administrative Theories of Hamilton and Jefferson* (1944), p. 45. Hamilton was willing to have a Board of Trade, but whether from genuine belief that trade regulation required 'prudence and experience more than other qualities', or from his often blind reverence for British methods can only be surmised.

[2] In *Myers v. United States* (1926), Chief Justice Taft, himself an ex-President, ruled, judicially, on the historical question of the intent of the First Congress, 'the Congress that launched the Government'. What-ever historians may think of this view, the Chief Justice was affirming a practice that was venerable and basic by 1926.

tary was to 'make report, and give information to either branch of the legislature, in person or in writing (as he may be required)'. He was 'to digest and prepare' plans for the improvement and management of the revenue and for the support of the public credit, and 'to prepare and report' estimates of revenue and expenditure. The Treasurer, too, was required to make an annual report to Congress.[1] Out of this special relationship with Congress and out of the exemption of the Secretary of the Treasury from complete presidential control, there might have grown up a kind of parliamentary relationship between Congress and the Treasury. But nothing of the kind came about. The President, the People's choice, was not a mere King. The Senate, representing the States, was not a mere House of Lords, and the possibility of reporting, in person if required, was not the same thing as the necessity of being a member of the House of Commons, sitting on the front bench and, in effect, liable to dismissal by his colleagues. For again, the power to dismiss was the power to command and the President, who could not be dismissed by Congress, and the Secretary who could be dismissed by the President, were holders of offices that were bound to evolve very differently from the offices of Prime Minister and Chancellor of the Exchequer.[2]

The text and the spirit of the Constitution worked together to ensure that the President would not, to quote Shelburne on the King of England, be reduced to being a mere 'Peshwa of the Mahrattas'—and that long before Caleb Cushing as Attorney-General laid it down in 1855 that it was American constitutional law that 'no head of a department can lawfully perform an official act against the will of the president, and that will is by the constitution to govern the performance of all such acts.'[3]

The establishment of the President as the effective head of all parts of the executive department was only one of the decisive interpretations of the Constitution made in these formative years.

[1] Leonard D. White, *The Federalists* (1948), p. 118.

[2] I do not wish to assert that the British Constitution of King George III's time was as purely parliamentary as it later became. But it was moving in that direction while the American Constitution began at once to move in another.

[3] Quoted in John A. Fairlie, *The National Administration of the United States* (1905), p. 19.

The Senate, then a body of only twenty-six members, had been given quasi-executive functions; it could confirm or reject all important presidential appointments; it could ratify treaties by a two-thirds majority and thus make them part of 'the supreme law of the land' or, by not providing that majority, make them nothing. But it was not clear how important was the function of advising the President. Treaties were to be made 'with the advice and consent of the Senate'. When was the advice to be asked, before or after the treaty had been negotiated? Need advice be attended to? That again was decided, negatively, in these years. Washington came to the Senate to counsel with that body about an Indian treaty. His reception was such that he never came back.[1]

President Polk later made a half-hearted attempt to revive this kind of consultation and wise Presidents have sounded out the Senate or, at any rate, important senators before committing themselves to treaties or other international agreements, but the role of the Senate as a kind of Privy Council was over.

There had to be a substitute and that was found in the meetings of the chief executive officers who came quickly to be called 'the Cabinet', a body unknown, even today, to American law. The Cabinet was and is composed of the chief executive officers, 'the secretaries', plus the Attorney-General. Very quickly something like cabinet unity was developed, the doctrine that a member who did not approve of and could not support the policy of the Administration should resign. But the Cabinet was, in 1790, in the days of President Washington, as it is in the days of President Eisenhower, a body inferior in prestige to the British Cabinet for, to be repetitive, all its members owe their official existence and so their power to the President; and, as Washington's successor, John Adams, showed, even an unpopular President could act against the wishes of Alexander Hamilton, the most popular leader of his own party outside the administration, by dismissing Hamilton's allies in the Cabinet without any risk of causing a 'cabinet crisis'.

It was, perhaps, accidental that the anticipated superiority of the House over the Senate did not come about. But soon after the beginning of the new government, foreign affairs, in which the

[1] According to tradition, he said that he would be damned if he ever came back.

Senate had a duty to intermeddle, became of paramount importance. In 1796 the House failed, in the great debate over the
ratification of the Jay Treaty, to divide power with the Senate.
Had Madison's view prevailed, the view that the treaty power
(which lay in the President and the Senate according to the constitutional text) was limited when, in fact, the treaty required legislation
coming from the *whole* Congress, the predominance of the Senate
might have been delayed. But it was not to be, and even if it was
only by the skill of the Administration's supporters, above all, Fisher
Ames, in pinning the label of warmongers on their opponents that
the question was decided against the House, it was so decided.[1]

Another accident that had permanent importance was the advantage that Alexander Hamilton got in organizing his department
(and more than his department) according to his own authoritarian,
centralizing views while Jefferson, who was to head the 'Department of State', was, as Minister to France, still busily supervising
and observing the first stages of the French Revolution. Hamilton
had six months' start in his dealings with the President and with
Congress, as well as six months' start in taking over the old
Treasury of the Continental Congress and organizing a new one.[2]
His renewal of his old association with General Washington enabled
him to implant in the President's mind the proper, i.e. Hamiltonian,
ideas of the powers of the federal government and of the proper
administrative and economic means to carry them into effect.
This would not necessarily have occurred if Jefferson, like Washington a Virginia gentleman, had been on the spot for, as is often
forgotten, Washington and Hamilton had broken off their wartime association on less than amiable terms.[3]

[1] Today, the fact that foreign policy so often requires vast expenditure
has given the House new importance in this field.

[2] Hamilton became Secretary on September 11th, 1789; Jefferson
arrived in New York to take over what had become the State Department on March 21st, 1790. When he discovered how completely
Hamilton had replaced him in the President's intimacy, Jefferson might
have reflected on the French saying: 'les absents ont toujours tort.'

[3] Hamilton at that time took a poor view of his late and future chief,
as he tended to take a poor view of human beings in general. 'I shall
continue to support a popularity that has been essential—is still useful.'
Quoted in Nathan Schachner, *Alexander Hamilton* (1946), p. 130.

As it was, Hamilton in nearly every important difference in the Cabinet, had the President's support in the matter of substance if not of form. He had it in two most important and closely connected matters, essential to the establishment of the new government as a vested interest, the assumption by the federal government of the war debts of the states and the establishment of the Bank of the United States.[1] Hamilton, too, was successful in setting up and getting to work what was, for the time, an elaborate administrative machine directly nominated and controlled by the new government. On paper, the Department of State dealt with more than foreign affairs. It was a kind of Department of the Interior as well. But the pressure of foreign policy and, perhaps, an inadequate interest in the administrative possibilities of his department, led Jefferson to neglect this side of his duties. The only important, all-pervading federal department was the Treasury (the War Department, in fact, was almost as much under Hamilton's control as was the Treasury).[2]

And it was this administrative predominance of Hamilton that made it certain that the new government would meet the wishes and the needs of the creditors of the States as well as of the Union. By getting the new federal government to assume responsibility for state debts, Hamilton made it certain that the moneyed interest would not be divided. By straining the constitution to create the Bank of the United States, Hamilton provided a centre of financial power connected with the new government. He knew that where is the treasure there is the heart also. He knew what a part in preserving the liberties won by the Glorious Revolution of 1688 the English national debt and the Bank of England had played. It was accidental

[1] In the assumption of state debts, Jefferson's opposition was bought off by Hamilton's agreeing to support putting the new federal capital in the South. It was, as Jefferson later realized, a bad bargain, the main sufferers being the inhabitants of Washington who for so long were forced to live in an unhealthy swamp with an odious climate. It still has a summer climate that many find barely tolerable but is no longer unhealthy.

[2] The distribution of minor offices was rather haphazard. Thus the Mint came under the Department of State, not the Treasury. Possibly the only important consequence was that the Mint stayed on in Philadelphia, where it still is, when all other offices were moved to Washington.

but in the strict sense of the term, ominous, that Washington took the oath of office as first President of the United States in Wall Street.[1]

The phrase used by a historian is unkind but it did describe Hamilton's methods and object: 'his plan to make the self-interest of the rich a cement to the Union'.[2] But in a less narrow sense, the self-interest of the rich had been one of the mainsprings of the movement that led to the creation of the new Constitution. This was reflected in the clause of the Constitution that forbade states to pass legislation invalidating contracts or to make anything but gold or silver legal tender. It was to be reflected in the attitude of the Supreme Court for well over a century. Again, it must be remembered that the rich, the Hamiltonian party, were genuinely frightened. They had seen one revolution and those who had profited by it had no desire to see another. They were what Albert Vandal called the profiteers of the French Revolution, 'révolutionnaires nantis'. They had hardly got the new government under way when the tremors of the earthquake in France alarmed them again. They saw a party that they called 'Jacobin', the disciples of Jefferson, organize opposition and prepare, legally, to take over power. They saw them do it in the election of 1800. 'The good, the wise and the rich', continued to be frightened, a characteristic that they have not wholly lost. They were to see political upheavals that threatened the achievements of the Constitutional Convention and the formative years of the Washington Administration. They could gloomily answer the question 'whether by means of its [the Federal Government's] peculiar modification, the conservative principles indispensable to the salvation of every government, could be maintained against the steam power of universal suffrage, and the ignorance and passions of the masses'.[3]

They need not have worried. Until very modern times, the steam power of universal suffrage and the ignorance and passions of the masses have been held in check. From that point of view the

---

[1] New York Stock Exchange was opened in 1792 after the capital had been removed to Philadelphia.

[2] Irving Brant, *James Madison Father of the Constitution* (1950), p. 304.

[3] Harrison Gray Otis to George Harrison (7 December, 1844). Quoted in S. E. Morison, *Harrison Gray Otis* (1913), vol. II, p. 303.

Constitution has been a success. No doubt it owed a lot to luck. By the time it came into effect, the worst of the post-war depression was over, and soon the outbreak of the great French War gave the United States and its government the early, easy profits of neutrality. Luck is not to be disregarded in the course of human events. But luck would not have sufficed if adroitness, legal and political acuteness, and a genuine concern for the general as well as for the particular good, had not animated the framers and operators of the new government. And the makers of the Constitution knew when to give way as when they accepted the claim for a federal 'Bill of Rights'.

The most famous Chief Justice of the Supreme Court was to remind his brethren that it was a Constitution they were interpreting. The drafters and makers of the new Constitution knew that it was a government that they had to make; they made it. The American people have to live with it; so has the world. Of how few political institutions in existence in 1789 can that be said!

Chapter Two

THE PARTY SYSTEM

THE American Revolution was made by a party, the 'Patriots', the 'Whigs'. It had its origin in party meetings, caucuses (the name dates from that time[1]), in 'committees of correspondence' linking the party members from state to state, and it had its governing body in the various Congresses of which the most famous, in 1776, published the Declaration of Independence. The Founding Fathers, then, knew a great deal about parties and party organization. The movement for a reform of the Articles of Confederation was the work of a party; so was the movement for the adoption of the new Constitution; so were the results of the first elections for the new Congress. Madison and Hamilton knew the seamy side of party politics and knew how skilfully a minority could organize to suggest and then impose its programme. And Madison, with his clear perception of the economic basis of politics, with his understanding of sectional and class interests, was apprehensive that party, or as he put it opprobriously, 'faction', might wreck the new republic as it had wrecked the republics of the ancient world and of medieval Italy. The division of powers between the states and the federal government, between the President and Congress, between the Senate and the House, and the giving of semi-executive powers to the Senate (confirmation of appointments, ratification of treaties)

---

[1] The word is one of Boston's contributions to the vocabulary of politics. It is from 'Greek *kaukos*, a drinking vessel' in allusion to the convivial or synposiac feature 'of the Caucus Club . . . No other equally plausible explanation has so far been made'. Mitford M. Mathews, *A Dictionary of Americanisms on Historical Principles* (1951), vol. 1, p. 286.

and of legislative powers to the President (his veto on legislation) were designed, among other objects, to prevent the domination of one faction, even if that faction were like the faction that had made the Revolution and the Constitution.

It must be remembered that 'faction' and 'party' were both words and institutions under suspicion in the years when the Constitution was being framed. It was not by going into politics and Parliament that Burke distressed his friend Goldsmith, but by giving 'up to *party* what was meant for mankind'. And we are still too prone, even after the work of Sir Lewis Namier and of other scholars, to see the problems of party through Burke's eyes, prone not to consider, sufficiently, whether Burke was not a Utopian, describing less what was than what should be, creating a fiction rather than describing a reality.

Be that as it may, party spirit, party organization were not words often used in a laudatory sense. Yet within a few years, party divisions, to Washington's distress, were very evident; he was, to his anger, the victim of a bitterly hostile party press that rejoiced in his retirement from office and, in the presidential elections of 1796, the third under the new system, the first in which he was not a candidate, there was no possible doubt that there were two national parties, one supporting John Adams, one Thomas Jefferson, that each was represented in greater or less strength over all the union and that elections for all offices, from local village jobs up to Congress and the Presidency, were fought for under party labels, formally the same all over the Union.

But for the appearance of these national parties, it is possible that the system of electing the President indirectly, through electoral colleges in the states, might have worked. It is also possible that, but for the appearance of a national party system, the election of a President really enough of a national figure to carry out his duties, might have been impossible. And it is certain that the greatest breakdown of the American constitutional system, the Civil War, came only when the party system collapsed. The last bond holding the sections together was the last remaining national party 'the Democracy', and when that broke in two at the Charleston Convention of 1860, war was at hand.

In contemplating American parties as they were and are, it is necessary to dismiss from our minds the ideal party of Burke's imagination or of the old-fashioned text-books. American parties have never been bodies of men united on some general principles of government and united to put these principles into concrete form by legislation and by administration. There have been moments when parties have looked like that, but they have been brief moments, and even in those moments, appearances have usually been deceptive. By taking the name 'Republican', the Jeffersonians hoped to pin on their rivals the imputation of being unrepublican. But the Federalists were republicans, although not Democrats. By taking the name Democrats, the majority faction of the Republican party hoped to pin on its foes the imputation of being undemocratic and by the time of the first election of Andrew Jackson, to be deemed 'undemocratic' was almost as fatal in American politics as it is to-day. By taking the name 'Whig', the opponents of Jackson hoped to get attributed to themselves some of the aura of revolutionary patriotism that clung about the honoured name.[1] And when it was necessary to find some common name for the old Whigs, 'Free Soil' Democrats, desponding 'Know Nothings' who were forced into common action by the introduction of the Kansas-Nebraska Bill in 1854, it was soon realized that a mere negative and, possibly, too concrete title like 'Anti-Nebraska', would not do and the coalition fell back on the sacred name 'Republican', to show that they, not the slavery-favouring Democrats, were the true heirs of Jefferson.[2] The new party soon became

[1] 'This name, thought to be so apt for those who criticized "King Andrew", and so bound up with the triumph of the Revolution as to be almost synonymous with "patriot" was first suggested for the united opposition by Colonel Webb in his paper, the *Courier and Enquirer*.' Dixon Ryan Fox, *The Decline of Aristocracy in the Politics of New York* (1918), p. 367.

[2] As late as 1856 when the new party, whatever it was to be called, was going to run a presidential candidate, some of its supporters still feared the new name. 'Still shying away from the name "Republican", a number of anti-Douglas editors met at Decatur on Washington's birthday. The sole non-editor at the convention was Abraham Lincoln. After issuing a general statement of principles, the editors summoned a general anti-Nebraska convention to meet at Bloomington on May 29.' It was this gathering that Paul M. Angle has termed "the real beginning of the Republican party in Illinois".' David Donald, *Lincoln's Herndon* (1948), p. 83, p. 87.

proud, almost inordinately proud of its new and increasingly meaningless name. Since 1868, the two major parties have remained the Democratic and the Republican, the latter, on the whole, preferring to forget its salad days when it tried to take over the assets of the Jeffersonians.[1] And the fact that all Republicans claim to be democrats and all Democrats to be republicans, makes the confusion of party names nearly complete. There may be significance, too, in the fact that parties with more meaningful names, negative or positive, the Anti-Masonic party, the Free Soil party, the Know Nothings, ('the American party' as they called themselves but not as they were called), the later Greenback, Prohibition, People's parties, the three alliances that, in this century, have run presidential candidates as 'Progressives' (in 1912, 1924 and 1948) have never, except in the case of the Progressives in 1912, looked like having any chance of national success and, for the most part, died within an election or two of their birth.

It is wise to begin by accepting the fact that the emptiness of the names of the two great American parties may be significant, not of the emptiness of the role of the parties, but of the fact that they cannot be understood if they are judged in European or, more strictly, in British terms. 'So different, indeed, are American from European political parties that they may be regarded as a distinct contribution to human institutions. It is a significant fact that the Federalists, the only American party that ever attempted to maintain the British social tradition, proved exotic, were sharply challenged at once by indigenous American forces, and persisted scarcely more than a dozen years.'[2]

Professor Binkley and other have attributed the special character of American parties to (among other things) the rapid disappearance in the United States of the kind of political issue that provided the raw material of politics in Europe. There was no dispute over the form of the state; there were different views about the meaning

---

[1] Pedantically, it could be objected that the Democrats adopted the 'Liberal Republican' ticket and candidate in 1872 and that the second party in 1912 was the Progressives who ran, or were run by, Theodore Roosevelt.

[2] Wilfred E. Binkley, *American Political Parties : Their Natural History* (second edition 1945), p. 4.

of the Constitution, but each side insisted that it was defending the true meaning of the sacred text. American political life had attained (and has kept) that *finality*, that universal acceptance of the legitimacy of its political institutions, that European nations have so vainly sought. There has never been even a formally revolutionary party of any size in the United States.[1]

Then the American Revolution and the years of the 'critical period' swept away most of the aristocratic barriers that were opposed to the rule of the 'People'. There continued to be disputes about the franchise, about the organization of state government, but by the time that the modern Democratic party emerged from the old Republican party in Jackson's second term (1833–37), the democratization of American politics was nearly complete. The heart-warming and heart-burning issues that filled European political life were missing in America. Politics was a matter of interests and of personalities. There was even a moment when party conflict seemed to have died out altogether, the 'era of good feelings', when under Monroe, the ideal then aimed at, by General Jackson, the extermination of 'the monster called party spirit'[2] seemed to be attained.

But as the career of Jackson was to show, party spirit was more hardy than it had seemed in 1816. For it fed on two powerful forces, ambition and economic interests. No moral suasion could make men like Jackson, Calhoun, Clay, Webster a band of brothers and no vague general formula could conceal the fact that the federal government, by its action or inaction, could profoundly affect the economic fortunes of states and, more important, of regions.

It was important, for instance, to decide how the immense inheritance of the 'People of the United States', the scores of millions of acres of fertile land held by the federal government, were to be disposed of. It was of great importance to decide whether the infant industries, begotten by Jefferson's embargo and by the war with

---

[1] Whether the Social-Democratic parties in Europe, between say 1880 and 1919, were really revolutionary except in words, may be doubted. But they were revolutionary in words. Jaurès, Bebel, Troelstra, Vandervelde had their revolutionary vocabulary. Even Ramsay MacDonald talked, at times, in revolutionary jargon.

[2] Quoted in Binkley, op. cit., p. 94.

Britain, were to be fostered by a high tariff. It was of great importance to decide whether federal funds and federal credit were to be
provided to finance the settlement of the West, to pay for roads,
then canals, then railways. It was important, and it became more
important, to decide whether federal policy should foster developments that would increase the population and wealth of areas settled
from the states that had abolished slavery or those settled from the
states that, since the discovery of the cotton gin in 1795, had found
that the apparently unlimited demand for the new staple made
slavery, again, a highly profitable proposition.

It became the business of the politician to build alliances, to
secure such a degree of control of the federal government as would
enable him to satisfy his own state and region and satisfy, as far as
was absolutely necessary, the regions whose support was needed
for victory on a national scale.

The combination that won was the Democratic-Republican
party that claimed to be the heir of Jefferson, but whose real maker
was Andrew Jackson and his Western and Eastern allies. On the
whole, Jackson's party was the party of small man, of the worker in
the growing industrial cities of the East, of the sections of the
country, mainly in the South, that thought they needed nothing
from the federal government but to be left alone. Sentiment and
interest combined to make this alliance very powerful, to make it,
except in moments of internal division, the natural majority party
and to establish the rule that once a winning combination of this
kind is established, it remains the majority party for a very long
time, only losing its place as a result of incurable internal discord
or of an evident failure to deliver the goods that it had promised to
its customers.

Against the Democrats were ranged various groups, the National
Republicans, the short-lived Anti-Masonic party[1] and other
dwellers in the Cave of Adullam. Together they took the felicitous
name of Whig. They had the greatest orators and the most respectable sections of society on their side. Yet they only briefly
occupied the seats of power and in them were ineffectual, disappointing their friends even more than they angered their enemies.

[1] The ostensible grounds for the formation of this party were the dangers to a republican government of secret societies.

Yet the Whigs were a true American party in the sense that the Federalists had not been. They were national; they had strongholds all over the Union from Vermont to Kentucky and Georgia. They accepted the necessity of adopting a democratic manner to defeat the Democrats. The old Federalists had been more of the temper of Coriolanus; even when they wooed the plebs, they did it ungraciously and unconvincingly. And the Whigs, unlike the Federalists, saw the importance of the rising factory industry. The Federalists were the old 'good, wise and rich', landowners and merchants and shipowners. Except for the prophetic Hamilton, they rather despised the 'rude mechanicals'. But the alliance of the 'lords of the lash and the lords of the loom', as the enemies of slavery unkindly put it, the political conjunction of the greater planters of the South with the rising textile interests of New England, was not sufficiently strong, politically, to overcome the alliance of the ever-expanding West with a great part of the South and with great areas of the North, still dominated by the memory of Jefferson and by economic interests not identical with those of the nascent, tariff-hungry industries. The Whigs did not lack for talent. In Henry Clay they had the most popular, the most 'glamorous' of demagogues. In Webster, they had the most adroit of orators, the most skilful of advocates, who once his supporters had turned from the sea to the factories, once they were identified with great economic institutions (and generous paymasters) like the Bank of the United States, saw the light, supported high tariffs and bank money and managed to invest this policy with a glow of patriotism that came a little oddly from the spokesman of the regions that had contracted out of 'Mr. Madison's war' and seemed on the eve of its ending to be about to contract out of the Union. Websters do not grow on every bush, but what Webster did with such mastery is what many lesser Websters have tried to do since and still try to do, give to sectional interest the appeal that comes from wrapping it in the flag. It is a job of packaging, an art in which American industry excels.[1]

But Webster and Clay did not succeed in leaving a viable Whig

[1] 'In his classic reply to Hayne the godlike Daniel (Webster) has never been surpassed by any orator in capturing a developing national trend and utilizing it to rationalize a set of interests and the flag.' Binkley, op. cit., p. 137.

party behind them. As an effective opposition it died in 1852; the party and its two great orators going to the grave at the same time. Local leaders, like Lincoln in Illinois, practically gave up politics; national leaders like Senator Seward of New York were in danger of having no political home. The Democrats seemed to be in unshaken control. But the forces that were undermining the Whigs were dividing the Democrats. In the decline of one, in the division of the other, the great American crisis that led to the Civil War was most clearly revealed. For the alliance of Northern and Southern Whigs was threatened by the increasing pressure on the 'peculiar institution', on slavery. The most respectable and economically impressive Bostonians might try to keep down the public temper, put an end to the glittering generalities of the Declaration of Independence. But, more and more, in the South only one question mattered; the defence of the South against a possibly hostile federal government. Tombs and Cobb, Stephens and Jefferson Davis had to forget their past party divisions in face of the gathering storm.

The divisions of the Democrats were even more significant, more revealing of the nature of federal party politics than the decline of the Whigs. For the power of the Democratic party had been based on an alliance of West and South with the poorer rural and the poorer urban elements of the East. The West wanted, the East began to want things that the South did not need or did not know it needed. As the United States stretched westward, sectional conflicts over the disposal of national assets took more and more divisive forms, for it made a great deal of difference whether a given area was to be open to slavery or not. It made a great deal of difference whether the public lands were to be sold or given away; it made a great deal of difference whether federal resources and credit were to be used to push railways westward or even to remove obstacles to navigations in the great lakes. And it became more and more difficult to hold South and West together; southern leadership became rigid as fear became greater. The proposal to open the Kansas-Nebraska territory to settlement, leaving the question of the acceptance of slavery or its prohibition to local option, to 'squatter sovereignty', split the Democratic party and led the way to the formation, in 1856, of a party that was sectional (it could hope to have no serious support in the South); that was opposed to compromise; that insisted on the intrusion of moral principles into the day-to-day sectional bargaining and the reiteration of comfortable and empty formulas. It was as a 'party of moral ideas' that the Republicans fought their first presidential election in 1856. They did not win but the range of their support, the degree to which they successfully forced the sectional issue was ominous and from the foundation of the party dates the modern American party system.

The description of the Republican party as 'the party of moral ideas' became, in the decades after the Civil War, a joke in bad taste for the Democrats and a joke to be enjoyed by the more cynical members of what was, by then, 'the Grand Old Party', the triumphant 'G.O.P.'. But not only did many members of that party, like Senator Hoar, sincerely believe that it was still a party of moral ideas, the legend (if it was only that by 1900) represented a once important truth.

For the Republican party that came into existence between 1854 and 1856 was a party of a moral idea, a party based on the proposition laid down by Lincoln that 'if slavery is not wrong, nothing is wrong'. That there were other forces behind the break-up of the old party system is true. The futility of the Whigs, the sterility of the Know Nothings, the internal feuds of the Democrats all created a demand for a new party. So did changes in the economic structure of the Union; so did personal ambitions and the disappearance of the great veterans, Clay, Webster, Calhoun. But all of these were accidents or results of the basic conflict, the attendant circumstances of the situation that chattel slavery in the mid-nineteenth century was an institution incompatible with the kind of civilization, moral and material, that was becoming common to the whole western world.

The role of the anti-slavery agitators was merely that of calling attention to the more emotionally moving aspects of the problem, but had there been no Garrison, no Weld, no Grimké sisters, no Lovejoys, even had there been no *Uncle Tom's Cabin*, the cleavage between North and South would have been more and more visible, although it need not, necessarily, have ended in war. The Free Soilers of 1848, the great mass of Democrats who left their (as they thought) apostate party between 1854 and 1856, the Know Nothings who failed to maintain their unity and 'went with their section', all testified to the basic nature of the party revolution.

But the division of the country on such openly sectional lines was itself enough to alarm the conservative, the timid and the prudent. Nor could moral indignation, in itself, provide enough steam to keep the engine running. The defeat of Frémont in 1856 showed that and it took luck, skill and the suicidal blindness of the Buchanan administration to keep up an adequate head of steam to make the new party fit for a second attempt on national power in 1860. No party in the United States had ever won on a single issue and on a moral issue at that. This was seen by one of the chief makers of the Northern temper that was, in itself, one of the forces creating the crisis. Horace Greeley, by 1860, had learned what must be done. 'I want to succeed this time . . . yet I know the country is not Anti-Slavery. It will only swallow a little Anti-Slavery in a great deal of sweetening. An Anti-Slavery man *per se* cannot be elected; but a Tariff, River-and-Harbor, Pacific Railroad, Free-Homestead man, *may* succeed although he is Anti-Slavery. . . . I mean to have as good a candidate as the majority will elect. And, if the People are to rule, I think that is the way.'[1] Greeley was right and the 'conversion' of the Boss of Pennsylvania, Simon Cameron, was perhaps the most encouraging sign for the future of the new party for Cameron, unmoved by moral principles, represented great power and increasingly important interests. The transformation of the party was noted even by the time of its second Convention; the party that nominated Lincoln (as a middle-of-the-road candidate) was already significantly different from the party that nominated Frémont. Old Joshua Giddings, who could remember the time when he and John Quincy Adams, alone in Congress, opposed 'the Slave Power', noted the change and was alarmed by it. But the Convention, full of practical men as it was, could not, as George William Curtis declared, vote down the Declaration of Independence; it did affirm that 'the maintenance of the principles promulgated in the Declaration of Independence and embodied in the Federal Constitution . . . is essential to the preservation of our Republican institutions'.[2] And Giddings, like a new Simeon, saw, credulously, in this triumph, 'an era in Christian statesmanship.

[1] Quoted in Jeter Allen Isely, *Horace Greeley and the Republican Party, 1853–1861* (1947), p. 266.
[2] Kirk H. Porter, *National Party Platforms* (1924), p. 55–6.

The old theory of politicians had been discarded. The dictation of the slave power had been repudiated. The Government was to be regenerated and redeemed'.[1] These were illusions, indeed, but illusions shared by millions and illusions destined to a long and potent life.

It can hardly be doubted that the immediate cause of the greatest breakdown of the American political system was the breakdown of the party system, the failure of the party machinery and the party leaders to remember their national function, which, if carried out, was the justification of the varied weaknesses and absurdities of the party organizations and policies. Not until the party system broke down, in the dissolution of the Whigs, in the schism of the Democrats, was war possible. 'Thus war came when the American people for the first time refused to abide by a national election. The parties which had been promoting the cohesive attitudes had broken down, and their disorganization had permitted the new Republican organization to win through direct appeal to the divisive attitudes. The constant heat generated in the frequent elections brought an explosion. The social, economic and cultural differences had been so used by the political operators as to produce secession and civil war'.[2]

Although it may be rash to suggest a belief in a national memory, it is at any rate possible that the American shrinking from doctrinaire parties, from people who knew their own minds, who would not compromise, who had a social theory to defend or attack, owed something to the recollection of the time when America *had* such parties, when, to the astonishment of each side, North and South found themselves at war.[3]

[1] Joshua R. Giddings, *History of the Rebellion* (1864), p. 447.
[2] Roy Franklin Nichols, *The Disruption of American Democracy* (1948), p. 516. By 'American Democracy' in this context Professor Nichols means roughly what we should call the 'Democratic party' or 'the Democracy', as old-fashioned Democrats called their party in not very remote times.
[3] 'Yet the lesson of the ruinous Civil War has been so well learned in America that it is many years since regional discontents have led to talk of secession. The political parties have learned to minimize such discontents, sometimes by concessions, sometimes by ignoring the evasion of the law. As usual when a political problem has been allayed, the

It is a much debated question whether the Republican party that re-elected Lincoln in 1864 and elected Grant in 1868, had much but the name in common with the agglomeration of 'Anti-Nebraska' men of 1854, or even with the Republican party of 1856 or 1860. At any rate, it was no longer a party of a moral idea; for some it was not a party that needed moral ideas. It had something better; it had possession of power in the federal government; it was linked with most of the rising economic interests of the country; and it had the immense advantage of an emotionally powerful stock of assets with which to win votes without paying anything very tangible for them. It was the party that saved the Union, freed the slaves; the party of the martyred Lincoln. It is easy enough to understand the importance of the first asset. So great a war as the Civil War necessarily distorted and promoted economic growth. Most bankers, railway men, iron manufacturers, textile manufacturers, the holders of the great federal debt, were natural Republicans. Not all bankers, not all manufacturers were Republicans, but most of them were.[1] Not all manufacturers had the same interests. Some not only did not want high tariffs but suffered from them, as did that eminent Democratic businessman and politician, Abram Hewitt.[2] Nevertheless, the Republican party became the

---

absence of friction is now taken for granted. The party system is given no credit; or is merely abused for the delays, the seeming inefficiencies, the endless regional compromises, which are the cost of exorcizing the demon of secession.' Herbert Agar, *The Price of Union* (1950), p. 85.

[1] Age told, too. The older generation had fewer Republicans, more unconverted Democrats in it than the younger. Thus one of the most eminent businessmen of Cleveland, Daniel P. Rhodes, objected, as a father and as a good Democrat, to the courtship of his daughter by a young man who was not only highly independent but a zealous Republican. ' I like you very well, Mark, but you are a damned screecher for freedom. ' Herbert Croly, *Marcus Alonzo Hanna* (1912), p. 47.

[2] Hewitt who had to keep his steel mill at Trenton wanted to bring 'the proper ores from Spain and Algiers to mix with their own. . . . He protested vigorously to influential Congressmen about the high duties. . . . The iron manufacturing interests to the westward, especially in Pennsylvania, profited heavily by it and were unwilling to reduce duties a cent'. Allan Nevins, *Abram Hewitt* (1935), p. 262. Hewitt never became a steel magnate on the scale of Carnegie or Frick, so he could remain a Democrat.

party of American business and claimed to be (and managed, to a large degree, to get its claim accepted) the party of American patriotism. 'Not all Democrats were rebels but all rebels were Democrats,' ran the saying.

Except for a brief and revolutionary period, the Republican party was sectional. It had little life in the South. It was weak, too, in areas settled from the South and in some of the great cities, above all in New York. It, too, faced difficulties arising from the different interests of the West and East. But its rulers were too sagacious ever to risk a serious weakening of their alliance with the new industrial leaders merely to placate angry farmers. The farmers could usually be held true to the good old cause by appeals to their emotions, by recalling to their minds the crimes of the South, 'waving the Bloody Shirt', as it was called, by appealing to dislike of the new, foreign and Democratic cities. The farmer, obviously, paid the cost of the greatest gift of the Republican party to the dominant sections of business, the high and mounting tariff, for he had, willy-nilly, to sell in an open world market and buy in a protected national market. It is the greatest tribute to Republican skill and to the genuine emotional assets that the party had managed to accumulate, that, in the mass, the farmers supported a party that did so little for them.

By 1880, the pattern of Republican strength was fixed. Territorially, it was strongest in Pennsylvania, New England and the northern states of the Middle West. It was the party of ministers and doctors, of businessmen, small and great, of the colleges and of the 'better' magazines. A Democrat, over a great part of the North, had to explain his position; a Republican did not need to bother.

What the Republicans did not securely possess, they fought for with the Democrats, on the whole with great success. From the elections of Lincoln to the election of Cleveland (1860–84), the Democrats did not win a single presidential election. For twenty-four years, that is, at a time when the economy of the United States was being transformed, the Republicans were the 'party of government'. True, the Democrats quite often carried the House of Representatives, less often the Senate. True, they were powerful, locally, in New York, in Indiana, quite often in Ohio. But

Republican administrations became the rule. The Republicans had the habit of victory and the fruits of victory.

If the Democrats had come into power, even as late as 1876 when, some hold, they really won the presidential election, many political and business habits would not have been so set. It was certain that whatever group of politicians was in power would be cultivated by business. If the Democrats had been in power, they would have had favours to give away and if, for example, their low tariff policy had been enacted, the pattern of American business would have been altered though not transformed. But it was the Republican party that ruled; it was the high tariff policy that was enacted. The Democrats were, felt themselves to be, and acted like the underdog.

In the North, there were patches of Democratic strength. Even in New England, not only in great immigrant centres like Boston, but in mainly rural states like New Hampshire, there were plenty of zealous Democrats. Connecticut, the 'land of steady habits', was slower to abandon the party than is usually remembered. But not only was the party out of touch with the dominant trends of the economy and out of touch with much living political emotion bred by the War, it inevitably became the refuge of the fugitives from the minor parties who had their own panaceas. It was a kind of national Cave of Adullam or rather the place where the Adullamites went when the cave became uninhabitable. 'Greenbackers' who wanted to lighten the debtor's load by the issue of paper money; 'silverites' who wanted to do this by the free coinage of silver; farmers angered, for the moment, by bad harvests or low prices or both; dissident groups of various kinds, religious, racial, economic; all turned naturally to the Democratic party. But they did not turn in sufficient numbers and they did not stay turned.

The Democratic national leadership, for the most part, was safely conservative. It differed from the Republican leadership in being less ready to support government aids to business by tariffs, land grants and the like, by doctrinal differences about federal power, by being more ready to shout 'turn the rascals out', if only for the good reason that the Republicans (rascals or not) were in and the Democrats (rascals or not) were out. So the radical elements of the party, especially in the Middle West, were constantly fretting against a leadership that seemed to differ very little from the Republican leadership. What, for example, had the Western agrarians or even the discontented workers of the cities to expect from a leader like Speaker Randall (who was not even sound on the tariff)? What did they gain from the two administrations of Grover Cleveland? Not even an effective dealing with the tariff.

And when years of depression, rural and urban, put the radicals briefly in command, when Bryan was nominated in 1896, 'respectable' Democrats left the party in shoals.[1] On the other hand, when the party nominated an eminently respectable conservative like Alton B. Parker in 1904, against the 'dangerous' Theodore Roosevelt, business was not grateful; its habits were too well formed; its confidence in the congressional if not the presidential leadership of the Republican party was unshaken.

The 'solid South' was, for long, an identifiable political unit. It included all the eleven states that seceded in 1861, plus the four slave states that did not secede, Maryland, Delaware, Kentucky, Missouri. Disregarding the rigged elections of Reconstruction times, none of the 'Confederate States', except Tennessee, ever voted for a Republican presidential candidate before the Hoover-Smith election of 1928. But in the McKinley-Bryan election of

---

[1] Even in the South, the nomination of Bryan put a great strain on party discipline. McKinley did much better in Virginia than Harrison had done. 'The businessmen, with their increasing strength in the border-state economy, had either refrained from voting or had supported McKinley as had men in a similar position but north of the Potomac. The vote showed that by a powerful tradition Virginia was bound to the Democratic party of the South, yet that on economic issues her interests, though still predominantly rural, were approaching those of the East.' William Du Bose Sheldon. *Populism in the Old Dominion* (1935), p. 138. So in the East, the renascent and respectable Democratic party to which the independents, the 'Mugwumps' had rallied, withered away. 'In Massachusetts, the people who had followed Cleveland and William E. Russell and had won victories for them in a constituency that was normally Republican, soon gave over the reins to local free-silverites and to a near-Tammany element in the city of Boston.' Henry James, *Richard Olney* (1923), p. 176. It was, however, Olney's opinion, that among those who for all practical purposes left the Democratic party for good, was Cleveland himself. Olney formally supported Bryan in 1900 and in 1908.

1896, the fundamental conservatism of the border states put them in the Republican camp, revealing, what the twentieth century was to make more apparent, that the fact that a state had had slavery as an institution in 1860, was no longer decisive. Yet, all in all, it was convenient, until very recent times, to talk of the 'solid South' and give any Democratic candidate the whole electoral vote of the former Confederate states and a good chance for the vote of some of the 'border states'.

It is no longer safe to do so; the South politically is now what it has been for quite a long time now geographically, an ambiguous term.[1] Even when the solidity of the South could be taken for granted, it was not taken for granted that it was based on some necessary configuration of the region. It was easy to see the power, in the South, especially in the states of the Confederacy, of a sentimental attachment to the 'Lost Cause' as potent as the attachment of a great part of the North to the party that had 'saved the Union'. The region where the 'Bonny Blue Flag' was popular was opposed to the region where 'Marching Through Georgia' was the agreeable reminder of a great feat of arms, not of a crime against the laws of war. But the North had been, after all, victorious. It had, or parts of it had, the spoils of war. But the beaten, impoverished, highly political South, by clinging to what was soon seen as the minority party, seemed to many to be cutting off its nose to spite its face, to be permitting nostalgia and resentment to extinguish a rational attitude to politics in a region that could afford sentiment in politics much less than could the victorious North.

The South, it was argued, in 1865, accepted the verdict of arms. It knew that slavery and the right of secession were dead. It knew that it faced a terrible problem of adjustment and reconstruction. It knew that it was rash to antagonize the victors, still angry at the cost of victory. And, it is argued, the South was ready to accept the

[1] 'There is no longer in the United States any single entity which may be designated as "the South". More authentically, there is a Southeast and a Southwest, comparable to four other major regions designated as the Northeast, the Northwest, the Middle States, and the Far West. . . . It is, therefore, neither possible nor desirable to present a single authentic picture of "the South".' Howard W. Odum, *Southern Regions of the United States* (1936), p. 5.

decision of arms and collaborate in reconstructing the Union, even to the extent of giving the Republican party a hearing and an opportunity that it could not have hoped to have in 1860. It is possible that in a different political system, the South would have returned to the Union in more than legal form. But its possibilities of rational action were conditioned by the facts of the American political system.

One result of the abolition of slavery was to *increase* Southern political power. For under the Constitution, the so-called 'federal ratio' applied; the slaves counted for three fifths of their number in the allocation of seats in the House of Representatives. The freedmen would now count for five fifths and the South would gain from thirty to forty seats in the House of Representatives. Since the Republican party, with victory in the war to its credit (for the end was certain by the time of the election of 1864) had not won by any wide margin, even with eleven hostile states out of the Union, it was less likely to win with those states back in their old place. The Republicans would have saved the Union for the Democrats.

It was not merely the politicians who were alarmed. The beneficiaries of Republican economic policy; the newly protected industries, the land grant railroads, nervous public debtors, the easily frightened men who had done well out of the war, had as serious an interest in preventing the restoration of the old political system as had the politicians.

It is possible that a Southern combination hostile to the Republicans need not have been formed. It is possible that the old Whigs, as well as former Democrats disillusioned by the loss of the war, the collapse of the old system, the unwillingness of their quondam allies in the North to give effectual help, might have been won over and a local, representative and deeply rooted Republican party come into being in the South. 'The gradual disappearance of this reasonable expectation and hope was entirely due to Northern folly. Blinded by their course of vengeance the Northern Radicals, by making loyalty alone their touchstone of worth, threw away their chance to build up an intelligent and respectable following in the South, especially from the old Whig element.'[1] Maybe, but not

[1] E. Merton Coulter, *The South During Reconstruction 1845–77*, in *A History of the South*, vol. VIII (1947), p. 44.

only were many Republicans reluctant to take the risk, but the attitude of the Southern leaders was unrealistic. Their view of what the war (and defeat) implied was very different from that which the victorious North held. Great wisdom and prudence, a Lincoln in the White House, men of his stamp in the capitols of the conquered states *might* have restored a two party system in the South that had died before the Civil War broke out. But Lincoln was murdered and he had no real successors and few imitators.

Republican 'reconstruction' was insisted on. The vote was given to all freedmen and denied to many of their former masters: State governments ruled by 'carpet-baggers' and 'scalawags'[1] took over the South and ruled it for the national Republican party and for the interests represented by the national party.

For the overwhelming majority of Southern whites, the sole political question became the restoration of white rule. State by state, the carpet-bag governments were overthrown until those that remained were only kept in power by federal military force. In the most closely contested of presidential elections, that of 1876, it was only the votes of states controlled by these governments that gave the Republican candidate, Rutherford B. Hayes, his possibly fraudulent majority. By a bargain, the Southern Democrats did not support their Northern brethren in a last ditch stand against the acceptance of Hayes and, in return, the troops were withdrawn, the carpet-bag governments collapsed and 'home rule' was restored.[2]

It is possible, again, that a new orientation of the parties might have occurred, that Hayes, in 1877–81, might have created a conservative, business-minded Southern wing of the Republican party, leaving the carpet-bag Republicans to their fate and, assum-

[1] Carpet-baggers were Northerners who, it was believed, had come into the South after the war with a carpet-bag as their sole possession. Scalawags were native Southerners who joined the victors from, it was assumed, sordid motives. Not all did so for this reason. One of the greatest of southern generals, Longstreet, became a Republican and we may assume 'in a general, honest thought and common good to all, made one of them'.

[2] Professor C. Vann Woodward in *Reunion and Reaction* (1951) argues that there was far more in the bargain than this, that the Southern leaders were as interested in tangible economic gains, railroad grants and the like, as in mere political 'liberation'.

ing that the Negroes would either follow the lead of conservative whites like Wade Hampton, or would be persuaded, in various ways, not to vote. But the times were unpropitious. 'Less than a year after the Compromise of 1877 an irresistible tide of agrarian radicalism was sweeping the South out of control of conservative leaders and into alliance with the West.'[1]

Indeed, the next attempt to give life to the moribund Republican party in the South took the form of 'taking into camp' the radical leader in Virginia, General William Mahone, leader of the 'Readjusters' who wanted, in effect, to cut down the cost of the state debt. He appealed both to Negroes and to discontented and impoverished whites. Mahone turned Republican, built up a formidable amount of support and was encouraged by a most lavish use of federal patronage. But, again, he was unlucky. 'A race riot' at Danville, in 1883, came at an opportune moment for the Democrats and probably accounted for their victory. It may have been only a coincidence but the Readjuster, 'contended that the uprising had been deliberately provoked by the Democrats for campaign purposes and Mahone was able to secure considerable evidence to support this contention'.[2] Mahone lost control of the state patronage; then, in 1885, the Democrats at long last came back into office and, of course, made a complete sweep of the Mahone federal machine in Virginia. The Readjuster leader lost his seat and ended his political (and financial) life in 'shallows and in miseries'.

By 1885, indeed, the pattern of the 'solid South' was set and with it the pattern of national politics. 'Conditioning all political activity was the fact that the parties had been shaped in the era of sectional controversy. The only issue that made division between Democrats and Republicans was the North-South rivalry. On the issues of

[1] Woodward, op. cit., p. 237. As an example of the passions that wrecked the prospects of the Hayes plan, Professor Woodward notes that the lower house of the Mississippi legislature (now safely white) thanked the surviving Negro Senator, Blanche K. Bruce, for voting for free silver, thus by implication censuring the white Senator, Lucius Quintus Cincinnatus Lamar.

[2] Nelson Morehouse Blake, *William Mahone* (1935), p. 227. It is probable that, even without this minor Reichstag fire, Mahone's dependence on Negro votes would have, in the not very long run, hurt him badly.

tariff, control of corporations, railroad regulation, finance, civil service reform, honesty in politics and labour organization, the divisions were intra-party rather than inter-party. Consequently all living issues were straddled or ignored, while easy retreat into the past was resorted to whenever and wherever the party chieftains felt that it would succeed.'[1]

The agrarian discontent that had wrecked the half-formed plans of the Hayes administration, and of the Southern conservatives, was not cured nor could it be, as long as the condition of the primary producers remained as depressed in the South as it was in the Middle West. That discontent might take the form of throwing up rural agrarian leaders like 'Pitchfork Ben' Tillman in South Carolina,[2] Tillman revolted not only against the rule of his state by 'Bourbons' like Wade Hampton, but against any threat to 'white supremacy'. He provided, that is to say, an outlet for all the passions and desires of the poor whites, resentment of their lowly economic status, social discontent with the manners of the old planter aristocracy and a firm, almost maniacal determination, to 'keep the nigger in his place'. That both the Negro and the poor white might have the same interests was too recondite an idea for a class that saw the freedmen as economic competitors, not as fellow sufferers from 'aristocratic' rule and saw in their votes, if permitted to be cast, a political asset of the Bourbons.

As party lines got confused, as the ruling class saw itself threatened, as the Republican party in the South saw in the discontent that led to the formation of the 'People's party' a chance to hitch its waggon to a rising not a falling star, the orthodox conservative Democrats

[1] Paul H. Buck, *The Road to Reunion 1865–1900* (1937), p. 264.
[2] Tillman got this name from a famous threat to stick his pitchfork into the person of President Cleveland, leader of the party to which Tillman formally owed allegiance. This threat got added news value from the fact that Cleveland was the bulkiest President before Taft. In thus attacking Cleveland, Tillman was, of course, appealing to the genuine resentment of the agrarian interests in more states than in South Carolina. 'I haven't got words', said Tillman at Rock Hill, June 18 [1894], 'to say what I think of that old bag of beef President Cleveland. If you send me to the Senate, I promise you I won't be bulldozed [by him].' Francis Butler Simkins, *The Tillman Movement in South Carolina* (1926), p. 181.

and the rebels against the party machines were each tempted to call in the Negro voter to redress the balance of power.

Flectere si nequeo superos Acheronta movebo

might have been the motto of both Populists and of Democrats in some regions where docile and venal Negro voters held the balance of power. If, in some states, the conservatives relied on Negro voters to turn the trick, they also, in general, clung to the Democratic party and saw in it, as the Democrats of Mississippi put it, 'the only security for the maintenance of white supremacy. . . . We therefore deplore the movement now afoot for the organization of a third party, to be known as the People's party, and we conjure all good men and true patriots to stand by the Democratic party.'[1]

In North Carolina, where there was a substantial white Republican vote, the Populist alliance and the acceptance of Negro support had more to commend it. But 'Fusion', the alliance of Republicans and Populists, was only too successful. 'There the Republicans and Populists had won in the election of 1896 not only the legislature and the state offices but many local and county offices as well. In some of the eastern counties, where the bulk of the Republican voters were negroes, this meant negro office-holders in large numbers.' It was exactly the issue that had provoked the Danville riot and begun the ruin of Mahone's party. 'Even the Populists were affected. If the existence of a third party was to mean in practice that the negroes were to have the upper hand many reformers were ready to abandon their third-party tickets.'[2]

And in the nation, the Populist tide was ebbing; the fusion with the Democrats in 1896 to support Bryan had not brought national victory. Populism was too tender a plant to survive this change of the weather in the nation and, above all, in the South.

The decision was taken. In all Southern states, the white population returned to the Democratic party and by law, quasi-law and intimidation, the Negroes were kept from voting. By 1900, the political rights of the Negro, given and guaranteed by the fourteenth and fifteenth amendments, were meaningless in all the states of the Confederacy, with the possible exception of Tennessee. And

[1] Quoted in John D. Hicks, *The Populist Revolt* (1931), p. 348.
[2] Ibid., p. 392.

the most famous American Negro, Booker T. Washington, had advised his people to wait for the restoration of those rights till they had made the economic progress that was their greatest need. 'The time will come when the Negro in the South will be accorded all the political rights which his ability, character and material possessions entitle him to.'[1] But that time was not yet.

The effect on the Republican party of the South was catastrophic. There remained a few states in which there was an indigenous white Republican party, Virginia, Texas, North Carolina, Tennessee. But nowhere was it strong enough to carry the state for a Republican presidential candidate, to control the state government, to elect a United States Senator. In most states, it consisted of non-assimilated Northerners, a few cranks, a few zealots—and federal office holders and office seekers, in most cases Negroes; in all cases, cut off from the normal life of the dominant white community.

Until the political revolution of 1932, the United States had a stable two party system; one party, the majority party, covering all of the nation except the South. Over a great part of the nation the party label was all that mattered. Whoever was the official Democratic candidate always won in Georgia, whoever was the official Republican candidate always won in Vermont. There were not only states that were forever faithful to one party; there were faithful counties, sometimes embedded, like some Republican counties in the South, in the midst of hostile territory, but unshaken in their allegiance.

The consequences of this traditional allegiance were very important. Since, in fact, the interests, the problems, the contemporary passions of these areas were not unified, the same party label might cover very different political principles and practices. It was not only that the right wing of one party overlapped the left wing of the other; the left wing of each party overlapped the left wing of the other. The whole range of politically important opinion was represented in each party and men in South Carolina and New Hampshire voted for the same types, the same attitudes, while never thinking of voting outside the formal party organization. The national and local party managers knew that practically every-

[1] Booker T. Washington, *Up From Slavery* (1901; World's Classics edition 1945), p. 174.

body in a state would vote for the nominee of the party that, traditionally, dominated there. An intending politician knew that if he wanted a political career, he could only have it inside the dominant party.

Inevitably, then, the real fights were for the party nomination. And, again inevitably, the politicians who wanted in any fashion to upset the *status quo*, had to upset the nominating system. The method they chose was the 'direct primary'.

'Primaries', the election by party voters of delegates to nominate candidates were an old institution in most American states. Even the 'direct primary', the choice of candidates not by delegates to a state convention but by the voters in the primary, has a fairly long history. But it is only with the turn of this century, that the direct primary became the instrument for reforming or, as some thought, for destroying the party system.

It was generally the radicals, the spokesmen of discontent, who fought for the direct primary. Such diverse types of leaders as Tillman in South Carolina, La Follette in Wisconsin and later Woodrow Wilson in New Jersey, made of the direct primary a democratic panacea. It is not at all certain that they were wrong. For the direct primary turned the flank of the historically in-expugnable party system. Voters in South Carolina, voters in Wisconsin still cast their ballots for the nominees of the sacred Democratic (or Republican) party. But the real election became the primary. In the contest for the nomination, the formal unity of the party was disregarded; live issues, local and national, were fought over. Reality was restored to local and national politics and, in very different parts of the country, very similar programmes of legislation and administration were put into effect. Mere appeals to the memory of Lincoln or Lee did not work in the decisive election, the primary. The victor, of course, was sound on Lincoln (or on Lee) but he might be very unsound on other more recent personalities and problems than those made classical during and after 'the war'.

Time was to show that the direct primary did not necessarily foster radicalism; that it could be used by conservative as well as by radical demagogues. But it was, in its early years, opposed by conservatives and for good reasons. The old system suited them, for the less realistic the party issues, the less danger there was of legislation or administration that would upset the *status quo*. And the leaders, North and South, thrown up by the direct primary (especially after the adoption of the seventeenth amendment providing for the election of Senators by the voters not by the legislatures of the States), were in general men who wanted to upset the *status quo*, to regulate railroads and public utilities, to alter the tax system to the disadvantage of the great corporations, to spend public money, in states and in the nation, for the benefit of the 'unprivileged'. The possessing classes, politically speaking, even in the days of Harding, 'never had it so good' as in the few years when the triumph of Bryanism inside the Democratic party gave the Republicans an unshaken superiority and gave power inside the Republican party to the veteran Senators, chosen by handpicked legislators in safe states.

But the critics of the results of the direct primary had more valid arguments than that the new system did not suit them. It did break down party discipline in Congress, since the victor in a Democratic primary in an agricultural state had more in common with the victor in a Republican primary in an agricultural state than either had with Republican or Democratic Senators from industrial states still dominated by business. From 1910 on, with few exceptions, party control of the old type became more and more difficult, and where leadership was supplied, it came from the White House rather than from Congress.

Alliances between radical groups were not always confined to Congress and there were an increasing number of cases in which conservative elements in the traditionally Republican states of the Middle West, defeated in the primary, went over, in the final election to support a conservative Democrat, still further confusing the party pattern.

Another group of critics, while they had to welcome the primary as being 'democratic', deplored its results as far as they prevented a rationalizing of the party structure. The direct primary saved people from the necessity of making up their minds. It allowed them to accept the irrational loyalty of the voters to meaningless party traditions, party traditions that had a hold even on staunch radical reformers like Borah and Norris. And it is possible that the existence of the primary, by making the intra-party struggle real without upsetting the traditional distribution of party strength, did destroy what little chance there was of the more fundamental changes in the party structure hoped for, by radicals and by some theorists, from coming to pass. For if the old order had survived, if party leadership in the Congress and in many of the states had remained as rigidly conservative as it was between 1896 and 1910, the mere pressure on the dikes might have brought about a re-alignment like that of 1854–60.

But the fact that, in this century, three attempts to launch a new party have failed, shows that those who advocated and advocate working within the existing system have shown prudence, if they have not shown sufficient regard for logic. For each attempt to launch a new party has failed, and the first attempt was more success-ful than the second, the second than the third.

The three important third party movements of the twentieth century had in common the fact that they were centred on the personalities, the ambitions, the programme of three leaders, each with his own following of admirers. The Progressive Party of 1912 was the party of Theodore Roosevelt; the Progressive ticket of 1924 was the 'party' of Robert M. La Follette, Senior; the Progres sive Party of 1948 was the party of Henry Wallace. This was not to say that the parties had no other roots than in the admiration of many thousands of members of the old parties for their leader and resentment of his wrongs. There was plenty of material for dis-content with the existing party system and its working in each of these years. The big vote polled by Debs as the Socialist candidate in 1912; the wide-spread insurgency of the politicians of the farm states and of the voters in 1924 and the emptiness, from that point of view, of the programmes and leadership of each of the old parties; the frame of mind represented by the Labour Party in New York, by the attitude of some important union leaders, the nostalgia for the great days of the New Deal in 1948; all these were serious political phenomena. But these discontents could not have been focused, could not have been so effective in stirring men and women to engage in the hazardous task of launching a new party had there not been a hero to act as a catalyst, a myth to exploit, a hero and myth of the first order in the case of 'Teddy' Roosevelt, of the

second in the case of 'Bob' La Follette, and of the third in the case
of 'Harry' Wallace. For that reason, the parties seemed more formidable, were more formidable than the political forces they pro-
fessed to represent would have been by themselves and, also for that
reason, the parties were ephemeral, sterile.[1]

It is probable that each of these candidates polled a bigger vote
than a protest party, without a standard-bearer of that magnitude,
would have done. It is probable that, given the circumstances, there
would have been a third party movement of some importance in
each of these years. But 'Bob' La Follette in 1912, or substitutes for
La Follette and Wallace in 1924 and 1948, would not have had the
charismatic appeal that made the third parties, for a brief moment,
appear serious threats to the old order and, in the case of the
Progressives in 1912, actually displace the Republicans in the
popular vote for President.

On the other hand, once the parties as national parties had failed;
had failed to elect Roosevelt in 1912, had failed to intimidate the
Republicans into nominating him in 1916; had failed in 1924 to
make any serious impression on the Republican predominance and,
in 1948, failed to defeat Truman; the parties, as national organizations, withered away. They might have had an important role as
regional groups or as national pressure groups within the existing

[1] Thus in the 1924 campaign, the 'Council for Progressive Political
Action', the 'CPPA', soon became submerged in the personality of the
elder La Follette. 'As the campaign progressed, it became increasingly
the "La Follette movement" and the terms "Progressive" and "CPPA"
were much less in evidence. . . . The 1924 progressive movement, under
these circumstances, became as vulnerable and as mortal as La Follette'.
(Kenneth Campbell MacKay, *The Progressive Movement of 1924*, (1947)
p. 251). The same fate befell the more important Progressive party of
1912 as was belatedly seen by one of the most combative members of it.
'The Progressive party, in large measure, was the outward expression of
the love and the admiration, amounting almost to idolatry, that the
overwhelming majority of its members felt for Theodore Roosevelt.
. . . Personally or politically, with only a relatively few exceptions, none
of the people who took their political lives in their hands when they left
the Republican and Democratic parties in 1912 to follow Roosevelt had
a thing to gain. Yet they were willing to risk all, if necessary to sacrifice
all, because of their faith in one man.' (Harold L. Ickes, 'Who killed the
Progressive Party?', *American Historical Review*, January 1941, p. 329.)

party system, but as the parties of one man they died with that one man's hopes of national leadership. And as the parties had put all their money on one man, they found it difficult to cut themselves down to size and to resign themselves to reconciliation with the older parties, to working within them or bargaining with them.[1]

Even regional, deep-rooted parties are handicapped by the character of American political organization. For nearly a generation, the La Follette family in Wisconsin was able, most of the time, to keep hold of the local dominant political machine. But, in Congress, a result of preserving formal independence would have been the exclusion of Robert La Follette Junior from his place in the committee hierarchy with resultant diminution in effective power, so 'Young Bob', who succeeded to his father's seat with ease, went back to the Republican party. He and his brother, Philip, later launched a new Progressive party when it would have been more prudent to have done a deal with the Democrats. The result was that the increasingly conservative farmers of Wisconsin stayed in the Republican party while many of the old progressive elements and an increasingly large number of new voters went over to the 'New Deal'.[2]

[1] There was some plausibility in the argument of some progressive Republicans who had not joined the Progressive party, that the schism had only succeeded in electing a Democratic President and in giving control within the Republican party to its most reactionary elements.
' "If the progressives will remain in the Republican party and work in the future as we have in the past, we will dominate in Kansas. . . .", Senator Bristow wrote a friend in May 1914. "But if they go into a side show and organize a third party and divide up our strength, you can readily see how it will put us to a disadvantage. The third party movement in Kansas is the most unfortunate and unjustifiable of any political movement I have ever known." ' Walter Johnson, *William Allen White's America* (1947), p. 220–1.
[2] As early as 1934, the second year of the New Deal, the problem was acute, for the conservative Republicans were fighting the La Follettes with great energy and the Democratic party had suddenly revived. I was told, in Wisconsin at the time, by some Democratic leaders that they were willing to go along with the La Follettes 'if they would be reasonable'. But Governor Philip La Follette came, it is believed, to count on the discrediting of the Democratic party as the New Deal was stalled.

The same fate befell the Farmer-Labour party in Minnesota. With the death of Floyd Olsen and the revival of the Republican party under Harold Stassen, it was forced into alliance, then into fusion with the Democrats. The attempt to create a 'New Deal' party in New York, the 'American Labour party', although it had important results for a time in state and city politics, did nothing to alter the national pattern and in the not very long run ceased to be decisive even in New York.[1]

It is roughly true that every attempt to keep up an effective state, much more an effective national third party has failed and that, more and more, the remnants of the third parties find themselves driven into the Democratic ranks or out of politics. Thus 'Young Bob' La Follette made a fatal mistake in 1946 in formally returning to the Republican party and running in the Republican primary. He misjudged the realities of the situation when he declared that he saw 'the unmistakable signs of dissolution and disintegration "in the Democratic party. . . . I am convinced that we have a better chance to put our progressive ideals on the law books if we go into the Republican party" '.[2]

He was beaten in the primary by Joseph McCarthy, his political career was ended and the remnants of the once invincible La Follette machine or party were swallowed up by the once negligible Democrats.

There remains one historical problem of the American party system, why there has been no evolution of radical thought and action in a socialist direction, why there has been no equivalent of the British or Australian Labour parties or even of the semi-Socialist parties of Canada. But that is a long and complicated story.[3]

Some of the reasons for the failure of the American socialist movement, taking it in its widest sense, to gain more than a local

He forgot that the magic once attached over a wide region to the name of La Follette was now attached over the nation to the name (and party) of Franklin D. Roosevelt.

[1] For the role of the American Labour party in New York see p. 86.

[2] William T. Evjue, 'Wisconsin' in *Our Sovereign State,* edited by Robert S. Allen (1949), p. 233-4.

[3] See p. 362.

and temporary foothold, are bound up with the difficulties that beset all third parties in America. Party success is measured in the successful election of a President, of a Governor, of a Mayor. The fact that these offices cannot be divided makes concentration of effort, and the effective means to that concentration, the two party system, especially strong in America. The linking up of national and state, and often of municipal elections, forces some degree of common action on politicians at all levels. It requires a great deal of tenacity to hold on while a party slowly builds up enough support to win the offices that make it more than a mere body of organized protest. Most voters do not have that tenacity; most politicians do not have it either.

Then the law, in most states, is weighted against third parties. In some, a party cannot easily get on the ballot unless it has polled a certain proportion of the votes at a previous election, an application of Cornford's law of academic politics: 'nothing should ever be done for the first time'. In other states, a very large number of signatures is needed to effect a nomination and they must be collected all over the state. Neither major party has an interest in making things easy for a third party and neither party tries to make it easy. The American voter, used to traditional voting, to the real political life of his state or city taking place inside a dominant party, used to a division of authority that makes it natural for the supporters of a programme to hope to get it enacted by pressure on the elected officers of the party normally in power, is hard to convert to the view that he should postpone immediate gains for a long-term political transformation. Then the higher proportion of the population that was and is rural and the fact that the farmer is grossly over-represented in the states and seriously over-represented in Congress, meant and means that the organized workers have to made a deal with the organized farmers and that their feelings often conflict even more than their interests. The American farmer has been even less inclined to socialism than the farmer in other countries and yet no victory of the economic underdogs fighting as a class party is possible unless farmers and workers are allied.

And, most important of all, the main reason why a class-based party has not taken root in the United States is that the simple class division of the Socialist and Communist theorists does not exist.

'The tenacious hold which the two-party system has in the United States, successfully resisting numerous attempts to establish third parties is due primarily to the multiple-group character of our society. . . . Political interests are not economic alone. Matters of taste, habit, culture and morals cut across economic group lines at times to establish strong affinities between voters in widely separated economic groups. . . . Democracy signifies government b y consent of the majority. It precludes government by an economic class, for no distinguishable group, no segment of the population possessing common economic interests, is big enough to be, or has prospect of becoming, the "majority" in our complex society.'[1]

'Labour', the 'workers' are forced to be content with being another pressure group, content with using, not changing the permanent party system, for if they undertake to change it, the other groups in society will 'gang up' on them and they will lose, as a pressure group, without the prospect of adequate gains as a political party to compensate them at least in any foreseeable period of time.

This is not to say that there are no visible class lines in American politics. It is less untrue than it was, twenty years ago, to see the Democrats as 'left', the Republicans as 'right'. The last time that any large number of the prosperous did not vote the Republican ticket was in 1932. By 1936, class lines were more clearly drawn in politics. This was revealed in not only the amount, but in the source of contributions to the funds of the two parties. It was reflected in the growing disproportion of press support for the two parties until, in 1948, only one newspaper in the firmly Democratic city of New York supported President Truman and until, in 1952, there were whole states in which the Democratic candidate, polling many hundreds of thousands of votes had no serious press support at all. This did not necessarily do the Democrats much harm.[2] But it did reveal the degree to which the party lines were becoming

[1] Dewey Anderson and Percy E. Davidson, *Ballots and the Democratic Class Struggle* (1943), p. 255-7.

[2] After the election of 1936 when many traditionally Democratic newspapers (like many traditional Democrats) bolted the party, a famous editor of one of the bolting papers, noting that the Republicans carried only two states, wrote up 'Country 46; Country Club 2'.

class lines. All polls tell much the same story; the more prosperous, the better educated, the more completely 'assimilated' groups are, outside the South, more solidly Republican than ever. There are some rich Democrats; there are some poor Republicans. There are nominal Republicans in Congress and in power in the states who are well to the left of many Democrats. But those Democrats are, as a rule, either highly conservative politicians from the 'Solid South' or almost equally conservative Democrats from Middle Western farm states in which radical agrarian leadership was inside the Republican party and where the Democrats, coming from traditionally Democratic enclaves or from the cities, unsympathetic to the farmer's woes, often depended for success on the support of Republicans who had lost control of their own party to the radical elements in the primaries. And this class alignment might have gone much further but for the survival of the 'Solid South' whose peculiar political system affects the national pattern as well as its own. And the 'rationalization' of the party system depends less on the growth of an open 'labour' party, than on the chances of a two-party system in the South that will reflect the national divisions openly instead of covertly.

This political revolution may be coming about now. No one knows. It has been predicted before, notably in 1928 when Herbert Hoover carried five states of the Solid South. And it is possible, though unprovable, that but for the economic collapse of 1929, the 'Hoovercrats' would have been the first swallows of a Republican summer. But in the disaster that overtook the Republican party in the North, there was neither time nor thought or resources to devote to the party in the South. Yet the revolt was symptomatic. For it was not the rural, backward, 'Fundamentalist' areas devoted to Prohibition and fearful of the Pope that went Republican. It was not the regions that had spawned the Ku Klux Klan; it was in the main the richest, more economically advanced, most modernized areas that deserted the Democrats. And it was also, as Professor Key has insisted, the regions with the smallest proportion of Negroes in the population. For in the 'black belt', where the Negroes are in a majority, the staple of politics is still 'white supremacy' and that was identified in 1928 with the supremacy of the Democratic party. The areas that went Republican were those in which the economic interests of the ruling classes were nearly indistinguishable from those of the ruling classes in the rest of the country and the areas of small, white farmers, with few Negroes and sometimes an old Republican tradition. These areas, of course, sometimes over-lapped and in all of them the Republican party had a chance of becoming 'lilywhite', that is of excluding Negroes from the control of the party.

The next important split in the South underlined the lesson of 1928. For by 1948, the Democratic party was ceasing to be 'lily-white' in the South and had been committed by the Convention of that year to a 'civil rights' programme in the nation that made it a very uncertain ally of 'white supremacy' in the South. As the courts (and the federal government) destroyed, one after the other, the legal or quasi-legal barriers to Negro participation in politics and as the Negroes more and more voted in the only effective elections, the Democratic primaries, the pressure to quit the party was strongest just in those states where Negroes were most numerous, and above all in the 'black belt' areas of those states. So the four states that supported Governor T. Strom Thurmond were not the economically advanced states that had supported Mr. Hoover. They were states loyal in 1928 to the old party system, because the old party system was still doing what they wanted it to do.[1] In 1948, the old party system was for the moment, at any rate, not performing its function. A world in which Negroes were beginning to vote in large numbers in the South *and* to vote the Democratic ticket, or in the Democratic primaries, was a world turned upside down.

[1] In the four states carried by the 'Dixiecrats', the Democrats who refused to support Mr. Truman, the bolters were legally the official Democratic party of the state. Only they appeared on the ballot 'under the rooster' (the Democratic emblem in the South). It can be argued that this does not prove the power of traditional party names and emblems, that it merely shows that the most powerful elements in Arkansas, Louisiana, Alabama and South Carolina naturally were able to control the emblem and the party label. But Professor Key thinks that the man-oeuvres by which the 'Dixiecrats' got control of the trade marks were important and not a simple aspect of the realities of political power. 'The chances are that Thurmond carried Alabama and Louisiana only because of the manoeuvres that made him the "Democratic" nominee in those states.' V. O. Key, Jr., *Southern Politics* (1949), p. 342.

But it did not stay upside down for long, or at any rate not upside down in the same way. For the states, the classes, the individuals that went for General Eisenhower in 1952 were not the states, the classes, the individuals (by and large) that went for Governor Thurmond. They were much more like the Hoovercrats of 1928. They represented the groups and interests that had most in common with the ruling groups and interests of the national Republican party. They were groups that wanted to and, in the main, succeeded in taking, for the time being at any rate, the control of the Republican party in the South away from the 'lilywhite' politicians who had, in most states, dominated it since 1928. And the future of the Republican party in the South depended on their success in this endeavour, since a successful Republican party in the South not only needed far wider support than the old, limited Republican organizations could attract but would, by its success, deprive the old organizations of their only asset, the control of the formal party organization.

The results of 1952, not only the Republican success in such states as Texas and Virginia, but the success of newcomers to the party taking over control in states like Texas and Georgia, has revived hopes of the creation of a genuine two-party system in the South. Such a prospect is welcomed by two different sets of commentators, prophets and politicians.

The first group consists of those who see in a two-party system in the South the only effective way of getting an effective 'liberal' party system in the nation. For these critics, the neglected fact of American politics since 1938 has been the tacit alliance between the bulk of the Republican party, its conservative hard core, and the bulk of Southern members of Congress or, at any rate, of the Senate. Because they are 'Democrats', these conservative Southern Senators have very great power, power which they owe to congressional majorities provided by Northern Democrats and, until 1953, power in part due to Democratic Presidents elected by Northern voters. If there were a genuine two-party system in the South, these conservative Democrats would be forced into their true home, the Republican party and the Democratic party in the South would become more like the 'Fair Deal' party in the North.

For, the critics allege, there is no real party system in the South, no real 'Democratic party'. Each state is a law unto itself. Indeed, except in a few states like Virginia and North Carolina, there is no party system *inside* the states. There are groups of local office holders, 'the court house gangs'.[1] There are local politicians who may rise in state and then in national politics *if* they keep in close touch with their point of departure. There are dynasties of varying types, like the Bankheads in Alabama, the Longs in Louisiana, the Talmadges in Georgia. But there is no party system, no regular chain of command. Even the officers of the state organization, so important in the North, are neutral, rather dim functionaries whose allegiance is to the winners in the primary—whoever they may turn out to be. There are lobbies and pressure groups, ranging from county (farm) agents and school teachers to the great utility companies, oil companies, textile companies and (in Georgia) the owners of Coca Cola. There is no more a party system than there was a political system among the Irish and Scottish clans. An effective party system in the South would mean, so these critics believe, that the old radical traditions of the Southern agrarians could be adapted to the present age in which the South is being industrialized, that despite the lesson of the breakdown of Populism, of the degree to which, traditionally, rural radicalism has been associated with 'white supremacy', the common economic interests of the poor will drive white and Negro together.[2]

A more common and probably, at the moment, more correct view is that a two-party system would strengthen the conservative forces in the nation, that, if they *were* forced to choose, the natural rulers of the South would have to separate from the unnatural allies that the present party system imposes on them in the North. What is assumed to be the 'natural' conservative majority over the whole United States, would then triumph.

[1] 'Before the war', there were few small towns or even real villages in the South; the local political centres were the court houses and the handful of taverns and stores around them. So the 'Court House' meant the little political capital. The most famous 'Court House' was at Appomattox.

[2] There is some ground for this optimistic belief in the fact that before the Negro began to vote in primaries and elections, he was already voting under the New Deal in the elections run by the Department of Agriculture to determine crop allocations etc. under the various pre-war schemes for saving the farmer from over-production.

This argument is the converse of the other. It assumes, optimistically, that the Republican party in the nation is unified, that there is a natural conservative majority which, for long past, has been prevented from getting its share of power (the predominant share) by the unnatural character of Southern politics. But this not merely ignores the risk that in some Southern states, the result of a 'real party system' would be to unseat some highly conservative politicians who are beneficiaries of the tradition of always supporting the Democratic nominee. It also ignores the great range of opinion and interest represented in the Republican party and the possibility that a Republican party, reinforced by the conservative elements in the Southern Democratic 'party', might lose, in many regions of the North and West, the marginal voters it now attracts. But more serious is the objection that this conservative rationalization of the party system would not benefit the conservative interests in Southern society enough to make them take the risk of abandoning the Democratic party and taking to the uncertain high seas of a two-party system. 'Most southern Republican leaders see little reason to change the kind of government provided by the Democrats in the individual states. Conservative "safe" government customarily results from the one-party politics of the South.'[1]

It is too easily taken for granted that, with a two-party system, both parties would be dominated by the conservative elements. But the establishment of a real two-party system might give the groups in the South that have no very tangible economic reason for being conservative, a place to go. The minority party (it might in some states be the Democratic party) would attract the discontented; the radical elements; the Readjuster, Populist, Agrarian movements might have to be represented by a party which, because it was working in a two-party system that is permanent in the nation, might not be ephemeral in the South. Even to-day, the South is not a simple conservative bloc and it might be less so if its political life were more normal. But 'normality', for the South, may not be normality for the United States as a whole. Nor may the exceptional character of Southern politics necessarily be due, to-day, to the 'race' question. It may be due to the Southern social and economic structure. 'One does not create a two-party system

[1] Alexander Heard, *A Two-Party South* (1952), p. 99.

by concluding that it would be desirable. A two-party system must have two strongly based interests to maintain itself, each of which can recruit, train, and support leaders who periodically reach out and attempt to win control of the state as a whole. Given the social and economic structure of most southern states—the comparatively small working class, the absence of organization and political sophistication among the lesser agricultural peoples—it would be rash to suppose that a two-party system would change radically in short order the nature of southern political leadership.'[1] It would be rash, but it would also be rash to upset a system that, so far, suits so well the very sections of Southern society who have the present leadership under their control and it may not be rash to assume that this risk will not be taken until the advantages of breaking away, permanently, from the national Democratic party or the risks of continuing to adhere to it, justify conservative Democrats in unwonted boldness. And it is probable that what will bring this about, (if anything will), will be the assimilation of the South, economically and socially, to the rest of the nation. Political assimilation will follow on this, not precede or cause it.[2]

From 1896 to 1932 Democratic strength was limited in the North to certain great cities where the 'machine' was 'Democratic'; to others, like Cleveland where a great popular leader like Tom

[1] V. C. Key, Jr., op. cit., p. 181–2.

[2] Dr. Heard argues that the adoption of the Lodge-Gossett scheme of reforming the presidential electoral system might force both Democrats and Republicans to make far more effort in the South. The Republicans who would have some hope of picking up part of the electoral vote in several Southern states would campaign more vigorously. On the other hand, Southern congressional candidates would be under greater pressure to support the national ticket and the national organization would be forced to keep a closer watch on congressional elections since a weak or disloyal candidate might mean the loss of presidential votes. 'While state control over the nominating process would continue to restrict the disciplinary channels open to national leaders . . . the slack-rein relationship between the top leadership of the party and its fighting corps would be reduced'. Op. cit., p. 176. The success of the Republicans in carrying several important Southern states in 1952, on the one hand makes the old Democratic complacency less tolerable but, on the other hand, may have made the Republicans less anxious to divide the vote of Texas when they can hope to carry the state.

Johnson dramatized local issues under the Democratic banner; to regions of midwestern states largely settled from the South, like southern Indiana and 'Egypt' in Illinois. And of these sources of strength, the most important and the most embarrassing and, at times, dangerous was the support of the great city 'machines'.

The local role of these interesting organizations is discussed else-where,[1] but their existence and power provided and, to some extent, still provides one of the explanations of the oddities of the American party system. For the machines, controlling the voters of some of the largest (and many of the smaller) cities of the United States were and largely are an independent force in politics with which the party leadership must deal, must bargain, and it is seldom that the state or national issues that matter to the party, matter much to the rulers of the machines. The machines could neither be ignored nor controlled. They could not be ignored, for they controlled great blocks of voters and voters massed in strategically important places and they could not be controlled, for although every machine pro-fessed allegiance to one or other of the national parties, they never sacrificed, for a moment, the interests of the local organization even to the gravest necessities of the state or national parties.

The relationship between the great machines and the national parties or, indeed, the state parties that they 'supported', was often highly formal. This was especially true of the great Democratic machines like Tammany and the Democratic machine in Chicago during the long period between the end of the Civil War and the coming of the New Deal. For only during sixteen years was there a national Democratic administration to deal with. Tammany, there-fore, could not and did not put much reliance on federal aid and comfort. During four years of that sixteen, indeed, New York suffered (from Tammany's viewpoint) from a reform administra-tion and during Cleveland's two administrations it was on notor-iously bad terms with the White House. It had to pay some atten-tion to state politics, especially during the domination of New York state by the Democratic boss, David B. Hill. But as a rule, Tammany had to live off its own fat and fight for its own hand, which it did with notable success. As one of the greatest of bosses, Richard Croker, put it: 'Tammany Hall . . . could gain no mounting good

[1] See Chapter Four.

from a White House, however much the latter might be friendly or inclined to give it aid. The organization is entirely local in its domain of toil. It must, of course, be regular; and, therefore, Tammany must work its best in a national campaign for the general ticket, and it ever does. . . . Should the party succeed, the best we could have would amount to no more than a minimum of good to the organization; the most that we commonly hope is to escape without being hurt.'[1]

Republican machines in Republican states, during the long period of Republican supremacy, were more closely bound to the national and state high commands. They were necessary to both and federal and state patronage and supremacy were useful to the machines. Thus in Pennsylvania, the state organization tried to keep control of or in close touch with the machines in Philadelphia and Pittsburgh. Jealousies, natural difference of interests led to conflicts but the unity of the Republican party in the 'Keystone state' was something to wonder at and admire. In doubtful cities like Chicago, the Republicans might be under greater obligations to the state and national leadership than in a safe Republican state like Pennsylvania; this was true, also, in Ohio, in Cleveland and Cincinnati. But no city machine of any strength was without its own bargaining assets.

The coming of prohibition made federal and state toleration desirable, since it was impossible to conceive of a city machine that did not have any connection with the liquor supply. The degree of enforcement and, as far as state law went, the kind of enforcement provided for or not provided for, were important to the city machines. A Democratic machine was, presumably, at a disadvantage during an epoch when the federal agents could be turned on or off at the wish and needs of the party headquarters, as they were rumoured to be in Pennsylvania and in Illinois.

[1] Alfred Henry Lewis, *Richard Croker* (1901), p. 288. It is highly probable that these were Croker's sentiments, but highly improbable that these were his own words. This 'life' of Croker is one of the oddest and, almost certainly, most irrelevant biographies ever written. Its author (whose style has a decided resemblance to that of Baron Corvo) was a distinguished writer of western stories and an ornament of the Hearst press. He seems to have gone on the principle that a life of Croker had to be long, but the less said about its nominal hero, the better.

With the coming into power of the Democrats and the repeal of prohibition, this link between city, state and national politics became of less importance. But, so some think, it was replaced by another. No machine, some observers hold, can really be run with a scrupulous observance of the income-tax laws. Too much money changes hands without records, without avowable reasons, is paid to too many persons, for the machine to be kept running smoothly, if at the same time the pedantic book-keeping demanded by the Internal Revenue authorities is to be complied with. Every machine is vulnerable to a really rigorous investigation of its finances by a ruthless administration. So a friendly administration is not only desirable but a necessity. That, so it is suggested, is one reason why the great city machines supported the 'New Deal'. It was by calling off such an investigation of the Long state machine in Louisiana, that the Roosevelt administration, so it is said, both averted the danger of a radical movement and secured the allegiance of the Louisiana members of Congress.[1]

The conviction of Tom Pendergast, the boss of Kansas City, greatly weakened the Pendergast machine, but the downfall of the Boss was due less to the necessity of law-breaking imposed on a machine, than to his pathological passion for gambling.

Nor is it to be forgotten that vague, traditional, almost meaningless as was and, to some degree, is the allegiance of a machine to a particular party, the naïve rank and file voters may take it seriously. The voters of the Bowery certainly saw nothing odd or wrong in sending so corrupt, if genial a politician as 'Big Tim' Sullivan to Congress, but they might have thought it wrong to send him there as a Republican. A machine was, in most cities, better able to 'knife' the national or state ticket by a lack of zeal than by a switch of its voters to the other side.

Political reformers in general, reformers of the party system in particular, have usually regarded the alliance of the city machines

[1] 'For some of the cases, a judicial bargain basement was set up; and men, by payment of $1,000 fines and penalties, were freed of charges which might have brought years in prison. Civil cases were carried out, however, and the Government succeeded in collecting about $2,000,000.' Harnett T. Kane, *Louisiana Hayride* (1941), p. 184. This was known as the 'second Louisiana purchase'.

with the national parties as a great scandal and one of the chief obstacles to the creation of a rational party system. There was, therefore, great rejoicing in the early years of the New Deal at the visible decline of Tammany Hall, for if it could be permanently weakened, the example might make municipal politics less corrupt and less confusing than they were. Out of the decline of Tammany might come a new deal that would confirm the triumph of the New Deal.

The general difficulties that weakened machines over most of the nation, if only by limiting their power of really independent action, were at work in New York. But Tammany suffered more than most machines because of local conditions. After the death of 'Commissioner' Murphy in 1924, the leadership of the Hall grew feebler and increasingly less intelligent. Tammany had, indeed, by replacing John 'Faithful' Hylan as Mayor, by 'Jimmy' Walker, recovered control of the City Hall from the Brooklyn Democratic organization. And for a few golden years, Mayor Walker was first admired, then tolerated. He was just the Mayor for the boom years, the years when Tammany, by moving uptown from Fourteenth Street, showed that it shared in the general euphoria. When the smash came, Tammany had to give up its brand new premises and it soon had reason to regret its playboy Mayor. The Hall was not only involved in the general difficulties of civic politics everywhere; it had to fear a new rival in the growing power of the Bronx machine whose boss, 'Ed' Flynn, was far more intelligent than the series of incompetent figure-heads in office but not in power in Tammany. The rulers of the Hall managed to alienate Governor Roosevelt, whose friend and aid Boss Flynn had become; it also managed to quarrel with its most famous son, 'Al' Smith, by sulking and trying to prevent the nomination of Lieutenant-Governor Herbert Lehman to succeed Governor Roosevelt.[1]

[1] This was a double error. For Governor Lehman turned out to be a greater vote-getter than either 'Al' Smith or FDR and support for his candidacy united both ex-Governor Smith and Governor Roosevelt in hostility to the Tammany leadership. John F. Curry, the then leader of the Hall, apparently thought that he could hold out against this double pressure. According to one story, Smith threatened to run for Mayor 'and take the town away from you'. Curry asked on what ticket Smith

Compounding their errors, the leaders of the Hall refused to support a candidate of the Bronx machine and, as a result, the mass of the 'New Deal' vote went to a reform candidate, a former Republican Congressman and candidate for Mayor, Fiorello La Guardia, who performed the unprecedented feat for a reform Mayor, first of being re-elected and then of getting a third term. The national situation plus La Guardia's special talents and availability[1] counted for a good deal in this miracle, but the stupidity of Tammany counted for more.

Even in Philadelphia, the decline in machine efficiency was noted. Long accustomed to partnership with the state and national capitals, 'the Organization' was at a loss with Democrats in power, not only in Washington, but in Harrisburg and the great rival city of Pittsburgh passing permanently under Democratic control. Nor had the Organization any chief fit to replace the Vare brothers. Yet it managed to cling on, to defeat local attacks, even when in state and national elections, the city went Democratic. It was not until robbery of the old Tweed type, if not on the old Tweed scale, was revealed, that the patient citizens revolted.[2] That revolt carried energetic Democrats into office, but more recent elections suggest that, once the first indignation has worn off, the permanent assets of the Republican machine, the trained officers and non-commissioned officers can still get out the vote.

The alliance between the New Deal and some of the great machines gave scandal to the more zealous New Dealers and ammunition, or at any rate blank cartridges, to the Republicans. Liberals might denounce Frank Hague and talk of the Berlin-Rome-Jersey City axis, but Hague delivered the vote. Less scandalous was the conversion of Mayor 'Ed' Kelly of Chicago. The Kelly-Nash machine had not been noted for its liberalism and one of the most brutal police actions during the early years of the New Deal was the shooting of strikers by Mayor Kelly's trigger-happy police.

---

would run. ' "Hell," he said in his harsh rasping voice, "on the Chinese laundry ticket." ' Milton Mackaye, *The Tin Box Parade* (1934), p. 156-7.

[1] He was a Protestant of Italian and Jewish origin.

[2] I remember the indignation of a life-long, faithful Republican when he discovered that the taxes he had dutifully paid for years, had never reached the city treasury and he was threatened with an immense bill for arrears.

But the Mayor saw the light. The old days were done; the time for 'songs of social significance' had come and the machine changed its tune.[1] So did the Pendergast machine in Kansas City and no Senator had a better New Deal voting record than its representative in the Senate, Harry S. Truman. In accepting these allies and in giving them tangible proofs of federal benevolence with which to dazzle their voters, Roosevelt and Farley were playing sound politics. It would have taken years to build up voting machines of equal efficiency; the New Deal mandate might have been exhausted before the foundations of an alternative structure were well and duly laid. And in accepting support from machines, Roosevelt may have remembered that some effective support was given to the great Progressive crusade of 1912 by William Flinn, the Boss of Pittsburgh, for motives very unlike those animating William Allen White, Gifford Pinchot, Hiram Johnson, Alfred M. Landon, Harold Ickes and other more representative Progressives. And Woodrow Wilson owed his nomination in 1912 not only to William Jennings Bryan, but to Roger Sullivan, Boss of one of the competing Chicago machines, the ancestor of the Kelly-Nash-Arvey machine which was turning in such satisfactory New Deal majorities.

Nor was this all. The machines had to give and did give more than the old handouts to their clientele. Even before the first world war Tammany had begun to support social legislation. Young Tammany politicians took, and were allowed by their chief to take, a very different view of the content of politics from that customary even a decade before in machine circles. 'Alfred E. Smith and Robert Wagner, who later became great leaders in the state and nation in social justice achieved by legislative techniques, got their education as members of the Factory Investigation Commission, appointed by the state legislature after the terrible Triangle [Factory] Fire in New York City, March 11, 1911.'[2]

[1] There was also in circulation a story that Mayor Kelly's conversion had, in addition to the obvious political reasons, another cause in the advice given him by the New Deal Archbishop of Chicago, Cardinal Mundelein.

[2] Frances Perkins, *The Roosevelt I knew* (English edition, 1947), p. 19. Miss Perkins notes that the handsome young Democratic senator from

Not all machine politicians learned the lesson taught the young Al Smith and the young Bob Wagner.[1] But even the most backward of them did, though slowly. Thus the Hague machine in Jersey City for long sent to Congress one of its most useful members, Mrs. Mary Norton. And the machine politician, asked what was his present utility, could answer with another question, how was he to be replaced? For ways of overthrowing the machines without, at the same time, weakening the Democratic party were hard to find.

The history of New York, as usual, showed the problem in its true light. For there, an attempt was made, in 1936, to organize a block of New Deal voters not tied to Tammany or the other New York machines. The 'American Labour party' represented the political activities and ambitions of the two great clothing unions and of their leaders, Sidney Hillman and David Dubinsky, the reforming ambitions of many supporters of Mayor La Guardia and the secret weapon of the American Communist party. This last role was not visible in 1936 and the American Labour party, although its support was hardly needed in that year, soon was the holder of the balance of power in New York City and State. When it did not support regular Democratic candidates, they lost. It was the dividing line provided by the Ribbentrop-Molotov pact that opened the eyes of many innocent liberals to the character of many of their party brethren, for a great part of the Labour party membership switched from fierce opposition to Hitler, to bitter isolationism, only to return to the anti-Fascist front after the invasion of Russia. New York was the only city with a mass Communist voting block and this revelation of its power led to a schism and the foundation of the Liberal party. The Liberals did not want close association with such docile followers of the party line as the supporters of Repre-

---

Dutchess County, who was hitting the headlines by his opposition to Tammany, 'did not share in that educative experience'. Not till Franklin D. Roosevelt went to Washington in 1913 as Assistant-Secretary of the Navy and was thrown into contact with some of the socially conscious members of the Wilson administration, did he learn that reform politics was not simply a matter of 'honesty'.

[1] Later one of the most important New Deal leaders in the United States Senate and father of the present (1954) Mayor of New York.

sentative Vito Marcantonio.[1] And two 'third parties' had no chance
of seriously threatening Tammany or electing a new La Guardia.[2]

The main charge made against the present American party system
is that it makes it difficult to pin responsibility on the 'party in
power' and almost impossible to pin responsibility on the party not
'in power'. Indeed, it is sometimes argued that being 'in power'
in the nation, merely means that the President is head of the
Democratic or Republican 'party' but that no definite meaning can
be attached to the word 'party'. Thus a voter who is a loyal
Republican may vote for the presidential candidate and for the
Republican candidates for the Senate and the House with no
assurance that he is electing federal officers who have anything in
common save the party name. The Senator, the Representative
may oppose a great part of the President's programme and for its
success, he may have to depend on Democratic members of the
Congress. The case may be still worse in the case of the election of
state party officers. Their ambitions, needs, probable line of action
may be opposed to the views, needs and programme of the national
federal party. A party 'victory' may, in fact, be a defeat, if party
victory is interpreted as meaning the victory of a legislative or
administrative programme.[3]

[1] Professor Bone points out that Representative Marcantonio, originally elected as a Republican, was nominated in 1940 in the primaries of
the Democratic, Republican and American Labour parties. What was
more important, he had 'begun to organize his own machine, keeping
the support of many Republican captains. . . . Since then he has had little
opposition from Tammany'. Hugh A. Bone, 'Political Parties in New
York City', *American Political Science Review,* April 1946, p. 272. It was
only when all rival bodies combined to run a strong candidate against
him, that this versatile politician was defeated.

[2] The election of Vincent Impellitteri as Mayor in succession to Mayor
O'Dwyer who had prudently retreated to Mexico (as Ambassador)
showed that there was plenty of hostility to the machine, but no effective
expression of it. In the mayoral election of 1953, all kinds of New Deal
support, ranging from that of Mr. Averell Harriman and Representative
Franklin D. Roosevelt, Jr., to union leaders and ex-Labour and Liberal
party members assured the victory of Robert Wagner, Jr., the official
Tammany candidate.

[3] Thus it is possible to argue that a defeat of the candidate of the Byrd
'machine' in Virginia in 1953 by a 'Republican' candidate would, in

It is not surprising that the *Report* of 'the Committee on Political Parties' of the American Political Science Association was given the title 'Toward A More Responsible Party System'. It was the explicit and implicit argument of the report that effective democratic government in the United States could only be achieved by making the parties more like-minded, by improving the discipline of the parties in federal politics, by improving the facilities that the parties have for creating a common policy, a policy that the party members can help to create and which, in consequence, they can be expected to support by their votes and for whose implementation they can hold the party's elected spokesmen responsible to a far greater degree than is possible or would be reasonable at present.[1]

It is easy to see how real are the evils or, at any rate, the imperfections of the party system as it exists. The will of 'the People of the United States' expressed in federal politics, is often, apparently, thinly or not at all connected with the national party system. The voter cannot have a reasonable expectation of getting what he, presumably, orders by his vote, a coherent programme which will be carried out. However much the doctrine of the mandate is open to criticism in British politics, it represents a political reality. A party *can* issue a programme and guarantee that most of it will be enacted if the party is returned to power. It can guarantee that the administration will not be hamstrung by legislative indiscipline. The will of the majority[2], if it is assumed that it is expressed in a general election, is carried out, nowadays, to a surprising degree.

It is easy (and valuable) to devise better methods of defining American party policy than exist at present. The National Committee may be very unrepresentative of the mass of the party and it

---

effect, have been a defeat for the Eisenhower administration, weakening support, in the South, for the general policy of the administration. It could be argued, too, that the victories of Governor Lausche in Ohio have been only beneficial to the national Democratic party in rare instances such as the nomination of a Democrat to serve out the unexpired term of the late Senator Taft.

[1] 'Supplement' to *The American Political Science Review*, Sept. 1950.

[2] Of course, the parliamentary majority may not represent a majority of the voters. In no British election since 1945 has it done so.

is only nominally the creation of the national Convention. A 'Party Council' representing the National Committee, the party in Congress, the state committees, state governors, organizations like the 'Young Democrats' or the 'Young Republicans' would certainly be more representative and more effective than the National Committee. But would the highly separated powers, the Senate, the House, the state parties combine to accept leadership from this body or contemplate admitting to it bodies like the 'Young Democrats?'[1]

More fundamental is the proposed limitation of the membership of the party. The test of membership laid down by Senator Borah is not thought good enough.[2] The candidate for the nomination must, somehow, represent a definite party line. So the closed primary (in which the voter has to make some declaration of party principle if it is only that by voting in that primary he does not vote in the other and in which the candidate opts to be the candidate of one party and not of another) is preferable to the free-for-all primaries of states like California and Washington. For in California 'cross filing' was permitted until 1954, a candidate, that is to say, can enter the primary of all parties. He may win (this happens not infrequently, in the politics of the Golden State) both nominations. And the stubborn party voter may find himself unable to vote, in the final election, for anybody but the candidate of the opposite party. In the Washington 'blanket primary', the voter has a completely free choice. It is an entirely *à la carte* system; he can vote for a Republican candidate for one office and for a Democratic candidate for another. Thus the minimum of party responsibility for the 'ticket' in the final election is destroyed. It is difficult, indeed, in such systems, to see what traditional meaning one can give to the word 'party'. If the party is represented by its candidates, it may change character at every election, depending on the luck of the primary.

[1] The chilliness of the regular politicians to bodies like the 'Americans for Democratic Action' reinforces these doubts.

[2] 'Any man who can carry a Republican primary is a Republican. . . . He might believe in the Communistic state, in the dictatorship of the proletariat, in the abolition of private property, and in the extermination of the bourgeoisie; yet, if he carried his Republican primary, he would still be a Republican.' Borah made this declaration in 1923. *Report*, p. 27.

Yet the evils noted by the Report are not seen by all observers as easily curable nor is the situation of which they are the results, seen by all as undesirable. For it can be held that, on the whole, the American people get as responsible a party system as they desire, that in a vast country, of continental range and variety, with sectional interests, traditions, passions to be allowed for, a highly integrated and responsible party system might mean the imposition, by a numerical majority, of its views and interests and passions on great minorities, spread over great territorial areas, creating in those regions a sense of outrage dearly bought by a symmetrical party programme. Such a sectional party triumph and such a sectional party programme brought about the Civil War.

It has often been argued that the ill-disciplined party system reflects the true spirit of the American Constitution, that its makers and the American people, then and since, did not and do not normally want a unified, omnipotent and omnicompetent party system any more than they want a unified, omnipotent and omnicompetent government. It would take more than a reform of the party system to produce a responsible government (in the British sense).[1]

An even more fundamental criticism has been made. If parties can, in effect, define their membership, the chance of minorities having a voice in politics by influencing the choice of candidates and of policies would be greatly lessened; the number of one-party districts possibly increased, certainly not diminished. For in many areas the candidate of a doctrinally rigid minority party could not hope to win. 'Only a Democrat who rejects at least part of the Fair

---

[1] 'In short, if the Committee really wishes to see genuinely effective and democratic government achieved in the United States, it must, however "impractical" it may seem, work for popular acceptance of the *whole* package of majority-rule democracy. . . . The problem we face is not one of deciding whether the constitutional system or the parties should be changed "first". The point is that the same popular beliefs about government which sustain our present anti-majoritarian constitutional system will continue to sustain (as they have for a very long time) our anti-majoritarian party system.' Austin Ranney, 'Toward a More Responsible Party System: A Commentary', *American Political Science Review* (June 1951), p. 499.

Deal can carry Kansas, and only a Republican who moderates the Republican platform can carry Massachusetts.'[1]

This necessity of adjustment is not confined to America. The party regular, the 'militant' as the French call him, may be indifferent (if he is not a candidate) to the need of winning the support of the independent, even of the merely indifferent voter. Party managers, in London as much as in Chicago or Detroit, know that except in the safe areas, it is by winning independents that you win elections, at any rate on a national scale. Accident, discontent may drive the independents to your side and induce the indifferent to turn out and vote for your side. But the regulars may have saddled you with a programme and a personnel that will anger and disappoint the very voters to whom you owe your triumph.

Then some of the characteristics of the American party system that are most difficult to understand from the traditional European (and still more British point of view) are, as has been suggested, necessary adaptations to the character of the American Constitution. It is not being excessively pessimistic to wonder whether, without the parties, the system of 'checks and balances' would work at all. The framers 'not only made it difficult for government to invade fields denied to it, but they made it difficult for government to operate at all. They created a system where deadlock would be the normal character of the American government—a situation from which political parties saved us'.[2]

That the parties played this role is highly probable, but they played it at the expense of their role as unified, consistent 'responsible' parties. For the parties had to get some harmony into the relations of three independent bodies, each with its own unalienable powers. It would be astonishing if, in carrying out this necessary but very difficult task, the parties had not had very frequently to resolve not to let the best be the enemy of the good or even of the barely tolerable. Only if the President or the House or the Senate gave up their powers, only if, in fact, two of the three surrendered their powers, could the unity of party command that is often

[1] Julius Turner, 'Responsible Parties: A Dissent From The Floor', *American Political Science Review* (March 1951), p. 151.

[2] Henry Steele Commager, *Majority Rule and Minority Rights* (1943), p. 7.

longed for, be attained. And it is hard to see how that surrender could be organized, that unity attained, except by something like the extra-legal centralization of power that has occurred often in great cities and occasionally in great states. One of the three units of federal power, possibly two, would have to atrophy. And, as far as the Supreme Court by its Damocles' sword, its power of vetoing legislation and administrative action as unconstitutional, introduces another element of uncertainty into the system, it would have to be *gleichgeschaltet* as well, if the ideal of that discipline which is the condition of real responsibility, is to be attained. It is not, strictly speaking, in the nature of the federal system, or even in the size and variety of the area ruled, that the difficulty lies, but in the constitutional system that the Framers chose to make—and it is not surprising that they made an effective party system difficult since they wished to do just that.[1]

The imperfections of the American party system, the merely traditional character of its membership in many areas; the consequent impossibility of attaching any precise meaning or conditions to membership and so the impossibility, in all but exceptional times, of creating a unified national policy; these are given by the character and history of American political institutions. These impose impediment to the marriage of true minds in a doctrinally united 'left' party or a doctrinally united 'right' party. American social institutions, the character of American society impose more impediments to a reconstruction of the American party system and all these known conditions breed despair of success and so prevent attempts by practical politicians to 'rationalize' the system.

But conditions change, even in the New World. For one thing, the hold of the old traditional party loyalties is not what it was. The recent history of the South shows that. Even in the rural North and Middle West, the glacial loyalty to the Republican party that immobilized politics for generations is not what it was. Mere hereditary party loyalty still plays a great role in the United States,

---

[1] Of course, a century and a half of working experience has made the chances of unity of command more remote by fostering customs that multiply the obstacles to unity and, on the other hand, has created many ingenious devices for minimizing the ill effects of both the constitutional system and some crippling customs that have grown up.

but a diminishing role. The looseness of party discipline bred by the direct primary sometimes conceals rather than prevents a real change in the party allegiance of a state or district.

Then as far as the parties were alliances of geographical areas which were themselves unified by one dominant economic interest, the greater and greater diversification of American economic life weakens the old sectional loyalties. It is not yet wrong to think of the 'cotton states' or the 'corn belt' as natural units operating inside the formal party system, but it is not as safe to do so as it was. Mississippi and North Dakota may still be states of one dominant economic interest, but Georgia and Kansas are not. In the days when it was safe to label great regions in terms of one economic interest, parties could be simply loose alliances of regions, adequately unified if the dominant interest of one region did not flagrantly contradict the dominant interest of another inside the party.

To-day, as industries spread all over the country, as the South and the far West cease to be merely primary producers, as agriculture itself becomes more diversified and develops competing interests inside the 'agricultural interest', the old role of the parties becomes more difficult and the need for giving the parties some other minimum basis of union more urgent. Moreover, the spread of interests all over the country nationalizes many interests, unites producers or consumers all over the Union, breaking down not merely state barriers but the much more important regional barriers. The diversification of industry and of farming works inside states like Texas to undermine the old party structure and links different groups in Texas with groups in other and distant states to whom the memory of the Alamo means little and the memory of Jim Hogg nothing.

This economic unification of the United States has been accompanied by a social unification. The movies, radio, television, the mail order houses, long distance buses, the network of airlines, the proliferation of private planes as well as cars have made the Americans even more mobile than they were. Millions are forever on the move, taking their politics with them no doubt, but often losing their simple faith and automatic allegiance in their new environment. All this integration is reflected in the creation of *national* interest groups, national pressure groups, in spokesmen of 'Big

Business' like the United States Chamber of Commerce, of 'Big Labour' like the 'Congress of Industrial Organizations', in 'Big Government', in the growth of federal power from Eastport, Maine to San Diego. The national parties are, it must be admitted, the least integrated, the least national of the numerous organizations that the Americans have invented for holding the country together. But they are national institutions; they are subject to the nationalizing forces that are steadily making for a 'more perfect union'. It is less the parties than the formal political institutions that they alone make it possible to work, that, in the days of supersonic flight, preserve the methods and the spirit of the politics of the rural America of the age of Lincoln, if not quite of Jefferson or Jackson.

Chapter Three

RACE AND POLITICS

DESPITE all the art and science of current sociology, the exact shading of race distinction in America is hard to describe with precision. 'Any man is a Jew whom Gentiles think is a Jew,' said an eminent Jew, and something of the same principle applies to other social or religious or ethnic groups. 'Mexican' is a vague term which *may* cover a 'wet-back' illegal immigrant or a descendant of a great Spanish-American dynasty in California or New Mexico.[1] In the same way, an aspiring Irish family in Boston has different ambitions and different chances from those open to an old Catholic family, even if Irish too, in Maryland. The French, of Canadian origin, in New England, are again a very different group from the French colony in San Francisco. It is, perhaps, safe to say that English, Scottish, Welsh, Irish blood (if Protestant) is highly desirable; so is Huguenot blood; so is membership in one of the great Dutch families of New York or one of the old German families of New Jersey or Pennsylvania.[2]

But it is a characteristic of American society that 'America is promises', and that immigrants from every depressed nationality

[1] Thus the descendants of General Vallejo hold reunions in California (most of them seem to have Irish names) and the senior Senator from New Mexico, Denis Chavez, is Chavez de los Chavez, 'Chavez of that ilk' as they would say in Scotland.

[2] There are, of course, variations even inside these groups. I have seen the automatic social pre-eminence of a member of a distinguished Maryland Catholic family in Rome and, *mirabile dictu,* some owners of the good Scots names of Pettigrew (or Pettigru) and Lamont hug a mythical Huguenot origin.

95

develop in themselves or in and for their children, ambitions that American society, however fluid, does not always make easy of fulfilment. One way to fulfilment is through politics.

The importance of politics has varied from group to group, as the interests and capacities of the groups have in turn varied. To many peasant immigrants from central and eastern Europe, the whole mechanism of democracy was novel and possibly meaningless. In Europe their opinion had not been asked and they could not believe it was being asked now. Their ignorance of English, their practical exclusion from all but the worst-paid jobs, their illiteracy made them, at best, mere voters at the behest of better adjusted groups. So, until well into the 20th century, the natural leaders of the immigrant groups, the 'governing classes' as apart from the 'ruling classes', to use William Allen White's useful differentiating terms, were the Irish. Their advantages and disadvantages alike adapted them to this role. They spoke English, or at least most of the men did, and all of the later Irish immigrants did. They were used, in Ireland, to the forms if not the realities of representative government; they had learned the mechanics of elections, the role of the press, of the meeting, of the political organization, public or secret, in Ireland. It was an advantage that few other immigrant groups had—who had the same handicaps.[1] For the Scottish, the English, even the Welsh immigrants had much the same experience, but the Scots and even the English were much more literate and had a range of leadership in American society that reduced their risk of being classified as a foreign and inferior group. Above all they were Protestants, moving into a profoundly Protestant society, a society in which their church connections, whatever they were, were sure to be represented, in which their church leaders would be pastors of a flock not necessarily foreign and depressed, but brethren of thoroughly assimilated and accepted Americans. The Catholic Irish had no such good fortune. If they settled in a new community as in California, or in some parts of the Middle West, they had few handicaps, but in the East and in the urban centres,

[1] The Catholic peasant in Ireland had the vote until 1829 and after he lost it, he had the intensive political education of O'Connell's agitation followed by the various other elaborate political mechanisms that, over some generations, brought about the Irish Revolution.

their religion cut them off from many of the normal roads to prominence and acceptance. The days of 'no Irish need apply' are not terribly remote and by Irish, Catholic Irish is meant.[1] The Irish were an anomaly, an English-speaking group cut off from the dominant tradition. Of course, non-English speaking Catholic groups were even more cut off, but as a rule they did not expect to enter, in the first generation, into the full political life of the country, nor in all probability could they have done so if they had wished. Carl Schurz would almost certainly have had a less brilliant career in politics had he remained a Catholic.

As it was, the Irish became, in most regions outside the South, the providers of a professional political class. They organized and disciplined the inrushing immigrant masses; not only did they provide a great part of the immigrant population, but they had an advantage of, roughly, a generation in entering American politics.[2]

Until very recent times, the Irish played this role, and it is only since the first World War that they have begun to lose it. This is due to two causes. One is the rise in the social and economic scale of new immigrant groups; the other is the rise of the Irish. They have, as down-to-earth political leaders, priced themselves out of the market. In the twentieth century, they have produced more party leaders than party workers, more senators and governors and other public officers than the old-fashioned saloon-keeper and political worker. What was real promotion to an immigrant or the son of an immigrant like Al Smith, the opportunity of a political career, is no longer automatically such to a third or fourth generation Irish-American whose education and economic position do not distinguish him from other members of what may be called the executive class or the professional class. He is at the top of the

[1] They are not totally dead. Not only is the Ku-Klux-Klan a recent memory, but, in some regions, anti-Catholic hostility is still strong. I have recently been told of a priest in North Carolina whose car was robbed of all four tyres and who complained, in vain, to a totally indifferent if not rejoicing sheriff.

[2] A not too fanciful analogy is with the role of the Greeks and Armenians in organizing for the benefit of the Turks, the less advanced Christian subjects of the Ottoman Empire. Tammany Hall, in this aspect, was a kind of *Phanar*.

D2

political ladder, and fewer and fewer of his own group are ready
to fight on the lower rungs with Jews, Italians, Poles, Negroes.[1]

The other great immigrant group drawn from outside the
British Protestant stocks, was the Germans. But their political
career was hindered by their inexperience in free political life in
Germany and by their loyalty to the German language. They were
a racial group that needed to be cultivated as that adroit politician
Abraham Lincoln, knew; but German-American politicians with
organizations like the *Turnverein* and the German press were a
special racial group, not a class providing lower echelons in the
political army. Leaders had to be rewarded; the German press had
to be watched and inspired; but the Germans did not take to mere
politics with the enthusiasm or competence of the Irish. After all,
they did not do it in Germany. Mr. Dooley's saloon-keeper
colleague, Mr. Schwartzmeister, may have been a trade rival, but
he was not a political rival.[2]

Before the Civil War, most non-British immigrants (classifying
the Irish as non-British) were natural recruits for the Democratic
party. It was by principle and policy their friend. The very danger
of revolutionary contagion that alarmed the Federalists was

[1] It is a purely subjective impression, incapable of verification, but it is
my impression that, other things being equal, Irish-Americans do still
take more interest in the mechanics of politics than do other Americans
of the same social and economic standing. Nevertheless, the trend is as I
have described it. There is a parallel from sport suggested by Mr. A. J.
Liebling. According to him, the reason it is harder and harder to get
good light-weight or feather-weight boxers, is that poor boys are not
hungry any longer. Unless they are hungry they will not undergo the
rigours of fighting their way to the top. There are few or no Irish professional boxers of merit to-day and few Jewish, although these groups, a
generation ago, provided nearly all the stars. They have been replaced by
Italians or Negroes, for whom the ring is still a way of ascent. And just as
many boxers with good Irish names are in fact of Italian or Polish origin,
at least one politician of Polish origin spells his name O'Konski in a
possibly unconscious tribute to the old dominance of the Irish among the
professional politicians.

[2] The Germans were content with rewards for their leaders more than
were the Irish. 'Doing something for Franz Sigel', was one of the chief
minor problems of Lincoln during the Civil War, for General Sigel was
no more successful as a Union General than he had been as a revolutionary General in Germany in 1848-9.

attractive to the party of Jefferson and then of Jackson. The allied fear of religious infidelity was not shared by Jefferson and his friends[1] and as the Jeffersonian-Jacksonian party cultivated the rapidly growing urban proletariat of the new, great cities, institutions like Tammany Hall became increasingly immigrant in their rank-and-file and even in their non-commissioned officers. But it was not only the cities that were soundly Democratic, many or most minority groups felt safer with the Democrats than with the Federalists or Whigs.[2]

The natural alliance between the Democrats and the immigrants was broken by the crisis that led to the Civil War. The greater part of the Protestant Germans or the free-thinking 'new Germans' became Republicans. The issue of slavery broke the bond that bound them to the Democratic party. The new Republican party was itself largely Democratic in membership, so that in moving over to it the Germans were not losing all contact with their old allies, and the Republican leaders were extremely anxious not to have the new party tarred with the Whig anti-foreign brush. Many of the old Whigs, indeed, clung to various 'nativist' groupings as late as 1860, to the advantage of the new political combination in its campaign for immigrant votes. It largely succeeded, and

[1] As Jefferson found, in his old age, his own state of Virginia was not as broadminded as he was, and the growing evangelicalism of the South put some strain on the tolerance of the Jeffersonian tradition.

[2] One of the most conservative groups in American history was, at that time, as completely devoted to the Democratic party as any Irish slum dwellers in Manhattan. The 'Pennsylvania Dutch', we are told, were kept in the faith by their German-language press. 'The editors of the German newspapers helped direct and strengthen in their columns this Democratic block of German-speaking voters and their opinions carried weight. Even many Pennsylvania Germans who could not read were accustomed to having their political thought formed by having the political articles in the German newspapers read to them. Many German editors were in demand as stump speakers. Some of them entered the legislature and became local political leaders. The old alliance between Pennsylvania German and the Democratic party is still the subject of much banter, at times good-natured, at times malicious. The country folks of Berks County, it is often asserted, still are voting for Andrew Jackson.' Ralph Wood (Editor), *The Pennsylvania Germans* (1942), p. 134-5.

some enthusiastic historians of German-American politics have attributed to this switch in party allegiance the winning of the western states by the Republicans and the election of Lincoln, an example of that over-estimate of the power of ethnic groups that has often led historians—and politicians—astray.

Many of the Irish too, of course, passed into the Republican ranks. By active support of the Union, by joining the Army, they were in fact taking sides in a civil war and committing themselves to a cause that was a party cause as well as a national cause. But on the whole the Irish (and many of the Catholic Germans) remained Democrats. The memory of Know-Nothing hostility was recent; the evangelical flavour of much of the Republican propaganda, the economic fact that, for the poor Irish labourer, the Negro was not so much an enslaved brother as a possibly dangerous competitor, saved the Irish from the seductions of Republicanism. In the great New York draft riots of 1863, the mainly Irish mob showed, in its attacks on free Negroes, a ferocity worthy of later years, in an explosion of economic fear as much as of race rivalry.[1]

Of course, there were variations on the pattern. Where the Democratic party for any reason stayed strong, active politicians, German or other, joined it. Where the political machine passed into Republican hands, as in Philadelphia, the Irish served as non-commissioned officers in the political army that kept the Quaker City 'corrupt and contented'. The most famous German-language

---

[1] *The Diary of George Templeton Strong* shows the horror which these events inspired in an intelligent and public-spirited New Yorker who does not seem to have reflected, much, on the justice of a draft that allowed the rich or even the prosperous native-born to contract out of fighting for the Union, an option not really open to a poor Irish immigrant in the Five Points. One of the most eminent Irish refugees, John Mitchel, exiled after the failure of the Irish 'Young Ireland' revolution of 1848, was a candid defender of slavery. He wanted a revival of the slave trade. 'In his *Southern Citizen*, just established in Washington, [he] adopted what he called the honest human flesh program, declaring that the trade would soon reduce the price of a robust fieldhand from $1,000 to $100, enabling every Southern farmer to buy one.' Allan Nevins, *The Emergence of Lincoln* (1950), vol. 1, p. 438. Mitchel removed himself to Richmond. His vehement defence of slavery later embarrassed his numerous admirers in Ireland where he was one of the saints of the Nationalist movement.

paper, the New York *Staats Zeitung*, was Democratic, and not only was it published in New York; its owners were Catholics. But in general the pattern was simple; the Irish outside the South were the backbone of the Democratic party, and there was more truth than tact in the famous *gaffe* of Dr. Burchard in 1884; it *was*, seen from a hostile angle, the party of 'Rum, Romanism and Rebellion'. The very importance attached to this episode shows how wedded to the Democratic party the Irish were assumed to be. For in 1884, the Republican candidate was himself of Irish origin[1] and he had carefully cultivated the Irish vote. He had the support of some of the most vocal 'friends of Irish freedom', and it is not improbable that he did win over more of the Irish vote than a normal Republican candidate could have hoped to do. The Democrats retorted by alleging that the Republican minister in London, James Russell Lowell, had not done his duty by the numerous naturalized Irish-Americans imprisoned in Ireland under the coercion acts, and martyrs like Daniel McSweeney were sent on tour to expose the hollowness of Republican claims to be friends of Ireland.[2] On the eve of the election, Dr. Burchard made his famous remark and, it was thought, lost enough Catholic votes to lose New York which Cleveland just carried, although there were and are others who hold that the necessary margin was provided by the technical skill of another Irish-American politician, Senator Arthur Gorman of Maryland. But for long enough the attitude of the average Irish-American was well summed up by 'Mr. Dooley', who declared that the people in the Archey Road would rather die than be buried by a Republican undertaker.[3]

[1] It is often forgotten that James Gillespie Blaine suffered, on his own side, from his Catholic associations. His mother's family, the Gillespies, were Catholics and he was charged with being one. One of Blaine's maternal aunts was a nun; an uncle was a (lay) professor at the University of Notre Dame.

[2] He was later rewarded by the incoming Democratic administration with a valuable job in the San Francisco Customs House.

[3] Over a generation ago, an Irish-Catholic politician in a New England state openly became a Republican. When he was seen the following Sunday at mass, a neighbour, in all honest surprise, asked him, 'You're still going to mass then?' His son became a Republican United States senator. Daniel McSweeney's son also became a Republican; but

The Republicans were not as uniformly successful in holding the Germans as the Democrats were in holding the Irish. For there remained in the Republicans a solid undigested mass of rural Puritanism that was unpalatable to the more lax Germans. Legislation against liquor, for the enforcement of the Puritan Sabbath, for putting impediments in the way of church schools, from time to time caused wholesale desertions from the Republican party and temporary Democratic triumphs as in Wisconsin.

These traditional affiliations had little general importance. There were no 'Irish' views on the national policies of the United States, not even on foreign policies. Both parties were perfectly willing to express pious hopes for the freedom of Ireland, but that was as far as they were willing to go. No politician worth his salt would have risked any serious American interest for the *beaux yeux* of Irish politicians and, if he had done so, he would have been rightly punished by the mass of the voters who were, after all, Americans and not Irish.

This is not to say that the nationalist passions of voters, Irish and others, have not from time to time played a part in American national politics. The defeated Democratic presidential candidate in 1920 attributed some of his discomfiture to the secession of national groups from the party.[1] In 1940, President Roosevelt's reference to Mussolini's attack on France as a 'stab in the back', alarmed party strategists who thought it would throw many normally Democratic Italians into the Republican camp. And a very acute student of contemporary American politics is convinced that German and Catholic isolationism, not 'Midwestern'

---

these were exceptions. In North Dakota in 1934, after the Democratic landslide of 1932, all important federal jobs seemed to me to be held either by Irish-Americans or by expatriated Southerners; they had been the faithful remnant of the Democratic party in the long dark years.

[1] 'Leaders of three racial groups, German, Irish and Italian, had gone over to the Republican side. The Germans were angry with Wilson because of the war. The Irish were inflamed because Wilson did not make the independence of Ireland part of the Versailles treaty. The Italians were enraged because Fiume had been taken away from Italy. The Italians were practically solid.' James M. Cox, *Journey Through My Years* (1946), pp. 272–3.

isolationism, explains much in the recent politics of the farm states.[1]

But the most obviously successful ethnic pressure group in recent American history has been the Jews, for if it is not quite certain that electoral necessities affected the policy of the Truman administration towards Palestine, the defeat, in the hitherto impregnable stronghold of the Bronx, of the official congressional candidate of the Flynn machine was a portent. It is probable, too, that in strongly Polish districts, the imputation that Poland was 'sold down the river' at Yalta has probably hurt the Democrats and helped such hammers of the Reds as Senator McCarthy.[2]

Serious thinkers and practical politicians have often condemned the intrusion of European feuds and passions into American politics. The menace of the 'hyphenated American' was much stressed in the first World War, the hyphen being that which joined 'German' and 'American', not that which joined 'English' and 'American' or 'Canadian' and 'American'.[3] Isolationists, after the first World War, argued, plausibly, that one good reason for keeping out of the League of Nations was that every question debated in the League would, inevitably, become a domestic issue. And although America was not in the League, the Abyssinian crisis of 1935 enabled such leaders of the Italian community as the late Generoso Pope to play on the national sentiments of the Italian population to rally support for the Duce and against American participation in sanctions.

But as this instance shows, formal 'isolation' does not secure that Americans will hold themselves aloof, be neutral in thought and

[1] 'This *memory of opposition to the last war* seems the real mainspring behind present-day isolationism. . . . The strength of the Republican appeal to the former isolationist voters is essentially one of political revenge.' Samuel Lubell, *The Future of American Politics* (1952), p. 152.

[2] On the other hand, the most strongly Polish district in the United States, the first Michigan, which contains Hamtramck, the most purely Polish free city in the world, the Cracow of our time, returned its Democratic member, Thaddeus M. Machrowicz, in the Republican year, 1952.

[3] The astonishingly high vote which Roosevelt polled in the rock-ribbed State of Maine in 1940 was attributed by some to the large number of voters of fairly recent Canadian origin in that state.

feeling as Wilson counselled in 1914 (without quite attaining that height himself).[1] Nor is racial origin a safe guide to attitudes in foreign policy. Wendell Willkie was of purely German origin on both sides, but he was far more hostile to Hitler than were such 'Anglo-Saxon' candidates for the Republican nomination as Senator Taft and Mr. Dewey. To imagine that religious, racial, class and other sources of bias can be eliminated is to imagine a vain thing.

Another charge as old as the first participation of immigrants in American politics is that, appealing to sectional, venal, and ignorant interests, the immigrant leaders debased the coin of politics. Tightening up the naturalization laws as a remedy was tried in the Alien and Sedition Acts of 1797. Political movements directed against the political activities of the immigrants have arisen in every generation since then, some—for instance, the Know Nothing party before the Civil War and the Ku-Klux-Klan after the first World War—being, for a time, very important political forces. Whatever the law might provide, the sentiment of many native Americans was hostile to treating naturalized Americans as anything but second-class citizens[2] and one reason for the complacency with which the 'rotten borough' system in state legislatures is tolerated is, more or less openly, based on the suspicion that the urban populations, which are under-represented, are 'un-American'.[3]

[1] It is sometimes forgotten that Washington's advice in the Farewell address to avoid 'permanent, inveterate antipathies against particular nations and passionate attachments for others' was completely disregarded by Washington's countrymen and that shortly after Jefferson warned them against 'entangling alliances', he was ready to make one with England to secure the mouth of the Mississippi.

[2] This attitude is sometimes justified by citing an alleged command of Washington at a critical moment. 'Put no one but Americans on guard tonight.' All the great traitors in American history, Benedict Arnold. Aaron Burr, James Wilkinson, have been native born.

[3] When it was proposed to reduce the congressional representation of Southern states that effectually disfranchised Negroes (a procedure provided for in the Constitution), Senator Black of Alabama retorted by proposing to cut down the representation of states whose congressional strength owed a good deal to the large number of resident aliens. Senator Black is now Mr. Justice Black and has put away these vestiges of his past.

That the immigrant leaders have not always been statesmen of the highest calibre may be admitted. Many of the spokesmen of immigrant groups have lamented this fact. But it is a gratifying fantasy and no more to attribute the corrupt character of many areas of American politics to foreigners. They learned most of the tricks of the trade from native masters and the deeper sources of corruption were not to be explained in mere ethnic or religious terms.[1] But since activity in politics was and is an accepted way to the promotion of individuals and 'races', the character of first-generation leadership will be coloured by the political environment. The Irish who flocked to New York in the mid-nineteenth century would have been miracle workers, not merely saints, if they had cleared up the politics of the city of Fernando Wood and James Gordon Bennett.[2]

Promotion for other groups came later. Senator Lehman was the first Jewish Governor of New York and he was elected in 1932. Fiorello La Guardia was half-Jewish and half-Italian; he was the first non-Irish and non-Anglo-Saxon Mayor of New York, and he was elected in 1933.[3] The rise of the Italians and Poles has come later, but it has come. Politics, that is to say, both registers and facili-

[1] See p. 36.

[2] Bennett had been educated for the priesthood in Scotland, but by the time he founded the *New York Herald,* he had ceased to be a representative Catholic. There was, in fact, very little place for an Irish Catholic immigrant in city politics in these generations except at the lower, less reputable levels. This was lamented by some Irishmen. An Irish M.P., John Francis Maguire, in his book *The Irish in America* (published in 1868) asserted that 'the Irish injure themselves seriously by not in all cases putting forward their best men to represent them, whether in municipal or other offices; and by allowing men to speak and act in their name who are not the best qualified, indeed in some, and too many instances, not in the least qualified, to do the one or the other. . . . This, however, is an evil that must cure itself in the course of time, when the Irish-American witnesses the happy results of a policy consistent not only with reason and common sense, but with the most ordinary self-respect'. Op. cit., pp. 305–6.

[3] 'Anglo-Saxon' is a term of art. It means any Protestant of old colonial stock, say Dutch or German or even Irish (like the descendants of General Sullivan of New Hampshire) and, of course, any descendant of any British Protestant stock such as Charles Evans Hughes, even if of recent American origin.

tates individual and group promotion, and as far as it does this, it performs an extremely useful function in so diverse a society as the American.[1]

As has been suggested, the character of Irish political leadership has been changing. It was a portent when a fairly eminent lawyer, George Olvaney, became leader of Tammany Hall in 1924.[2] It was a sign of the times when a judge of General Sessions was made head of Tammany, even though the judge accepted the post reluctantly and was far from a success in his new office. The change was not confined to New York. David Walsh was the first Catholic Governor of Massachusetts and the first Catholic Senator, the latter a post which he held, with a brief interval, for nearly thirty years.[3]

[1] The classical example of the rise of a group is furnished by Mr. Lubell's case history of the Italians in Rhode Island. It was facilitated by the resignation of Howard McGrath to become Solicitor-General. 'But for McGrath's resignation, one shrewd Rhode Island politician has estimated that the Italo-Americans might have had to wait another ten years before gaining the governorship. Although they didn't like the idea, the Irish Democratic leaders could not deny Pastore the chance to run for governor in his own right. When Pastore was born in 1907 the Italians were only one-thirteenth of the state's population. By 1915, one of every five babies born in Rhode Island was Italo-American. In 1938, the state legislature declared Columbus Day a legal holiday.' Lubell, op. cit., p. 73. It was not only a question of numbers. It was a question of fitness. 'From 1906 through 1924 only eighteen Italo-American lawyers passed their bar examinations, an average of one a year. In 1925 alone seven made the grade. . . . Since 1947 the number of new Italo-American lawyers in Rhode Island has averaged eight a year. Italo-American political activity has quickened proportionately.' Ibid., p. 70. Italo-Americans are members of a group that finds it harder than most to gain admission to medical schools; the law is more open and leads to politics. It is a change from nearly thirty years ago when I was talking to an Italo-American bootlegger who dabbled in politics (as was necessary in his profession) but at a low level. I asked him, ironically, why his father had left Calabria: 'A political refugee?' 'Yes; shot a guy at an election.'

[2] A wag reported a meeting of Tammany Hall at which some humorist shouted 'Alderman, your saloon's on fire'. In a moment the room was empty save for Judge Olvaney.

[3] The significance of the rise of Walsh was not lost on competent observers. 'Mr. Lodge is an aristocrat by birth and training. . . . If he had not given up to politics what was meant for mankind he might have been a distinguished historian and writer of essays. . . . The junior Senator is

Another charge made against the mixture of racial loyalties with politics is that it leads to the making of lists of candidates, based not on fitness, but on a 'dosage' that will bring out, in support of the ticket, all the competing racial groups. This is done, and is done openly.[1] It can, of course, be done too openly. Thus it was probably a mistake for Mayor Impellitteri, running, unsuccessfully, for renomination in the Democratic primary in 1953, to reproach Mr. Carmine De Sapio, Boss or at any rate head of Tammany Hall, with race disloyalty in supporting a German-American, Mr. Robert Wagner, against a fellow-Italian. But this naïve appeal to race solidarity was made in Harlem, to a Negro audience for whom 'race' loyalty is the cardinal political virtue.

The 'seeding' of the party ticket presents great dangers as well as great possibilities. For that reason, political leaders of the 'new' groups have often compromised on an 'Anglo-Saxon', an 'old

---

David Ignatius Walsh, a graduate not of Mr. Lodge's fair Harvard but of Holy Cross, a member not of the Massachusetts Historical Society but of the Irish Historical Society of America. . . . It is safe to predict that he will be succeeded by many more of his own race and kind. There will be no more Lodges. That breed is passing.' John Macy, 'Massachusetts A Roman Conquest', in *These United States,* edited by Ernest Gruening, (First Series, 1923), pp. 230–1. Mr. Macy was, in part, an inaccurate prophet. Mr. Lodge was, at a remove, succeeded by his grandson, Henry Cabot Lodge junior, and for a time the two Senators from Massachusetts were a Lodge and a Saltonstall. The Saltonstalls (according to an Adams) are the only Massachusetts dynasty entitled to coat armour. In 1952, Senator Lodge lost his seat to Representative John Fitzgerald Kennedy (Harvard '40) whose father was Ambassador at the Court of St. James's and maternal grandfather, 'Honeyboy Fitz', Mayor of Boston. Senator Kennedy's sister was the Marchioness of Hartington, married to a Cavendish, a family alluded to in Shakespeare, an honour beyond even Saltonstalls. Senator Lodge's brother is Governor of Connecticut.

[1] Mr. Edward J. Flynn admirably illustrated the system in his book, *You're the Boss,* when he described the nomination of the slate in his bailiwick of the Bronx. The names of the candidates, in order of importance of office were, William O'Dwyer, Lazarus Joseph, Vincent R. Impellitteri, James J. Lyons, Samuel J. Foley, William Lyman, Christopher C. McGrath, Charles A. Loreto, Michael N. Delagi, Agnes M. Craig. 'Our ticket shaped up as a well-rounded one; Lyons and Foley were Irish, Joseph and Lyman were Jewish, Delagi and Loreto were of Italian descent.' Op. cit., p. 223.

American', a 'Yankee' for, at any rate, the nominal leadership. In the northern Democratic party, there have been, in the eastern states at least, enough of these to be useful and not enough to be a nuisance. In a feud between Irish, Italians, Jews, Poles, Germans, a distinguished name may be an asset. It was as the bearer of a famous name that F. D. Roosevelt was first invited into Democratic politics in what was thought to be a safe Republican district. It was as a Yankee Democrat (and also Dean of the Yale Graduate School) that Wilbur Cross was invited to be candidate for the Governor of Connecticut. After their election, each developed political strength of his own, but at the beginning of their political careers, their 'race' helped.

This preference for the older stocks, which often led to the choice for high office of men who had not been active party workers, used to infuriate many Irish politicians who, realizing that the group to which the candidate belonged would provide few votes, did not see why it should get jobs.[1] Yet there were good reasons for this policy. The mass of the American voters was and is impressed by historic names and claims to 'Americanism'. It is even impressed by names that are historic only in the sense that they show or purport to show that the candidate belongs to old American stock.[2] As far as politics is promotion, it is necessary to have, in the organization of the promotion process, undeniable evidence of social progress. The ostentatious display of a few distinguished names is such evidence. And there are more of them than is some-

---

[1] Many Irish-Americans feel the same about having Italians as Popes.

[2] Thus it was probably wise for Mr. J. Parnell Thomas (former Chairman of the House Committee on Un-American Activities, recently released from the penitentiary where he was sent for graft) to change his name from Feeney when he decided to make a career in a prosperous, Republican district in New Jersey. The phenomenon is not confined to politics. Over twenty years ago the head of a very great New England business committed suicide and was briefly mourned as a victim of overwork. But when it was discovered that he had died highly insolvent, not only did mourning cease, but it was revealed that his real name was not Wood but De Silva, that he was not a Yankee but a Cape Cod Portuguese. I suspect that if he had died solvent, his ancestors would have been deemed to have come over in the *Mayflower* instead of in a fishing boat from the Azores.

times recognized by Republicans who are not quite sure of their own social standing. The Adams family has had Democratic members off and on for over a century; the name 'Payne Whitney' combines two great Democratic dynasties; and, of course, the Roosevelts of Hyde Park are more famous aristocratic Democrats still.[1]

The Irish, indeed, once they had arrived, began behaving like the Yankees. Senator Kennedy of Massachusetts is as much a 'Eupatrid', in any realistic sense of the term, as his colleague, Senator Saltonstall. Indeed, it is held by some that it was the over-reaching ambition of the Irish that, in 1936, made it possible for Henry Cabot Lodge, Jr. to enter the Senate in a year in which the Republicans only held Maine and Vermont. For the senior Senator, David Walsh, was an Irishman and a Catholic; and even if James Michael Curley, the Democratic candidate, foisted on the party by his Boston tail, had been less vulnerable on other counts, many electors, Italian, '*Canadien*', Polish, all Catholic, all Democrats, may have thought that enough was enough, and that a Yankee Democrat to succeed another Yankee Democrat, Marcus Aurelius Coolidge, would have filled the bill better.

It was one of the weaknesses of the Democratic party in the East, especially in New England, that the Irish leadership was exclusive. To the newcomers the Irish were a superior and intolerant class. To the very numerous French-Canadians, the political Irish were the brethren of the Irish priests and bishops with whom the '*Canadiens*' were involved in a constant *guerre sourde*. There were of course '*Canadien*' Democratic politicians like the unfortunate

---

[1] It is usually said that there are two Roosevelt branches, one, that which produced F.D.R., being Democratic, the other, which produced T.R., being Republican. But while there is no doubt about the Hyde Park branch's being Democratic, there is a good deal of doubt about the Republican orthodoxy of the Oyster Bay branch. For not only was T.R.'s mother a member of a stout Confederate (and, of course, Democratic) Georgia family, but his paternal uncle, Robert, though an enemy of Tammany, remained a stout Democrat while his nephew was in the White House. It was a member of an even greater (historically speaking) New York family who once told me that he was the only man who was a member both of the Racquet Club and of Tammany Hall. He preferred Tammany, or so he said.

Mr. Pelletier whose conduct scandalized everybody but the Knights of Columbus, but they were not many. As a result, '*Canadien*' and Italian leaders, as they began to appear, drifted into the Republican party, and might have stayed there but for the depression.[1] But the catastrophe of 1929–33 altered all that. The common misery drove all the victims together and into their common instrument of protest, the Democratic party. Probably, the depression only accelerated an inevitable movement. The Al Smith campaign of 1928 had seen the first effective, open, manifestation of the political ambitions of the new stocks. 'Al' Smith was Irish and a Catholic, but he got support from millions who were neither, Jews, Laodicean Italians, all the groups who knew that he was one of their own and that Herbert Hoover was not.[2]

Indeed, it might be said that the novelty of 1932 was the renewed adhesion to the Democrats of the poor whites who had moved into the northern industrial cities and who had, as a group, bolted the party in 1928 out of a real hatred of Rome and a theoretical hatred of rum.

This transfer of loyalties caught the Republicans unprepared. Even in states where it would have paid to cultivate the newcomers against the Irish, Yankee monopolizing spirit was too strong.[3] Even in Massachusetts it would not have been impossible to salt the ticket with a few non-Yankee names, even Irish names; but the rural Yankees, whose adherence to the Grand Old Party was emotionally based on its ethnic character, would have none of it. As a

[1] It is often forgotten that Fiorello La Guardia started life as a Republican.

[2] This point has been developed with great acuteness and a mass of information by Mr. Lubell. I hope I may be forgiven for saying that I stressed this aspect of the Smith campaign in my *American Political System* (1933). 'It is too early yet to dogmatize, but if Governor Smith lost heavily on account of his religion and origin, he undoubtedly gained heavily among the new immigrants of the great industrial towns, the Italians, the Jews, the Poles, the French-Canadians who followed the Irish in the campaign to prove that in America there were to be no half-citizens, no *perioeci*.' Op. cit. (1947 edition), p. 68.

[3] The '*Canadiens*' of Rhode Island had produced a Governor. His election was probably helped by the particular fury with which the religious war between Irish and '*Canadien*' Catholics raged in the state of Roger Williams.

result, at the moment of its direst peril, the Republican party was almost entirely deprived of leaders among the new and growing urban groups. There were tame Irish, Poles, Jews, Italians, but not only did many of them desert, but those who remained were about as powerful, politically, as the trade union leaders who clung to the party of Lincoln and Mark Hanna.

The lesson has been learned. Irish Republicans are more and more numerous and there has been a successful recruiting of leaders from most other races, including the Negroes. This process must continue if present Republican success is not to be a flash in the pan. The wiser Republicans know it. The descendants of those who had come over on the *Discovery* and the *Arabella*, not to mention the *Mayflower*, were no longer numerous enough to be the national rulers by right of ancestry.

The most obviously identifiable ethnic group in the American political world is that composed of the Negroes. Ethnologists may dispute how truly the Negroes constitute a group, and there is an immense range from the deeply black rural peasant of South Carolina to the light-skinned intellectual of New York who could and sometimes does pass for a white man and, though probably more rarely than in the past, sometimes 'passes' for good, that is, disappears into the white community. But these details do not affect the general picture. The American Negro is the only American whose ancestors, or part of them, were given a special, negative, status by law and whose status was not only the main cause of the Civil War but remained, until very recently, the organizing principle of party structure in fifteen states and a very lively issue in many more. 'Nativist feeling', hostility of the 'Gentile, Protestant' stocks to newcomers, especially to Catholic or Jewish newcomers, is a dormant issue that occasionally becomes live. But the Negro issue is never dormant in American politics, if only for the reason that the Negroes more openly, more consciously, more consistently than any other group turn to politics as a remedy for their disabilities. A good 'race man' is a good race man in politics above all, and an American Negro political leader is more in the position of an Irish Nationalist party member of Parliament than of an ordinary member of a normal American party. He is a Republican or a Democrat with a difference. He has to deliver the goods in some tangible form to his race brethren, and no plea of party loyalty will serve him if he fails.

Traditionally, the Negro was the most faithful adherent of the Republican party, the party that was believed to have been formed to defend him and which had freed him. 'The Republican party is the ship; everything else is the sea', was the sage counsel of the elders to the restless young who wondered whether it was a good thing to put all the eggs of the race into one political basket. Binding the Negro to the 'Grand Old Party' was not only the memory of Lincoln, but the memory of the Reconstruction in the South—and of the end of Reconstruction.

With the restoration of 'home rule' in the South after 1877, the Negro saw the gains of the period of Republican Reconstruction disappear. He lost the jobs he had got; he lost the protection of the federal law (and of federal garrisons); despite the promises of Southern leaders like Wade Hampton, he lost the vote. In the great wave of agrarian discontent in the 90's, both the insurgent Populists and the regular Democrats permitted or encouraged Negro voting; but by the end of the century both sections of the dominant race decided that this was too risky; ranks were closed, and by devices legal, semi-legal, and illegal, the political rights guaranteed under the Fifteenth Amendment were nullified. Some of the devices were so ingenious as to compel admiration in one sense of the term, but the most effective was the general adoption of the direct primary and the exclusion of Negroes from it. Since the primary was the real election, exclusion from the primary was exclusion from effective electoral power.[1]

This meant that, for effective political power, Negroes had to

[1] The drawback to basing electoral qualifications on literacy was that many Negroes were more literate than many whites. Tests of intellectual fitness often took the form of trick questions. Thus, in the enlightened Commonwealth of Virginia, questions more worthy of a quiz pro-gramme were put to disqualify otherwise highly competent voters. '"Can a minor hold office in Virginia?"—the catch in the last being that notaries need only be eighteen years of age.' Paul Lewinson, *Race, Class & Party: A History of Negro Suffrage and White Politics in the South* (1932), p. 118. More candid was the expression of the spirit of the laws. ' "It is an understood policy . . . that Negroes not be allowed to register in sufficient numbers to matter in any sort of election." ' Ibid., p. 118.

rely on their voting strength in the North and in the border states like Tennessee, Missouri, and Maryland where Negroes could vote fairly freely. But as the great mass of the race was still in the South, its real or supposed interests anchored the Negro, even in the North, to the Republican party. The Republicans had no serious political assets in the South except in a few isolated areas, and the Northern Democrats were dependent for any hope of power in federal politics on their Southern allies. So the Negro had no place to go until the great migration from the South began in the first World War.

This movement shifted the balance of power inside the Negro community. The greater number still lived in the South, but a far higher proportion of the educated and prosperous Negroes lived in the North. Automatic allegiance to the Republican party in the North weakened their bargaining position. And the migrants from the South who poured into New York, Chicago, and Cleveland had new problems and new needs that the local Republican parties could not meet or, at any rate, did not feel called on to meet as long as the Negro vote was safe.

But astute Democratic politicians in the North began to see that the Negro vote was a threat or an asset, and they preferred to have it as an asset. In the twenties, there were signs that Tammany Hall in New York was cultivating the Negroes, though these manoeuvres were kept in shadow as long as the idol of the hall, 'Al' Smith, had a chance of being President through Southern support. After the revolt of 1928 against the national Democratic candidate, there was no longer any motive for cultivating the South and some emotional reasons for defying it. The courtship of the Negro was resumed.

This process was accelerated by the onset of the depression. In the first enthusiasm over 'breaking the Solid South' in 1928, the Hoover administration began to cultivate the so-called 'lilywhite' Republicans, that is, the few remaining whites who were fighting for control of the Republican party in the South with the professional Negro politicians. This attempt to shift the traditional bases of political power was ruined by the depression; the Republican party, barely surviving in the North, was made more impotent than ever in the South.

In the depth of the depression for the Northern Negro to have remained faithful to the Republican party would have been heroic folly. The Republican party might still be the ship, but it was foundering; there was nothing for it but to take to the sea and get on board the broad Democratic raft. Everywhere from 1930 on, local, state, and then national government passed into Democratic hands, and the Negro thought, rightly, that no one needed help from public authority more than he did. Political action was almost his sole weapon; he used it and passed over, in wave after wave, into the Democratic party. Sometimes he left his old Republican leaders behind. Sometimes they were suddenly and prudently converted. By 1936, the day of automatic Negro allegiance to the Republican party was over. The ghost of Lincoln was laid.[1]

The one Republican Negro Congressman was replaced by a Democrat (himself a recent convert to the party of Jefferson). The Negro vote, no longer automatically 'deliverable' by the old-school leaders, became more and more independent, more and more insistent on tangible benefits for 'the race', not for race leaders. Better schools, parks, swimming pools; the effective opening of municipal jobs to Negroes; legal war against discrimination were the planks of the new Negro politicians' platform; and as, with all its faults, the New Deal, in most areas, opposed race discrimination in wages and opportunities of employment, and as no group needed social services more than the Negro, the alliance of the Negroes and the Democratic party in the North was soon as solid as had been the old alliance of the Republicans and the Negroes.

Other groups tried to profit by this foot-loose attitude of the Negro voter, notably the Communists. They cultivated the Negro by the ostentatious equality of their race attitudes; they nominated a Negro for Vice-President; they painted a glowing picture of the abolition of race barriers in the Soviet Union. They paraded

[1] Two acute observers of the Chicago scene point out that among the first groups to see the light were the organizers of the illegal gambling 'numbers' game. 'However, one group—the policy men—were quick to shift their allegiance to the new party. Political protection was necessary for them to carry on their business. By 1933, after a series of raids by the police, the " Jones Boys", who were among the largest operators, found it expedient to join the Democratic party.' Horace R. Cayton and St. Clair Drake, *Black Metropolis* (1946), pp. 352-3.

eminent Negroes who were party members or fellow-travellers such as Paul Robeson; they thrust themselves into race disputes and *causes célèbres* like that of the Scottsboro boys. They even painted, for a time, a rosy picture of a Negro commonwealth in the South. Naturally, they had some success. To the American Negroes more than to any other American group it might well have seemed that they had nothing to lose but their chains. But it is surprising how little success the Communists had. For one thing, the lavish display of affection may have reminded the Negroes of the old Republican attitude round election time. For another, there were signs that the Communist party was less anxious to save Negroes than to use them, as in the Scottsboro case. The rapid changes of the party line threw many Negroes, as well as whites, overboard. Eminent converts like Richard Wright left the party with as much publicity, almost, as they had joined it.

The Negro, whom hard experience had made a very practical politician, was not easily diverted from his immediate dire needs and bitter necessities by the Communist 'pie in the sky'. The new Negro commonwealth could have been created only by a civil war in the South which few Negroes thought they could hope to win. The Communists, even at the height of their strength, were a small, semi-alien body with more power for mischief than for construction. The Negro had enough handicaps without voluntarily taking on this new one.[1]

And, a point rightly insisted on by Gunnar Myrdal, the American Negro knows that the law is his chief ally, that the rights guaranteed to him by the Constitution, imperfectly enforced as the guarantees

[1] Gunnar Myrdal admirably illustrates the effect of Negro horse sense in immunizing the race against Communist siren songs. 'James Weldon Johnson makes this point: In the situation as it now exists, it would be positively foolhardy for us, as a group, to take up the cause of Communistic revolution and thereby bring upon ourselves all of the antagonisms that are directed against it in addition to those we already have to bear. . . . Every Negro's dark face would be his party badge, and would leave him an open and often solitary prey to the pack whenever the hunt might be on.' Gunnar Myrdal, *An American Dilemma: The Negro Problem and Modern Democracy* (1944), vol. 1, p. 509. The Negro, in short, does not trust any white man, even when he is red. 'Race' consciousness might, in Communist demonology, become a crime like Zionism.

are, are yet indispensable to his progress. He cannot afford to sneer at bourgeois democracy; the law and the formal electoral process, the loaves and fishes of politics, are things he cannot yet dispense with.[1]

In all Northern states, and in some areas of the South, the white politician, more or less openly, cultivates the Negro voter. He cultivates him by making careers possible for Negroes obviously discriminated against in the past, not in the old sense of giving a few 'traditional' jobs to Negroes, but by attempting, or pretending to attempt, to remove obstacles to general Negro advancement. This may take the form of putting forward Negro candidates for posts hitherto automatically reserved for white men;[2] it may take the form of filling important appointive jobs of all kinds with Negroes, otherwise fully qualified.[3]

[1] This realization may account for the Negro preoccupation with politics. 'The Negroes ranked highest in the proportion of their members belonging to political organizations. The Irish ranked second, then the Yankees, French, Italians, Armenians, the Poles and Jews, and the Greeks.' W. Lloyd Warner and Paul S. Lunt, *The Status System of a Modern Community* (1942), p. 87.

[2] In the autumn of 1953 all candidates for the post of Borough President of Manhattan were Negroes; this post is one of the most important in the New York municipal life. At the beginning of the primary campaign Tammany Hall made the mistake of not nominating a Negro, but hastily mended its ways as its rivals played up to the Negro vote.

[3] These nominations do not always win over suspicious 'race' men. Thus a Negro publicist, after listing a number of these appointments, goes on, 'These developments on the top-drawer level, while acclaimed, are chiefly class honors, rather than major advancements of the whole Negro community. . . . What often happens to these people is that they tend to form an aristocracy within the race and become jealous of their privileged position, and become chiefly concerned with maintaining it. They are unresponsive to the aspirations of the little fellow, and, in racial crises, frequently fail to speak out on behalf of their race, conscious perhaps that the security of their positions is dependent on the goodwill of the white folks. This, in its modern dress, is called Neo-Uncle-Tomism.' Roi Ottley, *New World A-Coming Inside Black America* (1943; 1945), pp. 216–7. This criticism may be justified, but a study made by me (in 1952 and 1953) of the Negro shiny-paper magazines convinced me that success of this kind is admired, is taken as a credit to the race, even though stories of successful jazz musicians or boxers may be more popular.

It also takes more general forms; there seems little doubt that as more and more Negroes vote, more and more tangible benefits accrue to the group. Indeed, the two forces, the law (as recently interpreted by the federal courts), and the making of the law and its administration, have been the chief instruments of Negro promotion.[1]

The comparatively sudden growth of Negro political power has led to some heady estimates of its potency. By calculations showing how close the margin was in decisive states in 1940 and 1944 (and, more recently, in 1948), it has been possible to argue that the Negro vote, by carrying New York, Illinois, Pennsylvania, Ohio, could be decisive. 'The Negro's political influence in national elections derives not so much from its numerical strength as from its strategic diffusion in the balance-of-power and marginal states whose electoral votes are generally considered vital to the winning candidate. In the 1944 elections there were twenty-eight states in which a shift of 5 per cent or less of the popular vote would have reversed the electoral votes cast by these states. In twelve of these, with a total of 228 electoral votes, the potential Negro vote exceeds the number required to shift the votes from one column to the other.'[2] But not only (as 1952 showed) are all elections not close; the obvious and noisy casting of the weight of one group, ethnic or economic, on one side, may provoke, by resistance or resentment, the throwing of another or of several other groups on to the other side, a fact of political life that Irish, Jews, Negroes, unions, even farmers sometimes forget, to their loss. But, without overestimating the power of the Negro vote, it is now important, occasionally decisive. In the North it seemed so solidly allied with the Democratic party that,

There is nothing odd in this. For long, the greatest Irish-American was not Philip Sheridan, but John L. Sullivan. Mr. Vito Marcantonio knew what he was doing when, as a fellow-travelling Congressman, he used to woo Negro voters in Harlem by badgering 'Happy' Chandler, the Baseball Commissioner, about the exclusion of Negro baseball players from the major leagues.

[1] Gunnar Myrdal points out, in this connection, the special importance of the vote in the South where the administration of the law is far more political, less neutral and objective, than in the North. The Negro needs the vote more in the South than in the North.

[2] Henry Lee Moon, *Balance of Power: The Negro Vote* (1948), p. 198.

except in local elections, the Republicans had little hope of detaching any serious part of it.[1] But this may be changing.

In the South, the question is involved in a wider one. What are the prospects of a party realignment? It has been, for the Negro, promotion to be allowed to vote in the Democratic primary and, where there has been a real contest, to vote the regular Democratic ticket. If a real two-party system grows up in the South, the Republican party, there, can only be a conservative party of the well-to-do. It can get mass support only by more or less openly supporting some kind of race discrimination. If it doesn't, what is Governor Byrnes doing in alliance with it? Not since the last act of Hamlet has there been such mixed scuffling as in the South since 1948, but the role of the Negro vote there is only part of a wider Southern problem.[2]

A very imperfectly assimilated group whose problems are more and more in the public, and in the politician's eye is provided by the 'Latin-Americans'. These fall into two groups: 'Mexicans' in all the border states, but above all in Texas, and Puerto Ricans in New York. The first group are mainly Indian in origin, and the problem of whether they were to be treated as 'white' is as old as the Republic of Texas. They drift to-and-fro across the border, one of the most artificial frontiers in the world. They have links both with Mexico and in Texas, and although all born in the United States are American citizens, their family archives are not well ordered. It is important to distinguish between New Mexico and Texas and Southern California. In New Mexico, there is in existence an important Spanish-speaking landed and professional class in whose veins runs 'the blood of Conquerors', to quote Harvey Fergusson. Of that ruling class, Senator Chavez is the most prominent representative. But in New Mexico, with the growth of the state the balance of population is probably tending in favour of the 'Anglos', with political results hard to assess. Nevertheless, so far, the New

---

[1] There is reason to believe that, in 1952, the Negro vote was the most unshaken in the North in its allegiance to the Democratic party. At any rate, competent observers thought that nowhere else in his tours did Mr. Truman get the same enthusiastic reception that he got in Harlem.

[2] See p. 78.

Mexicans of old stock are loyal to their native leaders and vote with commendable unanimity.

In Texas, the situation is different. There in the border counties the leadership of the Mexicans is in the hands of local 'American' bosses and landlords who get as loyal service out of their tenants and employees as an Irish landlord got from his before O'Connell stirred them to revolt. The balance of power in Texas is often in the hands of those who control the Mexican vote, a fact resented by those against whom the balance turns.[1]

As among the Negroes in the South, the urban areas are the first to develop independent voters. 'In Corpus Christi they vote; on the ranches they don't vote. In Corpus Christi they are proud of their political power.'[2]

The forces that have been elevating and liberating the Negro are beginning to work among the Mexicans too. They are developing their own leaders, and the increasing wealth and stability of Mexico reflects on the Mexicans in the United States—to their advantage.[3]

[1] 'The most famous of all Texas machines is that of the Parr family in Duval County. It gained national prominence in 1948 along with neighbouring Jim Wells County when Lyndon Johnson won the second senatorial primary by a state-wide margin of 87 votes. The vote in Duval was 4,622 for Johnson and 40 for Coke Stevenson. The boss of Duval and the leader in the 18-county twenty-seventh senatorial district, is George Parr, rancher and oil operator, who inherited his domain from his father, Archie, the "Duke of Duval". Following the 1948 election George Parr took offence at complaints by Stevenson about bloc voting in Duval and surrounding counties. He pointed out that in four previous elections Stevenson had solicited his support and his counties had gone for Stevenson with about the same enthusiasm then as they voted for Johnson this time. "And I never heard a complaint from him about the bloc vote in Duval County".' V. O. Key, *Southern Politics in State and Nation* (1949), p. 274.

[2] Paul Schuster Taylor, *An American-Mexican Frontier: Nueces County, Texas* (1934), p. 236. Another witness, quoted by Dr. Taylor, tells how on election day, Mexican and American flags float together with portraits of Washington and Hidalgo (the priest who led the Mexican revolt against Spain). As Mexican voters get more numerous, it will be necessary to find some way of celebrating Sam Houston and Santa Aña together.

[3] 'The Texas-Mexican is also waking up to realities. He is breaking away from domination by Anglo-American bosses and, under the dyn-

The Puerto Ricans in New York present a more serious problem. As natives of a poor and overcrowded island, they have many good reasons for emigrating and, as they are American citizens, there are no legal barriers to their emigrating to the continental United States. But unlike the Mexicans, they do not pass into the American economy, performing, under however bad conditions, tasks for which they are competent. They go from their rural slums into urban slums, overcrowding already over-crowded Harlem, and probably more handicapped in their struggle for existence than any previous group of immigrants.[1]

It is not surprising that the Puerto Rican slums provided the most steady voters for the fellow-travelling Congressman, Vito Marcantonio.[2] It took the combined efforts of all other parties—and machines—to shake Mr. Marcantonio's hold on this district, and the conditions will breed radicalism, if not formal Communism, faster than mere politics can undo their work.

Yet even the Indians (who have always been worth cultivating in Oklahoma) are now voters in relatively important numbers in Arizona. Issues are not only less and less sectional, but more and more, at the political level at any rate, American life is being nationalized and unified. Of course, political life is not all, but by performing a function that could be performed in no other way, politics, even 'mere' politics, deserve well of the Republic.[3]

---

amic leadership of such young men as Gus Garcia of San Antonio and Dr. Hector Garcia of Corpus Christi, is becoming an active and progressive political force.' Hart Stilwel, 'Texas' in *Our Sovereign State* (1949), edited by Robert S. Allen, p. 343.

[1] Messrs. Lait and Mortimer's description of the situation is not far off the mark. 'Puerto Ricans are not born to be New Yorkers. They are mostly crude farmers, subject to congenital tropical diseases, physically unfitted for the northern climate, unskilled, uneducated, non-English speaking and almost impossible to assimilate for healthful and useful existence in an active city of stone and steel.' Jack Lait and Lee Mortimer, *New York Confidential* (1948), p. 126. Puerto Ricans in New York bring to mind the Algerians in Paris.

[2] In the election of 1948 I inspected his district and was impressed by an apparent correlation between Spanish shops and speech and Marcantonio campaigning.

[3] Even inside the political system, there are social strains. It seems probable that some of the resentment that Mr. James A. Farley felt against

A problem that fascinates practising politicians is, what happens to individuals and groups when they *are* promoted? As more and more Italians, Poles and the rest move into full American society, leave the slums for the suburbs, encounter and mix with the 'old' stocks, will they keep the political allegiance that was, consciously or unconsciously, a way of ascent? If they do, many New York surburban areas now safely Republican will become, at best, doubtful. If they don't, Democrats will not recover on Long Island or Westchester what they lose in Manhattan. A good deal will depend on Republican adroitness and on the degree to which the newcomers are accepted.[1] The levelling of incomes, the creation of new communities where everybody is a newcomer, to be accepted at face value, are producing a new type of middle-class society very different from that into which the new stocks strove to climb.[2]

F.D.R. was due not only to the President's too low estimate of what he owed to the King-maker, but to Mr. Farley's exclusion from the President's private life. 'Strange as it may seem, the President never took me into the bosom of the family, although everyone agreed that I was more responsible than any other single man for his being in the White House. Never was I invited to spend the night in the historic mansion. . . . Mrs. Eleanor Roosevelt once said, "Franklin finds it hard to relax with people who aren't his social equals." I took this remark to explain my being out of the infield.' James A. Farley, *Jim Farley's Story: The Roosevelt Days* (1948), p. 68. Like the Duc de Guermantes, F.D.R. saw no reason to mix business with private life. Mr. Farley's resentment may not have been lessened by the knowledge that another Irish-American politician, 'Ed' Flynn, was a frequent guest at the White House.

[1] The least likely to be accepted, in the present state of American *mores*, are the Jews (and, of course, the Negroes). They, therefore, may remain faithful while Poles and Italians are seduced by the suburbs.

[2] 'Park Forest', a new suburb of this kind on the outskirts of Chicago, has been studied by *Fortune*. William H. Whyte, Jr., 'The Outgoing Life', *Fortune,* July 1953. 'In similar fashion, farm-bred Republicans learn to appreciate that all urban Democrats are not Communists. "The people who lived in the other half of our duplex", recalls one Republican, "were as different as could be from us. They were the kind who worshipped F.D.R.'s name. But we got to like them just the same. We just didn't talk politics. We used to go bowling together and that sort of thing. I didn't make him a Republican, but I think he appreciates my views a lot more than he did before." ' Loc. cit., p. 87. There is no indication that the Republican changed his views about F.D.R.

But whatever the effect on party fortunes, the national effect is to the good. The 'war between the races' is following the 'war between the states' into the shadows. It is not over; some wounds are still raw; there will be rearguard actions; but the making of a 'more perfect union' is a more hopeful project than it was as recently as 1928, and the chief makers of that union have been the politicians.[1]

[1] 'The thing we all sense, whether or not we acknowledge it, is that politically we are at last one nation. Our social cleavages have not disappeared—some have widened menacingly in recent years—but they are all national cleavages.' Richard R. Rovere, 'The Republican Prospects', *Harper's Magazine*, July 1953, p. 39. Mr. Rovere points out the importance of the acceptance of the new stocks, belatedly, by the Republicans. He thinks it has not gone far enough. 'So simple a thing, for instance, as making more frequent the incidence of names like O'Konski and Dworshak, and Cerano and McCarthy (repeat *names*) would strengthen the party enormously.' Loc. cit., p. 37. Without commenting on any of the names cited, it might be said that, to paraphrase Mr. Charles Wilson, whatever is good for the Republican party in this connection is good for the nation.

Chapter Four

MACHINES AND BOSSES

I

THE political machine is a decidedly American institution. Parallels can be found in other democratic societies, but the American political system is peculiar in that a great part of the political power is in what are, from a party point of view, non-political hands. For it is the main characteristic of the machine that it exists to secure and perpetuate power in the hands of a known organization. And that power is primarily used for the enrichment, or gratification in some form, of the owners of the machine. It is in this sense that the machine is non-political; it need have nothing to do with local or general policies and programmes. Its object is political control; its means the control of nominations and of elections. What it does with the control when achieved varies from time to time and place to place, but the true character of the machine is its political indifferentism. It is this that marks it off from political organizations like the old 'Birmingham caucus', from the Radical-Socialist *cadres* of the Third Republic, from the very elaborate political organization of the German Social-Democratic party under the Empire and the Weimar Republic.[1] The machine exists for itself; all other objects

[1] There is a good definition of a machine in *A New Dictionary of American Politics* edited by Edward Conrad Smith and Arnold John Zurcher (1949), p. 234. 'Machine. An organization controlled by a boss or a small coterie of leaders which subjects party organization and public officials to its will and operates efficiently and ruthlessly in exploiting governmental activities of nearly every sort for the private gain of its members.'

are auxiliary and are never allowed to interfere with the primary purpose of winning, keeping and using political power. Machines are not exclusively phenomena of city life. There have been rural machines, dominated by bosses or groups as ruthless and corrupt as any that the great cities have known. There have been state bosses whose power was based on such rural machines. But the rural machine, the rural boss, as a rule, had other sources of power than the mere control of the electoral machinery. Often it was because he *had* other sources of power, as a banker, lawyer, big landowner, agent for the railroad and the like, that he had political power. But it is the characteristic of the true machine that its rulers owe their power to their control of the machine. Nominations, elections, offices, these are the sources of the power that the machine wields and so often sells.

The machine has been the most obvious scandal of American politics for over a century and the death of the machine, the ending of boss rule has been proclaimed in every generation of that time. But the machines live on (though changed), the bosses are replaced by other bosses, and it is not yet certain that the day of either the boss or the machine is over although twilight may be upon both.

The character of the machine may be most easily illustrated by an examination of the most famous of all machines, Tammany Hall, the machine that, for more than a century, has, more often than not, ruled Manhattan Island.[1] Tammany began as a patriotic society in the *annus mirabilis*, 1789. Its patron was St. Tammany, a Delaware chief whose virtues were celebrated with the sonorous eloquence of the era.[2] The society of St. Tammany (or the

[1] Until the creation of 'greater New York' in 1897, the city was confined to Manhattan Island and the Bronx. Now it also includes Brooklyn, Queens and Richmond. Tammany, strictly speaking, is still confined to the borough of Manhattan.

[2] An early spell-binder described the virtues of the Saint. ' "There was no force, no violence, in his measures, but general consent and concurrence of sentiment conferred on him all the authority he possessed. . . . If he obtained influence, that influence was conferred on him by the citizens, and they trusted him with power because they were confident he would not abuse it." ' This eulogy was pronounced in the old Presbyterian church, on May 12th, 1795, by Samuel Latham Mitchill, M.D., F.R.S.E. Mitchill was a distinguished physician, much interested

Columbian Order) had branches in Philadelphia, in the new capital, Washington, in Ohio. But only the New York 'Wigwam' was destined for a long life. And although the Society was originally not affiliated to any party (parties did not, in fact, exist on a national scale in 1789), it soon became, under the leadership of Aaron Burr, the organization of the 'Republicans', the opponents of the Federalists, 'the good, the wise and the rich',[1] and it has remained formally attached to the party that claims descent from the early Republicans, i.e. the Democrats.

The real role of Tammany was to 'organize' the newly en-franchised voters of what was now the largest city in the United States. A great and increasing part of that city's population was composed of recent immigrants, usually indifferent to American issues, having nothing to lose but their chains and little to sell but their votes. The Tammany pattern was repeated in every great city, in Boston, in Philadelphia, even in Chicago as it emerged from its status as a village. For the machine performed a function that no other American organization performed at that time, or for long after. It gave some kind of coherence to a society in perpetual flux, in which even the natives were bewildered by the new problems of urban life in cities growing like the prophet's gourd. And it did this at a price. To the poor it gave favours; if it controlled the police, it could moderate its zeal; it could give and withhold minor favours like peddlers' licences; it could give minor jobs; it could arrange for naturalization; it could act as a kind of charity organiza-tion society, helping with coal and food in domestic crises; and, with its parades and excursions, it provided circuses as well as bread. There were moments in which genuine radical movements were on the edge of success in the new urban communities, equiva-

---

in Indian lore. The quotation is from M. Ostrogorski, *Democracy and the Organization of Political Parties* (1902), vol. II, p. 153. Tammany seems to be a vaguely historical character. The inventor of the perforated music roll, player piano and, appropriately, the voting machine, was John McTammany, a native of Glasgow, Scotland. He seems to have had no connection with the Society.

[1] Strictly speaking, Tammany is still a secret, friendly society, ruled by Sachems with a mock Indian ritual of a type popular in America. The political organization is the Democratic Committee of New York County, but the difference is hardly worth insisting on.

lents of Chartism and the like. But American urban society was too incoherent, changing at too great speed and in too many ways, to provide a basis for urban politics based on principles. The very success of the democratic movement helped the machines, not only by enfranchising its clients, but by removing from the field of politics such questions as the right to vote, to elementary education, to theoretically equal access to office. By 1850, there was little or none of the raw material of radical politics that kept the European working man politically alert.

That the rule of the cities was often in the hands of rogues was no secret by the time of the Civil War. Good citizens stung to self-reproach by some new scandal, would note that their neglect of municipal politics was one cause of the rule of Tammany or its kindred organizations, but that was all. It took a scandal on a very great scale indeed, like the plundering of New York by the Tweed Ring[1] or of Philadelphia by the Gas House Ring, to arouse the more respectable citizens. And they did not stay aroused long. Besides, there was no difference for the worse in the morals of Tammany (or of the Philadelphia Ring) compared with those of such business magnates as Jim Fisk and Jay Gould. A society that allowed the plundering of the Erie Railroad was in no very good position to protect the assets of New York. Within a few years of the overthrow of the Tweed Ring, Tammany, under John Kelly, was 'reformed' and again in control of the city. The machine rulers of Philadelphia got only singed, not burned, and there was no great city in the country that did not know the results of boss rule, though some, like Boston, did not get the benefits, such as they were, of unified machine control.

It was this repeated failure of the 'reform' elements to make their

[1] It is from the days of the Tweed Ring, after the Civil War, that some famous emblems of American politics date. The cartoonist Thomas Nast, of *Harper's Weekly*, made the elephant the emblem of the Republicans, the donkey the emblem of the Democrats, and the tiger the emblem of Tammany Hall. The tiger had been the emblem of the volunteer fire company to which Tweed belonged. 'Nast chose the tiger to denote . . . the ferocity of Tammany Hall and Tweed toward their prey, the people of the City of New York. The symbol stuck to Tammany Hall, and it has been adopted by the organization as part of its charm.' M. R. Werner, *Tammany Hall* (1928), p. 106.

reforms stick; the fact that, until the time of Mayor La Guardia, no reform Mayor of New York was ever re-elected, that bred despair. It also bred an unhealthy reliance on the state government to control the wicked cities, often by taking away their power over their police force (as in Boston) or dividing the functions of local government among a mass of competing authorities (as in Cook County, i.e. Chicago). But state governments were not necessarily any purer than city governments and, as often as not, the state government and the city governments were in corrupt collusion.

There was more than one reason for the failure of the Reformers, the sponsors of 'Good Government' Leagues, the 'Goos Goos', as the professionals contemptuously termed them, and the first was that they refused to see that the machines, corrupt and criminal as they were, did perform a function that the machine's supporters thought was worth the trifling price of a vote. It is very easy—and very tempting today—to see the faults and account for the sterility of the late nineteenth century reformers. They did assume that there was a known, vendible commodity called 'good government', that only fools or knaves could fail to recognize it and that, duly instructed by their betters, the urban masses would buy the panacea put on the market. They felt, much as James Mill had felt, that the natural leaders of the country were the public-spirited and educated middle classes and that, as education spread, as electoral laws were improved, as the mere distortions of the democratic process were dealt with by law and by 'public opinion', the power of the bosses, based on the fact that they could buy votes with petty favours, would wither away at the roots. It took them a long time to learn that this was not so, that the roots of the machines, of 'bad government' were deep indeed, that reform campaigns, even successful reform campaigns, merely burned the bracken; they did not kill it.

Partly, this failure to understand the political problem came from the unconscious class bias of the reformers. They thought (as middle-class reformers do in all countries) that the poor had middle-class wants, that only the limitations of their cultural status prevented their immediately demanding the cheaper goods their would-be mentors cherished. After all, the best things in life are almost free; some, like museums and public libraries, are, or can be made, quite free. That the poor might have tastes that differed from theirs, that literacy and even a rise in real wages might not increase the demand for higher things, was inconceivable.

In this the American municipal reformers were not alone in their innocence. They were no more innocent than the French intellectuals who brought the 'universités populaires' to the Paris workers, to discover that the Paris workers did not want the fine flower of the culture of the *École Normale*, that as far as they could be got to come to lectures at all, it was to be told how right they were in desiring to 'hang the rich at sight'. The reformers were no more wrong than the generous pioneers of the Workers' Educational Association in England, whose programme of transforming the mind of the English worker has run up against more formidable obstacles than poor wages and defective schooling: the dislike of most of the human race (at any rate in modern industrial society) for serious mental effort that does not pay in cash, prestige or tangible reward of some kind. The approach of the reformers was as amateurish as that of a church dramatic society boldly competing with the slickest Broadway or Shaftesbury Avenue producers. Tammany and the other great machines were the professional producers.[1]

The reformers forgot the wisdom of Shaw's counsel. 'Do not do unto others as you would they should do unto you. Their tastes may not be the same.' This truth was put in another form when the greatest commentator on American city politics set out to explain the failure of reform administrations. The reformer thinks, said Mr. Dooley, 'that we're achin' in ivry joint to have him drag us be th' hair iv th' head fr'm th' flowin' bowl an' th' short card game, make good citizens iv us and sind us to th' pinitinchry. So th' minyit he gets into th' job he begins a furious attimpt to convart us into what we've been thryin' not to be iver since we come into th' wurruld'.[2]

But it was not only that the reformers lacked an adequate knowledge of 'human nature in politics'. They knew little or nothing of

[1] It might be argued that television, the comics, the football pools, the dog tracks are the current equivalents as degraders 'of the democratic dogma' of the old city machines in America and the pubs and working men's clubs of the bad old days in England.

[2] *Observations by Mr. Dooley* (1903), p. 168.

the realities of life in the slums of the great cities. The dwellers in the 'old law tenements' of New York had problems, a social *ethos* and a social structure that could not be understood by the most public-spirited reformers. It was physically easy to walk east or west on Fifth Avenue, or down the wrong side of Beacon Hill, and come, quickly, to this unknown world; but the reformers were as cut off from the inhabitants as a European Christian walking through the Medina of an Arab town. Of course, the reformers who took the plunge, the men and women who entered the settlements in Hull House or Henry Street, learned the realities quickly enough. Jane Addams has told us how she began to understand the utility and, in a sense, the necessity of the machine. What it did for the poor may have been far less than what it did against them, but what it did was very visible; what it did against them was usually, though not always, invisible.

What the machine did was, however unconsciously, something that sociologists rank highly. It broke down, to some degree, the barrier between 'Them' and 'Us'. The policeman, the judge, the municipal official were still 'they' but, thanks to the Boss and his lieutenants, there was a human and understandable middle term; the machine was both 'They' and 'We'.

But there were reasons for the failure of reform other than the support that the machines earned. For the machines served more than the poor; they served some of the rich. They served some of them by adjusting the taxes in their favour (as they could threaten others by adjusting the taxes to their disadvantage). They served industries by being slack in enforcing factory legislation. They served others by providing votes for national parties that, in turn, served certain business interests. But above all, they served certain sections of the business world by selling valuable assets for substantial consideration, in particular by selling the monopolies of local transport, local water and gas supply. To control the transport system of a great and growing city was a standard way to a great fortune, as the history of New York, Chicago and Cleveland showed. And, innocently or not so innocently, reformers found that the 'better elements' were not united in favour of an honest, non-political government enforcing uniform law and vigilantly guarding the rights of the community. It was not enough to say that it was wrong of businessmen to stay out of politics, if it was not noticed that not all businessmen *did* stay out of politics. For as Lincoln Steffens wrote fifty years ago. 'The typical business man is a bad citizen; he is busy. If he is a "big business man" and very busy, he does not neglect, he is busy with politics. . . . He is a self-righteous fraud, this big business man. He is the chief source of corruption, and it were a boon if he would neglect politics.'[1] This, Steffens thought, was the answer to the problem that puzzled commentators like Bryce, the problem of why the 'best people' did not go into politics, why the better elements in a city like Philadelphia had so little apparent effect on its government. It was Steffen's opinion that there was no mystery; the best, that is the richest, elements *were* in politics.

Twenty-five years after Steffens expressed this unkind view of the role of the business man, a more objective observer came to much the same conclusion. It was the alliance of the 'Underworld' and the 'Upperworld' that explained the deep roots of graft and crime in Chicago, wrote Charles Edward Merriam. 'To the public much of this may sound terrifying and fearful but not so in certain regions of the Upperworld of business, where affairs are placed upon the hard and realistic basis of engineering. Obstacles must be swept aside at whatever cost in the interest of the greater efficiency, and among them are the obstacles of politics and the politicians whose whims and eccentricities and financial appetites are subjects of alternate irritation and amusement.'[2]

One of the model politico-business set-ups was to be found, as one would expect, in California. 'In California the subservience of politics to big business was especially facilitated by the dominance of a single great corporation in the state's economy. Most of the railroad mileage in California was merged under the name of the Southern Pacific, a holding company whose charter, granted by the state of Kentucky, empowered it to do almost anything except

[1] Lincoln Steffens, *The Shame of the Cities* (1904), p. 5.
[2] Charles Edward Merriam, *Chicago: A More Intimate View of Urban Politics* (1929), p. 53. I found the same attitude in Boston (Mass.), where many persons of the highest respectability regretted the infrequent reform administrations since, with these types, 'you didn't know where you were.'

to operate in Kentucky. The Southern Pacific, allied with lesser corporate interests, notably public utilities, maintained a confidential political organization of which the bosses of both major parties in California were satellites.'[1]

The same story could have been told of other states. In some, in North Dakota for instance, the 'invisible government' was not even located in the state, but in the capital of another state. To many Southern and Western malcontents, the whole of the United States was tributary in politics, as well as in the deeper realities of economics, to the Northeast. Senator Aldrich ruled more than Rhode Island; Senator Hanna more than Ohio. And no basic reforms that threatened the political dominance by business interests could be tolerated. Hanna, in all probability, knew that Tom Johnson was giving their common city of Cleveland a better government than a 'safer' Mayor would have done, but Hanna had more serious interests to consider than the municipal progress of Cleveland or, to do him justice, than the immediate interests of the Marcus A. Hanna Company.

II

'Work is done when the point of application of a force moves.' So the old-fashioned text-books on dynamics used to say. For the machine, work is done when the voters vote for the candidates hand-picked by the machine. And tireless industry is needed to keep both the voters loyal to the machine and the party workers loyal to the leaders of the machine. There are always 'four and twenty leaders of revolt' waiting for the first sign of weakness and, no more than the priest who guarded the golden bough, can a Boss afford to take any but an occasional nap. American history is full of stories of Bosses who grew slack, who alienated, without destroying, ambitious young men, who even overestimated the tolerance of the voters.

The main characteristic of the Boss, at all stages, is his indefatigable industry. Above all he must get out the vote; the election or,

[1] Walton Bean, *Boss Ruef's San Francisco* (1952), p. 5.

in many places, the primary is the pay-off. 'Stupid fellows, lazy fellows, slow-minded fellows, weak and timid fellows without ambition and courage do not rise in machine politics.'[1] The motives that lead men to adopt this laborious and risky life are various. In many districts a generation ago, politics, at least a minor political job, was social promotion. As the greatest product of machine politics put it, in describing his entry into the great game, 'I had a choice of hard labor at a small wage of ten dollars a week, or twelve at the most, in the kind of jobs that were open to me, or easier work at a greater wage. I had a fondness for politics and I liked the excitement of public life. I had plenty of friends and I always took much satisfaction in being able to help them.'[2] All of these motives counted with 'Al' Smith, but all practising machine politicians must have, or pretend to have, a desire to help, and they must help. They must be the bridge between the strange, unfriendly, or remote and meaningless, formal organization of society, and the poor and ignorant who had greater trust in the realities of luck and favour than in the empty formulas of justice that pleased, satisfied and, usually, served the more prosperous. It was put in final and classical form by Martin Lomasney of Boston: ' "I think . . . that there's got to be in every ward somebody that any block can come to—no matter what's he's done—and get help. Help you understand; none of your law and justice, but help." '[3]

Of course, for the member of a machine who wanted, or who wants to have a public political career of what is called the 'normal' kind, other qualities are needed, the gift of the gab, the gift of administrative ability, the gift of honesty and principle; and 'Al' Smith had them all. But it was possible and, in some places, it is still possible to be a power in politics without serving any known public purpose. But private purposes *must* be served, and the first private purposes to be served were and are those of the voters, for the boss is a buyer of votes. He buys votes in many ways, but above all by services.

In the old days of the free play of the American system of free enterprise, those services were very varied. The machine was the

---

[1] Frank R. Kent, *The Great Game of Politics* (1924), pp. 80–1.
[2] *Up To Now: The Autobiography of Alfred E. Smith* (1929), p. 56.
[3] *Autobiography of Lincoln Steffens* (1931), vol. II, p. 618.

social service state; the precinct captain and all the other members
of the hierarchy were the bureaucracy of that state. They gave
away coal and food, got the sick into hospital, the unlucky out of
jail. They got jobs for the boys leaving school, not only with the
municipal or state agencies, but with the business that dealt with
city and state. They made peace between husband and wife, or
arranged a quiet divorce if that was thought better. They were
always at hand as no state or civic organization was; the machine
and its officers kept no office hours. It is a long time since Martin
Lomasney gave the secret of his success. 'They the voters are
just my friends. I am with them all the time and that's what
counts.'[1] And long after Lomasney's day, the recipe for success
was still the same. The last great boss of Philadelphia, William
Vare, explained the success of 'the Organization'. 'The division
leader (or ward committeeman) must stay close to those that need
him. He must be on the job to help them. The average division
leader can always be found at a certain place—the corner cigar
store, the drug store, or some such place. He goes there every
night. When the voter wants him, he knows where to find him.'[2]
It was not only the minor officials, the precinct captains and the
like, who were available; as much as a French king, a Boss of the
old school had to be in touch. Commissioner Murphy, the greatest
recent Boss of Tammany Hall, standing under a lamp post, ready
to be accosted by all comers, was a great public officer though

[1] Harold Zink, *City Bosses in the United States* (1930), pp. 83-4.
[2] John T. Salter, 'Party Organization in Philadelphia: The Ward
Committeeman', *American Political Science Review*, August 1933, p. 621.
Elsewhere, Professor Salter gives an example of the lengths to which the
N.C.O.'s of the 'organization' went to serve their clientéle. One of
the minor Vare henchmen when asked where he met his people replied,
'Right here. . . . My door is never locked, day and night. I have
something here that not many of the men have—an extension on my
telephone that reaches right to my bed—it is about thirty feet long. But I
have seen myself transact business when I was lying with pneumonia.
. . . I feel that if the people feel I'm good enough to represent them in
the division, then I should be at their service just the same. This is the way
I look at it.' J. T. Salter, *Boss Rule Portraits in City Politics* (1935),
pp. 108-9. If not quite in the spirit that Lenin meant it, the agents of the
great machines gave to the party 'the whole of their lives'. Probably only
the Communists are equally zealous all of the time.

holding no legally recognized public office. Not all modern Bosses feel that this personal contact is necessary; they interpret the word 'machine' in a way that suggests a more literal meaning for the metaphor than was customary in the great days of the system. Thus the late Edward J. Flynn, for long Boss of the Bronx, and one of the most powerful figures in the New Deal, refused to play the game under the old rules. 'I intended to keep my personal life entirely separate from my political life.' This meant that the business of being a Boss would be 'conducted like any other well-run business. That meant I would not be available at night to any District group'.[1] But it is not at the top that the real work is done; the great and remote chief must leave a great deal to his lieutenants; his power and skill are shown in his choice of these lieutenants (as Commissioner Murphy's was when he chose young Mr. Flynn). But at the city equivalent of the 'grass roots', the old personal vigilance, the old personal service is as essential as ever. The N.C.O.'s cannot afford to keep regular office hours or to have a private life. They must get out the vote by the old methods.

For getting out the vote, no machine is stronger than its precinct organization. It is the captains of hundreds who produce the results. The most effective organization is that in which the precinct captain already has a large number of voters tied up. He has the votes of his own family; of such city officials as reside in his precinct; of the election officials. So for each of these offices it is a great advantage to be married and to have a family. Even the most loyal bachelor or spinster is at a disadvantage. It was usually assumed that each temporary or permanent recipient of the machine's bounty was good for five votes. In a well-organized city like New Orleans, the results were impressive.[2] The precinct

[1] Edward J. Flynn, *You're the Boss* (1947), pp. 60, 61. But Flynn entered politics from pretty near the top. He was a college graduate with a very different background from that of the old-school bosses. And, of course, lower down, his aides and lieutenants could not afford to be so aloof. They had to deliver the goods, the votes, by the old social methods. It was a new chain of command, that is all.

[2] 'In the average sized precinct of four hundred votes a leader controlled one hundred through his prerogatives and patronage. To carry the precinct such a leader had to have two hundred and one votes. The

leader has to keep his voters in good temper by services and, if that cannot be done, to keep them docile by threats. In normal times in the good old days, this was not too difficult, except where an ambitious aspirant for office was trying to upset the local leader. Yet, even before the great catastrophe of 1929–32 which upset the established order, there were signs of strain. In this as in many other things, the election of 1928 was ominous. In the great, unshaken Republican stronghold of Philadelphia, the Vare machine had to call on all its resources of disciplined service to hold the great slum and semi-slum wards in line. The voters there, party labels apart, had no doubt where their hearts were—with 'Al' Smith, not with Herbert Hoover. 'Al' was one of them; the end of prohibition was an aim that all of them, save perhaps bootleggers and prohibition agents, warmly sympathized with. Discipline did its work; Philadelphia went for the great engineer; but the precinct captains, the ward leaders had to be even more vigilant than usual. Some could not trust their wives; nearly all the voters had to be 'assisted'.[1] In 1932 it was worse. The Vare machine was cracking, so was the Republican party; there were even desertions among the N.C.O.'s.

It is in situations like these that the machine is tempted to tamper with the formal voting machinery. Compared with the scandals of two generations ago, American electoral methods are now reasonably clean. There is no great mass of raw, illiterate immigrants to provide such malleable materials. (Until the beginning of this century, in some states it was not necessary to be naturalized to vote.) Registration laws are much more severe, probably too severe in some states; federal control of elections is more and more rigorous. The 'mattress voters' of the old days, brought into a district for a night or two to qualify, the 'repeaters' who vote more

---

task then was to manage the campaign so as to get voluntarily one hundred and more votes out of the three hundred remaining. Compared to the task of the opposition, which ordinarily had no patronage to build up advance commitments, this was comparatively easy.' George M. Reynolds, *Machine Politics in New Orleans, 1897–1926* (1936), p. 116. Dr. Reynolds admits that these figures are perhaps higher than the national average.

[1] See p. 138.

than is legal are, if not things of the past, much greater rarities than
in the past.

The generally effective prevention of violence during elections
is in itself a preventive of the more gross frauds. It often took real,
physical courage to vote in primaries or even in elections in New
York after the Civil War, at any rate in the rowdier districts.
Primaries were usually held in saloons, and attempts to nominate
candidates not approved of by 'the lads' were foolhardy enterprises.
Electoral campaigns were often marked by serious violence.[1] The
police usually took a tolerant view of physical persuasion or the
intimidation of the official workers of the other party, in the rare
instances when the agents of the other party were not employees
of the machine they were 'opposing'. Now, elections cannot be won
simply by beating up. Since 1932, there have been no charges of
physical intimidation, on a big scale, in New York, although there
has been one election murder. Electoral laws have done a great deal
to bring about this change. In the old days, the parties provided
their own ballot papers, which were issued to the voters and offered
many opportunities for ingenuity. Now ballot papers are provided
by the State, which narrows the chances of fraud. Although padding
of electoral rolls is not unknown today, it is made harder by a more
rigorous state control of registration (at any rate in the big cities;
the countryside is more often left to its own devices, in the belief,
presumably, that this kind of fraud is difficult in a small community
where everyone is known). Some states insist on annual registration
a month or two before the election and the signature of the would-
be voter is compared with the signature made in the application.
This may check fraud, but it also checks voting and, in New York
City, almost certainly keeps down the number of voters—which
may be one of the motives of the rural and Republican legislators

[1] Richard Croker, one of the most famous and least attractive Bosses
of Tammany Hall, was charged with killing another politician in an
election row. He was acquitted, probably justly. He was, for once, on
the side of the angels, defending the rights of that eminent reformer,
Abram Hewitt. In a famous political tragedy, a 'repeater', Batt Shea,
was forced to kill a Republican worker in Troy (N.Y.) who showed
undue curiosity and was executed for his zeal. But these are nearly things
of the past; even slow-moving Philadelphia hasn't had an election
murder since 1917.

who prudently refrain from applying the same system to their villages.[1]

The adoption in most big cities of voting machines has had some of the effects that the coming of cash registers did in the book-keeping of saloons. It does not prevent fraud, but makes fraud more difficult and risky. A voting machine can be tampered with, but it takes mechanical ingenuity and a degree of general collusion now hard to come by. Voting machines have another unfortunate result from this point of view; they add up as the votes are cast so that the final result is ready almost as soon as the polls close. This makes impossible one of the classic tricks of olden time. It was customary, in close elections, for those in effective charge of the electoral machinery to wait till the last results were in, perhaps a day or two later and, if necessary, find the narrow majority required to offset an adverse poll. Thus, it was said, that great artist in politics, so admired by 'Mr. Dooley', Senator Gorman of Mary-land, 'carried' New York for Grover Cleveland in 1884. From this habit sprang the precept, 'Wait till all the returns are in and cry fraud'.[2] The voting machines get out the result too quickly for this waiting game to be profitable, save in the most exceptional circumstances.

[1] It can, of course, work against individual Republicans. I was in a Republican local headquarters on Manhattan Island on the night of the election of 1948. There was a stream of indignant citizens who had found that they could not vote for Governor Dewey and the ticket because they had omitted to register in September. The party workers were sympathetic but helpless.

[2] This precept was acted on in 1928 when F. D. Roosevelt, to the general surprise, carried New York state, although 'Al' Smith didn't. F.D.R.'s manager, 'Ed' Flynn, as soon as he was convinced that Roosevelt had been elected, issued a statement asserting that 'the Democratic State Committee has become convinced that fraud is being committed in an attempt to elect Albert Ottinger Governor of the State of New York'. Mr. Flynn announced that a committee was immediately being sent up-state to stop such knavish tricks. 'The fact is that this threat to send lawyers was a complete bluff. . . . But it was an effective threat. I made it because it had been a practice for many years in the rural counties to withhold votes as long as possible and in many instances to change them to supply a majority to elect a Republican Governor.' Edward J. Flynn, You're the Boss (1947), p. 72. Lawyers were actually sent up-state. They gained 640 votes for Roosevelt.

One last resort of the machine is to take advantage of the law that permits an illiterate or physically incapacitated voter to be 'assisted' in casting his vote. This is an effective method of controlling voters, especially in years like 1928 and 1932 in Philadelphia, when it was suspected that even the faithful could not be trusted alone behind the green curtain. To profess to be able to vote unaided was, it itself, ground for suspicion of intended treason and was effectually frowned on. As the number of foreign-born and of illiterates steadily drops, this device, though not impracticable, becomes more and more implausible.[1]

It would be idle to pretend that the days of fraud are over. But the easy ways of fraud are barred today. Even when districts vote with a unanimity equalling that of the citizens of a People's Democracy, this does not necessarily prove fraud; the districts concerned *may* be unanimous, or pretty near it. It is, of course, a mistake (which has happened under the Pendergast Machine in Kansas City, the Vare Organizations in Philadelphia, the Choctaw Club in New Orleans) for more votes to be cast than there are voters. A competent Boss deplores such excess of zeal as much as Talleyrand would have done. But the real strength of the machine (when it had it and where it has it) is in the genuine loyalty of the voter who cannot see why he should not do a good friend a trifling favour. Only when the electors begin to think that giving a vote is not a trifling favour do machines decline.[2]

[1] I myself was struck, while looking on at the Democratic primary in St. Louis in 1934 (I didn't waste time on the Republicans), by the number of voters who required assistance. It was this primary that sent the hitherto unknown Harry S. Truman of Independence, Missouri, to the Senate.

[2] It is a conviction of professional politicians that, in all but the most abnormal times, they know better than newspapermen, pollsters and political scientists how the vote is going. This may be an illusion like that shared by schoolmasters and professors, that they know what their pupils are doing, but I am inclined to agree with the politicians. I can remember being taken over his district by a Chicago leader during a presidential election. Driving to City Hall, he pointed out a house; 'Republicans live there.' I asked him how many Republican votes had been cast in the district in the last presidential election. 'Eight.' 'How many will be cast this time?' 'Twelve.' Regrettably, I did not check his

The average voter does not think that a vote is so important that he need worry too much about the results of the way he gives it, unless these results are intolerable and the connection between the vote and the result obvious. Then he can and does rise in his usually short-lived wrath. And in recent years, the favours the machine can confer have been rivalled by those given by other political organizations, notably by the federal government. But the foundation of machine power and of boss rule is public laziness and private industry, the voter being lazy and the machine and its employees tireless.

Democratic inertia is not confined to America but it is very marked there. The American, accustomed to think of himself as phenomenally self-reliant (as in many ways he is) is, as a social animal, passive, ready to respond to leadership, ready to turn over problems to 'experts' and to 'organizations'. This has been admirably put by one of the acutest foreign students of American life that the United States has ever known. 'In all America it is assumed that every group contains leaders who control the attitude of the group. Everywhere—not least in idealistic pursuits—the method of reaching a goal is assumed to be the indirect one of first reaching the leaders and, through them, influencing the masses. . . . The other side of this picture is, of course, the relative inertia and inarticulateness of the masses in America. The remarkable lack of self-generating, self-disciplined, organized people's movements in America is a significant historical fact usually overlooked by American historians and social scientists.'[1] This passivity (as Dr. Myrdal terms it) breeds the machine and gives admirable opportunities for the talents of those Americans who are not passive, who are leaders or who, merely, have the taste for the kind of dreary, repetitive, committee work, paper work which someone must do. If few are willing to do it, then 'in the country of the blind, the one-eyed man is king'. And American one-eyed men do well. This passing the buck, this laziness or boredom, out of which comes the party or philanthropic bureaucrat, is again not confined to America;

prophecy after the election, but I suspect he knew. For the value of the polls, see p. 260.

[1] Gunnar Myrdal, *An American Dilemma: The Negro Problem and Modern Democracy* (1944), vol. II, p. 712.

a great deal of tedious 'democratic' work must be done and most democrats are not willing to do it. They may trust or mistrust, admire or despise the man who is willing to do it, but because he does it, power flows to him.[1]

The machine politician not only flourishes because of this human trait, which is possibly exaggerated in Americans, but because of another aspect of American life, the comparative absence (by English standards) of a leisured class of which the more energetic members have many temptations to act as unpaid public servants. That class is now weaker in numbers, in economic resources and, possibly, in zeal than it used to be in England. But it never has been numerous in America where idleness has been frowned on, where a country gentry, free from the kind of economic cares that require constant vigilance in private business, has been rare (even in the ante-bellum South) and where, for a century past, the necessary docility in the rank and file of the population has been far to seek.[2] In a very fluid society, the public duties were left to 'mere' politicians, to clergymen, to wives and daughters and, in more recent times, to professional organizers, social workers, 'executive secretaries', the officers of the great foundations and, not infrequently, to mere frauds, for even today there is evidence that the American would rather give money than time or personal interest. The social system

[1] As one of the most acute treatises on applied political science points out, the problem and the solution exist in academic circles. 'The Good Business Man . . . is one whose mind has not been warped by and narrowed by merely intellectual interests, and who, at the same time, has not those odious pushing qualities which are unhappily required for making a figure in business anywhere else.' F. M. Cornford, Microcosmographia Academica (1908, 1953 edition), p. 8. The type is present (I am told) in business and in politics in Britain. It was these qualities (and others) that enabled Stalin to triumph over the brilliant Trotsky and earned Molotov the admiring epithet 'iron bottom'. The problem of passivity is not confined to America. As Mr. Herbert Morrison put it, 'Too many of our so-called democratic institutions are little better than shams which are run by small minorities in the name of large bodies of citizens who take not the least practical interest.' Quoted in Joseph Goldstein, The Government of British Trade Unions (1952), p. 59.

[2] The 'squire' in New England was not the great local landlord, economic and social master of the village, but the local justice of the peace who might be the local innkeeper, blacksmith, attorney or money-lender.

that turns over great charity drives to professional organizers on a commission basis, is the social system that turns over politics, local and state, to professionals on a commission basis. Society is lucky if the mercenaries take St. Paul's advice and are content with their pay.

III

Machine politicians are not in it for their health, and the first thing that they want and get is jobs and the power to give them away. A really great Boss, a Croker or a Kelly, may not want a job for himself once he has come to the top, but jobs are the easiest way of paying the running expenses of the machine. In this century, in more and more cities, various systems of civil service recruitment of public servants have been set up. They have not hampered the machines very much. They apply, for the most part, to minor jobs for which an examination is as convenient a way as any of dispensing patronage. But the really lucrative jobs, lucrative in salary or fees or opportunities, are not thus rashly opened to competition. Sometimes the civil service examinations are rigged; but the most astute of modern bosses, Ed Flynn of the Bronx, pointed out the advantage of having a number of exempted jobs at your disposal. It made it easy to reward and to punish.

These jobs are of two kinds; the mere sinecures, historical survivals of posts that once had utility or jobs that someone has to do but which are, in effect, held by two officials, one at a higher salary doing next to nothing in his office (but a lot outside it) and a lesser officer who does the actual chores of the job. Sometimes the sinecures are given as a reward for good and faithful service in financially unrewarding tasks. Thus Al Smith was nominated by Tammany (which was the same as being elected) Sheriff of New York County, a superfluous office half of whose fees the Sheriff could keep. 'My fees for the two years I was sheriff amounted approximately to $105,000.'[1] This particular bonanza

[1] Alfred E. Smith, *Up to Now: An Autobiography* (1929), p. 152. Smith had spent many laborious and ill-paid years in the legislature at Albany, and Tammany, rightly proud of its most distinguished son, gave him this present which enabled him to afford to become Governor in 1918.

no longer exists, but many plums remain and are given to the right people for good political reasons.[1]

Lawyers are, in most countries, more animated by a desire to serve the public publicly than is any other class. This is still more true in the United States, where the constitutional system makes many political questions also legal questions. But it is not because of the need for interpreting the fourteenth amendment that so many lawyers offer their services to the machines. There are valuable pieces of legal patronage to be given away by the machines;[2] there are opportunities of political advancement, especially for holders of drama-making offices like that of District-Attorney. And, even without pulling out any of these plums, an inspiring member of the bar is often quickly rewarded for his services. For the machine nominates the judges and the judges remember their maker. As one of the most reflective and respectable of modern Bosses put it, 'There are, of course, many lawyers who do not want political appointment, but who have law practices that take them into various courts. Because they are members of the organization, they have an opportunity to meet and become acquainted with the judges who are sitting. The judges often make appointments of referees or receivers, sometimes to the profit of the appointee. One can (and in the Bronx we do) frown on any attempt to influence a judge to commit an improper act without minimizing the part that personal friendships play in such matters as appointments.'[3]

Places on the bench are not only given in most cities as rewards for service, they are, in some, more or less openly sold. A current

[1] The new Mayor of New York, Mr. Robert Wagner, Jr., has nominated his predecessor Mr. Vincent Impellitteri, whom he defeated in the Democratic primary, to a well-paid judgeship, so proving that there is no ill-feeling and healing wounds made not only in the primary campaign, but in Mr. Impellitteri's successful revolt against the rulers of Tammany Hall in the previous mayoral election.

[2] Municipal judges in New York City receive higher salaries than do the Justices of the Supreme Court of the United States.

[3] Edward J. Flynn, op. cit., p. 24. If legal gossip is to be trusted, frowning has not been universal in other New York boroughs. And in the appointment to receiverships (more than 'sometimes to the profit of the appointee') the judges tend to act in the spirit of the Irish official of the old régime who, in reply to a colleague who said that, *ceteris paribus*, he always gave jobs to a friend, retorted, '*ceteris paribus* be damned'.

price quoted by the knowing in New York is one year's salary, paid in advance, the equivalent of the ecclesiastical 'first fruits' that Queen Anne piously gave up for the endowment of her bounty. It would be too much to expect that, in these circumstances, a New York judge automatically gets the respect given to a Justice of the Queen's Bench in London, not to speak of the reverence given a Senator of the College of Justice in Edinburgh.

A machine can survive, barely survive, without jobs, but not for ever, and the fact that jobs are in the hands of one machine and not of the other, is an effective means of keeping one machine in power and drawing to it the more aspiring young politicians. Only so can we explain the fact that the Republican machine in Philadelphia has been recruited exactly in the same way as Tammany Hall and has managed, with a few temporary setbacks, to survive years of Democratic domination in Washington and even in Harrisburg, the state capital, as Tammany survived Republican rule in Washington and in Albany. That is not to say that the opposition party, whatever it may be, is totally deprived of patronage. A well-run machine will save a few jobs for its nominal opponents, permit it to glean some of the alien corn, and 'opposition' leaders, thus favoured, seldom put up much of a fight to displace their benefactors. The law, too, provides that some boards must be bi-partisan, and that allows the machine to reward docile members of the other party and further improve discipline.[1]

Of course, in a great modern city, many jobs must be given to competent people merely to ensure that the inhabitants stay alive and are able to move. There is, even in machine-ridden cities, much more of a professional spirit in the local bureaucracy (at any rate in all but the top jobs) than was customary a generation ago. All the same, compared with the federal government, or even with some state governments, machine-ruled cities are still strongholds of the spoils system, a little more draped, a little more decorous, but

[1] Things got so bad, I am told, among the Republicans of the strongly Democratic city of Baltimore in the early years of the New Deal, that the jobs which the Republicans had to have by law, were rotated among them, each statesman holding a job for a month and then resigning in favour of a needy colleague.

basically the spoils system.[1] If the great machines had contented themselves with paying for their services by a lavish use of the spoils system, even by the creation of a large number of sinecures, this might have been written off as a necessary cost of working a democratic system of government in the new, overflowing cities. But these rewards were not enough. Some of the rulers of the machines were not office-holders and did not want to be and, in any case, no conceivable system of overpaid sinecures would have given to the machine leaders rewards commensurate with their abilities or ambitions. They thought themselves worthy of remuneration, if not on the scale of the great business magnates, at any rate on the scale of their representatives, the great corporation lawyers. This meant that machines exploited graft, 'honest' and plain.

Honest graft was the utilization of political knowledge and power to make gains in various forms of speculation and of business that could not have been made, or not made so easily, if political knowledge and power had not been available. To know where a new road, a new bridge, a new school was to be built and to buy land, whose value would rise as a result of the building, was honest graft. To make sure that a road or bridge or school or park was placed near property owned by you or your friends was also honest graft. It was no better or worse than admitting friends to make favoured bids for securities about to be offered to the less favoured at a high price. It was no better or worse than combining speculation in land values with the building of railroads, no better or worse than giving special and favourable terms to great corporations like Standard Oil. There was nothing, at this stage, to make 'politics' any different from 'business' and the shrewder businessman, while he may have resented the wealth accumulated by mere politicians, was less full of moral indignation at the methods than some moralists thought desirable. Nor were other forms of profit arising from political power necessarily so scandalous as to shock

---

[1] Even in jobs requiring some professional training and filled on a semi-permanent basis, the connection between jobs and politics in city politics is not yet a thing of the past. Mr. Dominick F. Paduano, Commissioner of Water Supply, Gas and Electricity in New York under Mayor Impellitteri, had served for over twenty years in the department; but he was also 'Democratic leader of Twentieth Zone of Tenth Queens Assembly District'. *The New Yorker*, 14 November 1953.

all right-thinking men, who really thought. Again and again, cities (and sometimes states) had to make administrative decisions that were bound to make money for X and prevent it being made by Y. And there might be nothing to choose, from any social point of view, between X and Y. It is conceivable that a Mayor or a group of Aldermen might, in a stern effort of self-denial, refuse to put the profit in the way of their friends. It was unlikely. It was possible that between two groups of strangers, the politicians would prefer those who made no offers of participation in the profits, who proposed (from the politician's simple point of view) to hog the lot, but again, it was unlikely. And it was possible that a group of businessmen, proposing, for example, to start a new street railroad, and knowing that only by giving the politicians a cut would their group and not another get the franchise, would refuse to offer a share to the politicians whose decision was final. This, also, was unlikely.

·Honest graft, that is to say, put temptations in the way of politicians and businessmen that could only have been removed by trusting all local power to an undemocratic bureaucracy which, even if *it* had been incorruptible, could not have avoided greatly enriching one group at the expense of another.

But (and it was an important but), the fact that the rulers, open and covert, of the city profited financially by their public service and on an increasingly big scale, was known to hundreds, to thousands of officials from the heads of departments to the policemen on the beat. Inevitably, as cities grew, so did regulation by law; so, too, did failure to enforce regulation in response to a tactfully offered tip. It might be no more serious than tipping a policeman not to report a failure to remove snow from a side-walk (an offence which one of the most vociferous reformers committed to the delight of the unregenerate), or other equivalents of paying a policeman to-day to tear up a ticket for illegal parking. But it might be more. And it might be more, especially, for certain types of traders whose businesses were legally regulated, saloon-keepers for instance. It might be more for shopkeepers or for the owners of great department stores whose lives could be made miserable by the arbitrary enforcement of regulations.

With a population far from law-abiding, with laws made by

state legislatures, often ill-informed, often unrepresentative, sometimes highly corrupt, bribery was often a necessary lubricant. But
the bribery of the various competing authorities was time-wasting,
did not always get results, opened the briber to renewed pressure.
There was one way out, a way taken in nearly all cities at some
time, the resort to the machine. The machine 'decasualized' graft.
The district leader, or for great matters, the boss, guaranteed for a
fee or a retainer, immunity from a horde of petty bribe-takers.
Men of high private moral standards welcomed an efficient
machine, as the nascent bourgeoisie of the early middle ages
welcomed the power of the rising kings as a shield against the
robber barons and were willing to pay a high price for the protection of the shield.

By this time, the difference between honest graft and plain graft
was blurred. Both paid well; each had become a habit. Of course,
there was a distinction between graft and open plundering such as
was practised by the Tweed Ring in New York and, in other cities,
by less famous bands of public robbers. The stealing of money from
the treasury, the criminal cooking of the accounts—and the criminal
prosecutions and, sometimes, convictions that followed, became
rarer by the end of the last century. Indeed, it is possible to argue
that business was slower to learn the advisability of, at any rate, best
policy honesty, than politics was, but then business has, in normal
times, had a better press and more automatic public acceptance.

At some time in every great city of the United States, the public
authority has passed into the hands of a man or group of men or of
rival groups of men who have managed to exploit within the
bounds of the law or just over the edge of the law, the great
economic possibilities of the growth of the United States, especially
of urban and manufacturing growth. And the possibilities of making
greater and safer profits by concentrating the political power in few,
known, sagacious hands, have created the great modern machines.
They are as 'American' as Standard Oil or United States Steel. And
where no more than this has been done, where political power has
been tactfully, responsibly, prudently used, even to the manifest
profit of its owners, as a rule, the machines have had more friends
and fewer enemies than the strict reformers or moralists liked or
like.

Yet in most cities, there have been revolts and some of them have been near-revolutions. If, on the one hand, the mass of the voters did not share the permanent indignation of the reformers; they did not share, either, the complete moral tolerance of the machines and of their allies. For, as the wiser of the machine leaders knew, there were limits which it was rash to overstep, especially the limit between graft and dirty graft, a more decisive and dangerous trespass than the more insidious and less resented move from honest graft to graft.

'Dirty' graft was graft whose profits came from the toleration of crime or vice. True, the crime might be technical and public opinion not very zealous in support of an effective campaign against it. The American passion for improving public and private morals by law often resulted in merely creating opportunites for excess profits for the machines. But again the transition from more or less tolerable 'dirty' graft to 'dirty' graft that the voters thought really intolerable, was very easily made and in the history of most machines, their defeats have come about from putting too great a strain on the ignorance or passivity of the electors.[1]

Notably, machines have suffered from suspected connections between their profits and the price of immunity paid by organized prostitution. When such charges are based on more than mere suspicion, the voters in many cases have revolted with more energy than they have shown in cases of proved corruption where the money was not tainted, as it was in the case of sharing the profits of prostitution. Machines and their leaders could afford to ignore charges of being crooks, but not charges of being pimps. Such charges, where there was evidence of their truth, shook even the strongest machines. Thus the investigations and sermons of the Reverend Doctor Parkhurst which almost wrecked Tammany in the nineties and drove Boss Croker to retire to Europe for a few years, had their parallel in other cities. They might be, what an official historian of Tammany called merely 'an outburst of unrestricted fanaticism',[2] but it was an outburst of a kind that prudent

[1] For the problems raised by moral legislation in general see p. 174 et sqq.

[2] E. Vale Blake, History of the Tammany Society or Columbian Order (1901), p. 158.

machine leaders feared. Many of the great bosses were of Irish Catholic origin and had scruples about profiting by prostitution that did not affect them when other forms of graft were involved. Thus Brooklyn, while it was still a 'city of homes', was sometimes called on by its local bosses to resist Tammany domination which would mean the invasion of Brooklyn by Tammany-protected prostitution from across the East River. One of the most notorious and most successful bosses of the twentieth century, Mr. Frank Hague of Jersey City, who has accumulated a large fortune in public service, boasted, truthfully, that his city was freer from commercialized vice than any other big city in the United States. It is probable, too, that, in the United States (as more recently in France), the giving of votes to women has made protection of the profession politically more dangerous. In some areas, special circumstances may alter cases. Thus in one Philadelphia district, the local leader resolutely cracked down on some voters who were not only running a small-scale brothel, but one in which white women were accommodating Negroes. Except in a few cities where the tourist trade is the chief commercial interest, the old, open 'red light' districts have disappeared. Probably there are many visitors to San Francisco's show place the 'Barbary Coast' who do not know how it got its name and fame in the remote days 'before the fire'. New Orleans, true to its 'Latin' traditions, long legalized and then long openly tolerated a *quartier* with some celebrated *maisons tolérées*. They were part of the *ambiance* and a campaign against them would have seriously incommoded 'the organization' and that was too serious a risk to run.[1]

One effect of a reform administration can be to make life easier for the profession. The police find both the collection of blackmail and the regular routine of raids and arrests 'for the record' no longer worth the risk of public scandal. Without the arrests and raids, the business can go on decorously, with no notice in the papers and

---

[1] 'Proof of the existence of wide-open vice conditions in the City seemed to have little effect on the fortunes of the machine. Tolerance in this respect was desired by many, and the controlling business interests could not well break the working arrangement between vice and government without endangering their own close relationship.' Reynolds. op. cit. pp. 129.

no public attention paid to the problem. We have the testimony of a most competent witness on that point who assures us that the 'clean-up' which followed the revelations of the Seabury investigation made business much less worrying and complicated. 'It could hardly have been what the reformers and citizens' committees and legislators had hoped to accomplish, but I found when I got back in business that the Seabury Investigation had sure as hell made *my* life easier. The police were no longer a headache; there was no more kowtowing to double-crossing Vice Squad men, no more hundred-dollar handshakes, no more phony raids to make up the quota. In fact, thanks to Judge Seabury and his not-very-merry-men, I was able to operate for three years without breaking a lease.'[1]

But such considerations seldom affect the reformers or the reform politicians. They know that hostility to what is romantically called the 'white slave traffic' is always a powerful force, that investigations of other irregularities, even of organized murder, do not really compete for the public interest. A mob organizer is more likely to be condemned by a jury and by an outraged public if he can be connected with prostitution.

Indeed, in one of the most famous and successful prosecutions of a mob leader, the conviction of Salvatore Luciano, better known as 'Lucky' Luciano, there was, at first, some surprise expressed that so great a man in the general field of illicit business should stoop to mere prostitution. He was 'so great a man in his field that Dewey had never suspected him of dabbling in a minor industry like prostitution'.[2] This surprise was felt by others and even survived Luciano's trial. 'There are those, even among his enemies, who claim that Luciano never got a dollar from prostitution in his life, and it is known that he was doing nothing more deadly than making book at Saratoga when he was surprised to learn that Dewey had crowned him King of Vice. Nevertheless, sex being what it is, the trial was an immense success.'[3]

[1] Polly Adler, *A House is Not a Home* (1953), p. 199.
[2] Rupert Hughes, *Thomas E. Dewey, Attorney for the People* (1940), p. 85.
[3] Wolcott Gibbs and John Bainbridge, 'St. George and the Dragnet' in *Profiles from the New Yorker* (Penguin Books), no date, p. 127. Something was owing, in this success, to the names of some of the female characters like Cokey Flo Brown, Jenny the Factory, Gashouse Lil, etc.

And the astonished curiosity with which American soldiers in London and Paris gazed on the open prostitution of Piccadilly Circus or 'Pig Alley' (the Place Pigalle) showed how successfully prostitution had been driven underground in America.

Yet the 'tenderloin' in some form or other is a problem in all great American cities and in some small ones. The very name which we owe to a New York police officer posted to the 'red light' district and rejoicing that he was now to get a chance at the tenderloin, reveals how much the oldest profession relies on police protections. Occasional scandals, especially if, nowadays, they involve 'socialites' call the attention of the public to a constant defiance of the law that suggests great incompetence or great corruption on the part of the police department, and, if the department is highly political, of the ruling administration. Few 'Crusades' pay better than a vigorous or at any rate noisy 'crack down' on vice.

The results of such campaigns are often disappointing. For one thing, they may merely put up the price of protection, or drive or encourage policemen to an excess of profitable zeal. It was the extortions of the 'vice squad' as much as the sins of the brothel keepers that angered New Yorkers with Tammany rule in the last years of Jimmy Walker.[1] It was another matter when the legal offences that the machines condoned were regarded by their voters as venial sins, if that. Notably, the machines profited by the resentment of the urban population, everywhere, at the imposition on the cities of rural views of the sin of drinking. As has been said, saloon-keepers were especially vulnerable to police persecution and so they paid for protection, or went into politics for themselves. Some of the most successful district and ward bosses were saloon-keepers like 'Hinky Dink' Kenna in Chicago. 'Big Tim' Sullivan of the Bowery owed his effective start in politics to his saloon which became a chain of saloons and centres of power.[2] Even a saloon-

---

[1] I remember a very honest and public-spirited reformer telling me with gratification, of the excellent co-operation he and his friends were getting from the police in their drive on vice. That co-operation, it was later learned, included a regular system of blackmail and the railroading to prison of innocent and helpless women.

[2] This once famous politician is today remembered, if at all, for two things, for the authorship of the 'Sullivan Act' making the carrying of a

keeper who was not in active politics, like 'Mr. Dooley' of the Archey Road, was a political force. It was in his saloon that politics were discussed and minor politicians made friends and influenced people.

Prohibition had naturally serious results in the organization of machine politics. The representative machine politician was a saloon keeper; he either became a saloon keeper in the course of his political career, or he drifted into politics because he was a saloon keeper. Needless to say, the mere adoption of the XVIIIth amendment and the enactment of the Volstead Act did not put all political saloon keepers out of business. But it made that business far more risky, far less open. Moreover, the machine could no longer give complete protection as it had done in the olden time. There had been periods of state aggression on local autonomy when the police was under state control; even New York had known dark moments of servitude. But, as a rule, the enforcement of such liquor laws as there were, about closing hours, Sunday closing, even such notorious intrusions on the liberty of the saloon keeper as the Raines Law, had left it fairly easy for the machine to guarantee immunity from harassing police activity. It was no longer possible to do this, for three authorities had to be squared, municipal, state and federal and only in the rarest circumstances did these three work or idle together.[1]

One result of prohibition was to give more importance to the political clubs which all the great machines ran. But contrary to popular belief, these clubs were not all speakeasies, though some of them were. But although they often sold beer, they were not

---

concealed weapon a crime in New York, and for a dictum that explains a great deal of the popularity of 'Big Tim'. 'God and the People hate a chesty man.'

[1] Thus in the great or notorious senatorial primary in Pennsylvania in 1926, it was asserted that the federal prohibition agents did nothing to hurt the chances of the candidate favoured by their chief, the Secretary of the Treasury, Mr. Andrew Mellon. And, of course, the city police of Pittsburgh was equally considerate. But a rival candidate to Mr. Mellon's nominee was the Governor of Pennsylvania, Gifford Pinchot, who was also a convinced dry. And the third and successful candidate, Mr. William Vare of Philadelphia, could only control his city. No wonder this primary was the most expensive election since Roman times.

usually centres of serious drinking.[1] It would be idle to pretend that all political clubs were centres of political organization and discussion and nothing else. But they served a useful function for the machine and possibly for the members. Professor Peel is remarkably philosophical in his estimate of one of the appeals of the political club. 'In giving their members access to games of chance, bars and brothels, political clubs create a feeling of communion. Like the appeals of the orator and the promises of the spoilsman, anti-social club activities are aimed at the lowest common denominator of social action. Thus large numbers of adherents are won to the club and to the party, attached to each other by bonds which cannot easily be severed by the sword of reason.'[2]

Repeal of prohibition restored some of the importance of the mere politician in the control and exploitation of the liquor traffic. The enforcement of closing hours, of revenue laws, of the serving of minors, of the tangle of federal, state and city legislation that the traffic labours under, renewed the old opportunities of political protection and profit. At least one famous machine has, as its nucleus, a highly successful brewery that might not sell quite as much beer if its owners were not politically so potent.[3]

[1] Professor Peel (from whose admirable work I take this verdict) admits that 'some of the writer's associates have objected to the moderation in tone which he here employs. Of course, it all depends on how one defines serious drinking.' Roy V. Peel, *The Political Clubs of New York City* (1935), p. 233. Professor Peel's standards seem sufficiently rigorous. 'In the spring of 1932 political speakeasies were selling standard brands of beer at fifteen cents per bottle, but Waxie Gordon's "high test" ale was still going at twenty-five cents a glass. Spirits were seldom sold in political clubs; wines only in a few Italian "associations".' Ibid., p. 76. As Professor Peel points out, quasi-political clubs were often more important (and profitable) than the regular clubs openly sponsored by the machine.

[2] Op. cit., pp. 245-6. Professor Peel also points out that in these days of high publicity for the sins of society, the common man, learning that, as Mr. Cole Porter has put it, 'anything goes' does not see why it should not go for him too. He is not content (this is a democratic age) to take vicarious satisfaction in admiring or deploring the sins of modern Charles IIs and Nell Gwynns.

[3] The O'Connell machine in Albany N.Y. The truth of the belief that much O'Connell beer is bought for political reasons is unsusceptible of proof. (A brewery was for long the centre of the Conservative party

But the great problem facing machines, the police, the public, the politician, today, is not the control of alcohol or of prostitution, but the control of gambling. In a sense nothing could be more American than gambling. The readiness to take a chance, to play double or quits, the resilience with which eminent Americans have recovered from total disaster is part of the character and part of the legend of America. In the ante-bellum South, horses were nearly worshipped and gambling went with this near idolatry. After the Civil War, the new wealth of the American rich led to the growth of such a highly fashionable English sport as horse racing. New race tracks were founded, one of them by Sir Winston Churchill's grandfather. The 'Kentucky Derby', from 1875, gave to American racing some of the glamour of the 'sport of kings'. But despite its social prestige and the romance associated with it, horse racing has always been suspect. For although it is well known that the object of horse racing is to improve the breed of race horses so that they may run faster in other horse races, this activity has, historically, been associated with wagers on the success of this endeavour. And this connection has led to hostile legislation, like that passed under Governor Hughes of New York in 1908 to implement a constitutional ban on 'bookmaking or any other kind of gambling', adopted in 1894 and 1895. Horse racing was left to flourish without the aid of wagering. It did not flourish.[1] There was, indeed, some danger that the improvement of race horses would be left entirely to those solely interested in the improvement of the breed of race-horses and there did not seem to be enough of these to pay the cost of the maintenance of tracks and horses. Nevertheless, in most states the ban on racetrack gambling continued and it was only with the wave of hostility to sumptuary legislation that followed the repeal

---

organization in Liverpool.) The Pendergast machine in Kansas City operated a cement plant and, so I was told by a newspaperman in that city, the cement was quite good and a lot of it might have been bought even if the machine had not been in control. This was an academic point as long as the machine was in control.

[1] At about the same time, the most famous of American professional gamblers, Richard Canfield, whose name has become a symbol of organized gambling on a luxurious level, was finally forced out of business.

POLITICS IN AMERICA

of prohibition that the ban was relaxed. And it was found, again, that the noblest friend of man was peculiarly subject to the attention of some of the less noble types of men, that the sport of kings was also the sport of crooks.[1]

Horse racing was peculiarly vulnerable to politics. As a critic pointed out it was more vulnerable than the drink traffic had been.[2] You can do something with an ex-brewery, but what can you do with a closed race-track? Moreover, a race-track is a semi-monopoly; a state full of race-tracks would be full of bankrupt race-tracks. And racing, if the most romantic, is not the only form of gambling and it is in competition with all other forms of gambling. A prudent promoter then will aim at monopoly, or, if that is unattainable, at oligolopoly. And that, in most cases, means that he must have the aid of the politicians who can ruin him by total prohibition or damage him by too much competition.[3]

The fears of the moralist have been, in great part, justified. Nearly every year sees a new scandal, involving politicians in the turbid finances of the racing business, including that peculiarly American branch of it, harness racing. Both parties in New York have found that important party leaders and office holders have

[1] I should not wish to assert that horse racing, in any of its forms, is the most corrupt sport. Horses have to be 'pulled', while professional runners or basketball players can 'pull' themselves.

[2] Professor Zachariah Chafee, Jr., of the Harvard Law School, *State House versus Pent House* (1937).

[3] 'If it was impossible for breweries to stay out of politics, it is even more difficult for a race-track to stay out of politics. It has far more at stake, and once it gets in has far greater resources with which to buy itself off from death. Consequently, the owners . . . are under a big temptation to preserve their enormous investment and annual gains by giving protection-money or race-track stock to state officials in all camps.' Zachariah Chafee also pointed out that a race-track owner's income is in cash. 'Consequently, it is far more available for campaign contributions and other political disbursements than the larger income of a manufacturer like Henry Ford, which is partly frozen in buildings and machinery and finished cars and unassembled motors.' Ibid., p. 12. Professor Chafee also foresaw the possibilities of patronage, the easy jobs to be given to political hacks. He did not foresee, I assume, that many of these hacks would also be criminals. He had not allowed for the peculiarly demoralizing effects of horses on human beings.

succumbed to the temptations of the patronage and the profits of the tracks. The Republican party in New York is the latest political organization to be forced to wonder whether racing and public purity can go together. But the difficulties with which Governor Dewey found himself faced when he tried to force out the acting President of the state senate whose tolerant view of race-track irregularities was a matter of record, shows how tepid is the public conscience in the matter. For it is normally difficult to get up or keep up indignation at gambling as such. This is especially true of the more relaxed cities whose tradition of publicly enforced morality is weak. It did Mayor 'Bob' Maestri of New Orleans no particular harm when the press pointed out that 'Mayor Bob' could see a handbook in operation if he went to his window in City Hall and looked across the street; again, that the district attorney need not go to that effort, had only to lift his head from his pillow at home to see another.[1]

There are other politically important forms of gambling. The 'numbers' have special attractions for the politicians and the professional gamblers. The 'numbers' is a simple form of lottery. Some figures which, it is believed, cannot be 'fixed', for example the daily clearing statements of the New York stock exchange, are chosen as the figures on which to pay off. Very small bets are accepted; there are numbers available every day, while there may be no local racing every day; the 'policy writer' is vulnerable and numerous. To control the 'policy racket' is to have a large political army organized at no expense and, indeed, at considerable profit.

---

[1] Harnett T. Kane, *Louisiana Hayride* (1941), p. 394. The tolerance of the Crescent City and its suburbs received a kind of official recognition in the *New Orleans City Guide written and compiled by the Federal Writers' Project of the Works Progress Administration for the City of New Orleans* (1938), p. 280. 'On the other side of the protection levee in Jefferson Parish the several *Gambling Houses* present a well-kept and prosperous appearance. Although prohibited by law, these places will be found open or closed according to changes in local political conditions; usually they are open from 6 p.m. to 6 a.m.' Mr. Kane notes that the police 'cracked down' on the handbooks' (i.e. the numbers racket) during the horse racing season. The organization had a great stake in all forms of gambling and they prevented ruinous competition quite in the manner of the first Rockefeller.

The operators must have political protection which they pay for in cash and in votes.[1]

Close to the numbers in importance come (or came) the slot machines. These 'one armed bandits' were more respectable than the numbers racket, for the machines were installed in highly respectable clubs as well as in saloons, pool halls, bowling alleys and the like. The political protection needed for their installation had to be handsomely paid for and the revenue from the slot machines became an important part of machine resources. Again, illegal toleration of the slot machines aroused little indignation. All classes of society were involved in their toleration, even the officers' clubs of the armed services. Some politicians, like Governor Stevenson of Illinois, might point out that it was impossible to suppress the slot machines in the slum saloons and tolerate them in the smart clubs. The answer was and might have continued to be, in that case, tolerate them in both, but for the popular association of gambling with mysterious and murderous crime rings. And these crime rings were seen not as mere protégés of the politicians, but as the masters of the politicians, as the owners of power which, for a consideration, they put at the disposal of politicians, police, judges.

That there is truth in this belief is undoubted; but it is much less easy to be certain what that truth is. Persons confident in their own competence tell different stories. Figures appear out of the underworld and are presented to the public as the Professor Moriarty of the national crime rings and then are declared, by other experts, to be, at best, lieutenants of the rank of Colonel Sebastian Moran. Names are flung about, Black Hand, Mafia, Unione Siciliano and the justification for these names is bitterly debated.[2] What is

[1] The numbers racket appeals especially to Negroes. And whereas the football pools in Britain encourage vain speculations in the theory of probability which delude investors into believing that their computations make any difference, the Negro 'policy writer', and 'investor', falls back on the equally scientific and aesthetically superior superstition of belief in omens.

[2] Thus one writer with first-hand knowledge objects strongly to the identification of the 'Unione Siciliano', a flourishing concern, with the Mafia. 'In fact, as a factor of power in national crime, Mafia has been virtually extinct for two decades. Unione, in the meantime, has grown fat on felony'. Burton B. Turkus and Sid Feder, *Murder, Inc.* (1952), p.

established is that gambling rings have replaced the gangs bred by prohibition and that, on the profits of gambling and armed with the resources that they need to protect those profits, they have 'muscled in' on a wide variety of businesses, especially entertainment businesses, have corrupted the police, have elected mayors and judges and, in some cities, notably in New York, have taken over some important trade unions.

It was the general realization that something was very wrong that led to the creation of the Kefauver committee, the 'Special Committee of the Senate to Investigate Crime in Interstate Commerce'. His role as Chairman made the Senator a national figure and a very strong contender for the Democratic nomination in 1952. He was aided in his task not only by his own ability, integrity and industry, but by the resources of television in whose light suspects squirmed, even if all that was seen by the viewers was twisting hands.[1]

Much of what was revealed was not new or news. The immunity which crime enjoyed in some cities was an old story. St. Paul had, fifty years before, the reputation of being an Alsatia where very tough guys could lie low in peace as long as they did not practise their business in St. Paul. Kansas City (Missouri) later got the same reputation. Connivance between gamblers and the police, crime covered up or even committed by the police, was no novelty. It was the murder of Herman Rosenthal by Lieutenant Becker of the New York police that blew Tammany out of power just before the first great war. Nor were highly opulent policemen a novelty, nor the sources of their wealth surprising. Nor was Senator Kefauver's conclusion that 'organized crime and political corruption go hand in hand, and that in fact there could be no big-time organized crime

---

61 (English edition). There is also confusion in the public mind between the Mafia (which almost certainly did play a part in American crime) and the Camorra whose role is more in dispute. There are those who hold that the real power in the New York underworld is not an Italian but an Irishman, like Professor Moriarty. But these are points of detail.

[1] When the Committee was in New York, business in department stores, movie houses and in other places fell off noticeably, since many of the normal customers were at home glued to the television sets.

without a firm and profitable alliance between those who run the rackets and those in political control.'[1]

What was a novelty was the revelation that crime had been 'trustified', that the pools and cartels which the great business magnates of around 1900 had organized and justified as putting an end to ruinous competition, had their parallels in the organization of the rackets. As it had been usually fatal, economically, to thwart Standard Oil or J. P. Morgan and Company, it was now widely believed that it was simply fatal to oppose 'the Syndicate' with its skilled and ruthless killers. What was more or less novel was the close interweaving of gambling and other forms of extortion. Gang warfare inside unions and between rival unions was no novelty. Criminal control of unions had not been unknown in the past nor had criminal collusion between unions and employers (especially in the building trades). What was a novelty were the ramifications of crime, the suspected scale of the operations of the gangs and of their political power. It was an age of Big Business, Big Unions, Big Government and Big Crime. And the more frightened or romantic of the citizenry feared that the one big union was the Unione Siciliano, that even its profits equalled those of General Motors or of General Electric.

The connection between the machines and crime on which so much attention had been directed, in recent years, may well be a sign of a permanent decline. For the machines today are, as has been said, often as much the junior associates of the rackets as their patrons and protectors. A number of social forces have been at work weakening the machines, driving them deeper and deeper into highly dishonest graft and provoking hostile popular reactions that may, in these new circumstances, be more permanent and effective than the revolts of the past have been.

The great depression shook the machines as it shook many other traditional American institutions. The revenues, legal, extra-legal, illegal, of the machines fell off, just at the time that the demands on it became unmanageably great. It was no longer a question of turkeys or coal at Christmas, municipal jobs or a good word to a municipal contractor for the unemployed, or help for a widow and her children. Hundreds of thousands of sound voters were un-

[1] Estes Kefauver, *Crime in America* (1952), p. 77 (English edition).

employed and they wanted and needed more than the most opulent and tender-hearted machines could give them. Machine charity, like organized philanthropy, collapsed before the overwhelming need.

But not only did the machines prove inadequate, but a great deal of what they had done was now being done by the state and above all by the federal government. The emergency measures of the 'First New Deal' did, on a far greater scale, what the machines had done. Some machines, as in Chicago and Jersey City, got credit for getting adequate funds out of the federal treasury. But in New York this redounded to the credit of Mayor La Guardia, not of Tammany, and in Philadelphia to the credit of the Democratic party in the state. Most Republicans and some Democrats saw in the use of the WPA (Works Progress Administration) by Harry Hopkins, a nation-wide buying of votes, putting Tammany to shame. Be that as it may, the political fruits of WPA were reaped by the Roosevelt Administration, not by Tammany. Indeed, success in getting federal funds was now one of the chief claims of a machine to the loyalty of the voters, but their loyalty, in such a case, was necessarily divided between the real benefactor and the mere intermediary.

When the hit-and-miss methods of the First New Deal were replaced by the extension of social services, by the creation of unemployment insurance, widows' pensions and the like, the role of the machines was again made less important. The voter now got as a right more than he had ever got as a favour. And, inevitably, the machines were driven to supplying extra-legal, if not totally illegal favours, driven over the borders of honest graft both in their manner of getting political power and merchandizing it.

Two economic forces combined to make machine profits depend more openly and completely on graft of an illegal type. The great prize of the old machines was the control of the city transportation system. In the mushrooming cities of around the turn of the century, the control of the 'franchises' given to *entrepreneurs* to operate street railways, or subways, or elevated railways were of great commercial value. The sale of them by the machines was common enough; cities were burdened with lavishly expensive and often inefficient systems of local transportation and great fortunes went to the businessmen who had, by hook or by crook, secured these franchises. But for over twenty years, all systems of local transportation have been white elephants which their owners are only too delighted to unload on the municipalities. Much against their will, in some cases, cities have been forced to take over and to build transportation systems and to run them at a loss.[1] There has been no comparable source of wealth to be marketed in recent years. No Yerkes or Widener has profited by the growth of the cities, no Patrick Calhoun has been the ally of a venal political gang.

Then the development of the cities has been more and more outwards into the suburbs. There an increasingly large number of the more prosperous citizens have moved; after them have gone the super-markets, the department stores, the chain stores. A strong community sense was never a marked feature of American urban life, but there is less of it today than there was a generation ago when the filth, danger, excessive tax rates, were burdens pressing on the middle classes and their wives. They still press; but they press on the poor who cannot move; on apartment house owners, not directly on their tenants; on business, especially on retail business. They do not come home as they did in the old days when, even on Manhattan, most people lived in houses and the 'better elements' lived on Manhattan, not in Southport or Rye.

How to weaken the machines is a problem that has long been studied in American applied political science. One method advocated was an alteration in the mechanics of local government. The traditional municipal organization in the United States was a parody of the state government, as state was of the federal government. A directly elected Mayor was provided, with two legislative houses and, in addition, some important executive officers were directly elected. The result was a baffling division of responsibility. The Mayor, formally head of the whole executive apparatus, could be easily thwarted. It was difficult, if not quite impossible, to pin the responsibility for corruption, crime, even mere ineffi-

---

[1] The prudent and far-sighted owners of the Boston 'rapid transport' system unloaded it on to the municipalities of the Boston metropolitan area. The original owners got guaranteed securities paying a high rate of interest. The tax-payers of Boston, Cambridge and the other cities concerned were left holding the baby. Such a *coup* would be difficult to bring off today when the sad economic truths about urban transportation are so widely known.

ciency on any one man or group. A mayor with great demagogic talents could, like Carter Harrison II in Chicago or Tom Johnson in Cleveland, dramatize the issues, especially if they were real issues, like the protection of the city's assets and rights from great financial interests. But, more often, the dissipation of responsibility meant the easy entrance of graft. Indeed, an argument for the machines that was not without weight, was that they *did* concentrate power and responsibility. Vare or Murphy were responsible bosses in a truer sense than a machine Mayor of New York or of Philadelphia was the real head of the executive.[1]

But the Mayor and council system was not the worst nor the system that gave most opportunities for graft. For in a local government system that centralizes all power in the Mayor or even in the Mayor and council, graft, honest and unadorned, is not impossible, but revolt against it is easier than in those systems of local government where, by artfully dispersing powers, the rural legislators have effectually made the task of the upright urban voter impossible. Here, as in many other ways, Chicago is pre-eminent. Cook County, of which Chicago is the heart and head, is provided with more overlapping, if not actually competing, governing bodies than any other area in the United States. The city of Chicago and its nominal head and ruler, the Mayor, are in the position of a medieval monarch faced with the rivalry or rebellion of a score of vassals when he is not as impotent as a mere Holy Roman Emperor. It is only in Chicago that the admittedly difficult job of keeping the city clean, has been made the basis for one of the oddest governing units on which great political (and cash) fortunes have been built. The 'Sanitary District', dealing with fundamental but not dramatic issues, has been, year in, year out, at least as valuable a prize as the City Hall.[2]

[1] Al Smith argued that Commissioner Murphy was not a Boss. But the only ground for this assertion seems to have been that Murphy always took advice from competent people before taking action. This shows not that he was no boss, but that he was an intelligent boss.

[2] Carter Harrison, five times Mayor of Chicago, in his reflective old age, wondered that so few of his fellow-citizens saw this truth. 'The citizens of Chicago have never realized what a gold mine the sanitary district has proved itself for the Order of Hungry Grafters; the trustees, employees and contractors this unobtrusive Golconda has converted into

To centralize authority was, it was thought, one way to weaken the machine. The first basic reform of this kind was the system called 'Commission' government, first adopted in Galveston after the great floods of 1900. A small elected council was given all powers. One of its members might be titular Mayor, but he was no more like the ordinary American Mayor than the President of Switzerland is like the President of the United States. He had formal precedence on honorific occasions, that was all.

A refinement on this system was the entrusting of control of the executive departments to a small city council. Again, a member of that council might be called Mayor, but his duties were purely honorific. Each of these systems concentrated responsibility and the second brought into municipal executive positions, as 'managers', men who normally would never have served in any really responsible capacity. There was, for a time, a hope that a new class of professional administrators like the German burgomasters of the old régime was coming into existence. A successful Manager, in a small city, might be called to a greater, bringing with him the experience gained for the benefit of his new employers. The commission system still governs some important cities; others have City Managers of deserved repute. Some brilliant careers have dignified the profession, notably that of Dr. Clarence Dykstra; but the early hopes have been largely blighted.

For one thing, voters got tired of hearing the Commission or the Manager called the just; and the elements always on the look out for power and plunder repeatedly took their opportunity to slip back into control. As the Pendergast régime in Kansas City showed, a City Manager system was perfectly compatible with rigid machine control. A City Manager, too, might build up his own political strength or the figure-head Mayor develop ambitions to be more than a *maire fainéant*.

The experience of Cincinnati has shown that more than a mere charter reform of the executive is required. The method of election

---

millionaires are generally unknown. Some have retired as *châtelains* of *châteaux* in France; others to live on the fat of the land in God's own country, California; some have contented themselves with palatial homes in Hyde Park, or country seats in the North Shore district.' *Stormy Years: the Autobiography of Carter H. Harrison* (1935), p. 184.

must make it harder for a machine to control the Commission or the Council. A large number of voters must be ready to cross the party picket line in local politics and, it may be suggested, the city must not be growing too exuberantly, its population not be too mobile. In Cincinnati, these conditions have been attained. Proportional representation makes it difficult for the machine to get, by its block voting, that safe control of the city government that it can use to undermine, destroy or exploit the formal constitution. That the machines dislike proportional representation is not enough to commend it to all right-minded observers, but it is a point in its favour.[1] It was the regular organization in New York that secured the ending of P.R. after ten years' experience, helped in their campaign by the fact that, under P.R., two Communists had managed to get elected to the Council, a charge made in all gravity by Tammany Hall that had been, a year or two before, quite ready to play ball with Communists and fellow-travellers who had votes to deliver.[2]

A long experience suggests that useful as mechanical reforms may be, they will not deal with the basic problem that explains and to some extent justifies the existence of the machines, the absence in American municipal life of real issues, the lack of social cohesion in the American city, the lack of critical responsibility in so many of the economic and other leaders of urban society. If there is less direct interference in municipal politics by the 'interests', if it is not as true as it was that business, as such, is one of the main corrupting forces in American urban life, business still tolerates much corruption lest worse befall. Business may now have no direct interest in

[1] Machines object both to proportional representation and to small legislative bodies for good reasons. A small legislative body means large election districts and it is at the street and block level that machines are strongest and reformers weakest. Proportional representation has a great disadvantage from a machine point of view, an insurgent or an independent can draw on support from a very wide range of voters; personality counts for a great deal and machine nomination for less than usual. 'One of the most important reasons why the party organizations repeatedly fought P.R. was that it deprived them of control over nominations.' Belle Zeller and Hugh A. Bone, 'The Repeal of P.R. in New York City', *American Political Science Review*, December 1948, p. 1137.
[2] See p. 120.

disorder or in corruption, but it has not or does not recognize itself as having enough interest in the basic reform of taxation, in the extension of the stifling boundaries of the cities, in the improvement of the condition of the public schools (to which fewer and fewer of the middle classes send their children, even when they live in the city and not in the suburbs). The American businessman is still an indifferent citizen.

Hopes were placed, too, on the effects of women's suffrage and it would be rash to say that there have been none. Machines have had to be less tolerant of organized vice, of ill-kept and ill-lit streets, of bad schools, of inadequate playgrounds, but the elevation of politics through the effects of women's suffrage has not been any more marked in city than in national politics.[1]

Nor is it certain that the rise of the labour unions has resulted in an automatic improvement in the standards of civic morality or order. A union, as such, need have no more sense of general responsibility than a business. A strong, incorruptible and objective city government that, for example, imposed taxes with unflinching justice might be unpopular with business; it might also be unpopular with some sections of labour. No doubt, today, the police think twice before they go into action against strike pickets, if the unions behind the pickets are strong. But they may also think twice before protecting weak groups and individuals against labour's leaders who acknowledge no duties to any but their own members and sometimes not even to them.[2]

[1] Giving the vote to women presented new problems to the machines. It was one thing, and a most obviously proper thing, to 'spring' a voter who had been officiously incarcerated on a charge of wife-beating, an old custom only calling for legal intervention when carried to excess. But it was another matter when the wife, as well as the husband, was a voter, so delicate decisions of the balance of advantage added to the already sufficient troubles of the ward leaders.

[2] In the early years of the New Deal, I was given an insight into an attitude not wholly dead today. I was talking to a picket in a great middle western city one of whose members was a fairly recently arrived Englishman. The picket had discovered, the day before, that one of the police officers guarding the struck plant had been stealing some of the property he was guarding. The Englishman was all for denouncing the peccant policeman to the Mayor, to the Governor, to public opinion. The Americans were adverse to any publicity. They had 'got the cop

For it is as naïve to idealize the American worker as the American business man, or to expect from him a type of civic virtue that little in his environment gives the American people any right to expect.

Thus the permanent and, until now, incurable scandals of the New York docks present a problem that mere moralizing cannot solve. For not only are the dockers a world apart, but the expense of fighting theft, smuggling, violent crime on the waterfront falls, immediately, on firms that risk very expensive strikes and on industries directly injured by those strikes and, on the other side, on union leaders and rank and file dock workers who risk ostracism, assault, murder. The whole economy of the New York harbour area pays for this situation, but it pays in not very visible ways; the cost of reducing this charge on the commerce of the greatest port in the world falls on those immediately concerned who prefer, naturally, not to be martyrs on such a scale.[1]

It is possible, though by no means certain, that the day of the machine is nearly over. Certainly there are far more big cities in which a single, unified machine is hard to identify, where political personalities, not mere machine 'stooges', play greater and greater roles, and where local issues of real moment are debated and voted

---

where they wanted him'. Any rash strike-breakers would find that police officer strangely unsympathetic. (I am translating more vigorous anticipations of the results of the successful blackmailing of the policeman.) The strikers didn't want an objective, incorruptible police. They wanted a police on their side.

[1] The dock workers, themselves, are usually represented as nearly innocent victims, possibly a little given to pilfering, as are dockers in a British port like Liverpool, but anxious to be relieved from the tyranny of the corrupt union bosses. Not all observers share this optimistic view. 'Neither the shipowners nor the majority of the longshoremen want a change in anything. Both have been brought up in the tradition of the waterfront jungle which glorifies the law of the survival of the fittest. The shipowners want a constant, controlled pool of labour, and the longshoremen live for the day of the "big killing". They are living in terror of their bosses, but the majority are hero-worshippers at heart and they believe that they should resist with all their hearts and souls any attempt by anyone to change the order of things.' Ed Reid, *The Shame of New York* (1953), p. 146 (English edition). It remains to be seen if the joint New York-New Jersey commission will do much to remedy this.

on. The long-term effect of the social services, of the practical cessation of immigration, of the political promotion of depressed nationalities and races cannot be assessed as yet.[1] Equally important is the changing economic character of the cities; the best days of the old urban centres may be over.

What is more certain is that the modern machine plays a less important and less useful role than it did in the past. The American cities may not, American life may not now provide sufficient forces for social integration, but it is unlikely that the machines can do that any longer, however much they did it in the past. The old social functions of the machine are as obsolete as the old clam bakes by which the faithful were rewarded on their rare holidays.

Nor is it particularly profitable to assess the degree of moral turpitude of the machines. They were highly representative institutions of the age of business; perhaps the cities, like the growing industries, could not have afforded too austere a system of government.

It is easy to indict the machines. There are few American cities that do not bear the scars of their rule in the past: atrocious and outrageously expensive public buildings like the Philadelphia City Hall from which William Penn looks, one may presume with astonishment, on the city he founded.[2] The New York public schools, in the older parts of Manhattan, are no credit to the richest city in the world. Badly sited, inadequate parks, badly planned transportation systems, defective water supplies[3] all testify to the

[1] See p. 122.

[2] The most magnificent and horrible example of building graft is in the same state, the capitol at Harrisburg. It is perhaps worth noting that Lord Bryce admired Philadelphia City Hall (from an architectural point of view).

[3] Nearly sixty years ago, the famous English correspondent, George W. Steevens, noted the silt in his bath spoiling the 'Sardanapalus luxury' of his great New York hotel; this, he thought, was the price of Tammany rule. But as usual the prize exhibit in this department comes from Philadelphia.

'Philadelphia water is unbelievably bad. . . . The only thing that can be said for it is that when spiked heavily with chemicals it is "safe". . . . Three dozen fine trout brought from Miami for a recent sportsmen's show died when they were transferred to a tank of Philadelphia water. . . . Philadelphia's water isn't even fit for ships. Acids and gases generated

price paid for turning the governing of the American city over to men who were 'not in it for their health'.

An equally serious charge is that the machines made civic politics meaningless. The wars of the 'Goats' and 'Rabbits' in Kansas City were no more meaningful than the wars of the 'Blues' and the 'Greens' in the Hippodrome of Constantinople. Not much more can be said of the fights between the leaders of the five boroughs of New York or the Boston wards. But, again, the cities were very American. All over the Union, political questions at any rate the election of public officers, were decided basically on issues and personalities dead nearly a century. It is only in recent years that the ghosts of Lincoln and Lee have shown signs of being prepared to cease walking. If it is true (and there is some evidence that it is) that where genuine local issues are fought over, as in the 'Socialist' city of Milwaukee, government *has* to be better, we cannot simply denounce the machines for preventing such developments (which they do). We have to ask why local parties, and national third parties, have such short lives and limited influence? It was not the machine, as such, that wrecked the American Labour party in New York. The power of the machines is explained by the failure of third parties, of 'Socialist' parties to get anywhere, and that is part of the total American party picture. The city machines rejoice that this is so, but they do not make it so, although they do all they can to keep it so.

It is only when the general political pattern changes that it will be safe to say that the machine is doomed and the way that will affect the machines is by depriving them of their power to attract the voters. For, as the most intelligent of modern bosses, Ed Flynn of the Bronx, put it, the voter is the boss. 'You're the Boss' was the title and lesson of his book and if the Boss, the sovereign People, prefer to contract out the business of local government, they will receive many tenders and the winners will be a machine.

---

by decaying sewage eat the paint off their hulls, corrode their metal work, and if they linger long enough, eventually eat holes in their bottoms. Visiting naval men and merchant mariners complain that river fumes turn green their gold watches and rings and tarnish their small change.' Thomas P. O'Neil, 'Philadelphia: Where Patience Is a Vice', in *Our Fair City*, edited by Robert S. Allen (1947), pp. 61–62.

The machine in its classical form, and in its main influence on American politics, is an urban phenomenon, and mainly a phenomenon of the great cities. That is not to say that there are no rural machines or small-town machines. There are plenty of each, but they have special characteristics that mark them off from classical models like Tammany or the Philadelphia 'Organization'. For one thing, their resources are far less great; they have less to plunder and consequently less with which to buy immunity. Many of their more enterprising sons made for the big cities early in life, there the rewards were better. And in small towns, the difficulties of hiding sin, sudden and probably ill-gotten wealth, are greater than in the great urban swamps and underwoods of New York or Chicago. Of course, even a not very large city might, for various reasons, acquire a political and social reputation that caused its neighbours to talk ill of it.[1]

It cannot have been with surprise, then, that the Kefauver Committee discovered that some quite small communities like La Salle (Illinois) were, for their size, quite as given to politically protected vice and illegality, as their big sisters. And this was not a case like Cicero, the fortress that Al Capone, the new Brasidas, planted deep in the heart of Cook County from which to raid neighbouring Chicago. This was genuine small town graft.[2] There

---

[1] 'We believed Galesburg was a decent well-behaved city compared to Peoria. In Peoria, we believed, were big distilleries and breweries making whisky and beer and the saloon-keepers ran the town. When a Galesburg man wanted a "bad woman" for the night it was safer to go to Peoria than to try it in Galesburg, where the police made raids. Gambling too was safer in Peoria.' Carl Sandburg, *Always the Young Strangers* (1953, English edition), p. 326. An historian has suggested that these differences in the *ethos* of towns go back a long way. Some have had a reputation of being tough and 'open' from the beginning. 'From the very beginning of Ohio River traffic some towns were recognized as being more dissolute, more lawless than others, and—perish the thought!—an unprejudiced visitor may still identify a few of them after two hundred years of progress and culture.' R. E. Banta, *The Ohio* (English edition 1951), p. 255. It is sometimes asserted, in places like Tacoma, Portland, Everett, Spokane, etc., that Seattle owed its astonishing growth to just such a well-earned reputation.

[2] In a book which I wrote some years ago, I used a small middle-western town as an idyllic background of peace, harmony and happiness

is also a great deal of rural graft, as investigation (in the rare occasions when it is provoked) shows. But graft in the small towns, in the countryside, corrupt political organization, even tampering with the secrecy and sacredness of the ballot, are aspects, as a rule, of the domination of the small town or the countryside by economic and social interests who owe their predominance in politics to their predominance as property owners, landowners, lawyers, agents of great remote economic interests and the like. Again, the cost of a real, full-time machine is more than the traffic will bear. Some person or some group in the small town or rural county may represent the dominating power in state politics, but that, again, is not a full-time job as a rule. The local legislator may be very corrupt, as corrupt as a Tammany alderman of the old days, but, again, his price is lower and given the rural *mores*, he cannot be rewarded with the valuable franchise of a saloon.

The reasons why it is rash to speak of state 'machines' are more complicated. There have been state 'bosses', leaders, in or out of office, to whom all the hierarchy of the party looked up, as far as state politics were concerned. Such was David B. Hill in 'upstate' New York and such was his Republican opposite number, Tom Platt. But the limitations under which Hill, during long periods of Democratic domination, and Platt, in the following years of Republican domination, worked, illustrate the difference between even the greatest state boss and the great city bosses. Neither Hill nor Platt could either ignore or boss Tammany. Hill, as a non-moralistic Democrat, could, as a rule, make a better deal with the Hall than could Platt, who was always tempted to plunder the plunderers to reward his rural supporters, materially and morally. But Tammany was there and potent because New York City was there and potent. It could be an enemy, an ally, or a neutral, but it was permanently a power.

Even in the more highly integrated state of Pennsylvania, when all the big cities as well as the state government were safely, impregnably Republican and the Senators from Pennsylvania were *ex*

---

in contrast with tormented and fear-ridden towns in Europe. I did not name it, but a friend who identified it sent me, a year or two later, a newspaper cutting reporting that all the civic officers of that 'Sweet Auburn' had just been indicted for various forms of malfeasance.

officio members of the real high command of the Republican party
in the nation, Philadelphia, Pittsburgh, Harrisburg were not mere
wards or districts or even boroughs on the model of New York.
Each had its own interests, its own resources, and state leaders, like
Quay and Penrose, knew that they had to persuade as well as order.
So it was with Chicago and Illinois, with Baltimore and Maryland.
In some states there was a triangular distribution of power, in Ohio
between the state, Cleveland and Cincinnati, in Missouri between
the state, St. Louis and Kansas City. The Governor might revolt;
legislators might hold out for higher prices; the permanent rural-
urban clash might upset discipline and what was called a Boss might
be more of an arbitrator, a prudent family lawyer advising against
dangerous litigation. Such seems to have been the role of Tom
Taggart, the Democratic 'Boss' of Indiana for so long. Men went
out to French Lick to talk to Tom Taggart and, if they were wise,
usually listened to what he had to say. But they could oppose him,
at their own risk. This was very different from Commissioner
Murphy asking for 'advice' in Tammany Hall.

There have, of course, been times when the whole political life
of a state has been highly disciplined and unified and where it has
been possible to identify one formal head of the state's political
life. But, as a rule, this state Boss ruled as the ally, or the nominee,
of great non-political interests, the great railroads that ran through
the state, like the Sante Fé in Kansas or the 'Octopus' (the Southern
Pacific) in California. It is a long time since P. T. Barnum called
New Jersey 'the state of Camden and Amboy'. But few states had,
or have, economic structures as simple as those of Kansas and
California two generations ago. Not only is there often more than
one centre of economic power wanting political privilege, but
there may be rival, conflicting centres of economic power neither
of which the formal 'political' rulers could afford to offend. The
Pennsylvania Railroad had to fight or deal with Standard Oil, as
later, it had to fear Carnegie. The very fact that what these great
corporations wanted was competitive privilege made the politicians
more important to them, but also made the politicians less able to
give exclusive privileges; the price might be the backing, by immense resources, of the rivals always waiting to take over the
'machine'. It may be doubted whether there has ever been a state

boss in the position of some of the great city bosses, able to sell political favours, confident that he had an effective monopoly of the supply, for the present and any future that it was worth calculating about. It is another matter when we turn to machines that are controlled by politicians holding high office and dominating their states and parties by reason of the powers inherent in their office, their powers of patronage, their powers of administrative decision, their powers of appeal by referendum, to the mass of the voters.[1] It is customary, and not totally misleading, to refer to the 'Dewey Machine' in New York. Certainly, Governor Dewey has constructed an extremely effective administration in New York, both from the point of view of the average citizen and from the point of view of the Republican politicians of the state. It has been discovered that thwarting the Governor, especially lending aid and comfort to his political enemies in his own party, is a highly dangerous practice. The legislature has been kept well in hand (although when one of its own members is involved, and is being treated harshly, it can sulk, if not revolt).[2] But even with complete command of the executive and great power over the legislature, Governor Dewey's control has very serious limits, above all those created by the existence of the incorrigibly Democratic or, alternatively, incorrigibly 'New Deal' city of New York.[3] And, more important, this power is a function of Mr. Dewey's office as Governor. Should he cease to be Governor and not become President, would his power continue, even should he become a United States Senator or a cabinet officer? It seems unlikely; he will remain important, but he is not in the position of a Simon Cameron or even of Oliver Morton of the old days. And they were Senators closely involved in the administration of the national policy of the Republican party and the United States, at that time almost indistinguishable.[4] The same story can be told of other Governors who have had great

[1] For the patronage resources of some Governors see p. 201.
[2] See p. 155.
[3] The limitations are illustrated even in the city of which Governor Dewey is first citizen. For Albany is as incorrigibly Democratic as New York, and a threatened investigation of the O'Connell machine was abandoned after that organization threatened reprisals.
[4] For the change in the role of Senators since the adoption of the seventeenth amendment, see p. 264 *et sqq.*

power in state or federal office, but whose power evaporated when they were mere party leaders without the disciplinary resources that official office gives. Such was the fate of Paul McNutt in Indiana; even were the Democrats still the leading party in that volatile state, Mr. McNutt (unless he got back into the capitol at Indianapolis or Washington) would not, necessarily, be their effective chief. But how few city bosses have needed office to control their cities! Wisely, they have preferred the role of Père Joseph to the role of Richelieu.

To this view that there are no true state bosses as there still are city bosses, the South, possibly, provides an exception. Some see in Mr. Roy Harris of Georgia, a state boss, but the troubled history of that state suggests that the power behind the throne has to be vigilant to watch what throne he is hiding behind. Huey Long was, of course, a true Boss, but he was more than that; he was something like a Dictator, ruling his legislature and his state officers with an open disregard of law and decorum that is probably unique and that rehearsal for dictatorship was ended by assassination.[1] Indeed, it is paradoxical, although not scandalous, that the state with the most perfect, perhaps the only perfect state-wide machine, should be no other than the 'Old Dominion', Virginia. For everybody who does not belong to it and some who do, talks of the Democratic party organization in that state as the 'Byrd machine' and no one doubts that its chief is the senior Senator, Harry F. Byrd.[2] 'Although many Virginians are too genteel to use the term, Senator Byrd is the boss of the machine and of the state.'

[1] Ralph S. O'Leary, 'Louisiana' in Robert S. Allen, *Our Sovereign State* (1949), p. 252, asserts that Mayor Behrman 'from 1912 to 1920 literally ran Louisiana's Statehouse in Baton Rouge from his office in the City Hall in New Orleans'. That he had great power in state politics is certain, but he could not run the state as completely as he ran New Orleans.

[2] Although the head of one of the oldest and most famous Virginia families, Senator Byrd, as a businessman and to some extent as a politician, is a self-made man, neither representing a dynasty founded on politics like the Talmadges in Georgia or the Longs in Louisiana, nor a locally entrenched family like the Wadsworths of Geneseo, in upstate New York. As his classically-minded ancestor, William Byrd of Westover, might have put it, he is *faber fortunae suae*. He describes himself in the Congressional Directory as a 'newspaper publisher, farmer and apple grower'. It was as an apple grower that he restored the family fortune.

That machine has proved invincible for a long time now, and it owes a great deal of its efficiency to Senator Byrd's remarkable powers of organization and of political judgment. The existence of a real Republican party in the state, its changing economic character, the extraordinarily complicated manoeuvres forced on 'regular' Democrats, in recent years, by the almost revolutionary changes in the national party's policies, have made it certain that only a man of great political sagacity and force, and only a machine admirably organized and commanded, could have won so long. But if Senator Byrd is a boss, again, even he is not quite a Boss in the city sense. Virginia is a special case (which most Virginians would agree is as it should be). 'The Commonwealth possesses characteristics more akin to those of England at about the time of the Reform Bill of 1832 than to those of any other state of the present-day South. It is a political museum piece. Yet the little oligarchy that rules Virginia demonstrates a sense of honour, an aversion to open venality, a degree of sensitivity to public opinion, a concern for efficiency in administration, and as long as it does not cost much, a feeling of social responsibility. Senator Byrd heads the governing oligarchy; he is less than a tyrant, a good deal more than a front.'[1]

Again, the difference between the best state machines and the best city machines (in terms of efficiency) is a difference that is more a difference in kind than in degree. For not only has the state machine to deal with the city machines, it has to deal with the federal government. As states' rights lose reality, as the legislative policy, the tax policy, the administrative policy of the federal government more and more affect state politics and policy, the mere machine, neutral, almost anonymous, content to be left alone, is more and more out of place in state politics, whatever life it may yet have in the cities.[2] It is not a question of morals or of 'good government'; it is a question of function and the old state machine is obsolete while the city machine is only obsolescent, if that.

[1] V. O. Key, Jr., *Southern Politics* (1949), pp. 19, 21.

[2] Of course, even a city machine has some interest in federal action, especially in the action of federal law-enforcement officers. During the depression, so many cities were virtually bankrupt that the Roosevelt administration often by-passed the states and found legal devices enabling it to aid cities directly. But no city's needs are so closely tied up with federal policies as are those of a big state or even of a small one.

Chapter Five

POLITICS AND MORALS

THE connection between morals, the law, and politics is old and not exclusively American. But, in America, the connection has been made closer by the religious inheritance of the American people, and by the American belief in the necessity and desirability of legislation to put down manifest evils. The American, from the beginning, has been quite willing to be his brother's keeper, and he has been ready to assume, in face of any clearly sinful activity, that 'there ought to be a law about it'. It is not quite accidental that the first great American novel deals with the public, legal punishment of adultery, and *The Scarlet Letter* has been more read than its lesson has been digested.

There were, however, special reasons in New England society for that intrusion of Christianity into private life to which Lord Melbourne later objected, for the New Englanders had been an especially selected and sifted stock. If that salt lost its savour? And if something like that savour could be produced by the arm of the law (in Massachusetts one could hardly talk of the 'secular arm'), it was the obvious duty of the magistrate to punish sin and so lessen its public opportunities of giving offence, if not to bring the sinner to true repentance. What Professor Perry Miller calls the 'jeremiads', the traditional sermons of the ministers, were full of lamentation over the fact that there was sin, even in Boston. Some of that could be attributed to the fact that Boston was a port on whose Common sailors, in the seventeenth century, misconducted themselves without necessarily implicating in their sins more than their immediate partners. But it was another matter when the sons of the elect

behaved in a highly indecorous manner and when, after the new
charter of the Bay Colony had been granted by William III, the
church and the state were no longer aspects of the same unified
body and tradition.[1]

The true source, however, of nineteenth and twentieth century
moral legislation is to be found not in the old semi-Calvinist theory
or practice of New England, but in the new evangelical zeal that
came in with Methodism and the spread of the Baptist and other
sects. By 1860, the Methodists, the Baptists and variants like the
Campbellites were more representative of the new religious conscience of the Middle West than were New England Congrega-
tionalism or Southern or Pennsylvania Presbyterianism. And the
older Protestant denominations, even in New England, were deeply
affected by the new view of the moral duty of the churches. The
more aristocratic denominations, Episcopalians, Unitarians, Dutch
Reformed, in New York, might resist the temptation (not among
them very serious) to discipline their opulent and self-satisfied
congregations.

> A solid man of Boston,
> A comfortable man, with dividends,
> And the first salmon and the first green peas,

was not likely to let his minister cut him off from his madeira.
The lower orders who listened to Lyman Beecher at 'Hell Fire
Corner'[2] might become teetotallers if they liked, but they could

[1] Professor Miller notes the increasing bafflement of the church
leaders. 'Drunkenness, for instance, not only was there more of it, there
was less shame; numbers were to be "seen in the open street, staggering
and reeling", and by 1713 it had to be admitted that women were no
strangers to the vice. "The town has cause to know the truth of this".
The vice itself had become a more complex thing; in 1673 Increase
Mather had addressed a *Wo to Drunkards* to imbibers of wine, but in the
preface to a revised edition of 1712 had to lament that so little wine was
drunk.' Perry Miller, *The New England Mind From Colony to Province*
(1953), p. 306. The view that wine, bad as it was, was better than hard
liquor suggests the campaign with which some semi-wets deceived
themselves in the twenties of this century, that all the American people
wanted was 'light wine and beer'.

[2] Park Street Church on Boston Common. It was not accidental that
Lyman Beecher was one of the most vehement defenders of the Trinit-

not be allowed to impose their whims on their betters. But they did; Maine went dry and, for a time, even Massachusetts, 'God forgive her, was a-kneeling with the rest', as Lowell might have put it.[1] But the dry tide (if the bull be permitted) ebbed; Maine alone remained formally constant to the cause.[2] It was in the Middle West and in the South that the next temperance (i.e. teetotal) move-ment made its conquests. After the Civil War, the prohibition of the liquor traffic by local option became an important issue in state politics, driving Irish and Germans together in defence of both their tastes and their pockets, for both groups produced a remarkably large number of saloon-keepers, distillers and, among the Germans, brewers. Some states went dry very quickly, in law if not in fact, notably Kansas which, in the nineties, produced not only Mrs. Mary Lease, the 'Kansas Pythoness' who advised the ruined farmers to 'raise less corn and more hell', but Mrs. Carrie Nation who went around enforcing the liquor laws by chopping up saloon fittings with her little hatchet. But local option, even state-wide prohibi-tion, was not enough. Both were, in fact, ineffective in the absence of federal authority to prevent the wet counties or states from flooding the dry. So in 1872, the Prohibition party made its first campaign, as it has continued to do down to the present day.[3] It

arian faith and also one of the first to protest against the tippling of the laity *and* of the clergy. He is now remembered as the father of the author of *Uncle Tom's Cabin* (and of Henry Ward Beecher).

[1] This dread era produced a famous Boston joke. An indignant mem-ber of a good club was lamenting the servile condition of the Common-wealth, in premises where illegal liquor was notoriously available on the top floor. 'What could I do if a friend, say from St. Louis, came in here and wanted a drink?' 'You could say, "Fils de Saint Louis, montez au ciel," ' retorted another proper Bostonian.

[2] One of the two most celebrated Maine politicians, James G. Blaine, expressed only partially humorous concern with a report that he had gout. He wished it to be reported as rheumatism.

[3] The platform of 1872 laid it down that: 'the traffic in intoxicating beverages is a dishonour to Christian civilization, inimical to the best interests of society, a political wrong of unequalled enormity, subversive of the ordinary objects of government, not capable of being regulated or restrained by any system of licence whatever, but imperatively demanding for its suppression effective legal Prohibition by both State and National Legislation'. Kirk H. Porter, *National Party Platforms* (1924),

was a one-issue party; so had the Republican party been in its origins. But the Republican party did not win until it became more than a single-issue party, and no prudent politician left either of the old firms for the new. The Prohibition candidates never polled more than a handful of votes and, if they had any effect at all, it was occasionally to weaken the Republicans enough to let a Democrat in.

More realistic crusaders than the leaders of the Prohibition party saw that their only chance lay in creating an efficient pressure group and, in 1895, the Anti-Saloon League was founded. Its principles were simple. It had no object but the adoption by the federal government of a prohibition amendment. It never allowed itself to add advocacy of other good causes to this primary one, thus avoiding an error of the Prohibition party. It was strictly non-partisan (in the American sense). It cared nothing about the party affiliations of Congressmen, Senators or Presidents. If they were 'dry', it was for them; if they were wet, it was against them; if all candidates were satisfactory or unsatisfactory, it was neutral. Thus it did not force the existing political organizations to resist it. All it wanted from politicians was legislation. All it could offer was votes and, in many regions, enough votes to make the difference between victory and defeat. The politicians took the hint, and more and more of the United States became formally dry.

The final triumph came during the first World War when state after state got on the bandwagon, a rush aided by the extraneous fact that the chief opponents of prohibition, in the Middle West at any rate, had been the Germans who were, from 1914 on, suspect, and from 1917 more than suspect, of an un-American attitude to the war in Europe. 'The world will be a more fit place to live in when autocracy, war and drink are all buried in the same grave,' wrote a leading dry propagandist in the climactic year, 1917.[1] This argument gained some plausibility from the fact that the most energetic organizers of the German-Americans had been the brewers

---

p. 77. Anxious to mitigate the hostility of the new elements in the population, the platform ended with a plank welcoming immigration.

[1] William E. Johnson, *The Federal Government and the Liquor Traffic*, 2nd edition (1917), p. 316.

and other enemies of the Drys. What had been a defence of an economic interest and a way of social life, became a defence of a particular foreign policy for the United States.[1]

In 1919, the XVIIIth amendment was ratified and the Volstead Act passed over Wilson's veto. In 1920, the dry era dawned, on one side, in expectations of a deliverance from the Demon Rum that justified all hopes, and on the other, in a state of gloomy resignation to enforced abstinence that seems comic today.

But the enactment of a law, even the adoption of an amendment, was one thing and an easy thing; enforcement of the law, the implementation of the amendment were another. 'Mr. Dooley' had noted, long before, that his countrymen were short-winded crusaders, sprinters rather than distance runners, and the American people got out of breath and out of temper with the dry régime almost at once. The Drys noticed, very soon, that the country was not dry. The Wets noticed, very soon, that the main effect of the social revolution was to raise the price and lower the quality of liquor. Politicians noticed that there were new profits to be earned, as protectors or as harassers of the new illegal traffic. And a new vocabulary and new arts, like home brewing, were revealed to millions of formally law-abiding citizens. The battle was not over; it was only begun. And the defeated and disgruntled Wets might have quoted Clough: 'Say not the struggle naught availeth', for certainly, within a year or two, it was possible to add 'comes silent, flooding in, the main'.

Indeed, even sound, 'dry' politicians, once they had voted for the XVIIIth amendment, were inclined to call it a day. They could see

[1] The dangers of this double role were seen by astute leaders. ' "War and prohibition", urged Judge John Schwaab, president of the Ohio Alliance, ". . . should be treated, so far as possible, as "separate issues". Bearing in mind that many opponents of prohibition were also opponents of Germany, those who addressed non-German audiences on domestic topics should always sedulously soft-pedal the war question. "Let us drive no friend out of our camp by making the European war our war." ' Clifton James Child, *The German-Americans in Politics 1914–1917* (1939), p. 17. As late as the November elections of 1914, organized German-American pressure was concentrated on the dangers to beer rather than to the fatherland. The German-American did not yet realize the danger that Germany was about to be in from American policy.

in the new jobs, created to enforce prohibition, untapped sources
of spoils. Some of them learned quickly that permits for industrial
and medical alcohol could be made political currency. And the
public, in the lush days of Warren G. Harding, was no more in a
mood of high moral endeavour than was the President himself. The
'realism' of the Anti-Saloon League had to be paid for. It is possible
that the more simple-minded of the Drys really believed that a constitutional amendment and a federal statute would eradicate, at
once, the whole wicked traffic. The new Prohibition Commissioner,
appointed by the Wilson administration, was a sincere and fanatical
Dry, and he believed that all was over bar the shouting. 'This law',
he proclaimed, 'will be obeyed in cities, large and small, and where
it is not obeyed it will be enforced. . . . The law says that liquor
to be used as a beverage must not be manufactured. We shall see
that it is not manufactured. Nor sold, nor given away, nor hauled
in anything on the surface of the earth, or in the air.'[1] There were
shrewder dry leaders than Mr. John F. Kramer, among them the
great lobbyist of the Anti-Saloon League, Wayne B. Wheeler. 'I
haven't been fighting for any prohibition amendment, I've been
fighting for prohibition. We haven't got it, but we're going to have
it if we stick it out.'[2] But even those who knew as well as did
Wheeler, that the battle was begun, not ended, were silent on the
realities of the problem. They had assembled and led an army under
the banner of federal prohibition. The good time had come, and to
discuss, realistically, making the good time stay would have been
to alienate Congress and disturb the faithful. 'Confronted by a
choice between arousing Congress and reassuring the country, the
prohibition organizations chose the second of these alternatives.'[3]
Wheeler himself, in public, had to pretend to an optimism that he
probably did not feel. He even assured the taxpayer that the government would actually make a net profit out of fines, forfeitures and
the rest of the penalties provided!

Within a year, the sad truth was out. Prohibition was going to

[1] Quoted in Herbert Asbury, *The Great Illusion: An Informal History
of Prohibition* (1950), p. 142.
[2] Quoted in Justin Steuart, *Wayne Wheeler: Dry Boss* (1928), pp.
160-1.
[3] Charles Merz, *The Dry Decade* (1930), p. 82.

require a great deal of expensive enforcement; mere law was not enough.[1]

It was part of the realist policy of the Anti-Saloon League to be content with the vote of a politician; it tactfully ignored how far the statesman's conduct was in keeping with his legislative record. To seek to secure both dry laws and dry lawmakers was to ask for the moon, and the League was not run by the moonstruck. This practical policy had its difficulties for, since the driving force behind the Prohibition movement was a deep and genuine moral sentiment, the news that some dry politicians were wet private citizens had a depressing effect on the more naïve supporters of the cause. Fortunately, the private conduct of the politicians was not usually public property; the Prohibition leaders were content with public decorum where they could get it.[2] It was not only during the campaign for the enactment of national prohibition that this tolerance was necessary; it was even more desirable when prohibition was enshrined in the Constitution and when dry statutes and lavish votes of money were necessary to make the XVIIIth amendment more than an empty moral gesture. For the City of Washington, then as now, was particularly rich in alcoholic temptation and it was widely believed that the solid dry majority in both houses included some weak vessels, and that the customers for the Senate bootlegger did not all come from the unregenerate statesmen of the cities.[3] But the cities, and those regions, urban and rural, where the 'new immigration' was strongest, were the centres of political resistance to prohibition. 'Rum, Romanism and Rebellion' were again allied, the rebellion, this time, being against the XVIIIth amendment. For prohibition, although the Anti-Saloon League paraded its Catholic members round and round like the Roman

[1] I have often heard Americans recall, with a kind of wondering amusement, how, in the first year or so of the dry era, they actually thought that they might not be able to get anything serious to drink!

[2] They perhaps remembered the story of John B. Gough, the most celebrated of American temperance orators, who was accused by another temperance advocate, during one of his English trips, of gross backsliding, a charge that was aired in the English courts.

[3] This appears to have been the view of an acute commentator. 'The radio is a great contraption for the dry candidate that's been out with the boys.' Kin Hubbard, *Abe Martin's Town Pump* (1929), p. 68.

army in a stage production of Julius Caesar, was much more a religious than a sociological movement. The identification of righteousness with total abstinence had, by the end of the century, become part of Protestant orthodoxy, even in fundamentalist sects which, on other matters, were strict in their adherence to Holy Writ.[1] As it was put by a learned student of the development of this dogma, 'there seems to be something distinctively American about the situation.'[2] And though prohibition was tried in parts of Canada and in Finland, and local option in Scotland, it remained distinctively American.

These truths were not ignored by the enemies of prohibition, who saw it as a sample of the general spirit of intolerance of which the Ku-Klux-Klan, the new immigration policy and legislation against Darwinian teaching in state schools were others. The Drys, in their more tactless moments, made no bones about it. Prohibition was the old American way that was to be forced on the inferior non-Nordic races.[3]

Then by a natural but costly error, the Drys and their political allies made two linked and fatal mistakes. They took credit for all the good economic results of the Harding-Coolidge boom and they insisted on regarding the election of 1928 as a plebiscite on prohibition. Both boasts proved highly lethal boomerangs as the market broke and the Republican party began to collapse. The cheerful

[1] Dr. J. Gresham Machen, the famous fundamentalist of Princeton Theological Seminary, was at least consistent. Water was not changed into 'raisin cake' at Cana for him, and he opposed prohibition *and* modernism. Few fundamentalists were so consistent.

[2] John Allen Krout, *The Origins of Prohibition* (1925), p. 300. A popular American author, looking about for a Scottish town to produce his mythical whisky 'Duggan's Dew', unluckily hit on Kirkintilloch, the only sizeable town in Scotland to go dry.

[3] Again and again in the so-called *Wickersham Report* (officially the *Report of the National Commission on Law Observance and Enforcement* (1931) 71st Congress 3rd Session), the sins of 'foreigners' are dwelt on. These foreigners, who by implication included Negroes, were preventing the acceptance of the law. If, in a city with a large 'foreign' population, any serious attempt to enforce the law was made, it was a matter for gratified wonder. An exhibit of a map of North Dakota showed a marked correlation between the incidence of wet sentiment and practice and the settlement of the state by 'lesser breeds without the law'.

boasting about the workers' cars, radio sets, new houses, new clothes was bitterly remembered as the cars were 're-possessed' by the dealers or credit companies, and the houses taken over by the mortgagors. The economic argument was even turned round. If the Federal Government was running a heavy deficit, that was due to the loss of excise revenue, now going into the pockets of the bootleggers and of their political allies. Reopen the (legal) breweries and give employment to brewery workers and farmers! That would give the jaded economy the necessary shot in the arm. And as for promoting the purity of politics, had they ever been more corrupt? Back to the days of legalized liquor.[1]

Equally disastrous was the linking of prohibition with the sinking fortunes of the Republican party. It had seemed safe and profitable, in 1928, to link the defeat of 'Al' Smith with the triumph of the cause. Mrs. Mabel Walker Willebrandt, who had taken a leading and not excessively scrupulous part in that campaign, rejoiced at the result. 'In another way, however, the candidacy of Governor Smith was *beneficial* to the cause of prohibition. Governor Smith centred national attention upon the subject. Nothing helped so much to clear the air as the last presidential campaign, deplorable as some phases of it were in some respects. . . . The prohibition discussion finally reached the "brass tacks" stage and a definite clear-cut issue was presented to American voters.'[2] It is doubtful whether the issue of prohibition was decisive in 1928. At any rate, the new administration showed no excessive zeal in plugging up the leaks in the dike through which liquor was pouring. It was not now a matter of leaks in dikes, so much as one of broken levees with the flood of booze pouring in like the Mississippi. The traditional remedy of bothered politicians was adopted. A Commission was appointed, the 'National Commission on Law Observance and Enforcement'.

[1] Few and frowned-on were those who went the whole way (despite Mrs. Parker's jest) and admitted that they would welcome or permit the return of 'the old-fashioned saloon'. In the evidence before the *Wickersham Commission* as in the *Report,* there is unanimity about one thing. No more saloons. That promise (a rare event in politics) has been kept. There are bars, cafés, taverns, inns, even public houses in abundance in America today, but not, as far as I know, a single saloon.

[2] (Mrs.) Mabel Walker Willebrandt, *The Inside of Prohibition* (1929), pp. 274-5.

But, despite the title, the Commission was regarded as a body that would find some magical way out of the dilemma that faced the people who had so resoundingly, it was said, rallied in 1928 to the good old cause. The 'Wickersham Commission', as it at once came to be called from the name of its chairman, a well-known lawyer George W. Wickersham, was put in an impossible position. For it was still thought impossible to talk of repealing the XVIIIth amendment and, without such a repeal, it was impossible to adjust the law. The most that could have been done was to repeal the Volstead Act, leaving the amendment with no legal penalties attached to violating it and thus, in effect, 'turning the question back to the states'.

This was to accept open nullification of a part of the sacred Constitution, for no one believed that states like New York or New Jersey would feel any obligation to step in where the federal government stepped out. Yet the evidence, however varying in plausibility, made it plain that, in very many cities and in a deplorable number of rural areas, the XVIIIth amendment was nullified. As the Commission cogently pointed out, this was demonstrated by the steady and not unreasonable price at which whisky could be bought. A national market had been created and was being efficiently and regularly supplied. This was a fact against which the more sentimental arguments of the Drys were ineffective. All that they could do, in fact, was to plead for more laws, more and better federal agents, more propaganda. The law would be enforceable if public opinion were really behind it, public opinion would be behind the law if it were enforced. Like squirrels, the witnesses went round and round this cage; the dry witnesses, that is, for the Wets simply insisted that public opinion had definitely turned against the practice, if not the theory, of prohibition. As Lenin said that the Russian army in 1917 voted for peace with its feet, a great part of the American public voted for ignoring the law with its mouth. Testimony before the Commission was conflicting enough. Prohibition was said, in North Dakota, to have done wonders for the morals of students at Yale; it was said, in Wisconsin, to have done harm to the morals of students at the University of Wisconsin.[1]

---

[1] At Wisconsin one fraternity (D.K.E.) was pilloried, but it was not the only sinner. 'The queen of bootleggers, an attractive young Italian

There were marked conflicts between the evidence and the *Report*. Thus the expert who reported on Virginia accepted the view that the excellent enforcement of the law, state and federal, in Richmond was due, in great part, to the fact that the 'governor (Byrd), his attorney-general and assistant, and the commissioner of prohibition were all non-drinkers (and also non-smokers)'.[1] The actual *Report* took a less cheery view. State and federal officials worked well together, Virginia had been 'a zealous prohibition state since 1914. . . . The number of convictions under the state law is impressive, and of seizures thereunder no less. Yet the number of arrests for drunkenness in Richmond has been growing steadily and has increased by more than one-third in five years. Also the testimony shows that the amount of liquor in circulation has grown steadily. Prices tell the same tale'.[2] The same tale could have been told of many more places than Richmond and, of course, a more depressing tale, from the dry point of view, could have been told of the states and cities that had no tradition of prohibition zeal and whose office-holders were not non-drinkers.[3]

---

girl, caters exclusively to a fraternity house clientele. [No song on the lines of "Sweetheart of Sigma Chi" is reported.] The Dean of Men was gloomy; but an assistant Dean of Women said "she knew of no drinking or revelry on the part of the young ladies under her supervision". This official impressed me as one who would not be likely to be cognizant of such conditions.' *Official Records of the National Commission* (1931), p. 1103.

[1] Ibid., p. 1069. Governor Byrd shortly afterwards became a Senator. What his famous ancestor, William Byrd of Westover, would have thought of a teetotal and non-smoking head of his family, is not beyond conjecture.

[2] *Report on the Enforcement of the Prohibition Laws of the United States* (1931), pp. 40-1.

[3] When a federal District-Attorney for New York announced that he would not drink while he held this office, his fellow citizens were more amused than impressed. The anger displayed by Wayne B. Wheeler showed that the great dry lobbyist understood the damage done to the fiction of enforcement by this naïve undertaking. He would probably have preferred that Mr. Emory R. Buckner had kept his mouth shut and continued to drink in a quiet way, than that he should have emphasized, by his self-denying ordinance, the bogus character of law enforcement in many regions.

The *Report* of the *Wickersham Commission* was a great disappointment to both sides. It dismissed the possibility of repeal;
its suggestions for amending the law were unimpressive; but the
whole tone was also infuriating to the fanatical Drys (of whom
there were still millions), for not only were some members ready
for repeal, but the *Report* dripped pessimism about the prospects of
enforcement.[1]

The formally 'dry' administration in Washington, like the often
genuinely dry state administrations, was in a difficult position. The
forces that had put over prohibition were still strong and, as they
were mainly rural, they gained from the over-representation of
rural areas both in Congress and in the state legislatures. But
politicians had, by necessity, to be realists. They did not live the
sheltered lives of clubwomen and the still more sheltered lives of
pastors. And the contrast between the moral aims of the legislation
and the character not only of the legislators, but of the enforcement
officers, the increasingly open defiance of the law by the 'better
elements' who still voted for it and spoke up for it, transferred the
genuine moral advantage to the other side or, if it did not quite do
that, removed the whole question from the field of morals to the
field of politics.[2] Something of the disgust with the results of the
Civil War that was provoked by 'Reconstruction', was now provoked by the results of what Mr. Hoover, in an unfortunate

---

A little before this, I had been taken by an eminent New York
lawyer to tea, on a Sunday afternoon, in the house of an eminent New
York judge. The eminent jurist gave me a long and highly Anglophile
account of a recent holiday he had spent in Britain, praised the deeply
law-abiding character of the people and, hardly stopping to take breath,
asked what kind of drink I'd like to have.

[1] The unfortunate chairman suffered the traditional fate of the
mediator. His *Report* was dubbed by the Wets, the '*Wickedsham*'
Report, a poor joke, but no worse than the 'Scofflaw' epithet with which
the Drys had tried to shame the Wets out of their wicked and illegal
habits.

[2] I remember being given a drink by a very well-known (and de-
servedly respected) American woman, who explained that she was a
Dry but gave drink to her guests since it didn't matter what happened to
the children of the rich (among whom I seemed to be temporarily
classed), as long as the law saved the children of the poor.

moment, called 'an experiment noble in motive and far-reaching in purpose'.[1]

The fact that the controversy over prohibition was more than a controversy over liquor legislation, became more and more evident. 'Moonshine' was an old southern comfort, and war against the 'revenoors' was part of the folklore of some of the most 'Anglo-Saxon' and 'Protestant' parts of the United States. But this was a traditional and very Anglo-Saxon evasion. That there was, at any rate, lip service paid to the religious taboo on alcohol met the case. The pastors and politicians knew that the homage hypocrisy pays to virtue was true homage. But in many regions, above all in the great cities, there was no homage paid at all. The old conflict that had flared up, from time to time, between the 'old Americans' and the Germans and Irish, was now a permanent and open war. That the saloon was always in politics and always a source of evil in politics was an axiom in the more moralistic circles. But the saloon had gone and the liquor business was more in politics than ever. If it had paid to vote dry before, now more and more it paid to vote wet. The Democratic party in the cities began to win new friends, as the Republican party was in office and was the instrument of tyranny, although, in many regions, the zeal of the federal law-enforcement officers could hardly have been more tepid. The question of prohibition was one of the underground forces undermining the old party alignments from 1922 to 1932.

It is possible that, in the long run, one of the causes of the Prohibition debacle was just this moral tolerance to which the Anti-Saloon League owed its initial success. After all, the Republican party, even at its lowest moral ebb, did not tolerate slave-holders among its leaders. And the necessity of playing ball with the run-of-the-mill politicians made for very strange bedfellows indeed.[2]

[1] Doubly unfortunate, since Mr. Hoover was misquoted as describing prohibition as a 'noble experiment', which he had not done, and because the noble motive was less and less visible or was, at any rate, covered up by the less than noble results.

[2] Thus to keep 'the Quaker City' in the ranks of the faithful, it was necessary to accept the Vare machine as an ally although it, like all city machines, was dripping wet. Yet such was the force of organization discipline that wet leaders delivered the vote not only for Mr. Hoover against 'Al 'Smith (a difficult enough feat), but for local, dry candidates.

It is probable that the *status quo*, with less and less enforcement at a local and national level, combined with lower prices and better quality 'wet goods' would have continued, but for the linking of prohibition with the depression and with the Republican party. It is difficult to say which partner suffered more from the partnership. The Republicans were as helpless as the Ancient Mariner, and the Drys (much of whose support had come from the Democratic South) found that many of their allies were more anxious to win the next presidential election than to support the cause. By the end of 1931, no one was thinking of the *Wickersham Report* and, though many astute politicians, dry and wet, did not see it yet, prohibition, like protection in England a century ago, was not only dead but damned.

The Republicans wriggled, but could not escape their *damnosa hereditas*. Their plank in 1932 was a non-masterpiece of ineffectual evasion. The Democrats wavered; some of their most respected leaders like Senator Thomas Walsh and Senator Cordell Hull were still convinced Drys. But to the surprise even of ardent Wets, the platform came out for pure and simple repeal. As an observer, Mr. H. L. Mencken noted, Prohibition died 'a much quicker death than anyone seems to have expected. . . . Prohibition is left without a salient friend in either party'.[1] It is as certain as such things can be that the Republicans were doomed anyway, but the epithet of 'dry' increased the completeness of their debacle. As far as national politics were concerned, the issue was dead.

The good of prohibition was indeed interrèd with its bones and the evil lived after it. It would be almost as absurd to attribute to prohibition the great increase in lawlessness that marked the twen-

---

Yet one of the Vare officers who performed this near miracle had been insulted when one of the Vare brothers offered him a job as a prohibition agent. ' "I told him I was raising children and that I needed work, but no one would be able to point to any of my children and say their father was a prohibition agent and a grafter." Another less austere supporter got the job. "He made a lot of money, but today he hasn't a cent. He ran around —high life and everything else. It was ill-gotten money, and it went." The concept of an honest prohibition agent who did not "shake them down" did not occur to any of the actors in this little drama.' J. T. Salter, *Boss Rule* (1935), p. 109.

[1] H. L. Mencken, *Making a President* (1932), pp. 119,130.

ties, as it was to attribute it to the dreadful experiences in the first
World War that, in face of all the evidence, the 'flaming youth' of
the era was deemed to have undergone. Prohibition, looked at historically, was a rearguard action, fought by the elements in American life that urbanization, the motor car, the decline in the 'old-time
religion', were steadily weakening and would have weakened,
nearly as fast, if prohibition had remained a rural fad. It was said
that the South, in 1861, went to war against the Census of 1860
that showed the immense economic superiority of the North. The
Drys, in a sense, went to political war against the Census of 1910
which revealed, for the first time, that the American farmer was
now a member of a declining minority group. Almost everything
economically, socially, philosophically, was against him. Radio, the
movies, the cheap magazines, the comparative ease of travel were
undermining his traditions and his way of life. He was a man with a
grievance, and prohibition was, among other things, an expression
of that grievance. It was also, and here it deserves more sympathy,
an expression of a real and genuine alarm that the new urban world
would eat away the habits and beliefs on which rural America had
prospered. The fear was well-founded, the remedy was imbecile.

Prohibition was not the only legal expression of the moral zeal
of the American tradition. Long after the time of Hester Prynne,
sexual sinners, when they were caught, felt the arm of the law.
At a time when the medieval conception of the duty of the state
to punish sin, as such, was dying out in Europe, it was being reinforced in America. The common law was strengthened until there
were few states in which extra-marital sexual intercourse was not a
criminal offence, and even between lawfully married couples what
the Victorians called 'the secrets of the alcove' were legislated
against. It is doubted, by serious students, that this legislation had
any marked effect on the standards of American sexual morality.
These went down (if they went down) under the impact of a
slackening belief in the 'old-time religion', of the generalized
knowledge of methods of contraception, of Freudianism, of the
financial and legal 'emancipation of women'. All that legislation
could do was to impose impediment, not very serious, to amorous
enterprise, and provide a fine field for blackmailers and for grafters,
as did the act that bears the name of an otherwise forgotten Illinois

Congressman, James Robert Mann.[1] This statute, passed in 1910, was designed to put an end to the so-called 'white slave traffic', the transport of women across state borders for immoral purposes (crossing the border made the transaction part of 'interstate commerce' and so subject to federal jurisdiction). It is probable that the authors of the law had in mind interfering with the activities of pimps and procurers. But the Supreme Court held (*Caminetti v. United States*, 1917) that the transaction need not involve cash, only immoral design. Not only *Venus meretrix* was banned, but *Vénus toute entière*. As the dissenting justices pointed out, this was a handsome present to blackmailers or to nuisance-makers, and it created a number of interesting problems in moral and legal casuistry.[2] Whether it had any other beneficial effect is unknown.

State law went further, and many millions of American citizens have, more or less innocently, violated solemn statutes designed to impose a degree of decorum on the American people not aimed at even in Ireland.[3] Literary censorship was imposed by legal action, or by threat of legal action, a system that reached its heights in Boston where the 'Watch and Ward Society' made an effective combination of Yankee and Irish puritanism. But the Society overstepped the limits of the prudent, especially when it attacked Mr. H. L. Mencken whose *American Mercury* was seized. Mencken insisted on selling a copy at 'Brimstone Corner', and was duly

[1] Mann was part-author of a good deal of important legislation, apart from the statute which has made his name immortal. He was a co-author of the Mann-Elkins Act, of Isthmian canal legislation, of the resolution providing for the woman-suffrage amendment, etc. He was also, we are told, 'a formidable antagonist to anyone trying to put through loose, unwise or Democratic legislation'. *Dictionary of American Biography*, vol. XII, p. 244.

[2] Thus it was not a federal offence, in the days when the ships still ran, to voyage to Cythera on the Hudson River Night Boat, famous in song and story, as the voyage was entirely in the waters of New York State. It was a federal offence to make the same type of voyage from Boston to New York and, presumably, in the other direction, although I have never heard of the trip being taken that way. The Mann Act has been used to harass Mr. Charles Chaplin and others.

[3] Thus I learn from Dr. Alfred Kinsey (*Sexual Behaviour in the Human Female* by Alfred C. Kinsey and others, 1953, pp. 261–3) that 'petting' is illegal in some states but is nearly universally practised in them.

arrested and acquitted. *The American Mercury* was, for a time, banned from the mails, but the uproar made the censors look silly.[1] The decisive case, however, was fought over *Ulysses*. The court ruled that 'whilst in many places the effect of *Ulysses* on the reader is somewhat emetic, nowhere does it tend to be an aphrodisiac'.[2]

General moral vigilance reached its height in the activities of Anthony Comstock of the 'New York Society for the Suppression of Vice'. The indefatigable Secretary gave a word to the language— 'comstockery', and, in his old age, added to the gaiety of nations. He was, of course, backed by men and women genuinely concerned with the commercial exploitation of the sexual instinct, as well as with other human passions, but Comstock's methods, his ability to see obscenity in harmless if worthless pictures like 'September Morn', irritated the more cultivated, gratified the vendors and made his patrons ridiculous.[3] He did not confine his activities to

[1] This is not the opinion of Mr. Mencken's biographer. But he admits that 'the stature of the Watch and Ward Society . . . suffered terribly since Chase's double defeat, and the secretary was widely blamed for it.' William Manchester, *Disturber of the Peace: The Life of H. L. Mencken* (1950), p. 205. I was at Harvard during all the *brouhaha* and, indeed, knew the innocent and neglected vendor of the original copy of the *Mercury* that began the action. An eminent professor in the Divinity School told me, at the time, that he passed round a copy of the incriminated number and not one of his students spotted the article that had offended J. Frank Chase.

[2] An appeal against Judge John M. Woolsey's decision was made to the New York (federal) Circuit Court of Appeals where he was upheld by Learned and Augustus Hand. The Chief Judge of the Court, Martin Manton, dissented, holding that 'good work in literature has its permanent mark—it is like all good work, noble and lasting. It requires a human aim—to cheer, console, purify and ennoble the life of people'. Judge Manton later achieved the distinction of being the only federal judge of his rank ever to be convicted of receiving bribes. The opinions of both courts are printed in the Bodley Head edition (London, 1937), pp. 749 ff.

[3] The ability of policemen and law enforcement officers to see and smell dirt was and is remarkable. I was present at a vaudeville show in Los Angeles when the authorities of that then puritan city had just shut down a touring performance of *Desire Under the Elms*. A comedian rushed on the stage, stopped a most innocent act and announced, 'I'm from the District-Attorney's office; I know dirt when I see it.' As Mr. Ogden Nash has noted, 'smut when smitten is front page stuff' and politically saleable.

New York, but visited the Chicago 'Columbian Exposition' of 1893 to give an expert opinion on 'Little Egypt', the celebrated 'belly dancer' who was packing the crowds in on the Midway.[1] He condemned three 'acts' and expressed his conviction that 'the Managers of the World's Fair will gladly purge the performance. The Lady Managers, good and pure women as ever lived, went down there to see the horrible exhibition, so that they might realize how shameful a thing it was. They stayed clear through the sickening spectacle, utterly overwhelmed with a sense of degradation of all that is pure and noble in womanhood'.[2] But the Gentlemen Managers of the World's Fair could not afford to underwrite, in a depression year, the losses that would have followed taking Comstock's counsel and 'Little Egypt' remained to add an item to American folk memory.[3] Shaw, Brieux, Eugene O'Neill, the Follies, the Vanities, all finally escaped the censors although, in the interests of war morale, Mayor La Guardia was able to close the famous Minsky burlesque. Strip tease was an obstacle in the way of victory. In more recent years, as Mr. Cole Porter points out,

> Good authors, too, who once knew better words,
> Now only use four letter words,
> Writing prose, anything goes.

It is in film censorship that the pressure groups, above all the Catholic Legion of Decency, are most active, sometimes succeeding in suppressing, in New York, films shown with impunity under a Catholic ministry in Rome. Equally potent, on paper, is the Catholic ban on the dissemination of contraceptive information to which the rulers of that Church devote much energy, with no very visible result, even in Boston.

[1] Now the site of the University of Chicago.
[2] Heywood Broun and Margaret Leech, *Anthony Comstock* (1928), p. 245.
[3] The same problem arose, in 1933, when Chicago was having another World's Fair, this time not to celebrate the discovery of America, but the 'Century of Progress' since Chicago became a city. It was again a depression year, a worse depression year than 1893, and the chief attraction was Miss Sally Rand dancing clad only in a largish fan. Again the fear of bankruptcy drove out the fear of the moralists, Miss Rand continued to pack them in.

For the clergy and the professional moralists in all fields, as the history of prohibition shows, are victims of a *déformation professionelle*. Their business is to be, like Coolidge's preacher, against sin, and they are constantly tempted to call in aid the arm of the law, an arm in these matters, almost always and in all countries, a clumsy and often venal auxiliary. Frequently too they are the victims of reformers whose motives escape the eye of the clerical and lay zealots.[1] Politicians who have much else to answer for have found that purity, as much as patriotism, can be the last and safe refuge of a scoundrel. The victories thus won by pastors, even by Cardinals, have a way of back-firing; men of the highest character may find themselves sleeping partners in odious exploitation; and censors, and other enforcers of moral standards by law, have a way of making themselves and their employers ridiculous. And, all the while, the highest desirable social virtue of respect for and obedience to the law, is worn down by the spectacle of laws, either unenforced, or enforced occasionally, arbitrarily, or corruptly. The real lesson was taught by a New York politician over fifty years ago.

'The experience of mankind confirms what common sense would at once suggest, that the manners and morals of a people can never be moulded by legislation. If a law harmonizes with the opinions and prejudices of the people on whom it is to be enforced it will be honoured and obeyed. If, on the contrary, it is repugnant to their sense of right or in restraint of their taste and habits, it will be a dead letter, or an object of derision and contempt.'[2]

[1] The reformer by law should ponder the sad history of the Raines Law. Its author, an assistant of that tepid moralist, Senator Platt, induced the New York legislature to make saloon keepers turn their premises into 'hotels'. They had to provide sandwiches and bedrooms. The saloon keepers obeyed. The sandwiches remained uneaten, the bedrooms did not remain unused. 'Raines Law Hotel' soon became a synonym for a house of assignation. The legal results of the law were profitable both to Senator Platt and to Mr. Raines.

[2] Matthew P. Breen, *Thirty Years of New York Politics Up-To-Date* (1899), p. 107.

Chapter Six

THE NATIONAL CONVENTION

The National Conventions of the American political parties are among the most characteristic institutions of the American political system. Other democratic systems have bodies that in appearance, and to some extent in reality, can usefully be compared with them. But the party conferences or congresses of Great Britain or Canada, France or Australia, are bodies differing in very important ways from the American conventions. For the congresses and conventions of the other democracies mentioned do not have, as their main function, the choice of an officer like the President of the United States. They may have, at times, as their function the choice of a party leader who, because of that choice, later becomes Prime Minister, but their nominating function is only occasionally called into play and their function as an organ for the discussion and decision of party policy is more real and important than the corresponding function of the American Conventions. For the Conventions are bodies whose only real justification is that they present to the nation one of the two, occasionally one of the three men who will take over all the executive powers of the United States, that, by this nomination, give to the candidate the formal leadership of the party for four years, the command of the national party machinery, such as it is, and, for at any rate the months of the presidential campaign, allow the nominee to make party policy and ignore or interpret with practically complete freedom, the declaration of policy, the 'platform', that the Convention presents to the voters as its formal programme of action.

The Conventions came into existence as the realities of the

American political system were revealed in the generation of the successors of the 'Founding Fathers'.[1] From 1800 to 1824, there had been an apostolic succession, the Virginia dynasty, two terms for Jefferson, two terms for Madison, two terms for Monroe. The succession was not uncontested, but it was not broken. Apart from the lasting influence of Jefferson, even in old age and retirement, the basic claim to nomination was the consent of the 'congressional caucus'. It was a crude approximation to parliamentary government, but it could not last when it was discovered that the United States had been given institutions incompatible with parliamentary government and when it was also discovered that the most popular candidates might not be members of Congress or liked by or, a little later, even well known to the congressional leaders. For the Union was growing in extent, the old, fairly unified, if not united national political class was being replaced by a much more loosely organized political class, not all of whose leaders were great figures in Washington although they might be great figures in Albany or Nashville. The secret of empire was discovered, that Presidents could be made outside Washington and against Washington. John Quincy Adams was the last President chosen not only in Congress, but in accordance with congressional sentiment.[2] Even had Crawford, the caucus candidate, won, even had the West not thrown up so formidable a frontier leader as Andrew Jackson, the system was doomed as the exclusive right of the Romans (or Italians) to accept Emperors would have been doomed even had the Julio-Claudian house not ended with Nero.

But if Congress was not to organize the presidential election, who was to do so? The loose coalition that won with Jackson in 1828, the much tighter alliance that won with him in 1832 were still not adequately organized to deal with situations in which there was no Jackson, in which a winning candidate had to be picked from a dozen possibles. It was this difficulty that produced the Convention system, that is the by-passing of Congress and the

[1] A term we owe to that indefatigable phrase-maker, Warren G. Harding.

[2] Since no candidate in 1824 had a majority of electoral votes, the election was thrown into the House of Representatives which chose John Quincy Adams.

entrusting of the nomination of presidential candidates to an *ad hoc* body meeting only every four years, for a few days and with very limited objects. The result was to force the recognition of the presidency as a power really, not merely formally, separate from Congress, often in opposition to it, and able to claim a direct mandate from the people that neither Senate nor House could plausibly assert.

But the Convention system did not destroy a national party system in the making. It provided for an emergency that the Constitution had not provided for, the maximum integration that the national party system was capable of, formal unity every four years to nominate and, if possible, to elect a President of the United States. This, strictly speaking, is all that a party need do to be national and so the Convention is one of the really fundamental institutions of the American political system.

Its weaknesses are easily seen and easily condemned. It is the nearest approach in the American system to parliamentary government. It is the master of its own rules, unregulated by federal law, little regulated by state law. All power is in one body and its decisions, for four years, are final; their results irrevocable. Yet it is poorly organized for its basic functions. It is too large; numbers vary according to the rules of apportionment but there are always well over one thousand delegates.[1] These delegates come from an area of over three million square miles; many have never been delegates before; many know no politicians outside their own states; in the case of some large states, the delegates may only get to know

[1] Sometimes there were nearer two thousand delegates (or fractions of delegates). 'The Democratic call of 1924 provided "that in order that opportunity may be afforded the various states to give adequate representation to women as delegates-at-large, without disturbing prevailing party customs, there may be elected from each state four delegates-at-large for each senator in Congress from each state, with one half vote each in the National Convention".... The innovation of 1924 was applied to the next four conventions. Without achieving its purpose, it led to serious abuses. Some congressional districts sent six or more delegates, one Mississippi district sending 54 (instead of 2) in 1940, with one twenty-seventh of a vote each. The Convention of 1940 had 1,884 delegates, with 1,100 votes. Henceforth, by a rule of that year ... "no delegate will have less than half a vote".' Howard R. Penniman, *Sait's American Parties and Elections* (Fifth edition, 1952), p. 397.

each other at the Convention or on the train taking them to the Convention city. Nor is there any effective organization into which the new delegates can be accepted. Every new House of Commons or House of Representatives has its quota of new members who have to learn the ropes, but the gap between one House and its successor is now always short in time; the high command of the old House takes over in the new. There is adequate continuity and there is also time in which the newcomers can learn. And if it is complained, as it often and rightly is, that the two years' life of a House of Representatives does not give the new member time to learn his business, how much more can this be said of a Convention that lasts, as a rule, from three to four days.

Of course, there are Conventions which are admirably disciplined and organized from the moment they open. But these are the Conventions that are almost superfluous, Conventions in which the candidate is already chosen to all intents and purposes, either because he is the President in office seeking a second term, or because he is the choice of the dominant forces in the party, or is himself a great political power who has managed to line up a majority of delegates before the Convention meets. On such occasions, the Convention is purely formal and finds it hard to invent ways of passing the time. But these Conventions are not only nearly superfluous, they are not usual and it is rare, indeed, that both parties are in this happy state.[1] One at least of the national parties has to do its very important business in very difficult conditions. It has to find a candidate and (much less important), a platform on which this inchoate mass of delegates can agree; and to find both in ways that will not destroy the unity of the party, such as it is.

Normally, a Convention has before it several candidates, each with a plausible claim to being an adequate standard-bearer, that is a plausible claim to being 'available'. Being 'available' means having some assets and lacking some handicaps which, by tradition or in the circumstances of this election year, are thought indispensable in one case, fatal in the other. The Convention's first job

[1] William Howard Taft and William Jennings Bryan in 1908, Mr. Herbert Hoover and Governor Smith in 1928 were, in effect, nominated before the Conventions met.

is to decide which candidates are available and then decide which of the available candidates is most available. For, to amend *Animal Farm*, all serious candidates are available, but some are more available than others.

Certain rules for availability are fixed. The candidate must come from a state with a large electoral vote and from a state that is not certain to vote for the party candidate. For, by the system laid down in the Constitution, each state votes by itself and, by state law, all the electoral votes of the state go to the winner, even though his majority be trifling.[1] It is thought that state pride and the interests of the state machine (if there be one) will ensure zealous support for a 'favourite son'. On the other hand, it is pointless to waste the nomination on a state that can be relied on. These considerations have ensured that, in this century, only one candidate has been nominated from a small state, Mr. Landon of Kansas in 1936. And 1936 was a year of the most dismal Republican prospects when any expedients were tolerable.[2] And, since both are or were safe, no Democratic candidate has been nominated from the South since the Civil War and no Republican candidate from Pennsylvania since the party was founded. It is possible, with the shifting allegiance of the South and of Pennsylvania in recent years, these rules will not apply, but at the moment they do. It will, indeed, probably need the alteration of state electoral law to break down the monopoly of the large doubtful states, what is, in effect, the overwhelming preponderance, in this century, of New York.[3] But it is not enough to be a 'favourite son' of a state with a large number of electoral votes; the delegates (and their leaders) must be convinced that the mother-son relationship is really warm. Thus two formal 'favourite sons' of Ohio, Salmon P. Chase and John Sherman, were not nominated because there was grave doubt whether Ohio felt any more than the most tepid maternal affection for either of them. To be available, a candidate must persuade the Convention that his local supporters *really* want him. If they don't, who will? To give a recent example, Senator Taft's overwhelming victory in the senatorial election in Ohio in 1950 made him a much stronger

[1] See p. 223 for a description of the electoral system.
[2] Mr. Landon carried two states, neither of them Kansas.
[3] See p. 226.

candidate for the nomination in 1952 than he had been in 1940 or 1948, when his local majorities had not been impressive. So Al Smith, in 1928, was a stronger candidate than in 1924, since he had been elected Governor of New York for the fourth time in 1926 with an overwhelming (and deceptive) majority.

In recent years, the votes won in primaries, the preferences expressed in polls increase the availability of a candidate, but if primaries or polls cast doubt on his vote-getting capacity in his own state, the old rule still holds, a tradition that may rule out a candidate whose national strength may, for good and creditable reasons, not be fairly represented by his strength in his own state. A candidate may, for example, be something of a national hero for his opposition to a machine in his own state, but the machine's hostility or tepidity may chill the enthusiasm of the delegates all the same.[1]

Availability has other and more negative aspects. Lord Bryce devoted a famous chapter of *The American Commonwealth* to the question of why great men were not elected President. He was writing at a time when Gladstone and Salisbury were alive and when Disraeli was not long dead. He had not to consider the forces that produced some twentieth century British Prime Ministers. But the kind of excellence that, theoretically at any rate, makes a British politician a possible Prime Minister does not pay nearly so well in the United States. No congressional leader of the very first rank, save James Madison, has ever been elected President and apart from Polk, Garfield, McKinley and Truman no parliamentarians of the second rank either.[2] It is not accidental that great parliamentarians who sought the nomination after the modern Convention system developed, Webster, Clay, Calhoun and, after the Civil War and at a lower level, Blaine, Reed and Robert Taft either were not nominated or were defeated. For in Congress, it is often necessary to take a line; to choose sides. The leading congressional candidates

[1] A famous case on the other side was the failure of Tammany to prevent the nomination of Grover Cleveland in 1884. As General Bragg of Wisconsin said 'We love him for the enemies he has made.' But Cleveland barely carried New York all the same. Tammany was suspected of not having done its darndest.

[2] Mr. Truman was not elected from Congress to the presidency, but it was his senatorial reputation that made him a strong candidate for the vice-presidential nomination in 1944.

are almost certain to have angered some group, injured some interests, to be associated with some legislation or with opposition to some legislation that may, so the timid fear, cost many, many votes in a presidential election. Forceful leadership, whether in Congress or out of it, may be a serious handicap to a candidate for the nomination simply because the delegates think it may be a serious handicap with the voters. What many delegates want is another William McKinley:

> That respectable McKinley,
> The man without an angle or a tangle,

as Vachel Lindsay put it.

Of course, availability means one thing in a year when a party is certain of victory and another when the fight is expected to be close and when it may be more important to find a candidate who will win votes than one who will not lose them. But even so, parties have seldom plumped for the bold, aggressive, opinionated candidate when they could find something a little more safe and equally marketable. Franklin D. Roosevelt, when he was first nominated in 1932, was not expected to be an innovator or a daring pilot in extremity and no Republican candidate in this century, save Mr. Hoover and General Eisenhower, came to the Convention with a generally accepted national reputation and neither of these had a political reputation.[1]

There are minor laws of availability which are still valid, although they may be losing their force. After the defeat of Governor Smith in 1928 it is unlikely that a Catholic will be nominated in the foreseeable future and *a fortiori* a Jew or a Negro is ruled out on the simple grounds that such a nomination would alienate more voters than it could possibly gain. The same consideration rules out the nomination of a woman who would probably lose more female votes than she would gain male.[2]

---

[1] Theodore Roosevelt was in the White House, having succeeded as Vice-President, when he was a candidate in 1904. He could not, as President in office, have been beaten for the nomination, but he did, to some extent, pull his punches until he had been nominated and elected for a term in his own right.

[2] The anti-Catholic feeling which lies never far below the surface in America, will be a handicap to the presidential ambitions of Senator

There are, of course, more specific forms of availability than being a male Gentile, White, Protestant from a large and doubtful state. In this century, there is no doubt what office provides the best springboard for a presidential candidate. It is being or having been (being is much better), Governor of a large, doubtful state, especially the State of New York.[1] The Governor's mansion in state capitals is far more the natural habitat of a future President or presidential candidate than is the Senate or any other public office. Indeed only one member of Congress has been nominated in this century, Senator Harding in 1920.[2]

The reasons for the popularity of Governors as candidates are of two kinds. First of all, a Governor is an administrative officer, so is the President. It is a perfectly reasonable argument that the experience of running a large state, dealing with the legislature. with the public employees, with the manifold daily and often unforeseeable problems that pass over a Governor's desk, is a better training for the White House than any that can be acquired, even by the most hard-working and zealous Senator or cabinet officer. The governorship of a great state is the presidency in miniature or something near it. This is especially true in states like New York where the state machinery is reasonably well articulated and the Governor, though not even relatively as powerful as the President, has yet very great powers.[3]

McCarthy assuming that he has any or that he develops any. The fact that he is a Catholic *Republican* will also hurt him since the American people is traditional in such matters. See p. 97 *et sqq.*, and p. 252.

[1] For technical reasons for the predominance of New York see p. 226.

[2] Of the ten persons who have held the office of President in this century, five have been former Governors (one of them, McKinley, with a long congressional record as well). Former Governors have occupied the White House for thirty-eight years. No President, not a former Governor, has been twice elected. Much the same result is obtained by listing the defeated candidates. There has been only one election (1908) in which neither of the main candidates was a Governor or former Governor.

[3] Of course many Senators have been Governors and have thus a double qualification. On paper, that is to say, Senator Bricker, as an ex-Governor, was better qualified than was Senator Taft who had never held any executive office.

There is, in practice, a more compelling political argument. The Governor of a great state, if he is ambitious, has far greater opportunities to create a body of zealous and interested supporters than has a Senator or cabinet officer. (Every President except Mr. Eisenhower elected in this century has been either a serving or former Senator, Governor or cabinet officer.) It is true that the power of independent action in the states has steadily declined all through this century, but the functions and the budget of the states and so the number of employees has greatly increased. So has the power of the Governor to help or harass cities, counties, individuals and institutions. He is, at any rate in some states, a dispenser of patronage of the same type as is the President. Even where elaborate civil service regulations exist, the higher echelons of the state service are his to command. He can not only fill the big jobs, he can use, for his own political purposes, the services of some, at any rate, of the job-holders.[1] Moreover, the duties of these state officials can be carried out in ways that, without being in any way scandalous, can yet make friends and influence people for the benefit of the political ambitions of the Governor. Thus labour can be conciliated by an efficient and generous administration of workmen's compensation; business can be won by an efficient tax system, or at any rate by a tax system that suits business interests.[2]

A cabinet officer or a Senator cannot compete with this. A Secretary of the Interior may be powerful all over the Far West; a Secretary of Agriculture all over the Middle West; but that power is not concentrated in one area—and it is held at the will of the President. A Senator, if his party is in power, has an important share in federal patronage in his state, but he shares it with the other Senator (if of the same party) and with Congressmen and other federal politicians. No Senator, today, can hope to have the

[1] 'In 1946, for example, Alger B. Chapman, chairman of the New York State Tax Commission, resigned that job to run Dewey's campaign for re-election as governor. . . . As soon as Mr. Dewey was re-elected, however, Chapman was reappointed to his old post. . . . Some might consider his original resignation a subterfuge.' Warren Moscow, *Politics in the Empire State* (1948), p. 68.

[2] Other departments appear to have possibilities, thus the Commissioner of Agriculture and Markets in New York, according to Mr. Moscow, licenses 'stallions, bulls and dairymen'. (Op. cit., p. 190.)

complete control of his state that an effective Governor has. Before
the direct election of Senators he often could. Indeed, if he were an
ambitious man, he *had* to control the state to control the legislature
which sent him to Washington. But there are no modern instances
of a Senator with the power of an Aldrich or a Platt except, possibly,
in one or two southern states, notably Virginia.

A presidential candidate who is a Governor comes to the Convention with great advantages. He has given proof of a state-wide
appeal like that which is needed to win a presidential election and
he has the political resources of his state at his command.[1]

The rules of availability are, however, wide enough for it to be
customary for a Convention to start with several candidates who
are highly available and who refuse to give way to each other. Each
of them is a 'favourite son' (though he may be more of a favourite
in other states than his own). Each has secured support from other
states whose delegates have been instructed by a primary, or by a
state convention, or by their leaders to vote for such-and-such a
candidate until he 'releases' them or their leaders 'release' them,
which normally means lead them into another camp. If one candidate arrives with something near a majority, it is in his interest to
rush the voting, to make such a demonstration of strength that the
other alliances will surrender or melt away.[2]

[1] The fact that Senator Taft was so formidable a presidential possibility
in 1952 was not only due to his great abilities, to the record he had made
in Congress, to his industry and party loyalty. He gained also from the
fact that the last Republican Governor of Ohio was his junior colleague
in the Senate and that the Governor was a Democrat, Mr. Frank Lausche,
with whom Mr. Taft was supposed to be on excellent terms. He also
gained from the fact that the two most 'available' Governors, Mr.
Dewey in New York and Mr. Warren in California, had been defeated
together in the disastrous election of 1948 which Republicans had thought
to be a certainty.

[2] Until 1940, the Democratic Conventions worked under the 'two-
thirds rule'; a candidate could not be nominated if he had not got
two-thirds of the delegates on his side. This rule prevented the nomination of Martin Van Buren in 1844 and had helped to produce the deadlock of 1924. It had prevented, too, the rush nomination of Franklin D.
Roosevelt in 1932 and it was he who secured its abrogation in 1936. Its
chief importance, however, was not in its effect on individual fortunes,
but that it gave the South what amounted to a veto on the presidential

It is equally the interest of the other leading candidates to see that the position is *not* carried at one rush, that the delegates from states with no candidate, or no available candidate, are not tempted to jump on the bandwagon. Convention history is full of delaying actions that, many hold, prevented the nomination of the first favourite, one beneficiary of such tactics being Abraham Lincoln and another Woodrow Wilson. For this reason, the 'organization' of the Convention is often as important an indication of how the Convention will decide as the first balloting for candidates. It may even help to decide the balloting, for the 'Committee on Credentials' decides between contesting delegations and the permanent Chairman, if he is a good, adroit and resolute parliamentarian, may aid the side he favours or, by being genuinely neutral, give the Convention time to think more than once and so give other candidates time to overtake the favourite. For it must be remembered that there is little or no permanent organization of the national party except when it is a question of nominating a President in office, or when a President in office goes all out for his nominee as Theodore Roosevelt did for William Howard Taft in 1908.

It is while these first skirmishes are being fought, skirmishes which may prove to be, in fact, the decisive battle, that the leaders of the main candidates go out hunting for votes. Of course they have been out for them for months, possibly for years before. Mr. Farley set out collecting votes for Franklin D. Roosevelt early in 1930 for the Convention of 1932. But if any candidate had collected enough, the Convention would be a walkover and it seldom is.

Again there is much legend about the methods used to influence delegates. With one exception,[1] the stories do not, as a rule, suggest that money passes. But the candidates' managers, without believing or at any rate asserting that every man has his price, do act on the assumption that

> Every man hath business and desire
> Such as it is.

---

nominations of the Democratic party. Some of the restiveness of the South in recent years has been due to the resentment of the loss of this veto power and to the discovery that a Democratic President can be elected without the support of the 'Solid South'.

[1] See p. 229.

Some local leaders are promised jobs; others are promised support in their local campaigns; others are promised forgiveness for not having joined the 'winning' side sooner, or politely threatened with the consequences of delaying their rally to the certain victor. If they join now, they will share in the honour, the power and the spoils. Cassius is always present at a Convention telling the hesitant that:

> Your voice shall be as strong as any man's
> In the disposing of new dignities.

But the doubtful delegate or delegation must first answer the question:

> Will you be prick'd in number of our friends
> Or shall we on and not depend on you?

And if that is the answer, then the risks and penalties will have to be accepted.[1] Despite the risks and penalties, there are plenty of cases of devoted supporters sticking to their candidate when all was lost, as did the Smith supporters in 1932 and the Taft supporters in 1952. But in general, the attitude is based on the old maxim 'if you can't beat 'em, jine 'em'. It is not only desirable to have credit in the White House if the party wins, it may be dangerous to local party control if the party leaders in command at the Convention can be taxed with backing a loser by a faction that wanted to back a winner.

But the delegates' difficulty is that it may be uncertain who is to be the winner. For in politics, as in racing, many sure things come unstuck and the decision in the Convention may depend on a series of negotiations going on all over the Convention city at the same time; a bargain may be clinched at just the wrong moment; a deal be refused just before the news that makes the deal essential, arrives. Rumours fly from hotel to hôtel, from bar to bar, from the floor of the Convention hall to the committee rooms and back again. It is easy to make a post-mortem of almost any Convention and point

---

[1] Mr. Farley is supposed to have kept a list of applicants for jobs who were entitled to the magic initials 'FRBC', 'For Roosevelt before Chicago'. Then came those who were for Roosevelt *at* Chicago and then those, in outer darkness, who had not provided any part of the necessary two-thirds majority.

out the errors that lost the nomination for a highly favoured candidate or permitted the victory of a candidate who might have been
defeated if his rivals could have got together. But what was missing,
at the time, was just this post-mortem knowledge. Candidates have
been blamed for holding out too long, but it was because Wilson
did not yield to the panic that overtook his nervous manager,
McCombs, that he was nominated. Candidates have been blamed
for not co-operating more speedily and warmly in movements to
'stop' somebody or other, thus Al Smith was reproached with
wrecking the plans of the 'Stop Roosevelt' forces in 1932 and Mr.
Stassen with wrecking the plans of the 'Stop Dewey' forces in
1948. But in all probability, neither Al Smith nor Mr. Stassen was
much interested in a mere stopping of a rival which did not directly
redound to his own benefit.

The delegates, the press, the spectators in the galleries know that
a great deal is going on which does not appear on the Convention
floor and the faces of leaders are scrutinized with the zeal of Roman
augurs watching the flight of birds for clues to what is going on.
Often, of course, the leaders don't know. It is not, indeed, till a
decisive delegation throws its strength to the favourite son of
another state that the omens are clear and the stampede to the
victor begins. It was the switch of the California delegation to
Governor Roosevelt in 1932, the switch of the Pennsylvania delegation to Governor Dewey in 1948 that convinced the experts that
the game was up.

It must not be thought (although the theory is very popular in
America) that nothing done on the floor of the Convention really
affects the result. So much of the ritual is both meaningless and now
purposeless that it is tempting to write the whole show off as a
mere show. Of course, a great deal of Convention oratory is
delivered simply as ritual. Many speeches are specimens of 'rich
badness' in oratory that should (and often do) drive the delegates
off the floor in swarms. Not even in a big formal debate in Congress
are the organ stops of the old-style rhetoric pulled out more noisily,
the *vox humana* more abused. But some very good speeches have
been made at Conventions in support of candidates and in support
of policies. Sometimes the speeches had unforeseen results. Horatio
Seymour in 1868; James A. Garfield in 1880; Adlai E. Stevenson are

all examples of delegates and speakers who were not candidates, finding themselves candidates against their will. The speech made by Franklin D. Roosevelt nominating 'the Happy Warrior', Al Smith, did not win the nomination for Governor Smith, but it brought Roosevelt back into politics. Robert M. Ingersoll's speech nominating Blaine, in 1876, gave that ambiguous politician the not very appropriate title of 'the Plumed Knight' to offset the name later conferred on him by his enemies of 'the tattooed Man'. And the most famous Convention speech, that of William Jennings Bryan in 1896, not only won him the nomination, but contributed the famous slogan 'You shall not crucify mankind upon a cross of gold' to the American political anthology.

But the delegates are more than an audience; they are actors as well as patients, for they have to cheer, shout, march, even sing in order to impress on the other delegations their firmness of purpose. They also wish to impress the galleries and, through them, the real audience, the millions of voters who now can not only read about the proceedings but, mixed blessing for old political habits, can both see and hear them.

It is traditional for the delegations supporting a candidate to burst into uproarious applause when the candidate's name is finally announced, to leave their seats and march through the hall in a fashion recalling a great college football game. Elderly, dignified, weary politicians have to do their share in this ritual, however unlikely it may seem that they are in any marching or cheering mood.[1] The purpose of the long and noisy demonstrations of devotion at the Conventions is an aspect of the basic character of the Convention, its necessary limitations as the forum of the national political system. In any hotly contested campaign for the nomination, it is necessary to convince the neutrals or the waverers that Pelissippia is really behind her favourite son and that the allied

[1] Mr. Farley notes the surprise with which he saw at the Convention in 1940 'the austere, impeccable Under Secretary of State, Sumner Welles, jogging along. I could have been no more surprised if General MacArthur had trotted by in full dress uniform. Welles's creased trousers were getting a collection of wrinkles and his collar was wilting. He was going through the motions, but his wan smile was ample evidence that he wasn't really enjoying himself.' *Jim Farley's Story* (1948), pp. 279–80.

states are not using him as a mere stalking horse. Since one of the factors making for availability is just the power to inspire enthusiasm and devotion, it is important to show that the job has already been done for a sizeable number of states and voters. The parades, the waving of banners, the shouting of slogans and jingles[1] and all the other circus trappings have two objects to give the impression that the devotion of the supporters of Mr. X is like that of the Tenth Legion for Caesar or the Old Guard for Napoleon and to show that a candidate who has inspired such loyalty, is capable of winning it from the electorate, the millions of final customers outside the Convention hall.

The symbols are not necessarily all on view in the Convention hall. They are also visible, ostentatiously visible at the headquarters. It may be a gigantic portrait of the hero, like the long banner bearing General MacArthur's picture that was draped in the hall of the Bellevue-Stratford hotel in Philadelphia in 1948, or the immense inflated rubber elephant that was the emblem not only of the Grand Old Party but of Senator Taft, its true, uncompromising representative.[2] By every standard, the most famous and effectual emblem ever used in a Convention were the wooden rails brought into the Illinois Republican Convention at Decatur in 1860 which, it was asserted, had been split by Abraham Lincoln. These may not have given him the nomination but they gave him the name, 'the rail splitter'.[3]

[1] I have borrowed a term from modern radio and television advertising to describe the little verses that have been used to win acceptance for a candidate. I do not know what importance to attach to the fact that the two most celebrated jingles,

He comes from Appomattox and its famous apple tree
and
You gotta quit kicking my dawg aroun',

were both used on behalf of unsuccessful candidates, Grant in 1880 and Champ Clark in 1912.

[2] General MacArthur got a humiliating handful of votes when he was nominated and Senator Taft's elephant collapsed before the voting began, an event that might have made a Roman murmur, *absit omen*. Some cynics suggested that a Democrat had stuck a pin into it.

[3] A banner was stretched between the two rails with the legend 'Abraham Lincoln The Rail Candidate for President in 1860'. Benjamin

But it is the cheering and marching of the supporters of the candidate that is the oddest feature of the ritual. When parades were a part of the presidential campaign, there may have been something to be said for forcing middle-aged and overweight delegates to march round and round what is usually a desperately over-heated hall; if they can march like this in the summer, they will do better in the cool weather of the Fall. But 'motorcades' have replaced the old torch-light processions and the ability to march no longer counts. Nor is the ritual of cheering when the candidate's name is finally announced (by tradition it must be the last word of the nominating speech) now a very convincing proof of popular support. It may be a little more convincing than the applause of the *claque* in a Paris theatre or the laughter of the audience in a radio show, but that is about all. As far as this ritual has any utility it gives an advantage to a leading candidate who is nominated late. His partisans know what target to shoot at.[1]

It is not only the delegates who take part in this ritual of conversion by noise. The spectators do, too. It has long been thought that the degree of warmth shown by the spectators affects the delegates and so candidates do their best to see that their supporters are on hand in the galleries to support the efforts of the delegates on the floor. Thus in 1860, the rumour that the Seward managers were packing the 'Wigwam' with loyal and loud supporters from New York, led the Lincoln managers to issue a large supply of forged tickets and take up all vacant places in the galleries before the Seward men had recovered from their debauches. To have the Convention in your home town is supposed to be an advantage,

---

P. Thomas, *Abraham Lincoln* (1952), p. 206. Professor Thomas points out that the rest of the information given was erroneous. The public memory has transferred the episode of the rails from the state convention at Decatur to the National Convention at Chicago.

[1] In 1912, 'the Wilson men were determined to out-shout the Clark supporters; and at 3.15 the Wilson noise had exceeded the length of the Clark demonstration. At 3.20 Chairman James had almost brought order out of the chaos when some Wilson man sounded an electric horn and the bedlam broke out again'. Arthur S. Link, *Wilson The Road to the White House* (1947), p. 447. The zeal of the supporters of 'the scholar in politics' is all the more remarkable when it is realized that this demonstration, which lasted one hour and fifteen minutes, began at 3.20 a.m.!

although there are some who think that the practical unanimity of the spectators in Madison Square Garden for 'Al' Smith, in 1924, alienated more waverers, already afraid of Tammany, than it impressed. At the last nomination of F. D. Roosevelt, the stentorian voice of one of the agents of Mayor Kelly's machine, calling for spontaneous outbursts of enthusiasm, was unfortunately magnified to inhuman proportions by some fault in the public address system, to the merriment of the delegates. But as these demonstrations have hardened into rituals, they have lost much of their effect and it is reasonable to suppose and hope that they are on the way out.[1]

Sometimes the enthusiasm at the Convention is both genuine and a real force. Probably the most passionate manifestations of devotion to a candidate, in modern times, were those poured out by the supporters of Theodore Roosevelt in 1912, both at the Republican Convention that did not nominate him and at the Progressive Convention that did. The Roosevelt delegates were filled with a passionate conviction that their hero was the necessary man, the new Samson who had been shorn by treacherous Delilahs like Taft and Elihu Root. They believed that they did 'stand at Armageddon and battle for the Lord'.[2] The fact that experienced politicians, for the

[1] The theatrical aspects of the Conventions sometimes take odd forms. At the Republican Convention of 1948, I descended to the underworld of the Convention hall in Philadelphia and found, to my surprise, a full pipe band waiting to go on. There was, as far as I knew, no notably Caledonian candidate in the running so I asked what candidate the band was supporting. The Pipe Major, in a very pure Glasgow accent, told me it was Mr. Stassen. He seemed to know no more. His second in command was more vocal and I asked him how long he had been active in American politics. He replied, in an equally pure accent 'Me? I only cam' aff the boat a fortnight ago.' Since Mr. Stassen is, I believe, of pure Scandinavian descent, I can only assume that the pipers were called on to prove his devotion to economy. As any student of American advertising knows, tartan is the symbol for thrift.

[2] There were irreverent people who made fun of this, the most famous Convention slogan of modern times. The *New York Sun* found in it material for jeering wit. 'In spite of some hesitancies of pronunciation the brethren got a holy joy out of "Armageddon". There is a mystic wonderful charm to it; it is like "Abracadabra" or "parallelopidon", a word of might with magic in the vowels and the bowels of it. Seth Bullock believes it to be a township in Oklahoma. The Hon. Angelo Perkins is positive that it is Welsh. Medill McCormick holds that it was

most part, saw no future in the movement, saw it as a revolt, not a
revolution, only excited the passion and devotion of the faithful
all the more. To the tune of 'Onward Christian Soldiers', sung
with equal fervour by Jew and Gentile, the faithful followed their
leaders, politically speaking, down a steep place.[1]

Even when a Convention can have hardly any hope that it is
nominating a winner, or when the nomination is decided long
before it meets (as when President in office is a candidate or one
candidate leads all the rest as Mr. Hoover did in 1928), the ritual
must be gone through. For a Convention needs a subsidy and the
city which plays host must recoup the money put up by the
municipality, in special terms for the hire of an auditorium, and
by the local business and hotel interests in direct subsidy. A Convention must last three days, and usually lasts four. If it lasts more,
as in the interminable Democratic roughhouse of 1924, the long-
drawn-out battle royal not only bores or angers the voters, it
nearly ruins the delegates, most of whom are poor men and women
and many of whom pay all their own expenses. It may be questioned
whether a convention is any longer a great spending spree, that is
whether a city gains much by playing host.[2] The delegates gain

---

an early skirmish in the Revolution.' Mark Sullivan, *Our Times The
United States 1900–1925* (1932), IV, p. 509.

[1] Perhaps the Democratic party at the Philadelphia Convention of
1936 was equally starry-eyed. But Franklin D. Roosevelt was President,
had only a faint quiver of opposition in the party, not to fear, hardly to
note, had all the working politicians on his side, and was sure of re-
election. Fervour in fact of such demonstrated miraculous power as
FDR's was natural enough. But Theodore Roosevelt was out of office,
his was a doubtful if not a forlorn hope, and yet the fervour was as great.
It was demonstrated or parodied by a handbill put in circulation 'At
Three o'clock Thursday afternoon Theodore Roosevelt Will Walk on
the Waters of Lake Michigan.' Mr. Mark Sullivan, who prints a
facsimile (op. cit., p. 511) is not absolutely decided whether this came
from friend or foe, or when it was circulated. It is pretty obviously the
work of a hostile humorist. The same device was used to deflate General
MacArthur on his joyous entry into New York after his recall by
President Truman in 1951.

[2] I was told by a barman in Philadelphia, that the Republicans spent
little, the Democrats not much more and that neither was a patch, from
a commercial point of view, on the Elks or the American Legion.

little by playing guest except an honour and an excuse to get away from the home town. They suffer in more than their pockets. For Conventions are held in high midsummer and usually in places with deplorable summer climates, Chicago, Kansas City, Philadelphia. Only once in modern times has a Convention been held in a tolerable spot, the Democratic Convention of 1920 which was held in San Francisco and which connoisseurs recall as a Capua or a 'pleasant isle of Avès' compared with the furnaces in which other Conventions have been held. It is impossible to estimate how many nominations (especially of Vice-Presidents) have been made because of the heat. One Convention is very like another in its climatic tortures and the description of a Convention in 1948 would fit most. 'From floor to ceiling, in tight rows, there are men in white shirts and women in cotton dresses. It is hot: it is stifling, sticky, moist hot, all the time. Fans in the upper corners of the stadium stir the hanging flags, and there is an unceasing flutter of folded newspapers from the galleries and the seething floor, but little can be done to relieve the heat. A man can take off his tie, but the back of his shirt will be stained with sweat from shoulder blades to waist. A woman can dab at her face with a damp handkerchief, but she will be red and shiny and wisps of hair will stick to her forehead and neck.'[1] What heat and financial stringency did not do to shorten the rituals of the Convention, television threatens to do. As more and more of the ritual is performed for the remote worshippers (or, at any rate, spectators), the views of viewers and of television chains become of the first importance. Even in 1948 when the newest of the arts was in its first childhood, it was strongly rumoured at Philadelphia that the Republican high command was warned to get its act over, as the channels were required for the world championship fight between Joe Louis and Jersey Joe Walcott, an event that, it was thought, would eclipse the Conventions for many viewers.[2] But

---

[1] Robert Waithman, *America The Sun is High* (1952), p. 103.

[2] As soon as it was clear that Governor Dewey was going to be nominated, I took a cab to his hotel to see him emerge. As soon as he had done so, I took another and asked the driver to step on it as I wanted to be at the hall when the candidate arrived there. I got no answer, so I asked whether he didn't care who got nominated. (In Philadelphia as in other cities most drivers seem to be Democrats.) 'Me care? I don't even

while the ritual is gone through with, the party managers and, in recent times, the candidates themselves are trying, under increasing pressure, to make the right, the winning decisions. Until 1932, the candidates stayed away from the Conventions, except in the case when they were present as delegates, not as open candidates. But at that time, the candidate, when nominated, waited for a month or five weeks till he was duly notified of his nomination. Franklin D. Roosevelt stopped this foolery by flying to the Convention and accepting the nomination on the spot. Since that time candidates for the nomination have been, as a rule, their own managers (General MacArthur and General Eisenhower have been exceptions). If a deadlock threatens, if the leading candidates neither lose nor give ground, the management tends to pass from their hands into those of the party leaders not directly involved who look for a compromise candidate, a 'dark horse'.

Again, popular legend has exaggerated both the importance of dark horse nominations and the darkness of some of those who have been so named. The first 'dark horse', James K. Polk, had been Speaker of the House of Representatives and became a good and historically important President. Even such drab specimens as Franklin Pierce and James Buchanan, Rutherford B. Hayes and Benjamin Harrison had, in different ways, a high degree of availability. The only really dark horse was Warren G. Harding in 1920 and his Administration was so scandalous and his unfitness so manifest that his nomination has cast a backward shadow over American presidential history. But the case of Harding was exceptional. The three chief competitors, General Leonard Wood, Governor Lowden, Senator Hiram Johnson, were, for various reasons, each strong enough to cancel out the others, but each had handicaps which they could not overcome. Moreover, the election was rightly regarded as a certain Republican triumph. The party could win with anybody and the party was controlled by a senatorial group, co-operating with some important state bosses, that wanted to do more than elect a Republican President; they wanted to elect a highly controllable President. They were the same men

---

care about Joe Louis.' This competition between politics and boxing was foreseen by the authors of *Of Thee I Sing*.

who had preferred defeat with Taft (and control of the party) to victory with Theodore Roosevelt in 1912, who had reluctantly accepted Hughes in 1916 and saw him lose, and who now wanted a docile winner. The deadlock gave them their chance and what was probably the most mediocre of candidates was duly chosen.[1]

If the nomination of Warren Gamaliel Harding marked the lowest ebb of a Convention's sense of responsibility, other Conventions have done odd things. It was odd for the Liberals and the Democrats to nominate Horace Greeley in 1872 to overthrow the discredited Grant Administration, but the Liberals who imposed him on the Democrats were amateurs and reformers. Fortunately for Greeley and, probably, for the United States, he was beaten, and died broken-hearted a few weeks after his defeat. It was odd for the Democrats, in 1896, to nominate a young ex-Congressman on the strength of one oration, and renounce the Democratic President then in the White House. But the Democrats in 1896 did represent a movement of passion and despair, the last great farmers' revolt:

> And all these in their helpless days
> By the dour East oppressed,
> Mean paternalism,
> Making their mistakes for them,
> Crucifying half the West,
> Till the whole Atlantic coast
> Seemed a giant spider's nest.[2]

[1] A witness who, if not as important an actor in this affair as he claimed to be, had yet a ringside seat, put the reasons for the choice of Harding fairly candidly. ' "There was", said Harvey afterwards, "no popular explosion for Harding. There was little spontaneity. He was nominated because there was nothing against him, and because the delegates wanted to go home. The delegates had become convinced that neither Wood nor Lowden could be or ought to be nominated, and they could not see anybody who would serve better as a candidate than Harding. There was no compromise about the matter. It was a fresh selection of the man *whom the delegates considered the best in sight*." ' (Italics mine.) Willis Fletcher Johnson, *George Harvey* (1930), p. 278. The words italicized are, of course, at best a rationalization. Harding was only the 'best in sight' in the terms in which his backers interpreted 'best'.

[2] Vachel Lindsay, *Collected Poems* (1925): 'Bryan, Bryan, Bryan, Bryan.' (The Macmillan Company, New York.)

That spirit of revolt (it was in fact only a *jacquerie*) found its golden voice in Bryan. No one else would have suited that mood.

But it was much odder for the Republican Convention, in 1940, to throw over recognized leaders like Mr. Taft and Mr. Dewey in favour of a businessman, only a few months in politics, only recently a Republican. A nomination like that of Wendell Willkie would have been more in the Democratic tradition;[1] a revolt of the amateurs was the last thing to be expected among the Republicans. But (and here the advantages of the Convention system were made manifest), since the delegates had been chosen, since Senator Taft and Mr. Dewey had taken their stand, Hitler had swept over Denmark, Norway, the Low Countries, France. A great crisis was at hand, and the doctrines and dogmas of a few weeks before seemed irrelevant. An amateur, like Willkie, could meet the crisis in a way the professionals could not or, at any rate, did not. And the Convention could meet the crisis, too, in a way a body tied to primary instructions would have been unable to do. The decision of the Republican Convention in 1940 was, in fact, very like the revolt of the Conservative stalwarts in the House of Commons a few weeks before, the revolt that brought down the Chamberlain government—another proof of the parliamentary character of the Convention system.

But if the Convention system seldom goes as far astray in nominating presidential candidates as has been suggested by many critics, the same cannot be said of the way in which it carries out two other functions both formally important, and one of which may turn out to be practically important. For the Convention has to nominate

[1] It is an accepted law of politics that the two Conventions differ deeply in their psychology. In 1932, Mr. Arthur Krock wrote, 'Democrats are excitable, difficult to lead, idealistic and reckless when in convention assembled. History demonstrates that they would rather fight among themselves than with the enemy. When Republican delegations are released from their home instructions, they go to their bosses. When Democratic delegations are released, they go to pieces.' Quoted in Edward McChesney Sait, *American Parties and Elections* (Third edition, 1942), p. 556. I can remember complaining to Mr. H. L. Mencken, at the Democratic Convention of 1948, of its dullness. 'Don't worry; it's a Democratic Convention. Hell will break loose somehow.' It did, over the platform, not over the candidate (Mr. Truman).

a Vice-President and to approve or amend a platform drawn up by one of its committees.

The office of Vice-President may be very important indeed, for, as is often being said (usually with real or simulated apprehension), 'to think that only a heart-beat stands between X and the White House!' It has normally no other importance. For apart from a few honorific duties, the Vice-President has nothing to do but preside over the Senate, occasionally give a casting vote, and ponder the question of the President's health. The emptiness of the office is an old story. The first Vice-President, John Adams, one of the greatest Americans of the revolutionary age, noted his impotence with disgust. 'I am very apprehensive that a desperate anti-federal party will provoke all Europe by their insolence. But my country has in its wisdom contrived for me the most insignificant office that ever the invention of man contrived or his imagination conceived.'[1] It is not surprising that such an office should have acquired a semi-comic aspect. There is a corpus of stories designed to illustrate both the obscurity of the office and the comparable obscurity of its holders. Alexander Throttlebottom, in the musical comedy *Of Thee I Sing*, anxious about the indignity of the office, is assured that in three months he will forget that he holds it, so there is no reason to worry about his mother's finding out. And the office has been deliberately pressed on at least one politician to reduce him to obscurity and silence. For although the motives that led to the nomination of Theodore Roosevelt for the vice-presidency in 1900 were mixed, among them was the desire to 'see Theodore Roosevelt take the veil', even if the desire to thwart Mark Hanna was a greater one.

Of course, there have always been plenty of politicians anxious for the job, even if the thought of a possible reversion never entered their minds. It is well paid.[2] The duties, if boring, are not laborious. It enables a politician to stay on in Washington and, if he has been an important member of either house, his parliamentary knowledge, skill and influence may be transmuted into something like power. Nor can it be said that the seven Vice-Presidents who

[1] *The Works of John Adams* (1856), vol. 1, p. 460.
[2] $30,000 a year plus $10,000 for expenses.

have succeeded to the office of President[1] have been notably inferior to any but the greatest of the elected Presidents. One of them (also the first to be elected President to succeed himself) Theodore Roosevelt, ranks very high in the second class of Presidents, and Mr. Truman, whatever the final verdict on his administrations may be, has played a role of the first importance in world history.

Nevertheless, the way in which the vice-presidential candidate is chosen is highly unsatisfactory. Usually he is chosen as part of a bargain involving the nomination of the presidential candidate. Thus, it is believed that, in 1932, the choice of Speaker Garner for the vice-presidency was the price of the shift of the Texas and (much more important) of the California vote to Franklin D. Roosevelt. At other times, a vice-presidential candidate has been chosen to placate a section of the party highly disgruntled over the presidential nomination, thus risking a political upheaval if the President dies, as happened when Garfield was assassinated in 1881 and was succeeded by the 'Stalwart' Arthur. Sometimes the vice-presidential nominee has been a candidate for the presidential nomination, as was Governor Coolidge in 1920 and Governor Bricker in 1944. But he is seldom a candidate who has much real chance of the nomination, seldom, at that time, a presidential possibility of the first order. It took, it is believed, a good deal of pressure to get Governor Warren of California to run on the ticket with Governor Dewey in 1948, for Governor Warren, as an immensely popular Governor of California, was a politician of Governor Dewey's own rank.

Sometimes, the Convention shows some spark of spirit; weary, and perhaps sulky, it revolts as it did in 1920 when, having swallowed Harding, the Republican Convention balked at Irving Lenroot and, to the astonishment of the bosses, nominated Calvin Coolidge. But however lucky the United States has been, the Conventions show their irresponsibility most clearly in their vice-presidential

---

[1] According to an ingenious and plausible argument by Mr. Horwill, the Vice-President becomes President on the death of the incumbent, not by law, but by usage. He is still legally Vice-President 'acting as President'. The office he leaves vacant is that of 'President of the Senate'. H. W. Horwill, *The Usages of the American Constitution* (1925), pp. 58 ff.

nominations. Neither the Conventions nor, it is to be feared, the voters, show any active interest in the fact that they may be electing a President *and* his successor. Not infrequently, the candidate for the vice-presidency is older than the candidate for the presidency.[1] Nor has fitness always been considered. Would the independents who voted for Cleveland have been pleased by Hendricks had he come to the White House? (He died as Vice-President.) Would the Republicans who barely swallowed Blaine have swallowed 'Black Jack' Logan?[2] In fact, voters, even if the vice-presidential candidate really strengthens the ticket (as he is supposed to do), seldom think of him as a possible President, though there is a respectable statistical possibility that he may be.[3] And while a first-term Vice-President need not be less well equipped for the presidency than is the President in *his* first term, he usually is so, as he is usually a politician of less eminence. More than that, he is not briefed as is a President-elect, and he may, without any notice, find himself faced with the most world-shaking decisions without any preparation at all.[4]

Yet it is unlikely that anything will be done to improve the system of nominating candidates for the vice-presidency. This consolation prize will be used as a consolation prize; this plaster will be

[1] In 1896, the Democratic nominee, Arthur Sewall, was eighty-one, the presidential candidate, Bryan, was just over thirty-six. Sewall lived, it must be admitted, until 1900.

[2] The team of Blaine and Logan was probably the worst assorted in American history. In 1940 Wendell Willkie and Senator McNary had never met before the Convention. Blaine and Logan had—and detested each other. As the poet put it (in the mouth of Logan):

> We never speak as we pass by,
> Me to Jim Blaine nor him to I.

> David Saville Muzzey, *James G. Blaine* (1935), p. 307.

[3] The Republicans in 1944 tried, more or less *sub rosa*, to make something of Roosevelt's ill-health and asked in quite loud whispers, 'Do you want Truman for President?' But although the probability of Roosevelt's dying in his fourth term was very openly talked of in Washington and elsewhere in 1944, it did not, as far as I could judge, affect the decision of the average elector. He was used to thinking of the vice-presidency as of little importance.

[4] Mr. Churchill has expressed his surprise that so little had been done to prepare Mr. Truman for the decisions that he alone could make, should he succeed to the presidency.

applied to bleeding egos; this near sinecure will be given to deserving veterans. The office held by John Adams and Thomas Jefferson, by John C. Calhoun, by Martin Van Buren and Theodore Roosevelt (to name only the dead) is also the office held by Daniel D. Tompkins, Henry Wilson, Garett Hobart and the lively and amorous Richard M. Johnson, *dauphins* whose reigns history knows nothing of.[1]

Nor can much more be said for the role of the Conventions as drafters or acceptors of platforms. These documents have, at times, been important. The exact implication of the Republican platforms of 1856 and 1860 was one of the 'war guilt' questions of the time and since. The Republican platform of 1920 was a masterpiece of ambiguity, drafted as it was to secure the votes of both those who wanted the United States to enter a reformed League of Nations and of those who wished to stay out.[2] The character of the platform has been described by the wit who said it was 'something to stand on but not to run on'. It consists, as a rule, of generalities, of appeal to the patron saints of the party (Lincoln, Theodore Roosevelt being the chief Republican saints; Jefferson, Jackson and Franklin D. Roosevelt being the chief Democratic). If the party is in power it praises the Administration;[3] if it is in opposition, it denounces and deplores the crimes and follies which have brought the Republic to the edge of ruin. But it is usually far from concrete in its suggestions of how to remedy these evils, undo these mistakes. Occasionally, a party does come out firmly on one side of a controversial question. Thus the Democrats came out in 1896 for the free coinage of silver at 16 to 1. But the Republicans did not come out *against* silver; they were forced on to the gold standard by the magnificent show put

[1] For the presidential succession (after the Vice-President), see p. 423, *n*.

[2] The relevant section shows the pleasant art of ambiguity at its best: 'We pledge the coming Republican administration to make such agreements with the other nations of the world as shall meet the full duty of America to civilization and humanity, in accordance with American ideals, and without surrendering the right of the American people to exercise its judgment and its power in favor of justice and peace.' Kirk H. Porter, *National Party Platforms* (1924), p. 452.

[3] Except in 1896 when the Democrats firmly refused to endorse the 'gold bug' Administration of Grover Cleveland.

on by Bryan, and by the need to appeal to the rich eastern interests which alone could put up the funds to save gold. The Republicans were definitely for keeping the conquests of the Spanish war in 1900, but as a rule the Grand Old Party has been cautious, steering between the 'Scylla of "yes" and the Charybdis of "no" ', as Cardinal Newman put it. In 1932, it was not *quite* for Prohibition and not *quite* against it. The Democrats, after a lively Convention fight, were definitely against it. But the Democratic platform, at the same Convention, came out for rigorous economy in federal expenditure and was of a Rhadamantine severity in condemning the extravagance of the Hoover Administration.

Within a year or two it was necessary for the supporters of the Roosevelt Administration to explain or explain away or just forget the platform. The best effort at explaining away (and one that does put platforms into their true perspective) came from one of the few big businessmen who had stuck to FDR. It was Mr. Joseph Kennedy, soon to be Ambassador at the Court of St. James's, who found the formula. 'It is unintelligent to compare an administration's performance merely with a party platform on the theory that the platform represents a covenant between the candidate and those who voted for him. If a party programme were all that counted in an election, then people would vote solely on the programme and let each party committee select the Presidential candidate. But the party platform is only one of several factors which foreshadow the probable future action of the elected man.'[1] It is that at best!

It is hard to see what can be done to make platforms more realistic (they have become, in the last twenty years or so, at least a little shorter). For their vacuity reveals and illustrates the character of American parties, their necessary character. They are not quite identical bottles and there are some fluids that would be at home in one bottle, but look and taste odd in another. But ideologically coherent and distinct platforms must wait until ideologically coherent and distinct parties fight for the presidency. For that reason, the minor parties can produce far more impressive documents, such as the best platform since the Civil War, the Populist platform of

[1] Joseph P. Kennedy, *I'm For Roosevelt* (1936), p. 111.

1892.[1] For they can afford intellectual virtues since they do not hope to win.[2]

This is not to say that disputes over the content of the platform in the Conventions are quite meaningless. The defeat of the compromise 'civil rights' plank produced by the committee in the Democratic Convention of 1948, showed the readiness of the rank and file to defy the Southern bloc and let it leave if it wanted to. The insurgents won and some of the Southern delegates did leave and some of the Southern states went for the 'Dixiecrat' candidate. In so far as the insurgents forced the pace, they were justified by victory and by committing the national Democratic party to a radical platform on the burning question of enforcing racial equality by law. And, by their revolt, they demonstrated that a Convention, even if it is committed to supporting a President in office, can yet have a mind of its own as to what he is supposed to be in office for.[3]

But if little can be done to reform the habits of the Conventions in such matters as the nomination of candidates for the vice-presidency and the drafting of the platform, a good deal can be done to make the Conventions more efficient, that is, more representative bodies for the execution of their basic function—nominating a candidate for the presidency. The basic defect of the Convention system is the imperfectly representative character of the assembly. The delegates represent at least as much the wishes of political leaders, pressure groups, city, county and state 'machines' as they represent the wishes of the rank-and-file voters who may be expected to vote the party ticket in November. Still less do they represent the views or sentiments of the millions of uncommitted voters who, in recent elections at least, are believed to have been

[1] Its author was Ignatius Donnelly of Minnesota, also eminent as a Baconian and a writer on Atlantis.

[2] Thus the Independent Socialist League in 1952 could expose the emptiness of the capitalist party programmes, the treasonable evasions of the 'Stalinoids', the irrelevant mischief-making of contemporary Trotskyites; but not even the most devoted believers in these truths really expected to win a presidential election, at any rate in 1952.

[3] I was told by one of the minor rebels that they expected the Democrats to lose anyway, so why compromise with the South, why not make a record for use in 1952? Victory upset that calculation.

the decisive factor. The Conventions are (with the state legislatures) the least 'reformed' representative institutions in the American political system.[1]

The visible defects of the nominating systems in the states, the rumours of deals and betrayals, the apparent anomaly of choosing the most important candidate in a body that is very imperfectly representative, all have led to many proposals to adopt national primary systems, as a means of giving a mandate to the delegates or, in more extreme proposals, to abolish the Convention altogether.[2] In his first annual message to Congress, Woodrow Wilson recommended universal primaries and the abolition of the Conventions. Wilson, who gained the nomination in 1912 by an ingenious use of the distrust of the professional politicians, then wide-spread, and who had fought for the principle of the primary in New Jersey, was naturally biased in its favour. But the movement, after some early successes, fizzled out and in not extending the system of mandatory primaries to the choice of presidential candidates, the American people has shown good sense. For these proposals presuppose conditions that do not exist, the existence of a class of national leaders among whom the voters can easily make a choice. There may be no such candidates available and there is no institution to provide them—except the condemned and distrusted Conventions.

Professor P. Orman Ray, indeed, suggested an ingenious variation on the proposals for the extension of the primary system to the presidential election. He argued for 'a presidential primary which should follow the national conventions, and at which the voters would choose the party candidates for President and Vice-President from five or six names submitted by the Convention for President. The person getting the highest popular vote of the party would be the party candidate for President, and the second highest would be

[1] 'Delegates are chosen directly by the voters of a party in only fifteen states. In twenty-nine other states, the delegates are picked at state or district conventions within the separate states. In four states, the choice of delegates is made by the state executive committee or the state committee of the party.' Clayton Knowles, 'Voter is Far Removed in Nominating Process', in *The New York Times*, 24 February, 1952.

[2] This proposal, in its latest form, comes from Senator George A. Smathers of Florida, a decidedly conservative statesman.

the party candidate for Vice-President'.[1] This scheme is much less drastic and much more practicable than the root and branch proposals of President Wilson and Senator Smathers. It allots to the Conventions an important function, the creation of a panel from which the party members can choose. It is, in effect, a proposal to restore the 'Electoral Colleges' to real power, but inverting the time table. Instead of the members of the colleges choosing among candidates presented by the 'People', the People would choose among candidates presented by a national 'Electoral College'. But it suffers, like other proposals, from over-estimating the degree of unity of American national parties; it gives to membership in the national parties a degree of legal fixity that is probably undesirable.

A Convention might present candidates none of whom had any real national following. It may do so today, but it is forced to consider what it is doing by the fact that it must decide on some *one* candidate. To allow it the freedom of nominating six would be rash indeed. The double campaign, first among the nominees and then between the two chosen candidates would add to the pressure and the cost, if not to the duration, of the campaign. And unless the method of choosing delegates to the convention was changed at the same time, the struggles and intrigues of the present system would continue. A group of not very strong candidates might combine, even more easily than today, against the really popular candidate and the bewildered party electors be forced to choose among six candidates, none of whom appealed to more than a minor section of the party in the nation. This, also, may happen today, but the party has time to rally, wounds have time to heal, the candidate chosen has most of a formally united party behind him. And, possibly only a minor objection, the candidate for Vice-President might refuse to run. More than once in American history, a political figure who was perfectly ready, nay eager, to run for the presidency, has refused to run for the lesser office and this popularity contest might make such refusals even more common.

The limit of practicable reform seems to be the extension of the system of 'advisory' primaries to all the states and the election of

[1] Edward S. Corwin, *The President: Office and Powers, 1787–1948*, 3rd edition (1948), p. 397.

the delegates to the Convention at the same time. This system exists in some states already. In some others, the delegates to the Convention are pledged to the candidate for whom they run. But that pledge is inoperative if no candidate wins on the first ballots, for if the Convention cannot quickly make up its mind, delegates pledged to blind obedience to the preferences shown in the primary would lose all influence in the Convention, would, in fact, disqualify their states if the candidates to whom they had been pledged proved to have no chance of the nomination.

The most that can be done to make the Conventions more responsive to the opinion of the rank-and-file voter is to give him a chance to express that opinion, and a chance to choose delegates who are to express that opinion as far as is prudent and possible—and the limits of prudence and possibility are not known and cannot be known till the Convention meets.

No part of the mechanics of the Constitution reflects less credit on the predictive powers of its designers than the provision made for the choice of the President. He was to be chosen, not by the mass of the voters (like the House of Representatives) or by state legislatures (like the Senate), but by 'electoral colleges' chosen, in each state, as the legislature should provide.[1] This scheme had a double advantage. It prevented, it was thought, the dangers of successful demagoguery; it allowed the electors to take stock of the situation, not only in their own states but in the Union, and as it was thought to be improbable that the various electors would concentrate on one man (George Washington apart), elections would frequently be thrown into the House of Representatives. There each state had, for this purpose, one vote; the three top candidates among whom the states would have to choose would be, presumably, 'favourite sons' of the big states. The big states would nominate and the small states choose. The Electoral Colleges were to perform the functions of the then undreamed of party Conventions.

None of these expectations proved to be justified. Washington was unanimously elected twice, but the third election, that of 1796 between Adams and Jefferson, was fought on national party lines.

[1] There is commonly said to be 'an electoral college', but, in fact, the presidential electors meet only in their respective states and send their pre-ordained decision in writing to Washington.

No elector thought for a moment of exercising his free choice, and this part of the scheme was dead born. No elector since, save in 1820, has ever voted according to his own judgment.[1]

In the great dispute over the presidential election of 1876, when sober men feared a renewal of the Civil War and others a permanent distortion of the Constitution, one Republican elector, James Russell Lowell, was asked to vote for Tilden and thus break the deadlock in the electoral colleges. His reply in a letter to Leslie Stephen states the duties of an elector in unexceptionable terms. 'In my own judgment I have no choice, and am bound in honor to vote for Hayes, as the people who chose me expected me to do. *They did not choose me because they had confidence in my judgment, but because they thought they knew what my judgment would be.*'[2]

If the office of presidential elector makes its holder no more than a postman, why is it retained? Little, it is true, is thought of the office. Sometimes an eminent figure is made an elector in a vague hope that he will strengthen the ticket, show support of a possibly unpopular candidate. More often, it is a cheap honour given as a reward. (It may not be cheap to the recipient, who is expected to contribute to the campaign funds.) But there is no office in the American system where the contrast between formal and real power is greater, no office less sought for or more obscure.[3]

Obscure as is the office and perverted as is the institution, the electoral college system, as it has developed, has real, practical importance. The Constitution leaves every state free to determine

[1] In the second election of James Monroe, only one vote was cast against him in the 'era of good feelings'. This was given by William Plumer of New Hampshire who justified his breach of what was already a firm convention by saying that only Washington deserved the honour of an uncontested election. But 'both Plumer and his son were known to be hostile to Monroe, on personal grounds, and letters of both reveal their dislike.' W. P. Cresson, *James Monroe* (1946), p. 352.

[2] Horace Elisha Scudder, *James Russell Lowell* (1901), vol. II, pp. 216–7. The italics are mine. In the original scheme of the Constitution, it was Lowell's judgment that was supposed to be trusted.

[3] At least one state convention adjourned, totally forgetting to nominate presidential electors, an omission more or less regularly dealt with by the executive committee in an hotel bedroom at 3 a.m. It is not even certain that a presidential elector need be an American citizen.

how its electoral votes shall be cast. All that the Constitution provides is that the number shall be equal to that of the Representatives and Senators to which the state is entitled. Since every state is entitled to at least three under this system, the rural areas are over-represented, although not perhaps very seriously, in the electoral colleges.[1] Much more serious is the growth of the system whereby the electors are chosen by the voters of the state in one general election and the winners, by no matter how narrow a margin, take all the seats. It could happen that a President might be elected with a large majority of the popular vote against him, because he had carried, very narrowly, a majority of votes in the electoral colleges against a candidate with very large majorities in states casting just half the electoral votes. No President has been chosen with a large popular vote against him; but on two occasions the President has received fewer popular votes than his opponent (in 1876 and in 1888), and on others it was a very near thing. Thus Hughes was nearly elected as a minority President in 1916. And another weakness of the system, even when it does not affect the result, is the gross exaggeration in the electoral vote of a majority or even a plurality in the popular vote.[2] The ordinary maps showing the results of presidential elections are usually highly misleading, giving an impression of solid blocks of 'safe' party territory that may be full of enclaves loyal to the other side. Even if the result is not affected, the losers feel annoyed and the victors unduly exultant and confident.[3]

[1] One neglected or, at any rate, not publicized objection to the admission of Great Britain as the forty-ninth state is that its electoral vote would be over 160 (the present strength of the electoral colleges being 531). The temptation to nominate only Englishmen would be very great.

[2] Americans, like the French, always distinguish between a majority, i.e. more than half the votes cast, and a plurality, i.e. the biggest single block of votes cast.

[3] It was not mainly (I think) the great popular majority rolled up by Roosevelt in 1936 (which was, in fact, less than Harding's in 1920), but his carrying all states but two, that bred a dangerous euphoria which helped to produce some of the defeats and discomfitures of the second Roosevelt administration. The misleading character of the electoral system has often been illustrated. 'The most devastating criticism of the electoral college system concerns the complete loss of minority votes in a

Then the 'winner take all' system increases the chances of no candidate's receiving a majority of the electoral votes. If that happens the decision is made by the House of Representatives, each state having one vote, with further possibilities of distortion of the popular will.[1] And, paradoxically, since the chance that this may happen is greatly increased by the existence of a third party, it works against third parties, for many voters who might have wished to vote for the elder La Follette in 1924 or Mr. Henry Wallace in 1948 probably abstained, or voted the 'regular' ticket, to avoid giving the House of Representatives an opportunity to carry out a duty for which it is not conspicuously well fitted.

A more serious consequence of the system is that it puts an excessive premium on the political weight of the larger states. To carry one of them is more important than to carry two or three smaller states. So money, organization, all kinds of political effort are lavishly expended in New York, Illinois, California, Ohio, Pennsylvania, and the chances of an ambitious politician from one of these states (Pennsylvania is an exception) are better than those of candidates of equal or superior claims from a smaller state. Thus, in the thirteen presidential elections held in this century, one of the two chief candidates has been a New Yorker on ten occasions; more than once both candidates have been New Yorkers (1904 and in 1944).[2] Only one state, Ohio, although one of the 'mothers of

---

state. . . . Many public figures headed by Senator Norris, are repeating customary appeals to fairness and equity. They maintain, and with reason, that this unique system of representative democracy violates fundamental ethical criteria. . . . The plight of the Republicans in the seven middle western states in 1932 illustrates this inequity in the operation of the electoral college. In that election, President Hoover received 5,440,493 votes in the Middle West. These constituted 43.83 per cent of its total poll. For these more than five million votes, the Republicans received not one electoral vote.' Cortez A. M. Ewing, *Presidential Elections* (1940), pp. 139–41.

[1] In 1948, 'A shift of only 3,554 and 8,933 popular votes in Ohio and California, respectively, would have thrown the election into the House of Representatives.' Frederic A. Ogg and P. Orman Ray, *Essentials of American Government*, 7th edition (1952), p. 187.

[2] I have counted Theodore Roosevelt as one of the two chief candidates in 1912 since he polled many more votes than the regular Republican candidate, William Howard Taft.

Presidents', has more than two entries (3). Only one small state in that time, Kansas, has had a candidate and that in the nearly hopeless year of 1936. (Mr. Truman, in 1948, ran less from Missouri than from the White House.)

The consequences in limiting the presidential potential candidates need not be stressed. But there are other consequences. Since it is double or quits, time and money are not wasted on states that cannot be carried; yet there may be, in those states, sizeable minorities of voters open to persuasion. The alleged educational effect of the campaign is limited by the fact that the national campaign is not really national; that, in a normal year, Democrats do not campaign very hard in Maine or Republicans in Georgia. And in the Convention itself, a feeling is often expressed that these hopeless states should not only have fewer votes than their size would justify, but that their votes are less worthy of respect. That view has, in some regions, especially in the South, some plausibility; although the double or quits system does not in itself explain the character of the Republican party in Georgia, it is part of the explanation.

In recent years, there has been increasing agitation against the system. Some radical reformers wish to abolish the electoral colleges altogether, to have one national poll, a proposal with no chance of adoption as long as federalism has even a faint flicker of life in it. Other proposals do not go as far. The most ingenious was that introduced by the then Senator Henry Cabot Lodge, Jr., and Representative Edward Gossett. This scheme had the merit of simplicity and of abolishing both the lottery system of the big prizes in the big states, and by giving the presidency to the candidate who gets the biggest vote, not necessarily a majority, avoids the necessity of throwing the election 'into the House'; and this frees the voter from the fear that his support of a third party, or his abandonment of his own, may lead to this unsatisfactory result. The electoral colleges and the electors would be simply abolished. (How fictitious the system has become can be seen from the fact that nearly half the states do not even put the names of the candidates for the electoral colleges on the ballot or the voting machine. The voter chooses the presidential candidate he favours and that is turned into a vote for presidential electors, a complete reversal of the constitutional provisions!)

Under the Lodge-Gossett scheme, electoral votes would still be allocated to the states as at present, one for each Senator and Representative, but they would be distributed within the states in accordance with the popular vote. It would thus pay a party to fight, seriously, in nearly every state; the chances of a minority President would be greatly reduced; and a candidate from a small state who had yet a wide-spread national following (a candidate like Senator Kefauver of Tennessee in 1952, for instance) would be far more 'available' than at present. If the nationalization of politics is desirable in the United States, such a reform is one way to that nationalization. But of course, no one is quite certain of the effects such a change would have inside some states, and the prudent politicians have so far refused to take the unknown risks of what is otherwise an ingenious way round a serious difficulty. Perhaps as fewer and fewer states remain absolutely 'safe', the most party-minded politicians will take the risk, since they can no longer be certain that the old system suits their party interest.

There is another aspect of the Convention system that has been often attacked, that has, at times, produced abuses, but which is defensible and indispensable if the true 'nationalizing' functions of the Conventions are borne in mind. This is the representation in the Convention of states that never cast a presidential vote for the party whose delegates they are, and the representation of territories and other areas which cannot cast a vote for the presidency at all— Puerto Rico, Alaska, Hawaii, the Virgin Islands, and the District of Columbia (i.e. Washington). Yet such representation is necessary if either party is to pretend, plausibly, to be national, and it is desirable since the President, when elected, represents the whole people of the United States, and that would be a bold claim if in addition to all the other accidents that may accompany the electoral mandate, the President had been nominated by a party Convention in which millions of American citizens were not represented, or were represented in such trifling proportions that the representation was purely and visibly nominal.

Until after the first World War, the Conventions allotted seats to delegates in proportion to their electoral votes. The Vermont Democrats (who had not carried the state since 1820) and the Georgia Republicans (who had, and have never carried their state) got the same representation, by electoral votes, as the most faithful and reliable strongholds of their respective parties. This was an abuse, but particularly an abuse in the representation the system gave to the almost non-existent Republican party in the 'Solid South'.[1] That party, although it had genuine local centres of strength in Virginia and North Carolina, among the Germans of Texas and in scattered areas of some other states, existed, in most southern states, as a group of federal office-holders, mainly Negroes.[2] It was visibly against the interest of this small group to extend the basis of the party, and in states like South Carolina, Mississippi and Georgia, it was virtually impossible to do so. Few respectable whites would dare join the Republican party and the Negro masses were not permitted to vote. The Southern Republican 'leaders', with between a fourth and a fifth of the voting strength at their command, had no public opinion to fear, and many of them were simply concerned to drive a hard bargain. As most of them were federal office holders, during the long period of Republican supremacy the President in office commanded them as his household troops. When there was a genuine contest, they were open to the highest bidder and were reported to be willing to take cash. To 'nobble' the Southern delegates before the Convention met was traditionally the first move of a presidential candidate who was not strong in popular support, but well provided with what Indiana politicians called 'the long green', i.e. money.[3] The only remedy

[1] There always were and are thousands of stout Vermont Democrats. The state produced, among others, George Brinton McClellan Harvey whose name speaks for itself and who had some hand in the election both of Woodrow Wilson and of Warren G. Harding.

[2] 'According to the *Democratic Text Book* of 1912 (p. 236), the southern delegates and alternates in 1908 included 220 federal office holders drawing $450,000 in salary.' Penniman, op. cit., p. 399.

[3] In the late nineteenth century, Indiana had the reputation of being about the most venal of the northern states, but it was a very doubtful state, so that it was necessary to issue money to voters, not merely to a group of leaders who could be relied on to deliver the electoral vote. Indeed, Indiana was so independent (if that is the word) that it was widely believed it had to be bribed, in 1888, to support the Republican candidate, although he was a 'Hoosier', a 'favourite son'. But Benjamin Harrison was probably the least favourite son ever to reach the White House. He was not re-elected.

open to candidates who had been late in the field was to apply to the delegates the test of an honest politician, a 'man who when bought, stays bought'. Not all the Southern delegates met this test.

The scandal flared into the open in 1912, when President Taft, as was traditionally his right, came to the Convention with the Southern vote already in his pocket. It *was* his right, but the case for Theodore Roosevelt was that he represented the real choice of the real Republican voters (which was probably true) and the normal exercise of the presidential prerogative was denounced with the genuine, forgetful fervour that Theodore Roosevelt commanded so easily.[1]

The first proposals and reforms were modest enough. The South had lost, by 1920, eighty-five votes in the Convention. Far more drastic proposals were put forward in 1920, tying the greater part of the representation of a state to the votes that it cast for Republican congressional candidates. But this reform alienated what was then an increasingly important part of Republican strength in the North, the Negro vote in the big cities. That vote was still faithfully cast for the party of Lincoln,[2] but the devotion of the Negroes to the party was rewarded, from the Negro leaders' point of view, only in the South. There they might not have votes, but they had the jobs and the power and dignity of the jobs. This drastic scheme was abandoned and, although the South was never restored to its old position in the Republican Conventions, and although states which voted the Republican national ticket or elected a Republican Senator or cast a substantial number of votes for Republican congressmen were given a bonus, the states which did none of these things were yet well represented.

[1] It was apropos of the alleged 'stealing' of delegates that Roosevelt declared that 'we stand at Armageddon and we battle for the Lord' (see p. 209). 'It was magnificent. It was epic, even if nobody knew where Armageddon was, exactly, and why the Lord had suddenly become an opponent of William Howard Taft. Roosevelt probably believed, as he spoke, that he was telling the truth. But the weight of the evidence is against him. He had forgotten that precisely the same methods had been used to achieve his own nomination in 1904, and that he had used them for Taft in 1908.' Henry F. Pringle, *William Howard Taft* (1939), vol. II, pp. 802–3.
[2] See p. 112.

It was these states that caused the great explosion in 1952 and, so some experts think, secured the nomination of General Eisenhower. Senator Taft, much stronger with the regular party members than with independents or disgruntled Democrats or plain Republican voters, had imitated his father and gone after the Southern delegates. But times had changed. In some of the Southern states, something like a genuine Republican party was springing up. Some of its leaders were very recent converts to the Republican party. Many were still Democrats in local politics. All of these thought it would be possible to carry their states for Eisenhower, but not for Taft. They fought the local Republican machines, and the opponents of Senator Taft were able, more successfully than the elder Roosevelt in 1912, to make this 'moral' issue a successful tactic in the Convention. Taft and his supporters were made to appear as thieves stealing the nomination by the aid of venal and totally unrepresentative politicians and so, paradoxically, the rotten boroughs of the South helped to nominate the candidate whose later victories in the South in 1952 gave grounds for hope that a genuine Republican party could be built up there.

The Democrats have always been a more truly national party than the Republicans, and they did not distort the party will, very much, by tying representation in the Convention to the allocation of seats in Congress. But latterly some attention has been paid to the real strength of the party in a state as shown by the election returns. In 1936 each state that had gone Democratic in the preceding election was given two extra delegates-at-large. In 1948, the bonus was raised to four. On both occasions the election that followed upset the calculations of the Conventions; for in 1936, only two states did *not* go Democratic and were penalized; and in 1948, four 'safe' Democratic states in the South bolted the party and voted for the States' Rights ticket.

There have, of course, been plenty of fights in Democratic Conventions over the rights of delegates to be seated. Anti-Tammany delegations from New York have fought Tammany delegations. Sometimes a state's vote has had to be divided among the claimants, and the immediate cause of Lincoln's election in 1860 was the setting up of two rival Democratic Conventions.[1]

Enough has been said to illustrate the grave limitations of the Convention system, the unrepresentative character of many of the delegations, the ludicrously short time the delegates allow themselves to make their choice, the accidents that mar the best-laid plans, the empty liturgies gone through. But the Convention system works, works as well, in its own sphere, as Congress does in its. It is plagued with notoriety seekers whose chances are nil. Even highly intelligent men let their names go forward when no one can see any chance of success, as did General MacArthur in 1948. The legend of the 'dark horse' deceives many who seldom reflect that the real dark horse, like Seymour, like Garfield, is usually entered from a very well-known stable, or is, like John W. Davis in 1924, the only entry the bitterly squabbling factions could agree on.[2] Time is wasted by these preposterous candidacies (there were twenty-two listed in the Democratic Convention of 1932).[3] But, as far as public proceedings go, time wasting is the badge of all Conventions. Yet the work is done, a candidate is selected, the newly invested party leader is at once clothed in the eyes of millions with qualities that only his warmest friends saw in him before. The

---

[1] In 1872, the 'Straight-out Democrats' who could not stomach the absurd nomination of Horace Greeley held a Convention and nominated the great New York lawyer, Charles O'Conor. In 1896, the 'Gold Democrats' who resented the nomination of Bryan nominated General John M. Palmer. But neither of these secessions was taken seriously by the voters, and there was no doubt who was the orthodox Democratic candidate. The supporters of Governor Strom G. Thurmond, who ran on the States' Rights ticket in 1948, claimed to be and, legally, were the Democratic party in some Southern states; but they had and made no claim to be the national Democratic party.

[2] In 1932, if Roosevelt had been stopped, it was believed that the 'dark horse' would have been Newton D. Baker, a very eminent Democrat. The 'dark horse', that is to say, is a candidate not openly entered or on whom the wise money is not being openly bet, but he is very seldom an outsider.

[3] Roy V. Peel and Thomas C. Donnelly, *The 1932 Campaign: An Analysis* (1935), p. 25–6. Of these, at least one was romantic, 'Alfalfa Bill' Murray, Governor of Oklahoma, who proposed to campaign on the platform of 'Bread, Butter, Bacon and Beans'. Ibid., p. 40.

platform and the vice-presidential nomination may be yet to come, but the Convention, as the great public understands it, is over. It is time to close ranks and so it is customary to make the nomination unanimous; in theory, all are good sports and accept with cordiality the decision of the delegates. Sometimes there is an approximation to truth in this idyllic picture.[1] More often the defeated candidates and their partisans go through the rite rather sourly. Sometimes, like 'Al' Smith in 1932, they do not even go through the rite. But if the wounds are too raw in the days immediately after the Convention, time, the great healer, and the need of party unity, usually force public reconciliation. Even Franklin D. Roosevelt and 'Al' Smith formally made it up before the election and it is highly desirable to get defeated candidates and their supporters to speak up for the chosen candidate, if only to give an impression of unity that may deceive the rank-and-file and encourage the lesser party workers to show zeal.[2]

The Convention has done its job. The attendants (if it is a Republican Convention) clear up the mess in readiness for the Democratic show, for both Conventions have of late met in the same city and the same hall, using most of the same decorations and most of the same clichés. The first act is over; the campaign is on.

Seen from Mars or Britain, it is an odd way to choose the men from among whom the American people will elect for four years their leader, the embodiment of their will and purpose. But so far the system has not visibly broken down, except, possibly, in the choice of James Buchanan whose feebleness and vindictiveness as a party leader may have helped to bring on the Civil War.[3] All this

[1] It was thought by some of the supporters of Mr. Stassen at the Republican Convention in 1948, that he overdid the role of the good sport by withdrawing himself instead of letting a lieutenant do it, as Senator Bricker withdrew Senator Taft.

[2] There are celebrated examples of a refusal to play the game. In 1884, Roscoe Conkling, asked to speak for the Republican candidate, James G. Blaine, whose financial reputation was somewhat clouded, replied: 'I am not in criminal practice.' And David Hill, the boss of New York Democrats, when asked if he would support Bryan in 1896, replied: 'I am a Democrat still, very still.'

[3] There is even a case for Buchanan, at any rate in the crisis that preceded the inauguration of Lincoln. Congress, Buchanan argued, would

can be admitted. Yet the Convention, imperfect organ of representative government as it is, is an essential part of the American system. It has rendered far more good service than it has done harm, and no really effective substitute for it has ever been suggested. For the Conventions do something that no other organ of the American system of democracy does: they provide a meeting place for a representative sample of all types of politicians, amateur and professional; they supply, however imperfectly, one great need of the American system, the nationalizing of party politics, and they are a substitute for a missing class in American political life, a group of universally recognized national political leaders. They are, in fact, a consequence of the separation of powers and of the federal system. If the presidency were subordinate to Congress or if great political careers could be made only nationally, the Conventions would not be necessary. As it is, they are.

---

not give him the necessary power to act. To act by himself, while Congress was in session, 'would have been to set at defiance both the Constitution and the legislative branch of the Government'. James Buchanan, *Mr. Buchanan's Administration on the Eve of the Rebellion* (1866), p. 161.

Chapter Seven

THE CAMPAIGN

THE American candidate is somewhat in the position of the young man in the English limerick. He is:

> A creature that moves
> In predestinate grooves.
> In fact not a bus, but a tram.

A British member of Parliament is never quite sure when he may have to fight an election, in a few months or in over four years. A British leader of the Opposition, with hopes of being Prime Minister ill-concealed in his bosom, never knows when the incumbent will 'pull a fast one' and dissolve at a moment highly inconvenient for the rival side. It is his right: as the Western poker player said to the tenderfoot who pointed out that the dealer was cheating: 'Well, it's his deal, isn't it?'

An American politician cannot be taken by surprise in this fashion. An American President cannot dissolve when his prospects are at their best. He must follow the calendar which, as far as federal elections are concerned, means that Congressmen must be thinking of elections virtually all the time, since their term is only two years; Senators must think of elections at least at the beginning of every sixth year; and a President must think of elections continually, since his peace of mind depends largely on the degree of harmony he can expect from Congress. In most states, state elections occur every two years; in some every four. But always local party politics and national politics are mingled, though, in a few instances, state politics may be more important. Even where municipal elections are held in odd years, as in New York city, the prize is, as a rule, too great for practising politicians, national or state, to ignore the campaign. This means that every two years in most states, and every three years out of four in some, important elections will be held on known dates, and active politicians will have to absent themselves from the felicity of public service to ensure their own re-election. Some months must be spent on this task, and this interferes with the efficiency of a Governor of a state, and even of a President of the United States.

Only a President (or Governor) not running for re-election and not caring much, or at all, whether his party wins, is free from pre-occupation with the will of the sovereign people. At the very least, a state campaign lasts two months, a national campaign nearly four, if the Conventions be counted as part of it, which they certainly are. But this is not all. For thanks to the primary system, the campaign for the nomination may begin far sooner. In absolutely safe states (of which there are now few), the primary may end the real campaign, but this is never so in a presidential election where the strain, cost, fatigue and, as some think, the folly of the system is most clearly demonstrated.[1]

The system can be justified on various grounds of differing plausibility. Quite often the presidential candidate is little known outside his own state; more rarely he is not very well known in it, save to the professional politicians. It is necessary that he be presented to the mass of voters, that his face, manner and speech should be made familiar. And as the United States is very large, that takes time or did, in the past, take time. It is, in fact, only in this century that the need for active presentation of the candidate in a series of campaign tours has been generally accepted. Some very successful presidential campaigns, like those of William McKinley in 1896 and of Warren Harding in 1920, were 'front porch campaigns'. The candidate received respectful delegations and less

---

[1] For example, in 1952, if either Senator Taft or Senator Kefauver had been nominated, they would have had to campaign for about nine months from the first primaries till the final election, nine months which would have left them exhausted in November and might well have interfered with the carrying out meanwhile of their functions as United States Senators.

respectful political leaders, but did not actively 'take the stump'. Only a candidate very sure of his party strength, or diffident about the additional strength he could give it, could afford this attitude. It is true that Presidents running for re-election have more than once assumed a high attitude of disdain for the merely political activities that might distract them from their exalted duties. But as election time gets near, even in war time, the President finds it part of his duty to show himself to the public.[1]

Next in importance to this exhibiting of the candidate to the mass of the voters, is the presentation to him of local but important party leaders whom he may know only slightly or not at all, among those leaders being, on at least one occasion, the party's candidate for the vice-presidency. The real powers in the politics of some states and regions may not be either Congressmen or Senators, but Governors or even unofficial persons. They must be seen, conciliated, if necessary reconciled with other local magnates. The rifts in the local lute must be put an end to—if there are any quarrels that might affect the national ticket. There often are, for as every, or nearly every, presidential nomination leaves some soreness behind it, so does every lost primary or mistaken backing of a loser at the Convention. It is a common charge against defeated candidates that they lost because they alienated local leaders by indifference, coldness, or taking sides in local feuds that did not concern them. Such charges were made against Governor Smith in 1928, for it was thought by many that he did not sufficiently appreciate the courage and loyalty of those Democratic politicians who stood by the national ticket even in the most doubtful areas of the South and West. The same charge was made in 1948 against Governor Dewey whose polished, but not very concrete speeches, did not help the local candidates much[2] and whose ostentatious

---

[1] This was literally one of the chief objects of Roosevelt's tour on the eve of the election in 1944. It was thought desirable, above all by the President, to show that the rumours about his failing health were false. They were, in fact, true, but the last and, in a sense, heroic effort of FDR pushed the question into the background.

[2] Governor Dewey did sometimes go out of his way to support, warmly, a candidate of whom he strongly approved, e.g. Senator Cooper in Kentucky. It was quite intelligible that he refused to do the same for the Republican senatorial candidate in the neighbouring state

ignoring of some Republican candidates aroused anger before the election and rage after Governor Dewey's defeat.

But the classical instance of the candidate alienating a powerful local leader and group occurred in 1916, and it was all the more dramatic that the election, whose result this error changed, was the closest in recent American history. Justice Hughes had been called from the Supreme Court to 'bind up the party's wounds', still bleeding from the civil war of 1912 when the supporters of Theodore Roosevelt and William Howard Taft had fought each other more savagely than either had fought Woodrow Wilson. The refusal of Theodore Roosevelt to run as the 'Progressive' candidate in 1916 had embittered many hitherto passionately loyal supporters, salt being rubbed into their wounds by the absurd suggestion of the nomination of Henry Cabot Lodge, Senior. Some of the leaders and more of the rank and file decided to support Wilson.[1] Others, bitter against Roosevelt, yet found it necessary to follow him back into the Republican camp, as did Johnson, Governor of California, towing the local Progressive party after him. This, in turn, infuriated the 'regular' Republicans out of office and jobs both in state and nation. These labourers in the vineyard had no intention of learning the lesson of the parable.[2]

It was a difficult situation for the Republican candidate who was, in nation and state, supposed to serve as a 'trait d'union'. Hughes had, in his two terms as Governor of New York, been unable to co-operate with the professional Republicans of that state, and his political austerity had angered the then head of the party, President

---

of Tennessee. It was possibly memories of this that induced General Eisenhower's advisers to insist that he could not ignore or snub Republican candidates, including those whom there was some reason to suspect then, and is more reason to believe now, he did not, as personalities, wish very strongly to have as colleagues in Washington.

[1] Bainbridge Colby became Wilson's Secretary of State and later a warm opponent of the New Deal.

[2] 'After eight years without political pap, the hungry Republicans saw Johnson's announcement as a brazen attempt to steal what they felt was honorably theirs.' George S. Mowry, *Theodore Roosevelt and the Progressive Movement* (1946), p. 364. According to my calculations, the regular Republicans had been deprived of all recognition and jobs for only around four years.

Roosevelt. He had been out of active politics for six years; he was badly advised and badly served by his staff. He arrived, injudiciously, in California, before the Republican primary decided who was to lead the party. A series of accidents left him entirely in the hands of the old 'regulars' who were fighting Governor Johnson for control. Johnson thought he had been deliberately snubbed. He continued to give formal support to the ticket, but when election day came round, he carried the state (as candidate for the Senate) by 300,000, Hughes lost it (and the presidency) by a little over 3,000. 'The severest test of the remarriage between the Republicans and Progressives had been bungled. The self-serving tenacity of the Old Guard and the vindictive attitude of Hiram Johnson had cast a shadow over the whole campaign.'[1]

It is memories like these that still stir fifty hopes and fears in the breasts of managers and candidates today, when there is more scepticism about much of the traditional political warfare of the presidential campaign. The new methods mean the expenditure (law or no law) of great sums of money, and only if a good show is put on will the money be forthcoming, or so many think. The feebleness of the national political organizations, at any rate of the opposition party, makes it desirable to create some form of party spirit over most of the nation at least every fourth year. Only by a great deal of 'ballyhoo' can what is, often, a fictitious degree of unity be achieved. American parties are not parties of doctrine, yet they must profess some degree of verbal unity in presidential years, and if the 'platform' is usually a verbose and vague document, it must be referred to and a great mass of reading matter must be (or at any rate is) issued to the party workers. The candidate has a free hand in the choice of the chairman of the National Committee and in the

[1] Merlo J. Pusey, *Charles Evans Hughes* (1951), vol. I, p. 349. As Mr. Pusey points out, although California decided the issue, given the distribution of voters in the other states, that line-up may well have been the result of the general mismanagement of the Hughes campaign. 'Hughes could have won if he had had a few thousand additional votes in New Mexico, North Dakota and New Hampshire or in several other states.' *Op. cit.*, vol. I, p. 363. But, as it was, till the California returns were in, Hughes was thought to be President-elect. California was the marginal unit with great though incalculable effects on the history of the world.

recruiting of such staff as he can afford to hire or keep. But this prerogative is far less important than the kind of control of the national party machine that a British party leader gets, especially a Conservative party leader, since there is far less of a national party machine to control. To inherit from Mr. John J. Raskob, his predecessor, the Democratic National Committee's famous publicity man, Mr. Charlie Michelson, was a windfall for Mr. James A. Farley when F. D. Roosevelt made him National Chairman in 1932. But the famous Democratic machine that Mr. Farley commanded by 1936 was not inherited by him; it was created by him, and it could not have been created if the Democrats had not won in 1932.

There hangs, therefore, over all American national politics, even in presidential years, an aura of the temporary, if not quite of the amateurish. What really needs years of tireless preparation, such as can be seen in some efficient state organizations, is rare indeed in a presidential campaign.

The federal character of the party system comes out in other ways. The presidential candidate may not be the political leader that the active politicians look to for leadership in a given state. They may not have much hope of his success; they may be primarily the liege men of the Governor or of a leading Senator. They will not waste state assets in a forlorn hope; besides which the victory of the presidential candidate may also be a victory for rebels inside the state organization. An unsuccessful presidential candidate cannot do good and may do harm to a powerful state machine, especially if it depends for local strength on non-party support.[1] Popular interest is focused much more on the presidential election than on those for state and municipal office. But it does not follow that the interest of the professional politician is similarly focused on the fight for the presidency. In many states, the local unit of a national party may be much stronger than the party is in the nation. During the long

[1] In 1944 it was much easier in northern California to find evidence of Governor Warren's political activities than of those of the Republican presidential candidate, Governor Dewey. This was not so noticeable in 1948, when Governor Warren was Governor Dewey's running-mate, and the chances of a Republican national victory were ranked very high. But in California, the strength of the Warren organization was most manifest in its success in keeping control of a nominally Democratic state. That control was incompatible with blind partisanship.

period of Republican dominance that ran from the end of the Civil War until 1932, the Democratic party only won the presidency four times, but it was strong not only in the South, but in New York, Ohio, Indiana and some of the Rocky Mountain states. Fights which the party had a chance of winning naturally excited more real interest in professional breasts than the presidential election that they had little hope of winning or, indeed, in some cases, much interest in winning. This was even truer of the great cities like New York and Chicago where the real prize was the patronage and other assets of the city hall and not the doubtful and often quite unprofitable triumph of the 'national Democracy'.

The period of Democratic supremacy that began in 1932 had the same results for the Republican party, for whom the control of Philadelphia or Minneapolis, of Ohio or of Minnesota, was, for the Republicans in these states and cities, a matter of greater urgency than a national victory. Party victories in local elections, that is, might have little connection with the national campaign even in presidential years and still less in 'off years'. Of course a great natural vote-getter like Franklin D. Roosevelt was an asset to the Democratic party nearly everywhere. He helped the Hague machine in Jersey City, the Kelly-Arvey machine in Chicago and, indeed, marginal Democratic candidates everywhere. But a presidential victory that was not accompanied by a local victory was nothing to stir uncontrollable exultation in the breasts of full-time politicians, except in so far as a 'friendly' federal government was an asset or even a necessity to the well-being of the local machines. Thus what, seen from a national standpoint, was one 'campaign', might in reality be a series of loosely connected contests and the apparently unified strategies of the national high command be, in grim reality, a series of desperate expedients and day to day adjustments to a series of local emergencies.

Of course, the strength of the local ticket may help the national ticket; thus Governor (now Senator) Lehman in New York was the greatest vote-getter in the history of the state and some of his strength was transferred to the national ticket. In an ideal set-up all the candidates, local, state-wide and national should add to the strength of each other, but it is very seldom that they do, all down or all up the line.

It is basically for this reason, that local elections cast an ambiguous light on national strength. A Senator or Representative or a Governor may have a local strength that has no national significance at all. Ohio has been especially rich in politicians highly popular in that state,[1] but either unknown or disregarded elsewhere. Both parties have provided politicians of this type, whose genuine local strength has had no national repercussions, at any rate not helpful repercussions. Indeed, it was in a contest with an Ohio politician of this type that Senator Taft scored his greatest triumph in 1950 when by defeating 'Jumping Joe' Ferguson in the senatorial election he showed that he had what all politicians want in their leaders, the power to draw out a great popular vote against a candidate whose long suit was just that personal popularity that Senator Taft was rightly thought to lack.

The basic object and the basic difficulty of the campaign is the presentation of the candidate to the nation, for, as fewer and fewer possible presidential candidates come to the front in the only national forum, Congress, the chance that a candidate is unknown or nearly unknown is not remote. When Governor Adlai Stevenson was nominated in 1952, he was little known outside his own state to a great part of the professional politicians whose collaboration he needed. The same was true of Governor Landon in 1936 and, although Governor Smith was a national figure, as the centre of a great deal of controversy when put forward in 1924 and still better known in 1928, he was not, in the British sense, a national leader.

It was the theory of the old campaign system that the delegates (many of whom might never have seen the candidate, for the custom of accepting the nomination at the Convention dates only from 1932) went home and spread the good news. They might have been part of the delegations which, six weeks or so after the nomination, broke the news to the candidate that he had been chosen as the peerless standard-bearer. They might visit the candidate with delegations pledging loyalty and asking for jobs.

[1] See p. 207. I am assuming that the recently discovered fact that Ohio was not formally admitted to the Union in 1803 does not affect its status as a state.

But they might have little news to give of the man they were recommending to the nation.[1]

Presenting the candidate involves more than getting him a platform or, today, a mike, and an audience, seen or unseen. Even before the coming of television, the candidate's appearance counted for a good deal. He might need to be humanized. Thus Charles Evans Hughes, in 1916, trimmed the 'forest of his beard', behind which critics had professed it difficult to see the personality of the candidate.[2] An article of dress may identify a candidate, but not necessarily favourably. Thus the emblem of 'Al' Smith as Governor of New York, the famous 'brown derby',[3] a great vote getter in New York was, some feared, likely to be a handicap in the hinterland west of the Bronx where the necessary votes lay. But the 'Happy Warrior' refused to abandon the equivalent of 'the white plume of Navarre', a decision that may have cost some votes, but a bogus rural costume might have cost more.[4] Mr. Hoover's high collars were a source of real or synthetic irritation to critics and Mr. Truman's lively taste in dress was subdued for the campaign.

Now with the rise of television, the candidate has to be as photogenic as possible for the devotees of 'video' and that means careful make-up, great care in gestures as well as in speech, a new hazard added to a sufficiently risky game. Of course the manners of the candidate have played a part in campaigns long before the coming of television. To represent a candidate as being unworthy of election to office because his manners would not grace the White House or the Governor's mansion is an old story. It was used against

[1] One of the difficulties of Lincoln's position as President-elect was that he was known to few of the national political leaders and scarcely at all to the mass of voters.

[2] The chin whiskers, which we associate with Lincoln, were adopted at the suggestion of a female non-voter after his election, although before his inauguration.

[3] *Anglice* bowler.

[4] 'He came buoyantly down to the luxurious special train at Albany that night of departure—and he had on a brown derby. So he was going to wear it after all. We discovered that this had been the subject of much controversy in the family. But Smith, like Abraham Lincoln with his Cabinet, voted his lone "Aye" and the Ayes "had it".' Thomas L. Stokes, *Chip Off My Shoulder* (1940), p. 238.

Jackson and Lincoln. So were the deficiencies, real or invented, of their wives. It was not only 'Al' Smith's crudities, but those imputed to his wife that aroused the indignation of socially-minded voters, especially prosperous women, most of whom would not have voted the Democratic ticket had Beau Brummell been running on it.

The press (the party press) does its best, and there is produced that special literary form, the campaign biography, designed either to win delegates at the Convention or votes after the nomination has been won. Most campaign biographies, in the nature of things, fail in their object and are quickly forgotten; yet well-known authors have written them: Hawthorne did one of his college friend, Franklin Pierce, and W. D. Howells one of Lincoln. One of them, James Sheehan's life of Stephen A. Douglas, is still of serious historical value, but the genre has fallen on evil days. The press, the 'profile,' the news reel, radio and television have reduced the market for the campaign life. It may be true that 'even the most extended campaign, with all the modern devices of communication, cannot give all the people of the country an opportunity to hear the whole story of any man's life and record'.[1] But in this age, the campaign biography is now merely a curiosity.

It is possible that the campaign train that rolled over all the doubtful states with its complement of secretaries, press officers, reporters, its more or less invited troupes of local and national politicians, the candidate's wife and, if there is one, a personable daughter, is also an obsolescent campaign instrument. It may be regretted; it was certainly fertile as a breeder of golden legends; 'we even had marimba when we played the Rio Grande'; but the coming of the plane, the radio and television diminish the utility of the campaign train without diminishing its costs. Indeed, the justification of the train was often and perhaps still is its local importance; it helps, so some think, less the national than the state ticket.

It was long believed that a presidential campaign helped the party ticket of the majority party. More people took an interest in the presidential election than in local elections. More people took the trouble to vote and, it was assumed, the majority party had more 'sleepers', more merely nominal members than had the

[1] Karl B. Pauly, *Bricker of Ohio* (1944), p. v.

minority party whose membership, by the very fact of their adhering to the minority, was obviously more zealous. Thus even in the long period of Democratic supremacy in the local politics of New York state, Republican candidates did better in presidential years when a presidential contest brought out the Republican vote.

It was thought, too, that the head of the ticket carried in with him 'on his coat-tails' many weak minor candidates who benefited by the natural tendency of the average voter to vote for the whole ticket, from President to Dog Catcher. The good and vigilant citizen might 'split' the ticket, but he was in a minority.

Recent elections, without totally destroying these beliefs, have made them less certain. For one thing, presidential elections do not necessarily bring out the vote. Many millions of more or less idle voters now stay away from all elections. Then it is by no means certain that the head of the ticket necessarily carries in with him a great mass of candidates who would otherwise have been defeated. Thus in 1948, Mr. Truman often ran behind the Democratic ticket; in some states like Illinois very badly behind it. In 1952, General Eisenhower ran very far ahead of the Republican ticket. It is probably true that, in a few narrow contests, he carried in with him Republican candidates who would otherwise have been defeated. But what was more conspicuous was his failure to do more for the Republican party than, in fact, he did. For his very great personal triumph was reflected in only a very narrow Republican victory in the House and Senate. The charismatic appeal could not be transferred to others. It is possible that had General Eisenhower not run on the Republican ticket, the congressional results would have been much the same. There were signs, not only of a great personal, non-party trust in and rallying to General Eisenhower, but of more exercise of critical choice than was believed to be usual.[1]

[1] Some of the results in 1952 were formally paradoxical. Thus General Eisenhower carried the state of Washington easily. But the sitting Republican Senator was even more handsomely defeated by a Democratic Representative whose safe 'Democratic' seat was, in turn, lost to a Republican. The Democrats did not carry a single congressional district, but elected the 'Representative at large'. (A 'Representative at large' is chosen in a state which has more seats in the House than it has provided congressional districts for. He is elected, like a Senator, by the whole state.)

This is not the only way that the traditional 'campaign' is changing. Just as the radio and, more recently, television have begun to change the character of the conventions, radio and, still more, television have changed, and will increasingly change, the character of the campaign. One justification of the length of the campaign is no longer valid. The most effective introduction of the candidate to the voters is now made on the air. It is not necessary for him to show himself personally to scores of small towns and hundreds of 'whistle stops'. His chief job is to present himself on the air. It may still be worth while to make a great speech from a great city, capital of a region. The television appearances go down better if they are part of a meeting and not mere studio jobs. The loyal party members who fill the auditorium provide the necessary warmth; but the real audience is elsewhere. Both candidates in the 1952 campaign went through the motions of the old traditional campaign. But their effective appeal to the voters was in great meetings seen by millions.[1]

The consequences of this change are only faintly visible. But it seems unlikely that the time and temper of the candidate will be wasted as much in the future as in the past by the formal 'presentation' to the voters which had become traditional in this century. A modified version of the 'front porch' campaign will be possible with no very serious loss, except to the minor politicians who glow in the presence of the great man and waste his time when they do not involve him disastrously in their own troubles.[2]

But there is more than the effect of mechanical progress to account for the increasing doubt with which some of the old-established rules of political campaigning are regarded. There is, for example, grave doubt about the effect of the last few weeks of the campaign. Has it any effect at all? Is there any evidence in recent times that

[1] I saw General Eisenhower arrive at an important city where he was to make one of his main speeches. The crowd welcoming him at the station would have seemed inadequate to a minor film star. But the hall where he spoke was jammed, and I have no doubt that he crowded everything off the television screens in homes and bars.

[2] It has been pointed out that the increasing tendency to use aeroplanes instead of trains, cuts the candidate off from the local politicians. The most pertinacious of the breed cannot 'hop a plane' as he can 'hop a train'.

electors do change their vote at the last minute, that the accidents that defeated Blaine in 1884 and Hughes in 1916 are any longer possible? That these last-minute changes do not occur, or do not occur in sufficiently large numbers to affect the final result, was very widely believed until the elections of 1948. One eminent 'pollster' shut up shop; refused to go on with what seemed to him the time-wasting activity of proving more thoroughly than it had already been proved, that Governor Dewey was as good as elected. The unknown factor in 1948 was how the voters who had not made up their minds how they would vote, would in fact vote. The doubtful for Truman proved to be more numerous than the doubtful for Dewey. But the scepticism remains. Perhaps the long-drawn-out 'campaign' *is* a waste of time, once the identity of one or both candidates has been established, once the 'issues' have been defined.

It is, however, hard to decide, at any rate the second of these points. As foreign affairs play a greater and greater part in American politics, the decisions of total outsiders may well affect the campaign. If the Truman Administration had got a truce in Korea or Stalin had died before the election of 1952, if there had been a change of government in Britain or a Socialist victory in Germany, the last weeks of the 1952 campaign might have been different.

There is, too, a domestic issue that is always important and may turn out to be decisive, the issue of 'prosperity'. It has been argued with great plausibility that the changes in party domination in America are the results of commercial crises. 'In the long-time political record we have found that business depressions are of primary importance in producing changes in party control.'[1] Even apparent exceptions seem to prove this rule. The most glaring is the Eisenhower triumph in 1952 in face of the highest and most widely-spread boom in American history. The saying 'you don't shoot Santa Claus' appeared proved to be wrong. But did it? Some hold that the continuance of the Korean War was the political equivalent of a depression; others that the boom itself destroyed for the time being the basis of Democratic support. 'There weren't enough poor for us to win,' a Democratic politician is supposed to have said. The Administration did not get credit for the boom, and there was no real fear that a Republican victory would endanger it.

[1] Louis H. Bean, *How to Predict Elections* (1948), p. 51.

Besides it is doubtful if there was a Republican as apart from an Eisenhower triumph. The real Republican revival came not in 1952 but in 1946, when the party got effective control of both Houses of Congress because of very high prices not yet accompanied by very high wages. 'The Republicans gained most ground in areas where living costs combined with reduced earnings, hurt most. They won about 55 lower-house seats in the urban areas when normally they might have added 25 seats in a mid-term election.'[1]

A local depression among the farmers of some middle-western states helped the Truman Administration, since the blame was put not on the Administration, but on what Mr. Truman called 'the do-nothing eightieth Congress', itself controlled by Republicans returned in a wave of economic discontent in 1946.

It is probably true that no Administration today can stand the impact of a great depression, and that is why, in turn, politicians of both parties are willing to abandon the formal economic doctrines of the party to avoid the political retribution that might result from their application. Politics, that is, is a permanently inflationary factor in the American economy. The economic state of the nation, especially as represented by farm prices and by the level of employment, is more important (to the politician) than financial soundness of the old type. And no campaign oratory can offset a fall in cattle prices or a sharp drop in employment. And neither of these disasters is necessarily under the complete control of the Administration that may suffer for them.

Yet whatever doubts the practising politicians may feel, whatever scepticism political scientists and social psychologists may express, the Campaign will remain for a good many years as (with the Convention), the most characteristic expression of the national character of American parties. It is obviously dangerous to link together in one electoral process purely local offices and the presidency. It is dangerous to let local or regional issues affect the composition of Congress and the chances of the President's being able to carry through his foreign policy. The secrets of the atom and the local jobs of Buncombe County are unfortunately linked. But the campaign is, as has been said, a great nationalizing force; it still arouses more excitement than do other elections and the winner

[1] Ibid., p. 52.

has at any rate the comforting reflection to support him in the inevitably difficult days to come, that his election was certainly not a thing 'done in a corner'.

He will need consolation, for the strain of the campaign is very great. He may have harboured to the end fears that something is going wrong, even when all seems to the outsider, not to speak of the loyal partisan, to be going admirably. Thus Theodore Roosevelt developed fears both for himself in 1904 and for his nominee, William Howard Taft, in 1908. Equally surprising, of course, is the optimism that comes over candidates with no real chance. The Democratic candidate in 1924, Mr. John W. Davis, was long confident; so was the Republican candidate in 1936, Governor Landon.[1] But there is panic as well as confidence, panic as bad news comes in from some quarrelsome states, as rumours of local leaders lying down on the job, as rumours spread of the enemy's secret weapons, above all of the last-minute scandal, the launching of a story, true or false, reflecting on the candidate and couched in a form that makes refutation difficult or, at times, impossible. Especially damaging is the 'roorback'[2] that imputes immorality, that is, fornication or adultery, to a candidate. In the campaign of 1884, the story was spread that the Democratic candidate, Grover Cleveland, had had an affair with a young widow who had a child whom she fathered on Cleveland. Cleveland accepted responsibility, but was by no means certain of the paternity. The scandal was not only spread by Republican partisans, but provided a topic for sermons by zealous, and possibly Republican, divines. But the

---

[1] This optimism was not generally shared even in Republican ranks. I attended a small meeting of Republican party leaders in the Middle West during this campaign. There was some desultory conversation about the national ticket into which one of the politicians broke suddenly. 'We all know Alf isn't going to be elected. He won't even carry Kansas. Harry Wallace will carry every county west of 100°.' He or the Democrats almost did.

[2] 'Roorback. A campaign falsehood. The name is derived from the publication in 1844 of extracts from the supposed "Travels" of a fictitious Baron Roorback reflecting on James K. Polk.' Edward Conrad Smith and Arnold John Zurcher, *New Dictionary of American Politics* (1949), p. 333. Despite Baron Roorback, Polk was elected and was one of the most successful Presidents of the second rank.

timing was bad[1] and Cleveland wisely imitated the Duke of Wellington and said, in effect, 'publish and be damned.' The Republicans chanted;

> Ma; Ma; Where's my pa?
> Gone to the White House
> *Ha! Ha! Ha!*

The Democrats retorted with verses reflecting on the much debated, if not much disputed, topic of the financial broadmindedness of the Republican candidate:

> Blaine, Blaine, James G. Blaine,
> The continental liar from the State of Maine
> *Burn this letter*[2]

Charges of this type have been made openly or *sub rosa* against many statesmen and have limited their appeal to their parties. Thomas Collier Platt, the 'easy boss' of New York, suffered from at least one story of indiscretion.[3] A more formidable and far from easy boss, Senator Boies Penrose of Pennsylvania, was thwarted in his ambition of becoming Mayor of his native city of Philadelphia because, it was said, his enemies had a most damaging photograph

[1] 'Had this scandal been brought out during the Chicago convention, it would doubtless have prevented Cleveland's nomination; had it been brought out in the last fortnight of the campaign, it would doubtless have defeated his election. But appearing when it did, it soon fell into the proper proportions.' Allan Nevins, *Grover Cleveland* (1932), p. 166.

[2] Ibid., p. 177. Most of the professional moralists were on Cleveland's side, and they found the revelation awkward. But the advice of an unknown reformer from Chicago was followed by the American people. 'The conclusion that I draw from these facts is that we should elect Mr. Cleveland to the public office which he is so admirably qualified to fill and remand Mr. Blaine to the private life which he is so eminently fitted to adorn.' Quoted from *The Nation* (25 September 1884) in James Ford Rhodes, *A History of the United States* (1919). vol. VIII, p. 223. It must be remembered that, in those pre-Kinsey days, the revelation of Cleveland's weakness was more startling (or could be made to appear so) than it would be today.

[3] Professor Gosnell puts the point delicately. 'Not being a candidate for popular elective office after his second election to Congress in 1874, Platt did not need in his work of political management such a spotless record of domestic tranquillity as Roosevelt possessed.' Harold F. Gosnell, *Boss Platt and His New York Machine* (1924), p. 330.

which would be used if he ran. Morals, good enough for the Senate, were not tolerable in the City Hall of Philadelphia.[1]

In more recent years, the national appetite for scandal had been fed but not satiated, and politicians, victims as so many are of the great columnists of the popular press and the peak hours on radio and television, have tended to huddle together for mutual protection, like so many newspaper owners. Yet this cannot account for the success with which the relationship between Senator Harding and Miss Nan Britton was hushed up; it is a little difficult to believe that the secret was kept completely.[2]

It is probable that the campaign in which mere scandal, whispering, slander and all malice and uncharitableness had fullest opportunities was that of 1928. The nomination of 'Al' Smith was a defiance of the dominant religious and social tradition. It came at a time when hostility to all forces threatening the old, traditional 'American way of life' was exacerbated by a barely half-conscious feeling that, perhaps, the battle being fought was lost in the long run. It was the age of the Ku-Klux-Klan and of the flapper, of the laws against the teaching of evolution and of the first general impact

[1] He had been photographed leaving a brothel. This misfortune fell particularly hard on a very cautious bachelor who once boasted, so it is said, 'that he never wrote a letter to a woman "that you couldn't chill beer on".' Walter Davenport, *Power and Glory: The Life of Boies Penrose* (1931), p. 200.

[2] The 'roorback' about Harding in the 1920 campaign was that he had a drop of Negro blood. The amorous secret, at any rate, was kept from the scribes who 'private dirt in public spirit throw', but perhaps the standards of public service were not so high in those days. It was later suggested to Miss Britton that she had been foolish in not asking the Republican party for a substantial contribution to the maintenance of her child. But by this time, Harding was dead and, as Miss Britton put it, 'such a request from me would have been as foreign to my thoughts as would have been the idea of threat of exposure of my sweetheart'. Nan Britton, *The President's Daughter* (1927), p. 351. It has been suggested that Miss Britton was aided by a more skilled female writer, now well known for her works of fiction. Miss Britton's second book, *Honesty in Politics* (1932), suggests a different stylist. 'And so my craft of well-purposed endeavour, instead of being duly and properly launched, was ruthlessly precipitated into a sea of miscreance and skepticism' (op. cit., p. 115) is a style of writing to which the alleged collaborator in *The President's Daughter* could not, I am sure, rise.

of Freud and other enemies of the old-time religion on the millions now exposed to a high school, if not a college, education. It was the age of prohibition, the 'experiment noble in purpose' as the Republican candidate, Mr. Hoover, was supposed to have put it, and the age in which the success of the experiment was more and more doubtful. All these fears and doubts were expressed in the hostility to the candidacy, to the impudence of the candidacy of a 'wet', a Catholic, an Irish-American of recent immigrant stock, a son of that incarnation of city sin, Tammany Hall. In such a cause what weapons were unusable, who dared say:

non tali auxilio nec defensoribus istis?

The Republican candidate could and did say it, but he was not heard or obeyed by all of his supporters.[1]

For there is plenty of evidence that some Republicans could see the advantage of rousing what Bishop Hensley Henson once called 'the Protestant underworld' and even of aiding ecclesiastics, whom it would have been impolite to regard as denizens of that jungle, like that leading Methodist bishop, James A. Cannon, Jr.[2] There is no evidence that this mixture of religious zeal, hallucinations, ecclesiastical competition and, in some, a taste for sanctified pornography, made any great difference. Only a miracle could have defeated any Republican candidate in that year and Mr. Hoover, as the leading businessman in politics, was a very strong candidate in the last days of the uncontested rule of the business community.[3] It was in the poisoning of the political streams, with results that are not yet over,

---

[1] Of course some of the most extravagant attacks on Governor Smith were made by Democrats like Senator Heflin of Alabama who saw the Pope everywhere and asked Governor Smith the $64 question. 'It has been shown that Roman Catholic whites and negroes are now worshipping together in the same Catholic Church. You are a Roman Catholic, Governor Smith, do you endorse that?' Michael Williams, *The Shadow of the Pope* (1932), p. 175.

[2] When, some time later, Bishop Cannon's adventures on the Stock Exchange got him into trouble and, as some thought, would have justified a Frenchman in calling his conduct 'indelicate', the Catholics felt the joys of *Schadenfreude*.

[3] Mr. Hoover argues that 'had he [Governor Smith] been a Protestant, he would certainly have lost and might even have had a smaller vote'. *The Memoirs of Herbert Hoover: The Cabinet and the Presidency, 1920–1933* (1952), p. 208. He may well be right (see p. 110).

that the campaign of 1928 was probably the least creditable in recent American history.[1]

The four campaigns of Franklin D. Roosevelt gave plenty of opportunity for printed and spoken slander as well as vigorous polemical writing within, if just within, the rules. Especially after Roosevelt had become the leader in the move away from isolation (he had earlier been a strong isolationist himself), he became the target for some astonishing examples of mythmaking. The elderly clubmen who had laughed over rather sour stories about 'Frank and Eleanor', were replaced by figures that Mr. Peter Arno would have found it hard to make appear funny. All the lunatic fringe of 'America First', all the anti-Semites and believers in the 'Protocols of the Elders of Zion', the spiritual kin of Streicher and Himmler, went to work. No one, probably, will ever be able to report adequately on this disturbing if not totally surprising phenomenon. But none of this affected the campaigns; it was an explosion of fanatical hatred, rather than the autonomous political force some previous campaign scandals had been. The very extravagance of the legends destroyed their power. Perhaps the only novelty was the degree to which the attack was levelled against Mrs. Roosevelt; but then, in American history, no other President's wife has had an independent political role like Mrs. Roosevelt's or has been a target worth attacking in her own right.[2]

[1] It is possible that a candidate as strong as Governor Smith was, could, in 1948, have been elected even though a Catholic. But by 1948, the boot was on the other foot and the chief intruders into politics were now Catholic, not Methodist, bishops.

[2] Perhaps the oddest example of the mythopoeic faculty of the Americans was the legend of the 'Eleanor Clubs'. These were organizations said to be fired by the example, if not by the actual orders, of Mrs. Roosevelt to encourage Negro women to quit domestic service for war work and so attain the objective of 'a white woman in every kitchen by 1943'. 'From Georgia it was reported that when army camp was started in my town and cooks were asked to cook for the soldiers, receiving as much as $15 a week, many housewives decided that this was a project of the Eleanor Clubs to get Negroes out of domestic service, and to give them higher pay.' Howard W. Odum, *Race and Rumors of Race* (1943), p. 74. Only Mr. Ogden Nash could do justice to this infamy:

> You ruptured the laws of God and man
> And made a pass at Matilda Ann.

In the 1952 campaign, the Republicans were, for a moment, seriously alarmed by the revelation of the fact that their vice-presidential candidate, Senator Nixon of California, had been the recipient of a large sum of money given to him secretly by supporters in his own state. There were even suggestions that he be dropped from the ticket. But, after a brilliant performance on television in which the issue, if there was one, was drowned in emotion-rousing rhetoric, Senator Nixon was discovered to be an asset, not a liability. Indeed, the attack was transferred to the Democrats, for it was discovered that Governor Stevenson, their presidential candidate, had also collected a secret political fund to augment the salaries of some state employees in Illinois. This was held, by Republicans at any rate, to cancel out the charges against Senator Nixon.

There is no real ground for believing that these whispering campaigns have ever vitally affected the course of history. But they are one reason why a prudent man (or woman) might hesitate to enter politics, and why some thin-skinned politicians get out. For an American running for office puts his character in the public domain and has no more reasonable expectation that it will remain unsoiled than it is reasonable to expect the goods at a department store sale to remain unpawed. Maybe the people to whom such things matter would not be good public servants anyway.

The new campaigning methods may save a candidate's time or reputation, but they do not save him, or his party, money. The fantastic cost of presidential elections has attracted the attention of moralists and politicians, but none of the measures so far adopted has done much, if anything, to cut down the expense of a presidential campaign, or if anything has been achieved, it has been by transferring the expense from the national party organization to state and local organizations and to *ad hoc* committees and leagues created for the purpose.

The first presidential election in which money was spent on a great scale was that of 1896. In other elections, notably in 1888, money had been used fairly lavishly, but the great Republican party manager of 1896, Mark Hanna, put the assessment of the big business interests threatened by the revolt headed by Bryan, on a systematic basis. It was not unknown, in previous elections, for funds collected to aid a presidential candidate to get no further than the pocket of the collector and the amounts contributed often depended on the sales resistance and the gullibility of the donors. Hanna altered all that. 'The customary method of voluntary contribution, helped out by a little dunning of the protected manufacturers, was wholly insufficient. Money in sufficient volume could not be raised locally [i.e. in Ohio, Hanna's and McKinley's state]. The dominant issue endangered the national financial system, and the money must be collected in New York, the headquarters of national finance.'[1]

The result was the swamping of the country and of the Democrats in a Johnstown flood of Republican money.

> Pouring out the long green to a million workers,
> Spondulix by the mountain-load to stop each new tornado.[2]

Legend grew around the McKinley campaign and, lavish as were the expenditures of the Republicans, they were not as vast as rumour reported. But to the defeated Democrats, all was plain. They had been beaten by money and, as they always had less money than the Republicans, the future looked grim. The nomination of Bryan in 1896 had some of the effect of Gladstone's adoption of Home Rule; it gave wealthy Democrats a chance to leave their party in a dignified way as the 'Liberal Unionists' left in 1886. Most of Cleveland's friends felt very much out of place in Bryan's party and it is, perhaps, significant that one of their moves to recapture control before the election of 1904, was to get one of their wealthiest members, Thomas Fortune Ryan, to pay off a great part of the party deficit incurred in the second Bryan campaign. But although the conservative Democrats nominated Parker, the results were not encouraging and Bryan was nominated again in 1908. It was this background that made Bryan's attack on Ryan (and others) as the

[1] Herbert Croly, *Marcus Alonzo Hanna* (1912), p. 219. James J. Hill, the great St. Paul railway promoter, took Hanna on a successful conducted tour of Wall Street, where, at that time, Hanna was hardly known.

[2] Vachel Lindsay, 'Bryan, Bryan, Bryan, Bryan,' in *Collected Poems* (1925). (The Macmillan Company, New York.)

backers of Champ Clark in 1912 so effective and thus enabled the liberals (and radicals) to nominate Wilson.[1]

The Democratic managers were as anxious as the Republican to heed Iago's counsel and put money in their purse; the question was where to find the money. They did not manage to do so on anything like an adequate scale until 1928, when John J. Raskob, of General Motors, undertook to manage and finance the campaign of his fellow Catholic, Al Smith, and, for the first time in a generation, the Democratic ammunition train was full. But of course the Republicans had even more money, and it is probable that not even a Democratic Hanna could have succeeded in Hoover's year.[2]

The coming of the New Deal changed the scene. The rich were more devoted than ever to the Republican party, for Roosevelt was soon seen as a menace worse than Bryan had ever been. Organizations to fight 'that man' sprang up, the most famous and unfortunate being the 'Liberty League'. This was founded as a non-partisan body in 1934; it especially welcomed leading Democrats who put country before party, and probably did the Roosevelt administration a great deal of good.[3]

The Roosevelt administration, of course, wanted money and it soon lost the support of the millionaires who had rallied to the call of John J. Raskob,[4] but lavish government expenditure, especially

[1] Wilson was less distasteful to the respectable Democrats than Bryan had been and he had some very rich personal friends like Cleveland Dodge, but the Democrats remained comparatively poor. The Progressives suffered from the fact that the 'angel' of the campaign, George W. Perkins, was head of the detested Harvester Trust. The other chief angel was Frank A. Munsey, the newspaper owner (and mortician).

[2] The long-term importance of the new solvency of the Democratic party was that Mr. Raskob did not dissolve his staff after the election, but kept on many employees of the National Committee on a permanent basis, above all Charlie Michelson, the master press agent.

[3] An eminent Republican, asked to join the Liberty League, refused, saying, 'I don't mind its being a rich man's lobby, but I do object to its looking like one.'

[4] Mr. James A. Farley, who succeeded Mr. Raskob as chairman of the National Committee in 1932, started his duties under the disadvantage that the party owed the former chairman a great deal of money and Mr. Raskob was still just a friend of Al Smith, not a dyed-in-the-wool Democrat.

under the 'Works Progress Administration' (the WPA), directed by Harry Hopkins, put some of the normal cost of getting out the vote on to the tax-payer and led the way to legislation that purported to cut down expenditure in presidential campaigns and to prevent a party in power from exploiting its hold over millions of jobs (including relief payments). The old-fashioned type of money contribution was far from being despised, and many persons of wealth, new and old, adhered to the policies and candidacies of the New Deal. But the Republicans still had the advantage in actual folding money. The Willkie campaign produced contributions from unusual sources and it did not suffer from financial anaemia. Indeed, at the end of the campaign, there was a surplus that was returned to the donors, another proof, if one were needed, of the incorrigibly amateurish nature of the Willkie management.

Attempts had been made to limit the amount of money that could be legitimately spent on federal elections long before the Hatch Act of 1939. Assessing 'civil service' federal employees had been banned by the Pendleton Act as far back as 1883. In the great fight over seating Truman Newberry who had beaten Henry Ford in 1918 when each was a candidate for the Senate from Michigan,[1] it was proved that Newberry had spent well over $100,000, perhaps much more; in any event, in the opinion of the Senate, far too much. The Pennsylvania primary of 1926 to choose a Republican candidate for Senator, was the most expensive state election in American history. It was a fight for more than a Senate seat; it was a fight for control of Pennsylvania, a fight between the ruler of Pittsburgh, the Secretary of the Treasury, Andrew Mellon, and the boss of Philadelphia, William S. Vare. More than $2,000,000 was spent. The methods, financial and other, of eliciting the popular will in this great state were investigated by a Senate committee under the vigilant and ironical 'Jim' Reed of Missouri and the winner, Mr. Vare (whom the Pennsylvania electors duly returned in the final election over a very respectable Democratic candidate), was never admitted to the Senate seat for which he had spent and sacrificed so much.

[1] It was this victory that allowed the Republicans to 'organize' the Senate and permitted Henry Cabot Lodge to pack the Foreign Relations Committee against the League of Nations.

There were other lavish elections, if none quite so scandalous, and the Hatch Act of 1939 (amended in 1940) was only the culmination of a legislative trend. No doubt, the motives of the act were admirable. If an effective way of reducing the exorbitant cost of elections could have been found, it would have been a gain for electoral purity and for democratic freedom of choice. But the method chosen was not very happy. For it consisted in limiting the amount of money to be spent on elections to federal offices; the most important provision being that a national party committee could not receive more than $3,000,000 in any one year and no gift from an individual could total more than $5,000. The motives for the enactment of the two Hatch acts were mixed and so have been the results.[1] What seems clear is that they have not substantially reduced the amount spent on elections. In the first place, since in presidential and congressional elections in most states, state offices are involved, and since it is very rare for the parties not to have a joint national and local ticket, money spent for state elections helps the national ticket. How much it helps, and how much it is intended to help, varies from state to state and from election to election, but as long as there are people who vote the 'straight' ticket (and there are millions of them) the total effect is to help both the national and the state ticket and, in many cases, the local municipal or county candidates. State law, varying both in severity and in efficacy of enforcement, may limit state expenditure, but it would be naïve, indeed, to make any assumption about the true cost of a presidential election based on the formal federal law.

Then independent bodies, existing or specially created, campaign either for special issues that help one set of candidates (thus the Anti-Saloon League in 1928 could not but help Mr. Hoover), or, specifically, for one candidate. In 1940, there was a sudden crop of bodies designed to help Willkie (the second Hatch Act became law as the campaign opened). There were 'Retailers for Willkie'; 'The Committee to Defend Life Insurance and Savings'; committees against a third term and so on. Today, enemies of federal housing or 'socialized medicine' help, as a rule, Republican candidates, and the unions, no longer able to contribute directly to campaign funds,

[1] For a possible reason for making civil servants more politically neutral, see p. 295.

set up other bodies to funnel money to their friends, normally the Democrats. It is doubtful, that is to say, whether the Hatch acts have done more than make legal ingenuity in even greater demand.[1]

Attempts have been made, from time to time, to get the rank and file party members to contribute to party funds, directly, or through special societies and leagues, but the American, normally so generous, normally so gullible, willing to subscribe to all funds, from community chests in very rich suburban communities to pensions for the widow of the unknown soldier, has proved curiously reluctant to contribute to his party. And the party has been forced to appeal to the fears and hopes of those with more to give than a few dollars.

The fears are usually fears of hostile legislative action or hostile executive discretion. In the good old days, great corporations subscribed to both parties if each had a chance of victory. In some areas, it was only worthwhile contributing to one party. 'In Republican counties I'm for the Republicans, in Democratic counties for the Democrats, but everywhere for the Erie Railroad,' is a traditional saying attributed to Jay Gould. Government contractors, however conservative their views, have often found it wise to transfer money, in some fashion, to Democratic administrations. High officials are expected to give handsomely if they want to remain high officials.[2]

Traditionally too, the more socially attractive embassies were conferred on generous donors to the party funds, the 'fat cats' as they were unkindly called, and this tradition has not died out; although more and more embassies of political if not of social significance, go to professionals. But the gaps to fill remain great. There were moments, in the 1948 campaign, when it was difficult, so rumour said, to raise enough funds to send the presidential train on tour, and Mr. Louis Johnson, who got the credit for raising funds for this and other purposes, was rewarded in 1949 by being

[1] For the role of labour, see p. 73.
[2] After Mr. Truman's victory in 1948, official Washington was full of stories, which if not true were *ben trovato*, of sceptical Democrats who had not wasted dollars on what they thought was a forlorn hope and of the faithful few who had—and of the rewards and punishments that followed.

made Secretary of Defence, a post held by the late James Forrestal
who was reported not to have thrown good money after bad by
contributing to the 'hopeless' campaign of Mr. Truman.

It is usual, too, for the national party organization to end up
badly in debt and there are those who think it pays better to help
to pay off the debt than to contribute lavishly in the first place. It
was transactions of this kind that helped to involve the first movie
censor, Mr. Will Hays, who had been Chairman of the Republican
National Committee, in some of the most depressing scandals of the
Harding régime.

The more realistic reformers give more importance to publicity
than to regulation of the amount spent. Others think that a great
deal of the cost of the campaign should be borne by the federal
government (and, for state offices, by the state). It can never be
cheap to campaign effectively for the American presidency, or for
the office of Governor or Senator of a great state. This sad truth
has had to be accepted; there is a place for a poor man in American
politics, but hardly for a poor party. And the cost of the campaign
rises; the cost of television (even when free time is allowed
for) is very great. The great networks, in giving time, are giving
time that they could sell; they naturally prefer to sell it. And it is
suspected that they will not, in future, be so lavish of free cover-
age, even of such great events as the Conventions, as they were in
1952.

The problem is not exclusively an American one. More than one
Canadian government has been involved in great scandals because
of party contributions. The British House of Lords has had many
recruits whose chief claim to honour was generosity to the party in
power. And it is not true that money conquers all in American
politics. The results of local and national elections show that;
repeated failures of high-power sales campaigns show that. But the
voice of the people is often distorted and magnified by a lavish use
of money, not so often now to buy votes, as to buy attention.

One new worry of the candidate (and of his staff) was provided
by the 'polls' which undertook to tell in advance, by scientific
methods, how the electors would vote, destroying the market for
the amateur guesses of newspapermen and 'political experts'. The
most famous of these polls was that conducted by the Literary Digest

which was run on a very large sample, but one heavily weighted against the poor who happened to have more votes than the prosperous and, in 1936, cast them in a markedly different way. This wrecked the *Literary Digest* poll (and the *Literary Digest*), for it had predicted the election of Landon who carried only two states.[1] The pendulum of approval now swung to the selective polls with their weighted samples, in which all identifiable groups were given a weight in the accumulation of the sample proportionate to that they bore in the total voting body. This gave much better results than the crude methods of the *Literary Digest*. At any rate it picked winners in 1940 and 1944. In 1948, the most famous poll of this type, that run by the Institute of Public Opinion headed by Dr. George Gallup, consistently predicted the victory of Governor Dewey and its reports were one of the main factors in breeding despair among all Democrats (except Mr. Truman and a handful of others) and complete confidence among all Republicans. This despair and confidence were equally ill-founded.[2]

In two recent elections, 1948 and 1952, the polls have been just off enough in one case to give a wrong answer to the basic question who was going to win and, in the other, to give a wrong answer to the question by how much the probable winner was going to win In 1948, they made a highly doubtful election look a walk-over, in 1952, they made a walk-over look doubtful. It is true that the main polling organization warned its clients of the limitations of its methods, and that its customers, editors, politicians, even voters were to blame for not noticing the qualifications and using their own judgement. But the very reason that editors and politicians and the public believed in (and paid for) the polls was to escape the necessity of using their own judgment and there was, in 1948 and again,

[1] The size of Roosevelt's victory in terms of states concealed the fact that Harding, in 1920, got a bigger percentage of the popular vote.

[2] One eminent journalist travelling on Governor Dewey's train told me that, having been on President Truman's train, it looked as if the President was drawing bigger and more friendly crowds than Governor Dewey. But he went on, he disliked Governor Dewey so much that his emotions were leading him astray. Look at the polls! His emotions were leading him right, but he did not act on them. At midnight on election night, I myself bet $10 on Governor Dewey (innocently breaking the law as well as losing $10).

though less violently, in 1952, a true *déception d'amour* in the attitude of the public to its once infallible guides.[1]

The result of the 1948 election was not only to lead to an improvement of the methods of the polls, but to dissipate a fear that many Democrats (and democrats) had sincerely felt. Believing that many voters who had no hope for their candidate stayed away and that many voted for the presumed victor, politicians whose own choice was not favoured by the polls, saw in the attention paid to them a threat to free democratic choice. 1948 showed that a majority of voters could vote for what, all the pundits said, was barely a forlorn hope. And in 1952, when the polls underestimated the Eisenhower majority, another comforting discovery was made. For it had been thought that many poor and insecure electors would deny their intention of voting for the Democratic candidate or evade the questioning. In fact, General Eisenhower must have got more support from the doubtful or evasive than had been allowed for. Again the voters were more independent than had been hoped for.

The polls, despite their errors, play an important part in campaign strategy. Within a fairly wide margin they do indicate where and in what groups it will be profitable to make an effort, where it will probably be merely wasteful. They also do keep interest alive as the long routine of the election drags on. And they are less open to misunderstanding when they deal with the fairly simple problem of for whom a given group will vote, than when they give decisions on policy or answers to necessarily vague questions bearing on party allegiance.[2]

---

[1] The limitations of the polls had been pointed out by an exceptionally competent observer before the disaster of 1948. 'The Gallup system seems to be designed to avoid an outright prediction of the election result, but to bury down deep enough data to support the correct conclusion. The sponsor later points to this with pride.' Warren Moscow, *Politics in the Empire State* (1948), p. 228.

[2] An eminent politician once explained to me why he took the results of the polls with some professional scepticism. 'We get all the polls, Gallup, Roper and the rest. We do our own investigations. We know all the pollsters know and something they don't. What are *we* going to do about it? We may decide, for good or bad reasons, to ignore some results in order to spend money and men elsewhere. And our decision may falsify the poll which otherwise would have been right.'

For these reasons a presidential election and, still more, a mid-term congressional election may be a very unsatisfactory way of testing the temper and the views of the American people. It is not only that local issues may affect that decision in the presidential election from which the victor draws his 'mandate' to lead the 'People of the United States', but that local issues, determining both the choice of candidates and their success in elections to each house of Congress may give the President a Congress with whom co-operation in the interpretation and execution of the mandate, may be nearly impossible. And it is because the American people feel that this is so, that they regard the President as the one national officer, and—a less desirable consequence—are not always very careful to provide him with the political allies he needs. All that can be said as the last returns come in, is that X rather than Y has been elected President and has, as Woodrow Wilson put it, the chance to make of his office 'anything he has the sagacity and force to make it'.[1]

[1] Woodrow Wilson, *Constitutional Government in the United States* (1908), p. 69.

Chapter Eight

PRESIDENT AND CONGRESS

═══════════

I

WHEN we talk of the 'government' of Great Britain, we mean either the great, anonymous bureaucratic machine characteristic of all modern states, or we mean a small group of men with a known head, the Prime Minister, who control (as far as any men can) the great bureaucratic machine, who combine, in their own hands, the law-making and law-administering functions of the state, with nothing but political controls and sanctions to fear. The limitation on their power (speaking in terms of internal policy) comes from the electorate which may punish errors, or bad luck, or unpopular but wise decisions, by defeat at a general election. A British government may retreat or reverse itself under a threat of future political disaster, but as long as it is in office, it has the Roman mandate to see that no harm befall the commonwealth and a practically completely free choice of means to carry out the mandate.

When we turn from London to Washington, we see a very different set of institutions. There is, of course, a 'government' in the first sense, an immense agglomeration of federal employees, of departments and bureaux, carrying on the business of a government that grows with every decade, perhaps with every year. But the other government that controls or professes to control the Administrative machine is not centralized, not omnicompetent and omnipotent, as in London. It is divided, competitive, not always capable of giving any answer to apparently urgent questions. There is, in the second British sense, no 'government'. There is 'the

264

Administration'; there is Congress (each house of it); there is the Supreme Court; there are the states. Each of these separate institutions shares in the total governmental powers given by the 'People of the United States'. Each has a share in these powers that the others cannot diminish; each shares some powers with other branches of the governmental set-up. Nowhere in this aggregation of 'governing' bodies, is there a single, unifying man or group of men. And the fact has to be accepted that the American people wanted it to be so and still want it to be so.

Of the division of powers, probably the least important today is that between the Union and the states. There is, of course, an irreducible minimum of federalism. The states can never be reduced to being mere counties, but in practice, they may be little more than mere counties. The Union may neglect to exercise powers that it has and so leave them to the states (subject to varying Supreme Court doctrines as to whether the states can legislate freely in the mere absence of federal legislation, on matters affecting interstate commerce for instance). But in a great many fields of modern legislation, states' rights are a fiction, because the economic and social integration of the United States has gone too far for them to remain a reality. They are, in fact, usually argued for, not by zealots believing that the states can do better than the Union in certain fields, but by prudent calculators who know that the states can do little or nothing, which is what the defenders of states' rights want them to do. Nevada can compete with Florida in hospitality to gambling, with Mexico in liberality in divorce, but no legal fiction can make Nevada a really sovereign state. The sovereign rights of the states are not quite as much a fiction as the sovereignty of Andorra or San Marino, but they fall far short, in reality, of those in the archaic legal picture painted by antiquarians and others.

Of the importance of the power of the Supreme Court to interpret the Constitution and so to exercise a veto power over state and federal legislation more is said elsewhere.[1] But it can be said that while the Court has, on the whole, extended federal power over the policy of the states in matters like 'civil rights', has assumed (or usurped) a corrective jurisdiction over state courts and

[1] See Chapter Nine.

the administration of justice, and has, in one or two cases, given back to the state courts powers long thought lost, it has ceased to preserve states' rights against the federal government in nearly all the fields that matter now. It will leave alone state jurisdiction over education (except where the rights of Negroes and the implications of the separation of church and state are concerned); it will leave alone jurisdiction over marriage (except where it is a question of forcing or not forcing one state to recognize the claim to jurisdiction of another); it will leave states free to tax to the limit of their economic capacity (which may be very limited indeed); but, all in all, the federal government is now little hampered by the fact that it is a federal government.

Where the federal 'government' *is* hampered, is by the fact that it is a divided government, that the President cannot abdicate all his powers in favour of Congress, that Congress cannot abdicate all its powers in favour of the President, that one house of Congress cannot abdicate simply in favour of the other. It is unlikely that the President, *any* President, the Senate, *any* Senate, the House of Representatives, *any* House of Representatives, would contemplate abdication, but, even if any did, they could not divest themselves of their share in the total power of the government of the United States. Whether the separation of powers (a doctrine implied but not stated in the Constitution) owes most to the doctrines of the eminent Baron de Montesquieu, or to the erroneous views of the nature of the contemporary British constitution held by him and others,[1] or to the memory of colonial practice, or to the horrible example of King George III, the framers of the Constitution wanted a government of divided, not consolidated powers, of divided not unified responsibility. And there is no sign that, today, the American people repent of the decision of the framers.

It is possible that had the separation of powers been more absolute, or even had the various organs of government always been rigid in the defence of their prerogatives, the system might never have worked. But doctrinaire statesmen like Calhoun have been rare

[1] Since the publication of Sir Lewis Namier's pioneer work, it is not quite so certain that Montesquieu, Madison, etc. totally misunderstood the British constitution of their time.

in American history; the *tact des choses possibles* that Cavour prized so highly, has been common, but, above all, the political system has forced a minimum of collaboration, has given a common interest to the political personnel, has normally made it profitable for the politicians to prefer adjustments to total victories or total defeats, so that, with the one great exception of the Civil War, there has been no break-down in the working system, though there has been wasteful friction and dangerous delay. But the American or foreign spectator, not excessively enamoured of symmetry, or of merely smooth working, has been forced to say, with Galileo in the legend: 'it *does* move'; it does work. And it moves because the government of the United States is so deeply political, because it has never been worked as a mere instrument of power or will. It has been worked by politicians, for politicians, but also for the people of the United States.

Central to the system is the office that is most political and also most above politics, the presidency. For the President, if only because his choice is the most dramatic and important function of the political system, is at the summit of the political system and his success as a President cannot be separated from his success as a politician.

Yet the present predominance of the President, taken for granted, even if resented and rebelled against by other politicians, was not, possibly, what the framers of the Constitution wanted or, at any rate, what they expected. The power and prestige of Washington and Jefferson were rather lent to the presidency than borrowed from it. The office declined under their successors as it had been only moderately effective under John Adams. Andrew Jackson, chosen from outside the normal national political personnel, seeing in himself the embodiment of the sovereign people, victorious in his conflict with the Senate, was yet such a novelty as a kind of elective monarch that Tocqueville failed to notice the revolution that was going on. The office can hardly ever have sunk lower than it did under Fillmore, Pierce, Buchanan. And, at the beginning of Lincoln's administration, his Secretary of State, Seward, was not the only leading politician to fail to perceive that power, especially in a great crisis, would be in the President's hands or nowhere. Lincoln's martyrdom added to the glory of the office

but, again, the almost successful impeachment of his successor
and the incapacity of Grant seemed to reveal the inadequacy
of the office except in rare circumstances and to justify the
observers who saw in Congress the real governing power for
the kind and amount of government the United States then
wanted.

It is difficult to realize, today, that the leadership that, even at the
lowest point of personal power and prestige, the American people
now expect from the President, was not expected from him,
automatically, between the time of Lincoln and the time of the first
Roosevelt. Even the strongest Presidents of that epoch (there was,
in fact, only one strong President, Cleveland), took a narrow and
negative view of their functions. It was possible for an acute
observer to see, or think he saw, the dispersal of the formal executive power in several hands and the concentration of effective power
in the hands of Congress, that is, in the hands of the leaders of
Congress. Thus the young Woodrow Wilson chose to study
'congressional government' as the key to the American system. He
saw the cabinet rising and sharing the powers of the President and
this joint executive losing ground to Congress. "But, though the
heads of executive departments are thus no longer simply the
counsellors of the President, having become in a very real sense
members of the executive, their guiding power in the conduct of
affairs, instead of advancing, has steadily diminished; because while
they were being made integral parts of the machinery of administration, Congress was extending its own sphere of activity, was
getting into the habit of investigating and managing everything.
The executive was losing and Congress gaining weight; and the
station to which cabinets finally attained was a station of diminished
and diminishing power.'[1]

One consequence of this diminution in the power of the presidency (whether it was rightly considered to be a single or a plural
executive) was the exaltation of the power, dignity and claims of
the Speaker. It was not absurd for Speaker Samuel J. Randall to
assert that he had come 'to consider that office the Speakership . . .
the highest office within the reach of an American citizen. . . . When

[1] Woodrow Wilson, *Congressional Government* (1885), p. 46–7. The
citation is from the English edition of 1900.

it fell to my fortune to occupy the Speaker's chair, I realized how true was my idea of the position.'[1]

Randall's great Republican successor, Thomas Bracket Reed, exalted his office at least as high. The Speaker was the embodiment of the will of the majority of the House and must be accepted as such. English parallels were misleading. As Reed rightly said, 'Our government has got to be the growth of the necessities of our people, and must be worked out under the principles of our government, and can never be adopted from any other land. If you want to mark the growth of our government you will mark it, if you study the history of the country, by the action taken by each House with regard to the Speaker at its close.' On the Speaker was concentrated the responsibility for putting into effect the party legislative programme. The alleged tyranny of the Speaker was a necessity of responsible government. 'Party responsibility has begun, and with it also the responsibility of the people, for they can no longer elect a Democratic House and hope the minority will neutralize their action or a Republican House without being sure that it will keep its pledges.'[2]

This exalted idea of the function of the Speaker was shared by many who, not being Speakers, had not the same temptation to glorify the office. He was seen as the equivalent of the English cabinet or, at any rate, of the Prime Minister. 'If still greater authority be given to the Speaker, if he become a recognized legislative leader responsible for the legislation of the United States, his office will be a prize little less valued than the Presidency.'[3] Even in 1900, Woodrow Wilson re-reading his book of 1885 and noting the increasing effect on the prestige of the Presidency of events like the entry of the United States on the world stage, as a result of the Spanish-American war, still attached great importance to the

[1] Quoted in M. P. Follett, *The Speaker of the House of Representatives* (1896), p. 112; Randall, it is true, as a Democrat from Pennsylvania, had few hopes of the Presidency.

[2] William A. Robinson, *Thomas B. Reed* (1930), p. 233.

[3] Follett, op. cit., p. 312. In the year this book was published, the greatest Speaker of this school, Tom Reed, failed, to his bitter disappointment, to get the presidential nomination which went to a much less vigorous parliamentarian, Governor McKinley of Ohio. Reed obviously did not share Randall's view.

Speaker who was 'now more than ever ~xpected to guide and control the whole course of business in the House'.[1]

But the tide was on the turn. It was partly on the turn for reasons that had little or nothing to do with the legislative machinery of the United States. In the twentieth century, from the beginning, executive action was increasingly important; federal power, in the form of executive power, grew inevitably as the federal government began to control business, conserve natural resources, as the representative federal employee became less the happy spoilsman, rewarded for services to Congressmen and Senators as much as to the President, than the executive agent using his own discretion in carrying out policies laid down by the President or, at most, vaguely sketched by statute. Nor was it unimportant that in the first year of the century, an accident should have put into the White House, a President of a kind very unlike those that the Republican party had chosen since the time of Grant, a President whom that party would certainly not have chosen deliberately.

But even had Theodore Roosevelt never entered the White House, the changing character of the government, and of the world, would have restored presidential power if only by making plain the irrelevance of mere congressional leadership for the new tasks. Some of the reasons for the failure of the Speaker to keep the high place given him by Randall and Reed and by scholars like Miss Follett were noticed by Wilson in his 1900 *Preface*. The Speaker (and the Rules Committee appointed by the Speaker) integrated 'the House alone, not the Senate; does not unite the two houses in policy; affects only the chamber in which there is the least chance that responsibility may be properly and effectively lodged and avowed.'[2]

But it was not only that the Speaker (and his nominees) had to divide authority with the leaders of the Senate. They had to divide it with a President elected by the whole people and possessed, if he had the skill to use it, of a representative character that no Speaker could have. For (and this is still true), the Speaker was not a true parliamentary chief of the English type. Reed certainly and Randall probably would have risen to the top in any parliamentary

[1] Wilson, op. cit., p. ix.
[2] Ibid., p. xi.

system. But that could not be said of many others. It could not be said, either, of many Presidents, but they *were* the direct choice of the American people, even if that choice had been limited to one between two mediocrities. And, as is argued elsewhere,[1] the nominating process was a more truly representative and, in the political sense, democratic method of choosing a leader than the complicated system that produced the high command in each House of Congress.

The twentieth century has seen Presidents whose authority was weakened by the loss of control over Congress; one President, Harding, terrifyingly incompetent for his job; moments in which Congress, negatively at least, has balanced the President and produced a stalemate; but if history can be said to prove anything, it proves that leadership and co-ordination can only come from the President. Only persons and groups which, for whatever reason, do not want either leadership or co-ordination, or Congressmen and Senators, for professional reasons, doubt this. Presidents, it is true, have sometimes acted on a naïve theory of the separation of powers, have simply waited to approve or disapprove congressional legislation, have allowed their own executive agents to be harassed and ordered about. But such Presidents are those whom American tradition has least delighted to honour and even they, the Buchanans and Pierces, or to take much higher examples, the Tafts and Harrisons, have found that there is a vacancy which a President can make but which no one but he can fill.[2]

[1] See p. 234.

[2] This truth was impressed on a President-elect by a great academic authority on American government. Mr. Louis B. Wehle tells us that he was present at a dinner given by the Harvard club of New York to F. D. Roosevelt in January 1933. A former President (of Harvard), Lawrence Lowell, told the President-elect of the United States that 'the most important principle for the Chief Executive is that he must always take and hold the initiative in his dealings with Congress, with his Cabinet, and generally with the public'. Louis B. Wehle, *Hidden Threads f History: Wilson Through Roosevelt* (1953), p. 134. Dr. Lowell, as the event showed, hardly needed to give this advice to his former pupil. At about the same time, a friend of FDR's commiserated with him on the great burden he was about to assume. He laughed and said, 'I shall enjoy every minute of it.' It is not necessary that a President enjoy his burden, but he must take it up.

It is probably the greatest claim to historical importance that can be put forward for Theodore Roosevelt that he dramatized the presidency. His flair for showmanship, his power of appeal to the mass of the voters that no President since Lincoln had had in the same degree, his enterprising spirit, all enabled him to make the presidency, visibly, dramatically, the centre of the American political system.[1]

Roosevelt assumed for the presidency a general power to look after the Republic not unlike, in peace time, the 'war power' on which Lincoln had relied during the Civil War. No politician could compete with him in popularity although some were able to thwart him or bargain with him. His successor, Taft, took a much narrower view of his functions, but his one term, during half of which the Democrats were in effective control of Congress, did not alter the trend of constitutional development. And Taft's successor, Wilson, as much as Roosevelt, saw himself the leader of the nation and of Congress.

Wilson had long pondered the problem of leadership in the American political system, hankering after the English cabinet system as described by his idol, Bagehot. But he had come to see more possibilities in presidential leadership than when he wrote his first book. (He began to see them, it must be said, before he had any reasonable hope of being President himself.) The President, he wrote just before his first inauguration, 'is expected by the Nation to be the leader of his party as well as the Chief Executive Officer of the Government, and the Country will take no excuses from him. He must play the part and play it successfully or lose the country's confidence. He must be prime minister, as much concerned with the guidance of legislation as with the just and orderly execution of law, and he is the spokesman of the Nation in every-

---

[1] This came out in small things that were, possibly, not so small. Thus T. R. dropped the cumbrous title 'the Executive Mansion' and called his official residence formally what it had long been called, informally, 'The White House'. He built the first office wing of the White House, giving the President for the first time adequate space to do his job. (The idea of making the White House an office and housing the President elsewhere seems first to have occurred to that rather dull President, Chester A. Arthur.) A second office wing was added by FDR.

thing, even in the most momentous and most delicate dealings of the Government with foreign nations'.[1]

It was Wilson who, making an opportunity that the first Roosevelt had unaccountably missed, revived the habit of addressing Congress in person. This had been done by Washington and John Adams, but Jefferson, a poor speaker, sent written messages instead; and presidential messages, read to an empty and inattentive Congress, were very inferior to speeches delivered not only to Congress, but to the sovereign people in the galleries and, more recently, to the nation by radio and television. Since that time, the President must lead or pretend to lead and he is able to dispose of unequalled facilities for publicity which he can use with all the adroitness he has at his command.

But parallel with the growth of the leadership inherent in the presidential office, has been the growth of the symbolic character of the office and of its incumbent. The White House was and is one of the few national sacred buildings in America, more sacred than the Supreme Court, much more sacred than the Capitol. The President embodies the nation as well as leads it. He combines the functions of active political leader and of constitutional monarch. Throwing out the ball at the first baseball game, lighting the White House Christmas tree, sponsoring Easter egg rolling on the White House lawn, receiving monarchs and delegations of almost reverential schoolchildren, the President is a dignified embodiment of the nation in a nation where official dignity is scarce and the supply normally exceeds the demand. No President, however idle or incompetent, can wholly divest himself of this representative character; no President, however great, can now add greatly to it. The American people need such a symbol and it is impossible that the symbolic character of the office should not strengthen its practical powers.

The charismatic character of the office is shown in many ways. Thus the moment that a candidate is elected (of course before the electoral colleges have formally acted) the Secret Service takes over the job of guarding him.[2] The moment the President takes office,

[1] *The Public Papers of Woodrow Wilson The New Democracy* (1926), vol. I, pp. 23-4.

[2] Thus in November 1948, the Secret Service sent up a detail to New

he becomes a man apart, being almost as inaccessible to the common man and woman as a King of France under the old régime and being almost as much a victim of protocol and ritual as a King of Spain under the old régime. Mr. Truman has told us of the comic embarrassment of a solitary meal in the presidential residence and the pre-eminence of the office is admitted even by those who may despise or detest the man.[1]

But the unique character of the presidential office is not best revealed in the case of an elected President, but in the case of one suddenly made President by the death of the incumbent. For the average Vice-President, whatever his official precedence may be, is not in himself an important figure and in the moment that he becomes President, he undergoes a change as dramatic as that which makes a subject the sovereign. 'Harry Truman, as the clock under the portrait of Woodrow Wilson in the cabinet room passed 7.09, suddenly ceased to be "Harry" and became "Mr. President". Then within the time it takes for the clicking of cameras, he was the almost superstitiously honoured man-symbol of America who can still, after our pattern of reverence, be described in the native argument in the American language as one angry truck driver would describe another. . . . He was not Harry Truman any longer; he never would be again. The prison of the Presidency dropped around him. The Secret Service scurried beside him as he moved. The personages shook his hand and fell away.'[2]

York to take over the guarding of Governor Dewey who was practically universally expected to be President-elect. When the unexpected happened, the Governor's safety was left to the New York State Troopers who had guarded him during the campaign.

[1] Not all have, in the past, respected this rule. Henry Cabot Lodge, Sr., during the first war dining with Henry Adams, was especially violent in his attacks on President Wilson. 'Suddenly Mr. Adams interrupted the tirade. He brought his fist down on the table and said sharply: "Cabot." There was a moment's silence. "I've never allowed treasonable conversation at this table and I don't propose to allow it now".' Harold Dean Cater, *Henry Adams and His Friends* (1947), p. cv. The fact that the British Ambassador, Sir Cecil Spring-Rice, was present may have reminded Adams of the very different attitudes of his family and the Cabot family in the last war with Britain.

[2] Jonathan Daniels, *Frontier on the Potomac* (1946), pp. 9, 12.

The office which this solitary and symbolic figure holds, is not adequately described in the mere text of the Constitution. For what the mere text meant was in many ways determined by the fact that the first President was General Washington and by important decisions made in the first years of the new government.[1]

Each generation, if not each administration, has seen the office further developed, its powers further interpreted and, over each generation, further augmented. For despite ebbs and flows, the movement has always been one way and the Presidents who have added to the functions and powers of their office might well murmur as Congress attempted a come-back;

> No winter shall abate this spring's increase.

Yet the essential character of the presidency was defined by the Constitution. He has powers that he does not receive from Congress and which it cannot take away and he cannot be a member of or directly employ members of Congress. In him is vested all the executive power of the Union. With few and not very important exceptions, all office holders of the Union owe their allegiance to him. Of course, no more than in an absolute monarchy or in a dictatorship are these powers always equally and effectively exercised, but they are there for use and no one else can use them except by presidential connivance or torpor and, it has been found more than once, that if the President does not use them no one can.

The most obvious example of the consequences of this concentration of executive power can be seen in the role of the Cabinet. This body is unknown to the Constitution. The President is, indeed, empowered to demand advice from the heads of the executive departments but he is not bound to ask it from them collectively, any more than he is bound to pay any attention to it when given. True, the custom soon grew up of having regular meetings of the chief executive officers and some Presidents, like Monroe, thought of themselves as merely a *primus inter pares*. But even Monroe was *primus* and he had chosen his peers. But the truer picture of the American cabinet is one that marks the contrast with the British system. It is in the story of Lincoln putting a question to the vote, announcing the result. 'Noes seven, ayes, one. The ayes

[1] See p. 35 *et sqq.*

have it'—an attitude so often contrasted with Melbourne's putting a question to the vote in his cabinet and saying 'it doesn't matter what we all say, as long as we all say the same thing'.

A consequence of this dominating position of the President is that as he is not bound by the opinion of his Cabinet, he can consult, regularly, not only Congressional leaders (that prudence drives him to do) but officials not of cabinet rank, ex-cabinet officers or members of Congress, in fact anyone he chooses. The late Harry Hopkins played an important role all through the Roosevelt administration but his importance at any given time had little to do with the official posts he held. Mr. Henry Wallace was brought into the Cabinet in the last Roosevelt administration, presumably as a compensation for having been removed from the vice-presidency, but his political importance was not much increased thereby, even if his feelings and those of his then numerous followers were soothed by this token of presidential esteem.

There naturally came into existence what, in the days of Andrew Jackson, was called a 'kitchen Cabinet', in which adroit politicians like Amos Kendall, played a role that irritated critics thought improper, but which was certainly legal. There have been equivalents of the Jacksonian 'kitchen Cabinet' since; 'tennis Cabinets' and 'Palace Guard' of the New Deal days. For as a monarch who is his own Prime Minister, the President cannot be prevented from seeking counsel where he wills. If he chooses to ignore the advisers who, by tradition, should have first access to him, that is his business. Like Louis XV, with his *secret du roi*, many a President has had his own policy and his own agents.

However overwhelming the prestige of a Prime Minister, he is bound really to consult his colleagues before proposing any important legislation or any important act of policy. Prime Ministers who do not do so, Lloyd George, Neville Chamberlain are examples, pay for it in the not very long run. But a President is under no such obligation. No more than he need take the advice or respect the vote of his Cabinet, need he consult them before committing the administration to a bold or even a rash course of action. It is his administration.[1]

[1] Thus we learn from the late Harold Ickes that there was no cabinet discussion of the highly dangerous and, as it turned out, unsuccessful

It is because it *is* the President's administration, that the rank of cabinet officer has not the prestige that the rank of cabinet minister has in England. A cabinet officer may be appointed merely because he is the friend of the President. He need have no personal or political weight. He may be appointed in spite of the fact that he is barely known to the President. Thus Wilson appointed Garrison, Cleveland appointed Olney, and F. D. Roosevelt, Harold Ickes. He may be appointed, in part at least, to make room for someone else. Thus one of Lincoln's reasons for making Fessenden his Secretary of the Treasury was to create a Senate vacancy for Vice-President Hannibal Hamlin who had been dropped from the ticket in 1864. And John Sherman, notoriously incompetent for any serious work, was made Secretary of State by McKinley to create a vacancy for Mark Hanna, the 'Warwick' of the 1896 campaign.

'A breath can make them, as a breath has made.' It can also unmake them and other eminent politicians besides Oliver Morton of Indiana have refused to accept any office that a man could dismiss him from. Probably only two or, at the most, three cabinet offices carry intrinsic prestige. The Secretary of State is still *ex officio* a person of great importance and dignity.[1] The Secretary of the Treasury, the Secretary of Defence hold offices so important

---

'court packing plan' in 1937. 'I have always deprecated the fact that President Roosevelt did not consult his Cabinet in advance and that nobody knew about the particular plan, except the President himself and the Attorney-General. The Cabinet was called together hastily at eleven o'clock one morning. The message was already on the way to the Hill [i.e. Congress]. Even if our advice had been sought, it would have been ineffective. We were confronted with a choice of supporting the President—and I did so because I believed the Supreme Court needed reform—or of resigning from the Cabinet and opposing it.' Quoted by Professor William H. Edwards, in *Principles and Functions of Government in the United States,* assembled and edited by W. Leon Godshall (1948), p. 365.

[1] I was present, towards the end of 1948, at a discussion of the new Cabinet Mr. Truman was expected to announce. It was suggested that Mr. Dean Acheson would be made Secretary of State and it was objected that he had resigned as Under-Secretary of State on the ground that he couldn't afford the job. A friend of Mr. Acheson's remarked, 'He couldn't afford to be Under-Secretary, but anybody can afford to be Secretary of State.'

that the prestige of the office passes in part at least to the holder. but this is not true of the other cabinet offices which rise and fall in prestige with their holders.

One consequence is that there cannot be a cabinet crisis in the English sense. A President can get rid of all his Cabinet, as Jackson did, he can get rid of his predecessor's Cabinet as Taft and Truman did. He can dismiss a cabinet officer as Mr. Truman did Mr, Wallace. He can let a cabinet officer down, with impunity, as Wilson did in the case of Lindley Garrison. The converse, is that cabinet officers and other high officials may talk very freely without committing their chief who, indeed, may know nothing of what they have said until he is asked about it at a press conference, or when an agitated ambassador calls anxiously at the State Department. And if cabinet officers need not or, at any rate, do not always consult the President, still less do they need to consult each other. Again, the only point of unity is the President himself. He may give a very free hand to subordinates, only insisting on the presidential right to make the basic decisions as Mr. Truman did. He may give a very free hand to several presidential agents in the same field and leave them, as long as possible, to fight it out among themselves as FDR did. But, as the notice Mr. Truman put on his desk rightly put it: 'The buck stops here.'

'The buck stops here' because, for many of his actions, the President is answerable to no one but the People of the United States. He may, in constitutional theory, be responsible before the Senate sitting as a court of impeachment, but that is a remote and unlikely sanction. The Senate can only try him on the impeachment by the House for 'Treason, Bribery or other high crimes and mis-demeanours,[1] and even the most partisan House of Representatives,

[1] *Constitution* Article II, Section 4. This article has only once been invoked against a President, though vague threats of impeachment are congressional common form. One charge against Andrew Johnson was the character of the speeches he made, 'to excite the odium and resentment of all the good people of the United States against Congress and the laws by it duly and constitutionally enacted'. (Roger Foster, *Commentaries on Constitution* (1895), vol. I, pp. 554–5.) But despite the fact that the Senate was thus mocked and despite the fact that Johnson was, politically, in the weakest possible position, with no party behind him, with a Congress in a revolutionary temper before him and all the passions

while bitterly resenting what a President does, is forced by law and tradition to recognize that there are many things he can do that no one can control. He has, for four years, in many departments of government:

the right divine to govern wrong.

Thus he alone decides whether to recognize or not to recognize foreign governments and that recognition may have important, internal, legal effects. He alone can decide when to support a 'Republican form of government' in the states. As part of the separate office of Commander-in-Chief, he commands all the armed forces of the United States and can use them, internally and externally, with great freedom. He has a pardoning power, limited only by the inability to pardon persons convicted on impeachment (who, in any case, only suffer the loss of office and the inability to hold office). The list of presidential powers could be extended, but enough has been said to show how much the President can do without or against the will of Congress. Even when Congress imposes special duties on him it is hard to force his hand or to compel him to act in the manner the Congress intended, as Mr. Truman showed by his effective reluctance to enforce the Taft-Hartley labour law. Congress may censure; Congress may denounce; but there is a substantial irreducible minimum of presidential power that Congress cannot take away.

Further power has been added, in these catastrophic times, by the nature of the world that the American people has to live in. One example of the inevitable increase of presidential and decrease of congressional power is the role of the National Security Council. This body was created by an act of 1947, but it is believed that it has become much more important under President Eisenhower. It has no congressional members and only some members of the Cabinet are members of the Council.[1] And as long as the cold war

---

of the Civil War still at blood heat, he was not convicted, a tribute to the strength, even at its lowest ebb, of the presidency and to the character of a third plus one of the Senate.

[1] Two are *ex-officio* members, the Secretary of State and the Secretary of Defence. The Secretary of the Treasury is at the moment (1954) a member, so is the Budget Director. So are the Foreign Operations

lasts, the Council will be more important than the Cabinet and not the boldest defender of the rights of Congress has suggested that either House should be represented on it. Yet on the judgement of the Council, Congress may have to act. But it is only to the President that the Council reports and only he can decide whether Congress is to be called on to act or not.

Then, the President is a part of the legislative process, if not of Congress, for he has a veto on legislation which can only be overridden by a vote of two-thirds of each house, cast after the veto has been announced.[1] It has been debated whether the veto power granted to the President by the Constitution is 'legislative' in character since all legislative power is vested in Congress. Historically speaking, the veto power is a relic of the royal veto power in England and the King was certainly part of Parliament. The Senate 'in impeachments, is a judicial and not a legislative body. In like manner the President acts as a part of the law-making power when he approves or disapproves an act.'[2]

More debatable or, at any rate, more debated, is the question of whether the President was given an unlimited veto power or simply a power to protect his own powers against congressional aggression. Again, practice has settled the question. 'It is clear that the power given to the President with reference to the vetoing of measures of Congress is one that, as a matter of propriety as well as of constitutional right, he may exercise upon any grounds he may deem sufficient.'[3]

Administrator and the Defense Mobilization Director. More important, the Vice-President is *ex-officio* a member. So should he succeed, he will not be at a loss as was Mr. Truman in 1945. Membership in this body may do something to make the vice-presidency an intrinsically important office.

[1] The President's veto does not apply to a constitutional amendment proposed by Congress to the states. But it is an extravagant novelty recently advanced by Senator Bricker that a President cannot advise against adopting an amendment.

[2] Edward Campbell Mason, *The Veto Power* (1891), p. 112.

[3] Westel Woodbury Willoughby, *The Constitutional Law of the United States*, second edition (1929), vol. II, p. 658. President Taft justified a veto of a bill on constitutional grounds by the argument that it was a bad habit of 'legislators and executives having any legislative

But although the law may have been the same from the beginning, the practice has changed in the sense that the veto has been more and more widely used, not only as a means of stopping legislation that a President for any reason may think wrong, or inconvenient, or politically dangerous, but as a means of controlling the action of Congress and as a means of appealing to the common master, the electors. And the reasons given for the veto may play and sometimes do play the part that minority opinions play in the Supreme Court, they give the President a chance to argue points, both of constitutionality and of public policy, with great effect.

The veto power has often been used for the rejection of very minor bills and there is something apparently disproportionate in the use of this great reserve power for such petty objects. But for reasons inherent in the working system of Congress, the only safeguard of the Treasury, the only barrier to jobs, has often been the veto which the President, representing the whole people, could use with a freedom and impunity that no Senator and, still more, no Representative who might at any moment need the votes of his colleagues, could dare to use. And vetoes preventing 'raids on the Treasury' in the form of private pension bills, endorsement of private claims, *ad hoc* (or *ad hominem*) legislation of all kinds, have been generally approved of by a public opinion that has no very high opinion of the ability of its representatives to resist pressure.[1]

---

functions to remit to the courts entire and ultimate responsibility as to the constitutionality of the measures which they take part in passing'. *Ibid.* Taft thought that since a Court was bound to give the benefit of the doubt to a statute, it was for Congress and the President to be more rigorous than the Courts in the interpretation of their constitutional powers, a view that few Presidents or Congresses have shared. For the opposite view expressed by F. D. Roosevelt, see p. 401.

[1] The numerous vetoes of Grover Cleveland were mostly directed at private bills, especially private pension bills. Cleveland had not served in the Civil War. He, as a Democrat, owed his election to the Southern states, i.e. to former 'rebels' who were not eligible for pensions, so that his motives were impugned by angry Republicans. They especially objected to the tone of veto measures, listing, as they did, the alleged sufferings of the heroes in a critical and unkind manner. These vetoes still make good reading and would provide material for an interesting essay on political or pension pathology.

But the general 'political' veto is more often criticized than not. Obviously, Congress has to pretend to be annoyed, even if the bill is one that it hoped and had reason to believe would be vetoed. Presidential vetoes that have upset party plans have provoked demands for amendments to the Constitution, either abolishing the veto or making it reversible by a simple majority of both houses. The theory has been advanced that a President cannot veto a revenue bill, a theory finally killed by President Truman who both vetoed a revenue bill and was not overridden.

It is sometimes argued that the 'strength' of a President can be assessed by the number of his vetoes, but the necessity for frequent vetoes may merely reflect inability to control Congress or an excessively scrupulous or fidgety view of presidential duty. Cleveland was a 'strong' President within his narrow view of what were a President's powers, but his lavish use of the veto power is not proof of it. F. D. Roosevelt was a strong President but his lavish use of the veto power is not the best proof of it. 'In contrast to Cleveland, who devoted his unfavorable attention to pension, military and naval relief measures, the range of subjects drawing the adverse action of Roosevelt has been as wide as the activity of Congress. Nothing too large or too small has escaped the penetrating eye of the President and his advisers. The following indicate that range of vision: agricultural relief, general appropriations, adjusted service compensation for World War veterans, interstate commerce, alien deportation, judicial review of administrative tribunals, flood control, protection of fisheries, homestead administration, Indian relief, tax and tariff policy, National defence, Philippine independence, Memorial Day observance, cemetery approaches, shorthand reporting, homing pigeons, District of Columbia street designations, parking meters, credit for beer wholesalers, control of funerals, and the exemption of religious periodicals.'[1]

[1] George C. Robinson quoted in Edward S. Corwin, *The President: Office and Powers*, Third edition (1948), p. 342. FDR was credited with diabolical skill in the use of the veto. A prominent New Deal congressman once complained to me that the President had vetoed a 'reactionary' measure on a Friday, knowing that many New Dealers from the eastern cities went off early that day to 'mend their fences', and that the more conservative members stayed on in Washington and, as he had foreseen, over-rode his veto. He thus got credit at no great expense.

Then vetoes are more common when Congress and the President are of different parties; each is acting 'for the record'; Congress sending up bills that will embarrass the President, the President rejecting bills that might aid the other side. These vetoes are often designed as campaign material for the approaching presidential election, as the bills also are. Thus Presidents Taft and Hoover were bombarded with bills that expressed less the considered legislative views of Congress than the tactical views of Democratic politicians.[1]

A President who has been defeated or is retiring can veto, in his last months of office, bills that are sure to be enacted in the next Congress, defying the opinion of the people as expressed by their representatives. But in electing a Congressman or a Senator, the voter does so in the knowledge (and often we may guess in the hope) that the President's veto will either prevent foolish legislation being enacted, or prevent its becoming law.

It is, of course, impossible to determine how many bills are not introduced or passed because they are sure to incur a veto. Congressional leaders may wish to spare the party the possible harm that an open breach between the party majority in Congress and *its* President may do the party as a whole. Even a Congress hostile to the President may wonder, at times, if it is prudent to give him a chance to appear before the public in a dramatic role as defender of the public interest or of some important voting group. The congressional retort seldom overtakes the presidential onslaught and the enactment of a bill over the veto is rare and may be politically expensive. At any rate, the argument that a veto is thwarting the popular will, seldom cuts much ice. The popular will is what,

[1] Miss Katherine A. Towle has shown that 'in the 12 years of politically divided or adverse Congresses the direct veto was exercised more than one and one-half times as often as in the 33 years of politically controlled Congresses: that, although within the respective groups themselves the percentages of both successful and unsuccessful attempts to over-ride the veto were almost identical, four times as many attempts at reversal were resorted to in the years of politically divided or adverse Congresses as in those controlled by the President's party; and that in the former period, congressional reversal occurred approximately four times as frequently as in the latter'. 'The Presidential Veto Since 1889' in *American Political Science Review*, February 1937, pp. 55-6.

constitutionally, passes Congress and the President; the President represents part of it.

There has not been, in recent times, any serious attempt to weaken the veto power; such changes as have been suggested have been directed to strengthening it by giving the President power to veto items in appropriation bills and thus prevent useless or mischievous expenditures being imposed on the country without forcing the President to veto what, as a whole, may be a useful or at any rate a necessary bill.

The great political advantage of the veto is that it gives the President an extra weapon against Congress, an extra means of influencing it. The knowledge that he will veto a bill may make Congress reluctant to waste time on enacting it. (It may also, of course, give Congress an excuse for enacting a vote-catching bill without having to fear the consequences of its becoming law.) The knowledge that he may veto a bill may induce Congress to accept amendments and may strengthen the hands of critics in Congress. The power of holding up legislation increases the importance of the President's role as a party leader and, above all, the inclusion of the President in the legislative process, 'nationalizes' legislation, gives a voice to the one national officer in the making of the laws of the nation.

If the President is, constitutionally, a negative part of the legislative process, he has also become one of the makers of law, positively. Of course, Presidents, even in the early days of the Constitution, had more or less influence over the legislative programme of Congress according to their political strength and adroitness. No modern President has had a more effective control over Congress than that exercised by Jefferson in his first term. But that influence was exercised behind the scenes, in private interviews with and letters to congressional leaders. In this century, the leadership has been open. The President is expected to put a programme before Congress. The 'State of the Union' speech is not quite like the 'Speech from the throne', not only because the speech really represents the speaker's views, while the Sovereign wisely keeps hers to herself, but because, except in rare circumstances, the President is much less certain of getting his programme through than is a Prime Minister here or in Canada. But although he does not control Congress, if it is of his own party he can give it a lead that it hesitates, openly, to refuse to follow (especially in an election year) and even if it is of another party, he can give Congress a lead that he hopes will put it on the spot, politically, for if it adopts his programme, he may get the credit of it and if it does not it can be denounced, effectively, as a 'do nothing Congress', as Mr. Truman demonstrated in 1948.

It is now part of the unwritten constitution that the President has a right to offer to Congress a legislative programme (including a budget). He cannot be sure that he will get all he wants or in the form he wants. But it is his duty to ask for it and it is to him, at least as much as to Congress, that the country looks for leadership, even in the field of legislation.[1]

It is easy to indicate periods in which presidential leadership was feeble, others in which it was strong. But it is harder to give the credit for a given piece of legislation even to powerful Presidents like Woodrow Wilson and Franklin D. Roosevelt in their first terms, for they (except in the first hectic days of the New Deal) had to compromise, cajole, follow as well as lead. Thus even the legislative history of the Federal Reserve Act of 1913, certainly a result of presidential leadership, 'should give pause to any one who glibly asserts that a particular act is the handiwork of this or that individual. Under our representative system of government the construction of a major piece of legislation is essentially a problem of co-operation and compromise. Certain individuals hold places of strategic importance and are thus advantaged in the competition for influence; but their advantage is relative rather than absolute for they also must yield many times against their will'.[2]

[1] Congressional leaders with responsibilities to their formal party leader, the President, sometimes find it hard to defend the independent judgment of Congress, of either house of Congress. Thus Senator Knowland, asserting that President Eisenhower 'does not believe that Congress should be a rubber-stamp body', was yet forced to admit that 'the public . . . from time to time may not understand the reasons that Congress takes certain action . . . but I think the American people strongly support our constitutional division of powers'. Interview in *U.S. News and World Report*, 24 July 1953, p. 40. This is the congressional theory, but whether it represents the public attitude or even a firm congressional belief is more doubtful.

[2] Lawrence H. Chamberlain, *The President, Congress and Legislation*

The power of the President to influence Congress has, in the last thirty years, been greatly increased by the coming of what are called 'the mass media'. A President can now, by means of the radio and of television, appeal over the heads of Congress to the mass of the voters. He can always make news and both Roosevelts, Wilson and, at times, Messrs. Truman and Eisenhower, have shown an admirable sense of timing. Congress cannot compete with a President giving a 'fireside chat' to millions of listeners or putting his cabinet through its paces on television.

Nor has Congress found an equivalent for the presidential press conference. This, as an institution, dates from the time of Wilson, but it was F. D. Roosevelt who made it an effective instrument of government. The advantages of the press conference for a President who knows how to use it are manifold. He can decide what questions to answer, what to put 'off the record', what is to be attributed directly, what to be credited to a White House spokesman. And all of this is done unofficially, to a body of which the law takes no cognizance. The contrast with question time in the House of Commons is obvious. There, the Speaker, not the Prime Minister, is in charge. The questioners are Members of Parliament with their own rights. They may be the leaders of the Opposition, they may be private members. But they are part of 'the grand inquest of the Nation'. They can put 'supplementaries' and considerable parliamentary reputations have been made by the display of skill in this art. The questions and answers are matters of official record; a refusal to answer is a more serious matter than a presidential 'no comment'. The average Washington correspondent is an abler man than the average Member of Parliament, but he is not a Member of Parliament. He is an unofficial person employed by the owner of a newspaper. He may have privileges but he has no rights.

(1946), p. 321. Professor Chamberlain calls attention to the odd way in which Wilson dropped the army projects of his War Secretary, Lindley Garrison, in 1916, an episode that led to Garrison's resignation and to the fact that later, he had to turn to the Republican leaders to get other military legislation through. And the Taylor Grazing Act of 1934, in the heyday of F. D. Roosevelt's power, was the work of 'Congressmen, administrative officials—political and otherwise—and lobbyists of varying degrees of self-interest. . . . The President was not an important factor'. Ibid., p. 410.

Congress, too, is at a disadvantage. *It* cannot question the President and he can arrange to answer in advance questions that one or other house might want to put by the cumbersome method of debate or investigation. The President can nearly always steal the show, and, usually, if he wishes, see that there is no show if that suits him.[1] For example, the President decides when a press conference is at an end. All that the correspondents can do is say 'Thank you, Mr. President', through their spokesman. The President is their host and can speed the parting guests. The Prime Minister is a member of the body that produces the questioners. He is not just their servant, but he is neither, during question time anyway, their master or their host.

Inevitably, the progress of techniques has led to suggestions of improvements in the system of the press conference that would, in fact, distort and possibly destroy its character. The conference is already tape-recorded, which a veteran reporter, Richard Strout of the *Christian Science Monitor*, thinks is a mistake. 'The old "off the record" system had great advantages for all concerned; it put the President at his ease, it placed the reporters in a livelier relationship to him and it created an atmosphere more favourable for turning up information—which is the true purpose of the meeting.'[2] A more radical change has been suggested, that the press conference be televised, but this has evoked even stronger opposition. For if the

[1] Roosevelt wisely (from his point of view) refused to act on a House resolution that 'asked for a transcript of a press conference for inclusion in the *Congressional Record*. The President voiced his thanks for the opportunity but doubted the advisability of creating a precedent. In a letter to Speaker Joseph W. Byrns he explained his desire to continue the conferences "on the free and open basis which I have endeavoured to maintain at all times" and to do as the resolution intended "would . . . bring to me a consciousness of restraint as well as a necessity for constant preparation of my remarks. The simple truth is that I do not have the time to give to such preparation for a press conference".' James E. Pollard, *The Presidents and the Press* (1947), p. 778. It may be doubted if the truth was as simple as all that, but FDR was undoubtedly wise in keeping the press conferences separate from any relationship with the *Congressional Record*. The transcripts of the nine hundred and ninety-eight press conferences he held are printed (although not in full) in the *Public Papers*.

[2] Mr. Strout stated his views in *The New Republic*. This version of them is from *The New Yorker* (6 February 1954, p. 21).

President had to perform before millions, he could not risk spontaneity, he could not be off the record, the temptation offered to
some reporters to get into the act might prove irresistible and
newspapers might begin to choose their Washington representatives
for their photogenic assets.[1]

A weapon that a President may still use but which has lost some
of its cutting edge is the federal patronage, the 'spoils system'. The
phrase, if not the institution, we owe to Senator William Marcy of
New York, who in 1831 boldly avowed the principle on which he
and his friends acted. 'It may be, sir, that the politicians of New York
are not so fastidious as some gentlemen are, as to disclosing the
principles on which they act. They boldly *preach* what they *practise*.
When they are contending for *victory*, they avow their intention of
enjoying the fruits of it. If they are defeated, they expect to retire
from office. If they are successful, they claim, as a matter of right,
the advantages of success. They see nothing wrong in the rule that
to the VICTOR belong the spoils of the ENEMY.'[2] Few, indeed,
in that age ever thought of giving jobs to any but partisans. What
was more novel was the policy of removal from office of those
already installed, although that, too, had been practised; what was
more novel still was the limitation of the term of office, even of good
party members, to four years. This principle of 'rotation' was the
real heart of the system.

The case not merely for the 'spoils system', but for the principle
of rotation, of limited tenure, was put with majestic simplicity
in Andrew Jackson's first annual message to Congress. 'There are,

[1] I do not wish to suggest that, as a body, the correspondents are less
photogenic than, say, Congressmen. One of the most skilful performers
at presidential press conferences is also one of the handsomest men in
Washington, but it is his brains, not his looks, that make him valuable to
his paper.

[2] Commager, *Documents*, Vol. I, p. 255. But Marcy was only more
candid than other politicians. In New York, the system went back long
before his time. 'It was the federalists who made the first step in the
direction of establishing the spoils system. . . . When John Jay became
governor he continued the work already begun by the Council. And the
policy pursued by Jay and the federalists was paralleled by John Adams
when he became President of the United States two years later.' Howard
Lee McBain, *De Witt Clinton and the Origin of the Spoils System in New
York* (1907), p. 157.

perhaps, few men who can for any length of time enjoy office and power without being more or less under the influence of feelings unfavourable to the faithful discharge of their public duties. Their integrity may be proof against improper considerations immediately addressed to themselves, but they are apt to acquire a habit of looking with indifference upon the public interests and of tolerating conduct from which an unpractised man would revolt. Office is considered as a species of property, and government, rather as a means of promoting individual interests than as an instrument created solely for the service of the people. Corruption in some and in others a perversion of correct feelings divert government from its legitimate ends and make it an engine for the support of the few at the expense of the many. The duties of all public officers are, or at least admit of being made, so plain and simple that men of intelligence may readily qualify themselves for their performance: and I cannot but believe that more is lost by the long continuance in office than is generally to be gained by their experience.'[1]

The principle was certainly acted on and federal office holders came and went in a fashion that showed either that Andrew Jackson was right, that experience didn't count, or that Adam Smith was right and that there is 'a great deal of ruin in a nation', especially in a nation like the United States. Probably no European

---

[1] James D. Richardson, *Messages and Papers of the Presidents* (1899), vol. II, p. 449. This doctrine has a curious resemblance to that preached by Lenin before the responsibilities of power sobered him. 'Capitalist culture has *created* large scale production, factories, railways, the postal service etc., and *on this basis* the great majority of the functions of the old "state power" have become so simplified and have been reduced to such simple operations of registration, filing and checking that they can be easily performed for ordinary "workmen's wages", and can (and must) be stripped of every shadow of privilege, of every semblance of "official grandeur".' *The Essentials of Lenin* (1947), vol. II, p. 170. Jackson and Lenin had good, though different excuses, for their illusions. Jackson had been a self-made planter, general, lawyer, judge, Senator and was now President, fulfilling each role to his complete satisfaction. He found it hard to realise that not everybody was an Andrew Jackson and still harder to realise that there were jobs that he couldn't do. Lenin when he wrote *State and Revolution* had the excuse of no practical experience of government or business. But Jackson's doctrines were at least more relevant to the America of 1829 than Lenin's were to the Russia of 1917.

nation could have survived the system, but the United States did. It represented the temper of the times for, in some states, the principle of rotation was applied to Congress as well; thus Abraham Lincoln got the one term in Congress that was his right, but no more.

The Civil War doubled the permanent size of the federal service, from 50,000 in 1860 to 100,000 in 1866. During the war, of course, the numbers were greater and Lincoln used the patronage skilfully and ruthlessly to reward Republicans, paper-over the cracks inside the dominant party and give support to factions within it. He had to employ Democrats as soldiers, but he firmly refused to let any pleas of national unity make him ignore the rigours of the game.[1]

But the system, at least the system of rotation, now had many critics. Had Lincoln lived, he might have kept on most of the appointees of his first term and by the time Grant was nominated, there was some talk of 'civil service', that is of an imitation of the system being created in England by which admission to public employment was by competitive examination. But apart from a few kind words and empty gestures from President Grant, the system remained and, if possible, was more rank with corruption than ever.

It was not a mere matter of giving jobs to good party men, for there were far more good party men than there were jobs. It was an elaborate system of allocation of jobs whose application needed a fine sense of discrimination. Cabinet officers had a right to some, though not to all of the plums in their departments and they used their powers in their own as well as in the party's interests. Thus Chase, at the Treasury during the Civil War, built up a Chase

---

[1] Even the greatest of Presidents, at least once, preferred his friend to his duty. He nominated Mark W. Delahay who had been a 'Lincoln man' before Lincoln himself was, to be Federal Judge in Kansas over the protests of the local bar. An opponent of the appointment wrote to Senator Trumbull of Illinois, Lincoln's own state, that 'the appointment is disgraceful to the President. . . . He, Delahay, is no lawyer, could not try a case properly even in a Justice's Court, and has no character'. Harry C. Carman and Reinhard H. Luthin, *Lincoln and the Patronage* (1943), p. 118. The critics proved right. Delahay had to resign under threat of impeachment.

machine which did not prevent him from asking for jobs in other departments. Representatives and Senators besieged the department heads and the White House[1] for their own clients and thus often involved the administration in intra-state feuds that harmed the party and, in their resulting appointments, harmed the country.

Allocations of jobs were systematized. Senators, if there were two of the dominant party, divided the big state offices between them, although if, as was usually the case, one of the Senators was more important than the other, he had the real plums. Congressmen divided lesser jobs and, of course, a great congressional leader got more than his share and an important Governor could not be indifferent to the views and loyalties of federal officials in his state. The results were usually, although not uniformly bad. The official had no hope of a permanent career so he was tempted to make a killing.[2]

Non-voters like the Indians were easy game and more than one Indian war was caused by the rapacity of the Indian agents.[3] The cost as well as the corruption of the Indian service was a national scandal and the *New York Times* once suggested that it would be cheaper to board all the Indian wards of the nation in the Fifth Avenue Hotel.

There were scandals in the Post Office; in the Customs Houses; there was comic inefficiency in the diplomatic service such as the appointment of General Robert Schenck as Minister to London where he distinguished himself by helping to float a bogus mine and

[1] Henry Adams tells us of a cabinet officer who broke out to him! ' "You can't use tact with a Congressman! A Congressman is a hog, You must take a stick and hit him on the snout." Adams knew far too little, compared with the Secretary, to contradict him, but he knew a shorter way of silencing criticism. He had but to ask: "If a Congressman is a hog, what is a Senator?" This innocent question, put in a candid spirit, petrified any executive officer that ever sat a week in his office.' *The Education of Henry Adams* (1918), p. 261.

[2] There is a possibly apocryphal story of an honest land agent in the West who wired Washington, 'Remove me at once, they're getting near my price.'

[3] It was noted as one of the few signs of grace in Matthew Stanley Quay, the notorious Senator from Pennsylvania, that his rapacity did not extend to his Indian kinsmen whom he even tried to protect from lesser spoilsmen.

introducing draw poker. But the great consulates were real rewards, for their incumbents were paid by fees.[1]

There also grew up the habit of allotting special jobs to given states and it was a breach of faith or, at any rate, a proof of presidential indifference if these traditional allocations were disregarded. Thus the combative Senator William E. Chandler of New Hampshire found that President McKinley was not paying adequate attention to the established rights of his state. 'The vigilant and ever-grasping Senator Proctor, capitalizing his flop to McKinley in 1896, secured for Vermont, the Pension Agency and almost obtained a consulate, supposed to be the property of the State, while Senator Elkins carried off the Colombian mission, occupied by New Hampshire men for a number of years. To add to the exasperation of the group, President McKinley sweetly proposed, in place of recommendations made by the delegation, that a personal friend of his, then not even a resident of the State, although he retained his voting rights there, should be made Minister to Persia and that appointment should be regarded as the State's share of the upper diplomatic posts.'[2]

More serious was and is the problem not merely of rewarding the faithful by foreign posts, but the filling of domestic posts, that, civil service or no civil service, are thought to be of political importance, if only as a sign of the power and prestige of the patron.[3]

[1] Thus Patrick Collins, one of the most important Irish-American politicians, was made Consul-General in London by Cleveland. He was ever after known as General Collins. Bret Harte, for literary services, was made Consul, first at Düsseldorf and then at Glasgow. Even this last appointment did not satisfy him.

[2] Leon Burr Richardson, *William E. Chandler, Republican* (1940), p. 550.

[3] 'Because Coos County at the tip of New Hampshire is part of the same federal district as Vermont the story is going around that U.S. Senator Bridges may have the say in the selection of a new collector of customs. Basis of the report seems to be the reported split between Senators Aiken and Flanders over this $6,000 a year plum and that of district attorney. . . . It is likewise rumoured that G.O.P. national committee members, Edward G. Janeway of Londonderry and Speaker Consuelo Bailey, have ideas of their own on these appointments. Guessing on political probabilities of this sort is nearly always hazardous, but that

The scale of federal patronage of course varied from state to state. There was, in the days before a federal income tax, before federal social welfare services, before federal aid to agriculture (and to agricultural agencies), much less patronage in a farm state than in a great city, above all if that city were a port, or could be (as some inland cities were) deemed to be one. New York Custom House, the Brooklyn Navy Yard, New York Post Office were teeming with politically useful jobs. Navy yards could, at critical times, suddenly increase their labouring staff.[1] 'The navy yard at Portsmouth was a large and unfailing employer at critical times'[2] and what was true of Virginia was true of Pennsylvania, Massachusetts (where the chief beneficiary was Henry Cabot Lodge) and of Maine where, in a poor state, the spoils of a small yard like Kittery were not to be despised.[3]

There were a few permanent officials who were kept on through all administrations, because there had to be some expert continuity.

---

of this newspaper is that Senator Aiken's wishes will prevail.' *The Brattleboro Daily Reformer,* 25 July 1953. Even in rural New England, in these times, a job paying $6,000 with very insecure tenure is only a 'plum' in the political sense.

[1] The Navy Yards were able to employ a great many men by concentrating on slow and costly repair work. 'Never was so little done by so many in so long a time', as a famous phrase was later to be amended. 'Between 1868 and 1885, the Government had spent more than $75,000,000 on its wooden fleet and had nothing to show for it. Whitney later pointed out that the worthless *Omaha* had been rebuilt at a cost of $572,000, while the *Mohican,* a 910-ton mite, had cost $908,000 for repairs in twelve years.' Mark D. Hirsch, *William C. Whitney* (1948), p. 262.

[2] Charles Chilton Pearson, *The Readjuster Movement in Virginia* (1917), p. 154. Control of the yard was one of Mahone's chief benefits from his alliance with the Republicans and the success of the Democrats and the appointment of Whitney, a disaster.

[3] The dockyard vote was a well-known phenomenon of British and French politics with Pembroke and Rochefort playing the part of Kittery and Charleston. But there were British and French navies to show for the expense while, when Whitney took office in 1885, it was doubtful if the United States could have fought a successful naval war with China and almost certain that she could not have fought one with Chile.

These were chiefly to be found in the State Department and in the scientific departments.[1] The War and Navy Departments evaded the full force of the system by employing officers.[2] But, all in all, the American government, as the United States was about to become the greatest industrial power in the world, was manned according to the simple principles of the America of Andrew Jackson.

Reform was in the air. The assassination of President Garfield by a disappointed office-seeker was a shock to the public for it was seen as part of the savage struggle between the President and Senator Conkling, between the 'Half-Breeds' and the 'Stalwarts', for the lush patronage of New York. Garfield, it was felt, had been murdered as much by the system as by Guiteau.[3]

It was the time for the reformers to strike while the public temper was hot and the first law creating a Civil Service Commission and opening some jobs to competitive examination, the Pendleton Act, was passed in 1883. It seemed to the more hopeful reformers, the dawn of a new day. It was, but not quite their new day.

For one thing, the Pendleton Act was the work of a Democrat, a member of a party with no share in the profits of the system. It was unfortunate for the reformers that, a year after the act was passed, the Democrats won a presidential election for the first time in twenty-four years and the new President, Grover Cleveland, was under exceptional pressure, on the one hand from the faithful as hungry for real food as the Israelites after a hardly longer time in the desert and, on the other hand, from the independents, the 'Mugwumps' who had supported him and were inclined to think

[1] Thus Lester Ward, the sociologist, spent most of his life in increasingly important scientific jobs in Washington. But he entered the government service as an ordinary clerk in the Treasury, after applying to Lincoln in a letter like that of many hundreds of other applicants. 'My necessities are great, I have no regular home, am an orphan, am physically disqualified for any laborious occupation and have been out of employment nearly all the winter.' Samuel Chugerman. *Lester F. Ward the American Aristotle* (1939), p. 32.

[2] See p. 369.

[3] A more remarkable politician than Garfield, Carter Harrison I, five times Mayor of Chicago, was also murdered by an office-seeker.

that they had elected him.[1] All things considered, Cleveland managed to steer a fairly successful course, offending both sides but not mortally. But the reformers could not have been satisfied in any case, for the reform they wanted was impossible in the American context.

The early reformers of the American civil service were profoundly impressed by the success of the English reforms associated with the names of Charles Trevelyan, Stafford Northcote and Gladstone. They wanted to see, in America, an equivalent of the new higher civil service, recruited by a severe competitive examination, that had first been tried out in India and then adopted in England. The organ of the reformers, *The Nation*, was deeply anglophile. Godkin continued to think that they ordered a great many matters better in England (if not in Ireland) than they did in America. No doubt, the reformers wanted a general reform of the civil service, less corrupt foremen in the Navy Yards, less venal customs inspectors at the docks. But their real aim was to see in America, a class of professional civil servants in the highest ranks, recruited from brilliant university graduates and, from the start, given opportunities of power and material rewards, that would, taken together, make government service as attractive as the opportunities of business, the law, medicine, even the press.

They tended to ignore the great social differences that made the simple imitation of the English system impossible. It was easy to plan an examination system based on that of Oxford and Cambridge, one which even some wandering Scots and intrusive Irishmen could cope with. But how was it possible to invent such a system in a country where the pre-eminence of Harvard was far from taken for granted? How was it possible, in the country of Andrew Jackson and Abraham Lincoln, to use Macaulay's argument to the House of Commons, that, on the whole, the brilliant university student did best in public life and public service? Where were the

[1] The Mugwumps were mainly readers of the two organs of righteousness, both edited by a pugnacious Irishman, Edwin Lawrence Godkin, *The Nation* and *The Evening Post*. The word is Algonquin 'mugquomp' meaning 'an important person; the high-muck-a-muck . . . used ironically'. Mitford M. Mathews, *A Dictionary of Americanisms*, vol. II, p. 1098. It was first used by the *Evening Post* on 20 June 1884. It was not used ironically by the *Post*.

American equivalents of double firsts like Peel and Gladstone? And although Macaulay argued that examinations in Ptolemaic cosmogony and Choctaw or Cherokee would sift out the talented as well as Newtonian mathematics and Latin and Greek, in fact the examinations were designed to suit the curriculums of Oxford and Cambridge and that just in the short period in the life of those two ancient universities when they most effectively excluded the really poor boy. One can find, at the time, plenty of references to the absolute equality of the conditions of competitions in the examination in England, but it was absolute equality as it exists at Wimbledon or Forest Hills, after a rigorous seeding.[1]

Nor was it likely that American society in the second half of the nineteenth century, would permit the offering of rewards in cash, power or prestige like those offered to the new civil service in England and India. Even in cash these rewards were substantial, especially in India. For the Indian Civil Service, nearly ninety years ago, offered to quite young men salaries which, when the value of money and the rate of taxation is considered, are not only far better than those offered today in the Home Civil Service, but better than those offered on the boards of nationalized industries.[2] It did more than that, it offered a career full of interest and power, both to be enjoyed young. 'There is no career which holds out such certain and splendid prospects to honourable ambition. . . . The real education of a Civil Servant consists in the responsibility that devolves on him at an early age, which brings out whatever good there is in a man.'[3]

[1] One of the reasons why the Gladstone reforms of 1870 were so easily put through, was that the great extension of the franchise in 1867, the reduction in the number of 'close boroughs', threatened the transfer of effective patronage from the magnates to the publicans and radical agitators who were beginning to create something a little like the American machine. The spoils were removed before these upstarts became the victors.

[2] See the mouth-watering figures in Sir George Otto Trevelyan's *Letters of a Competition Wallah* (first published in 1867) reprinted (in part) in *Interludes in Verse and Prose* (1912), pp. 177-8.

[3] Ibid., pp. 178, 180. This high opinion of the recruiting of the I.C.S., I have heard confirmed by the most famous of living Irishmen, or Irish-Americans.

The home civil service did not offer such splendid material rewards (the price of exile), nor did it offer them quite so young. It promised, too, rather less power and more influence (to use Lord Beveridge's distinction), but many prefer influence to power and its penalties. And, not a totally imaginary attraction, there were the decorations, the Bath, the Star of India, even the occasional peerage. No wonder the civil service examination stimulated the academic zeal of the young in Balliol and King's College. Tutors amending Dean Gaisford's sermon, could point out that academic distinction 'not only elevates above the vulgar herd but leads not infrequently to positions of considerable emolument.'[1]

II

The English system could not be transplanted then and has not been transplanted yet. Attempts have been made, especially in the last twenty years, to bring into the civil service young men of exceptional distinction and give them the kind of opportunities for rapid promotion and rapid accession to authority, open to those who pass high into the British civil service. But none of these attempts has really succeeded. American society is too egalitarian for such an open aristocracy of talent to be tolerated.

What has been done is to extend the area covered by civil service regulations. Nearly every administration has added to the 'classified service'; fewer and fewer jobs are now awarded on a spoils basis. There are many reasons for this. Few jobs, if any, now offer the lavish and legal rewards that were attainable in the past. As the federal government has extended its range of activities, more and more technical divisions, agencies and bureaux have been set up. With all the will in the world, the most zealous party worker is not thereby qualified for such jobs and he and his patrons usually know it. Who would think of putting a body like the Bureau of Standards on a patronage basis?[2]

[1] A former Cambridge tutor, Leslie Stephen, noted how the opportunities of the Indian Civil Service had increased the already considerable cash value of academic distinction.

[2] I have let this example stand, for although the present Secretary of Commerce tried to remove the head of the Bureau on grounds that

Then the mere scale of federal employment is too great for patronage to handle. With two and a half million federal employees of whom eight hundred thousand hold jobs that are, possibly, coveted by party workers, the whole political system would break down if Senators and Congressmen were not protected from endless solicitation by their impotence to interfere.

Lastly, Congress, more and more afraid of losing its powers to the President, is almost, if not quite, ready to give up its patronage, *if* that will hamper the President in using *his* to coerce and seduce. After all, the President alone can nominate and refuse to nominate and the powers of the President are already, most members of Congress think, too great.[1]

A curious custom, that now has practically the force of law, grew up as a result of senatorial suspicion of presidential power. This is the so-called 'courtesy of the Senate'. The courtesy is displayed when a Senator tells his colleagues when a nomination is sent in by the President for one of the offices that need senatorial confirmation (and all important offices do), that the nominee is 'personally offensive' to him. He need not explain why the nomination is offensive. His reasons may be strictly personal. They may be based on the character of the nominee; on his unfitness, in the objector's opinion for the job; or they may be based on the fear that the nomination will weaken the position of the Senator. And since every Senator fears that a President may sometimes nominate for high office someone falling under one of these heads of objection,

---

would justify dismissing the Astronomer Royal for refusing to cast horoscopes, public and professional reaction forced the Secretary to retreat.

[1] Mr. Spann rightly stresses this motive as one of those behind the 'reform' legislation of recent years. It was not only that the Democrats who passed the legislation were providing against the evil day, which they knew must come sometime, when the Republicans would get in. There was 'a newer motive, fear of the "sharp-pointed pic" that the President had made of the patronage instrument. The memory of the attempted party purge of 1938 and the approach of the 1940 elections acted together to stimulate reforms which ten years later had given competitive status to 92 per cent of federal offices inside the United States'. R. N. Spann, 'Civil Servants in Washington', *Political Studies*, June 1953, pp. 159-60.

all Senators, except in the most outrageous cases or where party and intra-party feuds are most bitter, support their colleague. Often, it is true, Senators have exercised their 'right' outrageously and have, for merely personal or plainly bad reasons, debarred good public servants from employment. But the right has been used, and used recently, by some of the most respected and deserving members of the Senate. And as long as it is believed that, in patronage, is one of the keys to political mastery, so long will the Senate allow its members the right to prevent a President from freely using a power that might weaken or ruin any one of them.

The presidential power *has* been an important source of presidential power and of congressional discipline. Traditionally, a new President holds up nominations until he has secured support for his programme from Congress. But this was much easier to do in the past, when mere jobs played a greater part in building-up political strength, especially in the days when a Senator was elected by the legislature instead of by millions or, at any rate, hundreds of thousands of voters. Cleveland could, by this means, force the silver Democrats to swallow their principles. But such pressure is not likely to be enough in itself to coerce Congress today and a President may wonder, as members of Congress are beginning to wonder, whether patronage is not more trouble than it is worth.

The presidential power of patronage made and may make more enemies than friends or even allies. Nothing was likely to have made Speaker Reed an admirer of President Benjamin Harrison, but the decision of the President to nominate as Collector of Portland, the nominee of his Secretary of State, James G. Blaine, instead of the nominee of the Speaker in whose territory Portland was, made relations between the two most important Republican official leaders worse than ever.[1] Another Reed, 'Jim' Reed of Missouri, opposed the Wilson banking legislation 'because the

[1] Reed commented in a famous gibe 'I never had but two personal enemies in my life. One of these he pardoned out of the penitentiary and the other he has just appointed Collector of the Port of Portland.' William A. Robinson, *Thomas B. Reed* (1930), p. 161. Maine, for its population, had too many eminent statesmen for its natural patronage.

President would not appoint his candidate as postmaster of Kansas City. Wilson finally named Reed's man'.[1]

If the spoils system is but a shadow of what it was, it is still a shadow with some substance. For, at the top of the American civil service, are a good many jobs that, in Britain, would be considered unpolitical, but about which, in the United States, there is doubt; and when a party comes into power, it naturally resolves the doubt in its own favour. This, the Republicans have done since they returned to power in 1953. But the more naïve of them have found out, with irritation or sterner emotions, that there are comparatively few federal jobs in the public political domain today. There have been incessant complaints about the unco-operative attitude of the Civil Service Commission and some ingenious ways round the law have been discovered. Thus if it is impossible to remove a civil servant, with status, from his job, it is possible to abolish the job. Whether this deprives the incumbent of all rights is a question now before the courts. But whether the Republicans succeed in re-making the Washington bureaucracy nearer to their heart's desire or not, they have succeeded in disturbing the peace of mind of the incumbents. For Washington is full of stories of 'riffing', 'bumping' and 'slotting'.[2] Civil Servants have found that their tenure is much less secure than they had fancied and that attractions of government service, at any rate above the lower levels, are less than had been believed. But there has always been a very big flow into and out of

[1] Arthur S. Link, *Woodrow Wilson and the Progressive Era 1910–1917* (1954), p. 52.

[2] 'Riffing' comes from 'reduction in force', the cutting down by an arbitrary number of the establishment of a department. 'Bumping' comes from the complicated results of moving a high-ranking incumbent down or sideways. These incumbents have usually high civil service ratings; they have to be found a place and that involves the further bumping of scores or hundreds of others. Like a remote earthquake in the Pacific reported from Fordham Observatory, an adjustment in the top ranks of the bureaucracy may be felt at great distances. 'Slotting' is finding a place into which someone 'riffed' can be fitted. Sometimes the official who is 'riffed' has no or low civil service status, but may have special talents or the 'bumped' official with higher rating who replaced him, may turn out to be totally unfit. The dismissed bureaucrat is then 'slotted', put back in his old job under a new title. I know of one case in which an official 'riffed' on Wednesday was 'slotted' by Friday.

the federal service and the numerical change in personnel may reflect more the natural mobility of American life, than the success of the Republicans in getting back to the days of Conkling or John Wanamaker.

Most of what was said against the spoils system was deserved. But there was something to be said for it. Andrew Jackson (and Lenin) were not quite wrong in stressing the dangers of an irremovable bureaucracy. And the spoils system brought into federal service many temporary servants of great ability who shook up routine (or prevented it from being established). The system of rewarding party services with jobs, and then making those rewarded pay part of their salaries to the party funds, was open to grave objection. But it was not morally or politically worse than the methods by which Mark Hanna raised funds for McKinley in 1896, by which the debts of the Harding campaign of 1920 were paid off, or funds raised for Mr. Truman's forlorn hope of 1948.

The spoils system is dying but it is dying hard and it will still have life in it as long as the average politician retains his superstitious belief in its necessity and efficacy. Some begin to doubt. Thus one of the most eminent of modern politicians, Mr. James A. Farley, has said that it is not necessary to have jobs to give away to create an effective political organization. The main necessity is the willingness to work hard. But not all politicians are as skilled managers of men as is Mr. Farley and no politician, as yet, has been willing or able to do entirely without patronage.[1]

One special power that the Senate shares with the President is

---

[1] A critical if friendly observer agrees that the importance of mere patronage in the growth of Mr. Farley's power has been exaggerated. 'There are better reasons for the flourishing state of Big Jim's empire than that its builder has had a hand in parcelling out somewhere between 200,000 and 300,000 federal jobs.' 'Big Jim Farley' by Duncan Aikman in *The American Politician*, edited by J. T. Salter (1938), p. 222. Mr. Farley justified his famous dictum 'patronage is the test by which a party shows its fitness to govern', by the argument that the executants of policies must be in sympathy with them. 'Take my word for it, no matter how conscientious an employee may be, or how loyal he thinks he is, if he is basically at odds with the policies of the department in which he works, the fact will show itself in his labors sooner or later.' James A. Farley, *Behind the Ballots* (1938), p. 230.

that of ratifying treaties. For that, a two-thirds majority of Senators, present and voting, is required (not, as was once asserted, a two-thirds vote of all the membership). The Constitution, indeed, goes further, for the Senate is to give 'advice and consent'. But with very few exceptions, the Senate has never been asked, as a body, to give advice until the President has negotiated a treaty and submitted it to the Senate.

The power given to the Senate was very deliberately given, for one of the dangers to the unity of the United States under the Articles of Confederation was created by the fact that each state, or each group of states, suspected the rest of being willing to barter away the rights of the others in dealing with foreign powers. Thus the states which looked to the Mississippi as their way to the outer world, feared that New England would give in to Spain (which then controlled the mouth of the Father of Waters) to secure fishing rights important to the industry of the 'Sacred Cod'. When Jefferson bought Louisiana from France, New England objected to the upsetting of the sectional balance of power. Sectional quarrels like these fully justified giving to just over a third of the states (for that rather than a third of the Senators plus one was the real safeguard) a veto on treaties. But states, and even sections, are not what they were and the two-thirds requirement has been under fire for most of this century. For the two-thirds rule was often used to gain political advantage, to cater to racial groups, and this could be done with impunity since to the average American, foreign affairs were very foreign indeed. Providence, to borrow from Andrew Marvell's description of English pre-Civil War isolationism,

> Which to exclude the world did guard
> With watery if not flaming sword,

could be trusted to see that its foresight was not frustrated.[1] But the

---

[1] 'The idea took hold that an all-wise Providence had set aside this empty continent as a refuge from Europe's century-old hatred and wars. Timothy Dwight wrote in 1794:

> See this glad world remote from every foe,
> From Europe's mischiefs, and from Europe's woe.'

(Thomas A. Bailey, *The Man in the Street: The Impact of American Public Opinion on Foreign Policy* (1948), p. 244.) The future President of Yale was not as good a poet as Marvell, but he had the same idea.

world insisted on butting in and the action of the Senate in rejecting the Treaty of Versailles and keeping the United States out of the League of Nations was only the most dramatic and the most criticized of the exercises of senatorial rights.

The orthodox case against the Senate was put in classical form by John Hay, or by Henry Adams reporting Hay. 'A treaty of peace, in any normal state of things,' said Hay, 'ought to be ratified with unanimity in twenty-four hours. They wasted six weeks in wrangling over this one, and ratified it with one vote to spare. We have five or six matters now demanding settlement. I can settle them all, honorably and advantageously to our own side; and I am assured by leading men in the Senate that not one of these treaties, if negotiated, will pass the Senate. I should have a majority in every case, but a malcontent third would certainly dish every one of them. To such monstrous shape has the original mistake grown in the evolution of our politics. . . . The fathers had intended to neutralize the energy of government and had succeeded, but their machine was never meant to do the work of a twenty million horse-power society in the twentieth century, where much work needed to be quickly and efficiently done'.[1] Even if we make allowances for Hay's impatience with a body that he did little to conciliate or study, there is no doubt that more adroit Secretaries of State have felt much the same.

That the requirement of senatorial ratification of treaties creates difficulties for American negotiators is obvious. Compared with the negotiators of a unified government like the British, they must be hesitant and possibly evasive.[2] On the other hand, the possible action of the Senate gives the Americans a joker to play; they can tell their opposite numbers how deeply they agree but remind them that the consent of two-thirds of the Senate has to be got and thus induce the other side to give way.[3]

[1] *The Education of Henry Adams* (1918), pp. 374–5.
[2] Not until about the middle of the nineteenth century, did treaties between Great Britain and the United States begin to refer to the need for senatorial ratification. One must assume that the Foreign Office knew that it was needed, but this was not reflected in the text where the United States was treated as a normal 'high contracting party'.
[3] We have evidence of this use of the Senate, or of a Senator, in very recent times. We learn from Senator Vandenberg's diary, that the late

Not all negotiators take so cheerful a view of the usefulness of the senatorial prerogative. A former Secretary of State pointed out, nearly fifty years ago, that the Senate 'is securely isolated from the other party to the proposed agreement. It debates in spurious secrecy. It adds or subtracts or otherwise alters and sends the proposal back to the President. . . . The point is not that the Senate should abrogate or conceal its views—it is immensely important that a legislative body should pass upon treaties, which are nothing more or less than law. It is rather a question of international good manners'.[1]

The two-thirds rule was an obstacle, in itself, to easy negotiation and to ratification, but it was made more of an obstacle by 'the peculiar rule of the Senate, which, since 1868, permitted amendments to be inserted or reservations added by an ordinary majority, although a two-thirds majority was necessary on the final vote of ratification'.[2] Thus a small group of 'irreconcilables' were able to vote first to impose reservations wanted by the large group of Republicans ready to ratify the Treaty of Versailles (i.e. the League Covenant) and impose these modifications by a simple majority,

---

Leo Pasvolsky told him before the Senator went to San Francisco as a delegate, that his record as a critic of Russia would be a help. ' "The big question mark in every foreign delegate's mind", said he, "will still be the same one that has plagued them in past experience, namely, What will the Senate do? Well—when we are pressing for something we don't seem able to get, we'll send you in to tell 'em that it has to be done if they expect to get their Treaty past the Senate." ' The *Private Papers of Senator Vandenberg*, edited by Arthur H. Vandenberg, Jr. (English edition 1953), p. 158.

[1] John W. Foster, quoted in Royden J. Dangerfield, *In Defence of the Senate* (1933), p. 315. (Mr. Foster's grandson is John Foster Dulles.) But international bad manners sometimes pay, in the short run anyway. The second Hay-Pauncefote treaty dealing with the building of the Panama Canal had to be negotiated because of the Senate's objections to the first. 'It seems evident that the Senate secured a better bargain for the United States than had the Department of State.' Ibid., p. 198. The British Foreign Minister was so impressed that he had suggested that the new Treaty should be submitted to the Senate before signature. 'This is the only suggestion of its kind coming from the foreign office of another country, the writer has been able to locate.' Ibid., p. 198.

[2] W. Stull Holt, *Treaties Defeated By the Senate* (1933), p. 296.

knowing that the Democrats following Wilson's lead would then vote against the adoption with the amendment. 'So the irreconcilables first joined one group in putting reservations into the resolution of ratification and then voted against the resolution with the third group whose opposition was caused by those reservations.'[1]

These manoeuvres succeeded, the Treaty was defeated and apparently the defeat was ratified in the elections of 1920, although the usually mixed character of the 'verdict' of the American voter was even more mixed than usual.

It is possible that the Senate's victory in 1919 and 1920 was too complete and too portentous. No one knows whether, had Wilson been less rigid, the Treaty would have been ratified or whether, if it had been, the history of the world would have been different. But the way in which the Treaty was defeated, the fact that the disasters prophesied by Wilson came to pass, all made the memory of that triumph odious. 'The Senate's triumph in 1919 was the most spectacular in its history; but indeed that was its fatal defect. For as the years wore on and the world seemed to be getting into worse and worse shape . . . people—who always look for a devil to blame—began pointing the finger of reproach at the body that had so lightheartedly assumed the responsibility for keeping the United States out of the League, the one great nation with comparatively detached outlook and hence the one whose participation, it was said, was absolutely indispensable.'[2]

Certainly the Senate, in recent years, has been more co-operative than it was and if it has now turned restive, that is partly an aspect of a general congressional resistance to presidential power and partly a protest against the kind of world that the United States finds itself forced to live in. But there is a special senatorial, as apart from congressional resentment of what it deems presidential aggression, for if the Senate does not or dares not return to 1919, it does not want to abandon its constitutional role in the making of American foreign policy. And it should be remembered that it was immediately after the rejection of the Treaty of Versailles, that the Supreme Court interpreted the treaty-making power in a sense that

[1] Ibid., p. 298.
[2] Corwin, *The President*, p. 266.

made it more important than the statute-making power of both houses of Congress.

The constitutional problem created by the treaty-making power was clearly stated in the classic case of *Missouri v. Holland* (1920). A treaty made between the United States and Great Britain (acting for Canada) empowered the legislature of each country to pass laws controlling the migration of certain wild birds and to protect them during their flight. Pursuant to this treaty, Congress legislated in 1918 and Missouri brought suit, alleging, wrote Justice Holmes: 'that a treaty cannot be valid if it infringes the Constitution, that there are limits, therefore, to the treaty-making power, and that one such limit is that what an act of Congress could not do unaided, in derogation of the powers reserved to the States, a treaty cannot do. . . . Acts of Congress are the supreme law of the land only when made under the Constitution, while treaties are declared to be so when made under the authority of the United States. . . . It is obvious that there may be matters of the sharpest exigency for the national well being that an act of Congress could not deal with but that a treaty followed by such an act could, and it is not lightly to be assumed that in matters requiring national action', a power which must belong to and somewhere reside in every civilized government 'is not to be found'.[1]

This doctrine, if not novel, was bold, for it gave to the federal government a method of extending its jurisdiction by treaty. True, Holmes had said that 'We do not mean to imply that there are no qualifications to the treaty-making power' and both Houses of Congress had had to act to give the treaty effect. But from the point of view of a devotee of states' rights, the doctrine of *Missouri v. Holland* was another nail in the coffin. The ratification of treaties, it was now evident, was a very special branch of the Senate's powers and, if the treaty power could add to federal jurisdiction, it was desirable that treaties should be made as the framers of the Constitution had intended.

The Senate has always hankered after the function it was intended to fulfil, that of a kind of Privy Council. The long history of failure to interpret 'advice and consent' as giving the Senate any right to advice before a negotiation was begun or a treaty drafted,

[1] Text in Commager, *Documents* (1948), vol. II, pp. 343–4.

has led to many suggestions of means to restore the constitutional relationship of the executive and the Senate in foreign affairs.[1] The nearest approach to a solution was the successful attempt made by Mr. Hull to get Republican senatorial support in advance for the post-war settlement then believed to be possible. He won over the most important Republican Senator on the Foreign Relations Committee, Arthur Vandenberg, to support of what was called a 'bipartisan' or 'nonpartisan' policy.[2]

But the co-operation of Senatorial leaders, based on private negotiations, however valuable, is not what the supporters of Senate prerogatives had or have in mind. They want each of the ninety-six members to have a right to an opinion, expressed at any length, at all stages of negotiations and a feeling that this restoration of the original role of the Senate is unlikely is, one may suspect, one of the causes for the widespread senatorial support for such novel proposals as the 'Bricker amendment'.[3]

If the treaty-making power, embedded in the Constitution by the framers and, presumably, representing the considered thought of those revered men, is to be treated with exceptional respect,

[1] Thus Senator Elbert D. Thomas suggested that 'the Foreign Relations Committee should be so constituted that it can function as the founding fathers intended the Senate to function in our foreign policy— as a council of state. . . . The practice of considering "advice and consent" as a single act makes it possible for an executive to conduct foreign policy which becomes law in such a way as to leave the Senate with the single power of accepting or rejecting'. 'Foreword' to Eleanor E. Dennison, *The Senate Foreign Relations Committee* (1942), pp. vii–viii. Senator Thomas went on to complain that 'the present Executive meets the Speaker, the Vice-President, and the two Congressional leaders on Mondays. If there is nothing vital, one meeting a week seems sufficient —because the President is busy. Busy with what?' Ibid., p. ix. The date of this foreword is 16 February 1942. The day before it was written, Singapore had fallen, so the question might have answered itself, especially as Senator Thomas had been a missionary in Japan.

[2] Dulles, according to Hull's memoirs, had wanted to use 'bipartisan', which would recognize that the two parties were collaborating. Hull argued that the responsibility for foreign policy could not be shared by both parties or avoided by the party in power. Vandenberg, op. cit., p. 113. Both 'bipartisan' and 'nonpartisan' were, in fact, used interchangeably.

[3] See p. 307.

it is said that no such sacredness surrounds the so-called 'executive agreements' or laws passed by both houses of Congress in fields normally thought of as reserved to the treaty-making power. Yet both substitutes for treaties have had, in practice, as much importance as most treaties and have, in more than one case, led the Senate to ratify them by a treaty, thus locking the stable door after the horse was safely inside.

The executive agreement gets its authority from the double role of the President as Commander-in-Chief and as sole organ of American dealings with the outside world. Beginning with the Rush-Babot agreement of 1817 demilitarizing the United States-Canadian border, down to the tangle of agreements made during and since the late world war, the power of the President in this field has grown as the commitments of the United States have grown. In any field in which the President as Commander-in-Chief, or a director of foreign relations can act, he can commit himself to act by an agreement and can carry out his agreement. Thus he can station troops in the British West Indies or in Iceland by agreement, arrange for the disposition of American troops in the occupation of Germany, in practice make war, even if he cannot declare it.[1]

In his role as director of American foreign policy, the President has large and vaguely determined power. The Supreme Court has held that there are 'political questions' which it will not scrutinize and one of them is the power to recognize foreign governments, a recognition which may have important, internal legal results over the ownership of property claimed by the government so recognized for instance. Anything that the President can do in the light of this prerogative which does not need a fresh grant of money, he can undertake to do in writing and that undertaking, until repudiated, binds his successor who has obvious reasons for not wishing

---

[1] This President Truman did in Korea. He sent in armed forces without congressional authorization (to the distress of constitutional purists like the late Senator Taft). A little later, it is true, the United Nations gave an *ex post-facto* sanction to these proceedings, but it would surely be stretching a point to claim that the United Nations charter could give to a President of the United States a power denied him by the American Constitution. His effective power was as Commander-in-Chief.

to depreciate the value of a currency he may, in his turn, want to use.[1]

Equally important are agreements which Congress (both houses of it) authorizes the President to make. Congress by-passes the treaty-making power by giving (as in the Hull trade treaties) the President power to make agreements having the force of internal law. And Congress may, by joint resolution, do many things that could also be done (if the Senate rules permitted) by a treaty. Again the constitutional plan is evaded, and sometimes in matters of great moment. One of these evasions, indeed, is by the people most affected, regarded as the most important event in American history, the union of the United States with Texas.

Why have these evasions been resorted to? They have been resorted to because of the difficulty of getting a treaty, *any* treaty through the Senate, since treaties can only be ratified by the vote of two-thirds of the Senators present.[2]

[1] Professor Corwin, while arguing that the American commitments under the United Nations cannot be dealt with as normal exercises of presidential power since 'Congress must be constantly asked to exercise powers which no President has ever ventured to exercise on any scale', notes that the danger of Congress being presented with *faits accomplis* increases. 'This is not because of presidential devising to that end, but because of the frightening risks which are inevitably incurred whenever our government takes a hand in, and thereby assumes a measure of responsibility for, events in Europe and the Near East—in those regions especially.' Edward S. Corwin, *The President Office and Powers* (third edition 1948), p. 271. This was written before the Korean 'war' which of course greatly reinforces the argument.

[2] So much emphasis has been placed on the two-thirds provision that not enough has been paid to difficulties arising out of other weaknesses in the Senate's way of doing things. 'The Senate's chosen mode of doing business by unanimous consent is open to still more serious criticism as conducing to executive agreements and to secret diplomacy. . . . In the field of domestic legislation the unanimous consent procedure . . . provides a sort of antidote to its own poison. For every Senator is well aware that he will wish sooner or later to get some pet measure of his own enacted and so cannot afford to stand in the way of similar enterprises of his colleagues being brought to a vote. But in the field of foreign policy no such automatic check operates. It took the Senate twenty-one years to get around to consent to the treaty receding [sic] to Cuba the Isle of Pines; and that fiasco was due far more to the practice of doing

Despite the attempts to secure a bipartisan or nonpartisan foreign policy, there has been growing up in the Senate a resentment of the way in which the treaty-making power has been evaded and so the rights of the Senate reduced, the way in which executive agreements have, in practice, committed the United States without any congressional sanction. There is some genuine alarm that the separation of powers is being undermined and that the safety of the United States is being endangered by the policy of the President, *any* President.[1] It is also possible that a deep-seated fear that *no* President will carry out the kind of foreign policy that a large section of the Republican party desires, lies behind the recent moves to limit the treaty and executive agreement power.[2]

The most famous of these moves is the so-called 'Bricker' amendment, called after its author, Senator John Bricker of Ohio. This proposal declares that any treaty provision conflicting with the Constitution is ineffective, which is already the case. But the heart of the matter is the 'which clause', providing that 'a treaty can become effective as internal law' only through legislation which would be valid in the absence of a treaty.[3]

---

business by unanimous consent than to the two-thirds rule.' Edward S. Corwin, *Total War and the Constitution* (1947), p. 159.

[1] It is probable, although unprovable, that some of the emotional force behind these projects is simply due to the feud that many Republicans are still carrying on with the dead Roosevelt. It is the equivalent of the amendment barring a third term.

[2] It is a sign of the depth of this feeling that a majority of the Senate was, for a time, ready to give away one of its own powers, for by denying to a treaty (for which the consent of two-thirds of the Senate is required) the 'enabling' power of *Missouri v. Holland*, and by insisting on legislation by both houses, the Senate has both shown its readiness to discard the important power of deciding what additions to federal authority it can make by ratifying a treaty, and further increased the danger of encroachment by the House of Representatives in the field of foreign relations.

[3] Morris D. Forkosch, 'What the Amendment Means', *The New Leader*, 1 February 1954. Professor Forkosch rightly asserts that 'the *Missouri v. Holland* decision is . . . at the heart of the Bricker amendment dispute' and he notes that even now the Senate has power, by a simple reservation, to declare any treaty non-self-executing. 'Since some treaties deal with subjects outside the federal jurisdiction, legislation to

Equally significant and, in practice, equally important is the proposed recognition by constitutional amendment of 'executive agreements' which are at present based only on implied powers. For, as Senator Hennings of Missouri has pointed out, the formal recognition of executive agreements as instruments of the same character as treaties, would tempt Presidents to make far more use of them than before in order to evade the slowness and uncertainty of the treaty-making process and, in so doing, further diminish the Senate's share of control over foreign policy in favour of the House of Representatives and thus remove one guarantee in favour of the small states, since executive agreements can be passed by mere majorities of each house.

The feelings, the anxieties, the constitutional doctrines that gained for the Bricker amendment such an astonishing amount of support, are still lively. But the times we all live in fight against the attempt to hamstring the President and to entrust either to the Senate, or to Congress as a whole, a really controlling power over American foreign policy. A majority of both houses may regret the situation in which the United States finds itself. It may blame it on Franklin D. Roosevelt, but to wish to ignore the situation is as vain as to wish away:

> all that the brigand apple brought.

And the American people, if not Congress, knows that and since it knows it, Congress protests in vain.

If the single most important thing to remember about Congress is that it is separated from the executive, the second is that it is divided, that its powers are shared between two bodies of approximately equal powers and that, if these two bodies are unequal, the more powerful is the smaller, less 'democratic' of the two. It was certainly assumed by the makers of the Constitution that the House would be more powerful than the Senate. On the English analogy, it would be more powerful as representing 'the People' and because it was given the sole right to initiate revenue bills. (By custom, which has now the force of law but has no formal consti-

---

implement them would have to be sought in forty-eight states, a problem of political management that would make foreign negotiators far more wary than even the Senate's power over treaties.'

tutional sanction, the House has the sole right to initiate appropriations as well.) But the House represents the people in a very
imperfect way, much less completely than does the House of
Commons; its seniority and locality rules are both proof and cause
of that comparative inferiority.[1] More important has been the
growth of the role of the President as *the* democratic representative
and embodiment of the People. And, lastly, the longer life of the
Senate, the new 'democratic' character that dates from the adoption
of the direct election of Senators and the emptiness of the special
constitutional rights of the House, as compared with the real
importance of the special constitutional rights of the Senate, are
enough to account for the superior position of the Senate, a
superiority not in any serious doubt in this century.

The special rights of the House of Representatives have turned
out to be empty. For the Senate can amend revenue bills and
appropriations in any way it chooses, striking out everything but
the enacting clause and since there is no power to coerce the Senate,
no equivalent of the making of peers in Britain, or even of the very
moderate powers of reinforcing the Canadian Senate open to the
leaders of the majority in the Canadian House of Commons, the
two Houses are equals in financial matters. On the other hand, the
special powers of the Senate, its right to ratify treaties and sanction
all important federal appointments are real, are not shared with the
other House and give the Senate special powers of bargaining with
the President. To this sweeping statement it is wise to add one
modification: most foreign policies now cost a lot of money which
the Senate, alone, cannot provide but which the House, alone,
cannot provide either.

There is something paradoxical in a democratic age, the age of the
common man, in the predominance of the Senate, even in the fact,
attested to by some, that the Senate has been even acquiring new
powers, in financial questions for instance, over the last twenty
years or so. For the Senate is absurdly un-democratic. Each state
has two Senators; the two Senators from New York represent
roughly one hundred times as many people as the two Senators from
Nevada. Lots of ingenious combinations of states have been made
to show that a fifth or sixth of the voters have an absolute veto on

[1] See p. 314.

the legislation desired by the rest of the American people. No one doubts that the extravagant oddities of the silver policy of the United States since 1933 have been mainly due to the fact that there are twelve Senators from sparsely populated states who must, if they are to survive, 'do something for silver' and the rest of the country has to pay ransom. And this power and prestige of the Senate is still more strange since the old quasi-nationalist idea of states' rights is nearly dead. Nobody thinks of Nevada or Montana as a sovereign state in the way that Calhoun thought of South Carolina or Lee of Virginia. But the fact remains, the Senate is the more powerful half of Congress.

The first and possibly most important reason is that a Senator is elected for six years, a Representative for two. A Senator, that is, normally serves during two presidential terms; a Representative can only be certain of serving through half of one. Elected in three groups, two thirds of the Senators, at any given moment, have no electoral worries less than four years away. Because not all the Senate is elected at one time, the Senate is a continuing body. Members lose their seats, new members arrive, but the Senate goes on. *Qui mange du Sénat en meurt* is partly true just because the Senate itself never dies.

The next source of senatorial predominance is the size of the Senate. It has ninety-six members. (Even should Hawaii and Alaska be added, it will have only a hundred.) This makes it too big to be a privy council, as it was destined to be. But it is still a small body, with its own intimate life, with its desks and arm chairs, its air of a club smoking room. It needs few rules and has even fewer than it needs. It gives every opportunity to personality, again, perhaps, more than it should. It is an excellent sounding-board, capable quite often of competing, although at a disadvantage, with the President.

Turn to the House. It lives for only two years. It always has a high proportion of new members learning their business and often doomed to be dismissed by unfaithful voters when the lesson is at best half learned. It has to organize and discipline four hundred-and-thirty-five members and, in order to do that, it has to have rigid rules, to risk suppressing personality (especially the personality of the new members). It can do little work as a body and has to do good by stealth and yet not find it fame. It is conscious of its inferior position, but can do nothing about it or nothing that would not upset its long-acquired habits by which alone, it thinks, it can keep going at all. It is not true to say that nobody marks it, but few mark it enough, and, last comment of all, its inferior status is underlined by the notorious fact that so many of its members lust after the greater ease and glory of the Senate which they long to share.

Both houses have, of course, much in common, especially the fact that they are not led, not organized by the executive. From that fact arises the importance and the character of the committee system.

All legislative bodies need a committee system; the complexity of modern political life, the range of governmental activities impose this solution. Not all of the house can be doing the same business at the same time, since there is so much conflicting business to do. Business must be broken up, members allotted to specific pieces of legislation or to the consideration of specific problems. The house, as a whole, deals with the work put before it by committees and, in parliamentary systems, above all with the work put before it by the committee of committees, the Cabinet. But in the United States Congress, there is no parliamentary Cabinet. Congress must control its own business.

Of course, a great deal of legislation is suggested by the executive departments; often bills come to Congress ready drafted. But there is no front bench, no government control of the time table to make sure that the executive proposals will ever be 'reported out', i.e. put before the House at all, or reported out in the form an executive department wants or in terms that make enactment likely. That depends on the committees and in normal times on the will, not to say the whims, of the chairman chosen under the 'seniority rule'.

Among the congressional institutions most difficult to explain or justify is the 'seniority' rule. This is a custom, not a rule in the strict sense, but it is a custom having nearly the force of law. By the rule, members of Congress acquire rights by mere survival, that is, a Representative or Senator takes precedence of a member junior to him, even if only by a few days or weeks. He has a choice of the more important committees and, more important, once he is on a committee, his rank in that committee is fixed for ever. If he lives long enough he will become either chairman or minority leader or, as his party wins or loses power, both. There is next to 'no damned nonsense of merit' about it.[1]

Next to no damned nonsense, for there are times when strict seniority is ignored, but they are not frequent. The rule means, in effect, that the very considerable power that goes with a committee chairmanship is conferred not by the Senate or the House, but by a combination of the faithfulness of states and districts, first of all to the party and then to the incumbent, combined with the vacancies caused by death and defeat among other members of the same seniority.[2]

---

[1] The importance of seniority is illustrated by the case of Bennett Champ Clark. Mr. Clark was elected with many other Democrats in the landslide of 1932, to take office on 4 March 1933. But the Governor of Missouri was induced to appoint him to the seat helpfully resigned by Senator Harry B. Hawes. Senator Clark, when the New Deal Congress met, had been a Senator for a month, thus getting the jump on all the other new Senators. When Representative Henry Jackson defeated Senator Harry Cain, in November 1952, some hopeful citizens of the state of Washington asked Senator Cain to resign before the new Congress met, so that the new junior Senator from the state would have some seniority. Even if the two statesmen had been of the same party, it is unlikely that Senator Cain would have complied, but that the request was made again shows the importance of seniority.

[2] The absurdities of the system reach their maximum when members with exactly equal seniority compete for a vacant chairmanship. 'When Congressman Edward Taylor of Colorado died, there were two members who could claim the chairmanship of the important House Appropriations Committee: Representative Clifton A. Woodrum of Virginia and Representative Clarence Cannon of Missouri. . . . Representative Cannon got the chairmanship because his name began with C. . . . Thomas L. Stokes, Jr., made this comment when, during the 79th Congress, Mr. Woodrum retired: "Neither the committee itself, nor the House had anything to say about the chairmanship of this most important committee, nor do they for any others. . . . In this case of rival claims, the alphabet was invoked." ' Estes Kefauver and Dr. Jack Levin, *A Twentieth-Century Congress* (1947), pp. 134–4. Representative (now Senator) Kefauver and Dr. Levin went on to note that when the chairmanship of the Military Affairs Committee in the House went to Andrew J. May of Kentucky over Robert Ewing Thomason of Texas 'there was no opportunity to choose between the two'. They kindly

Luck may bring a Senator or Representative up the escalator rapidly; bad luck, the unconscionable time taken a-dying or retiring by an incumbent chairman may keep an ambitious and able man out of a chairmanship (or at any rate the chairmanship he covets) for all his congressional life. And a newcomer who chooses his committees wrong, that is chooses those whose senior members defy the actuaries, has no remedy short of assassination. Since (although not quite so rigidly) seniority operates also to great effect in the choice of a Speaker and since the Speaker is now number two in the presidential succession,[1] this rule might give the United States a President whose chief, if not exclusive, claim was that he lived in a district that always held by one party and that he had managed, in a long political life, to avoid making enough enemies to lose the party nomination.

What justification is there for this escalator system, the simple moving up of the man with his foot on the step ahead of the next man? Basically it is that there *has* to be an escalator because there is no ladder. The House of Representatives, at least, offers no great rewards except the committee chairmanships. The real rewards are elsewhere; house members want to become Senators or Governors or, less commonly, cabinet officers and, of course, President, although there is even less chance of being nominated for President from the House than there is from the Senate. And as the Senate in recent times has had less and less room for former Representatives[2] and as the case of Representative Herter becoming Governor of Massachusetts is nowadays exceptional, the Representative must seek his reward in the House. But all Congressmen are elected equal. There is no 'front bench' as in Britain or Canada; there is no easy way of determining merit as there is in a parliamentary system where both the leader of the Government and the leader of the Opposition must, in their own and their party's interest, be allowed a fairly free hand in promoting the brilliant and necessary young. The House would have to make its own choice and to make

---

forbear to add that Chairman May was later sent to the penitentiary for graft.

[1] See p. 380.

[2] Only about a third of the present Senate (83rd Congress) is composed of former Representatives.

it in every Congress afresh would be to introduce into the House the spirit of an international sporting event or of the election of Miss Universe.

In any case, as an extremely knowledgeable observer has put it, this is the spirit of Congress. 'Congress is an institution in which power and position are highly valued. Seniority is not only a rule governing committee chairmanships, it is also a spirit pervading the total behavior. This is especially true between new members and the older ones. The latter want the former to seek their advice and have their own ways of clipping the wings of upstarts. This does not mean that a first-termer is not listened to in committee or even on the floor if he is really master of his subject, has something to say, and is not merely seeking prominence.[1] After one or two years, during which his colleagues have taken his measure, he may be entrusted with a subcommittee chairmanship dealing with some problem close to his heart or even with the chairmanship of a special committee. By these devices many of the admitted disadvantages connected with rigid adherence to the security rule are overcome and its good side preserved.'[2]

The admitted disadvantages of which Dr. Griffith speaks are not admitted by the beneficiaries of the system or by some rather uncritical admirers of Congress. 'If a congressman is returned election after election from a district where he is known over a long period of years, it is a very reasonable assumption that he is a man of some ability. My own impression, after many years of observation, is that the men in the Senate or House who have served a long time, with some exceptions, are usually able men.'[3] Even this not very warm praise is excessive, for the ability that may explain why a man is in Congress at all and has stayed in for a long time, may be quite inadequate justification for making him the often autocratic chairman of an important committee. For almost always, the mem-

[1] I remember asking a serious and powerful Senator about a young colleague who had hit the headlines with great regularity. 'He's a pinhead.' The later career of the infant prodigy justified this judgment, but it is possible that had the new Senator been more deferential, his pinheadedness would not have been noticed so soon.

[2] Ernest S. Griffith, *Congress, Its Contemporary Role* (1951), p. 19.

[3] John T. Flynn, *Meet Your Congress* (1944), pp. 71–2.

bers who have high seniority represent not only safe, but nearly ossified seats. This is more true of Republicans than of Democrats, not because of any superior Democratic virtue, but because, inside the safest Democratic area, the real party conflict is in the primary and Southern Representatives and Senators may embody very different social attitudes and yet be perfectly sure of election if they win the primary. In the same way, there are a good number of safe industrial seats in the North where the Democratic party has yet to cater to the needs of its voters. On the other hand, most of the safe Republican seats in the House and so most of the Republican committee chairmen come from seats which, held even at the lowest point of Republican fortunes, between 1932 and 1936, have shown their insulation from the contemporary world. Moreover, the fact that Democratic strength is territorially more widely spread than Republican, means that seniority is also more widely spread and so is power.

'Customs and practice insist upon a wide geographical distribution of committee appointments, but under the operation of the seniority rule the chairmanships are not so distributed. When the Democrats have been in power most of the committee chairmanships have gone to men from the South and when the Republicans have been in power most of them have gone to men from the North.'[1]

The consequences are, at times, serious. It is true, at present, that a Republican President can only be elected by winning over the millions who classify themselves as independents and, probably, some of the millions who describe themselves as Democrats. Yet some, perhaps most of the committee chairmen (at any rate in the House) will represent districts where it is only necessary to be the Republican nominee to be elected and where dangerously novel thoughts would be a positive disadvantage in seeking the Republican nomination. Thus the chairman of the Ways and Means Committee in the 83rd Congress was Daniel Alden Reed of New York

[1] Floyd M. Riddick, *The United States Congress Organization and Procedure* (1949), p. 172. Actually, Dr. Riddick's table shows that although the South predominated when the Democrats were in power, it had less of a monopoly of chairmanships than had the North (and West) during Republican dominance.

who first entered Congress in 1918.[1] Mr. Reed fought to the bitter end against the most important Eisenhower financial measure, the retention of the excess profits duty, and was only defeated and for that occasion only, by all the pressure of the White House and with the collaboration of the Speaker.

It is probably true that a member of Congress who is totally idle or incapable or unsuited in some other way, would not, seniority or no seniority, become chairman of an important committee. Probable, not certain, for during the last war, one reason why the Senate was not able to control the executive was that the chairmen of the Naval Affairs Committee and the Military Affairs Committee, each the product of seniority, were notoriously unfitted for their posts. But even though we may believe that Frederick the Great was wrong when he refused to allow much to mere experience: 'The General has seen twenty campaigns, so has an army mule': the real spirit of the seniority rule is shown not merely by the creation of artificial seniority, but by the fact that a member who loses his seat loses his seniority and, if and when he gets back, starts at the bottom again. Of course his weight in the party earned during his previous service means that he cannot, in fact, be treated exactly as a mere freshman, but he loses the formal precedence and probably some power.[2]

---

[1] Mr. Reed does not state the year of his birth in the Congressional Directory. He is thought to be 'rising eighty', which would make him a little older than Mr. John Taber who was born in 1880 and entered Congress with Mr. Reed, in 1918, the year of the midterm elections that showed that the Democratic usurpation under Woodrow Wilson was doomed. Although Mr. Taber does not say so in his biographical note, he is chairman of the Appropriations Committee. These two veterans, that is to say, hold the purse strings.

[2] 'In this respect, the seniority principle strictly applied defeats its own purpose of basing promotion upon experience. Both Joseph G. Cannon and Nicholas Longworth failed of election in 1912. . . . After his re-election in 1914 though he returned to the same Committee (Appropriations) he was given no rank higher than that of the two members who were then appointed to the Committee for the first time. Similarly Mr. Longworth . . . was compelled to begin again at the bottom of that Committee (Ways and Means) after he returned to Congress in 1914. His previous service did not avail even to give him preferment among the Members newly appointed to the Committee.' Paul DeWitt

What has been said only applies in all its rigour (and oddity) to the House. In the Senate, the seniority rule applies, but it does not have, as a rule, the same controlling effects. For one thing, the Senate is a small body. It can barely staff its committees and so a new Senator can at once get on an important committee and prove his worth early in his first term. More important still, the absence of effective control in the Senate means that a Senator who for any reason is deprived of what he thinks his due committee rank, has the floor of the Senate open to him. And lastly, there are fewer safe states than there are safe congressional districts.[1]

Then the new Senator usually comes to the Senate with a previous political career of some importance, as a Representative, Governor, cabinet officer, head of some great government agency or legislative leader in an important state. He is rarely a political novice. This is recognized by the Senate which, as a rule, pays attention to this experience in its committee appointments.[2]

The Senate's special committees are much more important than those of the House, if only because, since the Senate unlike the House never 'dies', they have usually a longer and more newsworthy life.[3] Thus Mr. Kefauver, whose attack on the seniority

---

Hasbrouck, *Party Government in the House of Representatives* (1927), p. 54. Cannon had been Speaker and Longworth was to be.

[1] Outside the South, only six states have been 'solid' over the last twenty years, Maine, Vermont, New Hampshire, North Dakota, Oregon and West Virginia. (All but the last being Republican.) And in the South, the frequently bitter primary contests have prevented the automatic acquisition of Senate seniority in states like Tennessee, Texas, North Carolina, Florida.

[2] Thus in the 83rd Congress, Senator Stuart Symington of Missouri, who had been Secretary for Air and Administrator of the Relief Finance Corporation, was appointed to the Armed Forces Committee and the Government Operations Committee.

[3] The Un-American Activities Committee of the House was an apparent exception, but its most famous recent member, Mr. Richard Nixon, used the reputation he gained on that Committee to enter the Senate and then to become Vice-President. When the Senate of the 83rd Congress began to hunt out the 'Reds', the parallel efforts of the House were almost ignored. Representative Velde tried, indeed, 'to get in the act' which was being hogged, in his opinion, by Senators McCarthy and Jenner, but he was promptly pushed back into the wings.

system, while he was still a Representative, was one of the most effective made in recent times, became a national figure in his first term as a Senator, as chairman of a special committee to investigate crime.[1] And Mr. Truman, who had been a fairly silent and obscure Senator in his first term, became as a result of his admirable services as chairman of the 'Truman Committee' to investigate waste in the war effort, enough of a national figure to be vice-presidential timber in 1944.[2]

Even in the Senate, as has been said, seniority sometimes produces results that weaken the power of that great assembly, but it is safe to say, that the 'rights' of the House of Representatives will never be recognized by the Senate, the President or the public as long as it is too tender-hearted to revolt against rule by age.

If the seniority rule has little to commend it save the convenience of the members of Congress, there is a good deal to be said for the role of the committees. A new Representative, still more a new Senator, can be sure that if he wishes to master the job, he will, from the beginning, be given an opportunity to see and to influence the working of some branch of government. His committee colleagues will all admire industry (it husbands theirs); if all the new member wants to do is to be useful, he is given the chance. Not for him the long years of mere opposition or of loyal support without the power, perquisites, or training that comes from holding responsible office. Few Members of either house of Congress could get along on as little real contact with policy and administration as is still possible for a docile Member of Parliament. An able member can build up among his colleagues, if not with the public, a reputation for capacity and industry that will not only impress them, but will impress the permanent officials of executive departments who will go out of their way to be helpful (as far as they can or dare) to one who is likely to be a permanent power.

[1] See p. 329.
[2] It is, presumably, significant that while it is easy to remember famous special Senate Committees by the name of their chairmen (The 'Reed Committee', the 'Nye Committee', the 'La Follette Committee', the 'Truman Committee', the 'Kefauver Committee') and to believe, as many do, that there is a special 'McCarthy Committee', it is practically impossible to remember any special House Committee by any name.

But despite this real claim of the committee system for respect, the multiplication of committees, the obvious decline of congressional control of the executive, the inability of Congress, especially of the Senate, to get its job done, has led to much discussion of the need for reform, to floods of pamphlets and books, as well as speeches and reports, and to the enactment of the Monroney-La Follette Act in 1946.

It took a good deal of public spirit for Congress to agree even to the comparatively mild reforms of the La Follette-Monroney bill.[1] For by cutting down the number of committees so drastically, the bill cut down the opportunities for reward, meagre as they were, that the old system gave to members of long service. Thus the 74th Congress had thirty-three committees for a membership of ninety-six, so there were reasonable opportunities for rewarding the deserving and, what was functionally more important, leading Senators who were not chairmen of important committees could be chairmen of something.[2] And being Chairmen of *something*, gave them not only dignity but better offices and other minor perquisites.[3]

'The Legislative Reform Act of 1946 not only cut in half the number of standing committees, but also in large measure made their several jurisdictions correspond to those of the appropriate

[1] Called after its authors, the then Senator, Robert M. La Follette, Jr., of Wisconsin, and the then Representative (now Senator) Mike Monroney of Oklahoma.

[2] Thus Senator James F. Byrnes was chairman of the 'Committee on Audit and Control of the Contingent Expenses of the Senate', Senator Alben W. Barkley was chairman of the 'Committee on the Library', Senator Tom Connally was chairman of the 'Committee on Public Buildings and Grounds'. Each of these was, of course, also a leading member of important committees.

[3] Mr. Hoover appears to think that these considerations affected the decision of the Republican Senate leaders to claim control in 1931. 'Senator James Watson, Republican Senate leader, rejected my advice that the Democrats be allowed to organize the Senate and thereby convert their sabotage into responsibility. . . . Watson, of course, liked the extra importance of being majority leader, and the Republicans liked to hold committee chairmanships and the nicer offices in the Capitol.' *Memoirs of Herbert Hoover*, vol. III (English edition 1953), p. 101.

departments and agencies in the Executive branch.'[1] This reform had the further advantage that it made committee systems in the two houses much more alike, except in nomenclature[2] and makes possible, if not probable, the holding of more joint hearings and the reduction of the time-wasting habit of getting executive representatives to give much the same testimony twice over or, in case of jurisdictional disputes, three or four times.

The reform, of course, has not wrought miracles. Some see in the proliferation of sub-committees, an evasion of the spirit of the act. Yet while there are still too many special committees, there are fewer than in the old days and, perhaps most important of all, the number of committees of which Senators or Representatives were nominal members has been healthily reduced. 'Including special committees the average Senator is a member of two, three or four committees, the Representatives of one or two.'[3]

Important additions have been made to the regular committee set-up. One of these is the 'Joint Committee on the Economic Report'. The Economic Report is that made to the President by the Council of Economic Advisers and sent by him to Congress. It is a specialized version of the message on the 'State of the Union' that the President has to send and, in theory, the Economic Report is an objective stocktaking of the situation, with suggested remedies based on economic science. But economic science, when exposed to congressional scrutiny, becomes political economy and neither the Committee nor Congress as a whole approaches the report in a scientific frame of mind. Yet the Report, by reminding politicians that there are other considerations than elections, weight of pressure groups, sectional interests or effective political slogans and campaigns issues to be considered, may have an educational effect.[4]

[1] Ernest S. Griffith, *The American System of Government* (1954), p. 32.

[2] Thus the Senate has a committee of 'Foreign Relations', the House a committee on 'Foreign Affairs'. The old explanation, that Senators are too old to have affairs, no longer explains, as the average age of the Senators is only slightly, if at all, higher than the average age of the Representatives.

[3] Ibid., p. 34.

[4] It is difficult to be more enthusiastic. A very friendly witness notes the limitations of the usefulness of the Joint Committee's work. 'The committee conducts important studies; the findings of these special

Still more difficult to assess is the work of the Joint Committee on Atomic Energy. For, inevitably, the work of this committee is done in secret. Its members are privy to some of the most important confidential information in the possession of the government of the United States. But how far they are taken into the full confidence of the President, the Atomic Energy Commission or the National Security Council is, itself, a state secret.

Congress, in its reforming mood, recognized that it was at a disadvantage in dealing with the executive departments which had large staffs of experts whom busy politicians could not cross-examine competently. The advantage, from the side of the executive, was evident; so was the disadvantage seen from the congressional side. Congress and each member of Congress have now far more adequate and competent facilities for research and information; so have the committees. How effective these additions to the staff of Congress and of members have been in arresting the decline of congressional authority, is hard to say. But that the decline would have gone further without this reinforcement of the knowledge and industry of the members is certain.[1]

If the basic problems of the two houses are alike, their domestic problems differ a good deal. The size of the House of Representa-

---

studies are duly sent to the relevant committees. In fact it is the policy of the chairman to consult the chairman of the appropriate standing committee before the Joint Committee undertakes a particular study. Its reports on the President's *Report* are widely circulated and publicized. So also are its minority reports. Undoubtedly the thought and controversy thus evoked are beneficial. Yet so far as the author knows, no standing committee has ever referred a bill to the Joint Economic Committee for comment nor has the Committee's *Report* figured materially either in floor debate on specific measures or in the deliberations of other committees.' Ernest S. Griffith, *Congress Its Contemporary Role* (1951), p. 127.

[1] Dr. Griffith thinks highly of the new services. 'It is my sincere conviction, based upon many, many more instances than I would ever be at liberty to disclose, that the enlargement and strengthening of the staffs of Congress have in fact been a major factor in arresting and probably reversing a trend that had set in in the United States as well as in every other industrialised nation. This is the trend in the direction of the ascendancy or even the virtually complete dominance of the bureaucracy over the legislative branch.' Ibid., p. 74.

tives in itself imposes discipline on it. Even were the bills and resolutions less numerous,[1] it would be necessary to cut down debate and impose a fairly detailed time table. As it is, the sponsor of a bill in the House has to get his bill 'reported out' (an adverse report is better than mere suppression), by the appropriate committee. That committee has to get a place on the parliamentary calendar from the 'Rules Committee', to get 'a rule' as it is called. If expenditure is involved, it has to be authorized in one bill and the necessary money appropriated in another. As a condition of appropriating adequate funds, the Appropriations Committee may make conditions, may alter the scope and even the character of the legislation and the Rules Committee may, and often does, inform the committee chairmen to whom bills are sent, that it will grant a rule only if certain modifications are made. Many bills, of course, are of no interest except to their supporters and if not stopped by a small group representing both parties called 'objectors', they go through unopposed. But general bills have to run several gauntlets and, thanks to the seniority rule, the men who decide on their fate may not represent the temper of the House or of the technically dominant party. If it is desirable that the voter should have some reason to believe that his Representative and his party will be able to deliver the goods, and if it is desirable that the American people should have some idea of who promotes or who impedes legislation, the veto power of the present system is hard to justify. And from time to time there are revolts against the veto power of the committees in general and of the Rules Committee in particular. These usually come when there is a more obvious and wider gulf than usual between the veterans of the committees and the mass of new or newish members from the doubtful districts. They are most likely to occur, that is to say, when the House is more radical than its elderly leaders, but since a really uncontrolled House would be a kind of Polish Diet without discipline or power of action, the revolts do not last long.

The power of the committee chairmen and, especially, the power of the Rules Committee, is sometimes defended, plausibly, as a way

---

[1] They average about 10,000 for the life of a Congress (two years). About 1,000 become law. Many of these, of course, are private acts affecting no general issues or interests.

of protecting Representatives from 'pressure blocs' or from powerful interests. The chairmen or the Rules Committee know that
many bills are brought in to placate such groups, that their sponsors
are delighted to see them die in committee, but dare not risk defying
the pressure blocs openly. The committee veto, that is to say, is a
version of the presidential veto and has the same formal justification.
But the presidential veto is exercised by a known elected officer; his
reasons for his action are usually given; his is a function that the
public understands. But not one voter in a thousand has heard of
the Rules Committee. It may be very unrepresentative; it may be
worse than unrepresentative. It is a third house unknown to the
people and the Constitution and it further weakens the House in that
it reduces the already inadequate time and facilities for debate.

For the great failure of the House of Representatives is not in its
performance of its legislative functions, or its investigatory functions, but in its failure to impress on the public mind that what it is
doing is necessary, is worthwhile, is interesting. The present system
of doing House business adds to the boredom with which the work
of the House of Representatives is regarded and reduces to a minimum the effective educational work of that body. For education is
one of the functions of a legislative body. It should remind its
electors of the greater issues that it deals with. If it is unlikely that
speeches change votes in the legislature itself, they may help and
should help to interest and inform public opinion outside. The
House of Representatives, with its comparatively infrequent
debates, with its rigorous procedure, with the exclusion from consideration of much that many of its members as well as the public
would like to see debated, makes of itself an exchange and mart
where local interests are offset, one against the other, and adds, by
its procedure, to the 'localism' that weakens the House (and sometimes the Senate) in any contest on a national issue between the
President and Congress.

In many ways, the Senate is the reverse of the House. With its
small numbers it does not need and, with its membership, it would
not tolerate a rigorous control of its time by committees or by
ruling officers. For one thing, the Speaker of the House is a leading
politician who can, if he chooses, take the floor and lead the House,
although it is far less common to do this today than used to be the

case. The 'floor leader' and the other chiefs of the controlling party share the high command with the Speaker. But although he is not as openly partisan as he was, he has still a duty and a power to see that the business of the House is done in terms of the general interest of his party (as he, not the President or other leaders), sees that interest.[1]

The 'President of the Senate' is the Vice-President of the United States. He is not chosen by the Senate; he has no vote except in the case of a tie. He may have no political weight in that body. Of course, if he is adroit, vigilant, with much parliamentary experience, he may play an important role, both as a presiding officer and as a conciliator and manipulator in the committee rooms and lobbies. But he is not a dictator or a chairman of a nearly omnipotent oligarchy. There is, nowadays, no such oligarchy. Committee chairmen are powerful, if only by preventing other Senators from being chairmen and by holding up committee business by sloth or indifference. But any Senator can, if he is pertinacious, get the floor and, under the rules, keep it as long as his lungs and feet, etc. hold out. The threat of an endless speech, of a 'filibuster'[2] often brings the Senate leaders to terms, especially at the end of a session when much legislation *must* be got through. It takes a two-third vote to impose a *clôture* and that two-thirds is hard to find in a body each of whose members may want to stage a filibuster himself, sometime. The fault of the Senate (if it has one) is that it sacrifices formal efficiency to the desire of its members to say all that they think and feel, to their desire to bring to the public attention all the aspects of any question that may occur or be suggested to a member. It is the Senate calendar, not the House calendar, that is usually in arrears. It is the Senate that does little at great length while the House does a great deal in brief and formal public performances. But the Senate, for all that, knows that its power and prestige depend, in

[1] The Democrats controlled the House from 1931 to 1953 with one interval of two years (1947–9). This meant that there was a succession of Democratic Speakers, not a series of Speakers of alternating parties. This not only made for continuity, but made the speakership less partisan. Mr. Sam Rayburn, the last Democratic Speaker, served in that office longer than any other holder of it in American history.

[2] 'Obstructing legislation by dilatory parliamentary tactics, such as speaking merely to consume time.' Mathews, *A Dictionary of Americanisms*, vol. I, p. 605.

great part, upon the fact that it does *not* limit debate, that it allows irrelevance, that it tolerates very dramatic and sometimes distressing exhibitions of senatorial vanity and other faults. But, in return, it gets attention; it does dramatize great issues; it does make it possible to expose abuses, to take skeletons out of cupboards, to make politics interesting. If it is slow as a law-making body, that is not necessarily attributed to it as a fault.[1] The Senate does fulfil one, at any rate, of the functions of a parliamentary system. It makes politics news, and is often a source of public education.

Especially, the Senate provides a way of enquiring into real or alleged abuses, a way which, though it can be and often is itself an abuse, is yet one of the most useful functions of that body. One important result of the separation of powers, is the freedom that it gives to the investigating committees of Congress, especially of the Senate. First of all, it is only by such investigations that Congress can discover what has been going on, as it has not the day-to-day contact with the executive departments that question time gives to the English House of Commons. Then, as the executive is not part of Congress, or in full control of it, Congress is not directly responsible for executive failures. And, since party lines are loose, members of investigating committees are not as tempted as are their opposite numbers in London, to find for the defence. A British government may have to give way, appoint a special committee or a royal commission but it is normally far more in command of the situation than is an American administration. Parliament may be the 'grand inquest of the nation', but the government, as a rule, is the coroner and in fairly effective command of the jury. Not so in Congress. A Representative, still more a Senator, knows that successful investigations are one of the most travelled roads to political fame and power. To be acute, fearless, competent, industrious and to see that these virtues are not hidden under a bushel, is to win a place,

[1] I once heard a Senator defend in private the right of unlimited debate. He asked what happened when you put up a 'no talking' notice in a factory. The output went up. The output of the Senate is laws. 'Does anybody want any more laws?' In a long career in the Senate, this statesman, now dead, added little if anything to the statute book but talked a lot.

fairly rapidly, in the front line of the political chorus. Even a comparatively junior Senator can do this, as Senator Truman and Senator Kefauver have shown. True, the results of the investigation may hurt not help the investigator's party. Thus it is thought that the defeat of the Democratic floor leader, Senator Scott Lucas, in 1950 in Illinois, was in part due to the tactless thoroughness with which Senator Kefauver investigated the interesting finances of Democratic officials in Chicago. Although the two most effective exposers of the Harding scandals were Democratic Senators, Messrs. Walsh and Wheeler, they could not have carried on their investigations without Republican support, and it was true and may still be true to say that it is to the Senate that we owe most of our knowledge both of the darker side of American politics and of administration. To the Senate, for the House, again, suffers from its short life. The Senate never dies; some members of a Senate committee are free, for the moment, from electoral cares and hardly any House investigations have compared with the great Senate enquiries. It is, perhaps, significant that some members of the American public began to wonder at the power, the methods and results attained by congressional investigations, only when a House Committee turned these methods not against 'Big Business', but against termites eating away, so it was asserted, the very ideological foundations of the Republic.

The 'Un-American Activities' Committee has a continuous history going back to 1937 when a member of the Rules Committee, Representative Martin Dies of Texas, introduced a resolution for a special committee to investigate anti-American propaganda. It was explained that the Committee ought to be able to do its job in about seven months. The problem of 'un-American activities' was first brought to the attention of the public by politicians worried about Nazi propaganda and the early investigations of the danger (if such there was) were directed to soothing the feelings of Jewish voters, as much as of the numerous elements who trembled at the threat of Communism. And, originally, the Committee *did* investigate both menaces and, during the period when the Nazi sympathizers in the United States were, in effect, the allies of the Communists in keeping the United States out of 'the imperialist war', an investigation of one easily slid into an investigation of the other.[1] But the Nazi groups were, as a rule, easily identifiable; they were German-American groups with a lunatic fringe of anti-Semites, cranks and crackpots, but, had the Committee confined itself to the Nazi elements, it might well have done its business inside seven months or so, instead of being still in active life nearly twenty years after its founding. For in the danger to American institutions and to national safety that came from the Communist conspiracy, the Committee found a far richer lode and one that possibly interested more such original sponsors of the Committee as Mr. John Thomas Taylor, Director of the American Legion's 'National Legislative Committee'. And, from the beginning, there were millions of Americans who agreed with Representative Joe Starnes of Alabama who 'warned that' the Communists, not the Fascists or the Nazis, were, 'the most dangerous dissident minority' in the United States.[2]

That was certainly the opinion of most supporters of the Committee and many who doubted that this was true, became enemies of the Committee, either because it insisted on being put off the real trail by a red herring or because of its methods.

These methods were sometimes odd enough. Especially odd was the habit of Chairman Dies and then of a successor, J. Parnell Thomas, of conducting what amounted to one-man committee hearings and issuing reports that, being simply the opinion of Representative Dies or Representative Thomas, did not commit the Committee, a legal point of little consolation to the witness summoned before the one-man show and faced with charges without previous notice or, worse still, reduced to reading in the papers of damning charges made by witnesses not cross-examined and not heard in private so that the charges might be weighed, instead of being merely publicized.[3] Then the habit of imputing 'guilt by association' hurt

---

[1] So the Committee in 1941 was able to point with pride to the fact that 'our work has been a type of public education whose importance cannot be exaggerated. Not a single one of the countries of Europe that have been overrun by Stalin and Hitler had the protection of a committee like ours during the years that preceded its supreme crisis'. Quoted in August Raymond Ogden, *The Dies Committee* (1945), p. 230.

[2] William Gellermann, *Martin Dies* (1944), p. 198.

[3] Mr. Alistair Cooke points out that the sins of the committee were often really the sins of the press. 'It is only fair, I think, to the Committee

a large number of innocent if gullible persons who joined, in good faith, one or several of the numerous 'front' organizations that the Communists controlled. But, and this is sometimes forgotten, not all who joined the front organizations were naïvely innocent. The naïve joiners, indeed, provided a kind of 'innocence by association' that helped to confuse the issue further. And, since the attack on alleged penetration of the federal government agencies from the State Department, up or down to the Federal Theatre Project, provided ammunition both for the Republicans and for conservative Democrats, there was a natural tendency for the Administration and its defenders to see in the charges made, merely mendacity, hysteria and politics. It was, said Mr. Truman in 1948, a red herring.[1] But with the indictment and conviction of Alger Hiss, a process begun by the Committee, the red herring issue became of the first political importance. In recent years, the House Committee on Un-American Activities has been almost eclipsed by the activities of Senator Joseph McCarthy of Wisconsin and, although the Senator now has the authority that comes to him as Chairman of the Committee on Government Operations, he was able to acquire fame, become a hero or, at any rate, a symbol, without that authority and although his chairmanship helps him (it allows him to employ agents at government expense), his strength comes not mainly from his powers or acuteness as an investigator, but as a demagogue increasing and exploiting, both the anxieties of the mass of the voters and the worries and resentments of the 'liberals'.

It is difficult to say what limits can be put on the investigating power of Congress or on its power to summon witnesses, force them to testify or commit them for contempt if they refuse.[2] The

---

to recognize that . . . in spite of its evangelical attacks and the jingoisms and scurrility of some of its members, the crimes of putting people into discreditable associations, and presuming guilt before innocence can be proved, were committed far more by the press than by the Committee.' *A Generation on Trial* (1950), p. 65.

[1] In the same way, it is still axiomatic in Labour circles in England that the 'Zinoviev letter' of 1924 was a forgery. It may have been, but there was nothing improbable in Zinoviev's writing such a letter or having such views.

[2] The most useful precedents (from the congressional point of view) were established by committees investigating the real or alleged crimes

habit of falling back on the protection of the Fifth Amendment and refusing to testify because it might incriminate the witness, was not invented by persons accused of being Communists. But the Courts refused to excuse Sinclair and he was in due course convicted. And, it should be noted, the protection of the Fifth Amendment applies only to the reluctant witness who does not wish to incriminate *himself*. He is not protected at all in a right to refuse to give evidence because it may incriminate others. The simple *ethos* of schoolboys or private soldiers does not apply; a witness must give evidence, even though it be to the detriment of a friend or comrade. If the legal authority of congressional committees is very wide, it is to some extent controlled by political considerations and historical traditions. Thus when Representative Velde, the Chairman of the Un-American Activities Committee, summoned Mr. Truman to give evidence, the first decision of the former President was to accept the subpoena. But wiser counsels prevailed and Mr. Truman refused to submit to interrogation by the Committee on anything connected with his presidency. As he wrote to the Chairman. 'It must be obvious to you that if the doctrine of the separation of powers and the independency of the Presidency is to have any validity at all, it must be equally applicable to a President after his term of office has expired. . . . The doctrine would be shattered, and the President, contrary to our fundamental theory of constitutional government, would become a mere arm of the Legislative Branch of the Government if he would feel during his term of office that his every act might be subject to official inquiry and possible distortion for political purposes.'[1]

---

of Republican politicians and Big Business, notably in the investigations arising out of the scandals of the Harding régime. Few 'liberals' had much sympathy then with the wrongs of Harry Sinclair or later of J. P. Morgan. In *McGrain v. Daugherty* (1927), the Supreme Court showed that it 'will construe an investigation to be a legislative one if possible, which means that most Congressional investigations will be presumptively legislative, and hence constitutional, unless there is a clear statement and avowal to the contrary.' Ernest J. Everling, *Congressional Investigations* (1928), p. 379.

[1] *New York Times*, 13 November 1953. It may be assumed that this new Truman doctrine will be a precedent, although Mr. Velde protested against a claim to an 'uncertain and ill-defined immunity', by those 'who

The extravagances, to use no harsher term, of some recent investigations have led to a deprecation of the investigative functions of Congress, especially of the Senate. There have been suggestions of a code of procedure to be adopted by Committees (a code already acted on by the more responsible committees). Charges, it is suggested, should not be made public before the person charged has been informed of them and has had a chance to rebut them. Chairmen of committees and of sub-committees should not become one-man shows. The final report, not the daily headline, should be the target aimed at by the committee. These reforms, obviously desirable, will be adopted when, and not before, ferocious patriotism ceases to be politically profitable and when, to adapt a phrase from the Dred Scott case, Senators recognize that it is not true that a man accused of Communism or fellow-travelling has no rights that a committee (or its chief) is bound to respect.

These scandalous abuses of necessary senatorial powers make many critics, despairing, perhaps, of making any important reforms in the House, attack the Senate which could, without any serious difficulty, adopt an effective system of closure and put an end to the filibuster and to mere irrelevant garrulity. It could refuse to let chairmanships go by mere seniority, this putting its reputation in sometimes very unsuitable hands. It could provide, so it is asserted, a running commentary on and control of executive usurpations without going off at wild tangents, as was done in the early days of the movement for the Bricker amendment. It could be what it was in its great days (those days differing according to the party and class and sectional bias of the commentator). For the Senate is not what it was; perhaps it never was.

The prestige of the Senate is still great; a Senator is not only a great man at home, he is an important man in Washington. And yet the Senate *is* not, perhaps, what it was, in the public eye and esteem. Its record in foreign affairs has been vehemently attacked. Indignant spokesmen for the densely populated states have made computations of how many western 'acreage states' live off the taxes paid by Pennsylvania or New York and yet swamp them in

---

have a continuing and sacred duty to co-operate in all respects where the public safety and public welfare are concerned'.

the Senate. The seniority rule is certain to bring to the top, and into the limelight, Senators whose judgement and egoism give the critics plenty of raw material to work on. And, humanly enough, the Senate is the victim of the *laudator temporis acti*. He dwells gloomily on the contrast between the great men who adorned the Senate in the past and the pygmies who usurp, but cannot fill their places today. And the rigid constitutionalist, the defender of the spirit of the Constitution, even now, after forty years of the new system, regrets the good old days when Senators were elected by state legislators, were chosen (so it is asserted) as Presidents were supposed to be chosen, not by mobs of ill-informed voters, but by competent politicians, choosing an ambassador to the federal government who would do them and the state credit. For the most important change in the character of the Senate has arisen from the adoption, in 1913, of the seventeenth amendment to the Constitution, providing that Senators should henceforward be elected by the people of the states, not by the state legislatures. The ratification of this amendment marked the triumph of an agitation that had gone on from the late nineteenth century. The movement for the direct election of Senators was a part and one of the most important parts of the general movement for making American political institutions more democratic. It was, in this, like the movement for the direct primary, for the adoption, in the states of the initiative, referendum and recall.[1] Like them, the agitation for the direct election of Senators reflected the growing suspicion of the honesty and independence both of the Senators and of the bodies that elected them. Politicians, it was said, were 'the best that money could buy'; their honesty consisted of staying bought, when bought. The Senate was 'the millionaire's club'. Scandals associated with senatorial elections, reaching their height in the great Montana

[1] The initiative gave the voters in some states the right to initiate legislation; the referendum gave them the right to sanction or veto legislation proposed by the legislature, the recall, the right to dismiss public officers. The initiative and the recall were distinctively western in their origin and never took root east of the Mississippi. The referendum became accepted over most of the Union as the proper way to amend state constitutions which became, in consequence, masses of detailed legislation, not 'constitutions' in the old-fashioned sense of the term.

scandals, weakened the prestige of the Senate and spurred on the advocates of reform. In 1913, they won at last.

Almost from the adoption of the amendment in 1913, the direct election of Senators has been attacked. It has been attacked as lowering the level of senatorial ability and character. The names of Clay, Calhoun, Webster, Seward, Douglas have tripped off many critical tongues. But there is no evidence and can, in the nature of things, be no evidence, that any mute, inglorious Websters or Clays are, in fact, kept out of the Senate by the need of appealing to the voters direct, instead of to a state legislature. A Senator in the old days, could only keep his seat either by being dominant in the local politics of his state, or by being the ally or the nominee of those who were. He was not more independent than he would be today. The double ordeal of the primary and of the election probably makes a Senator devote more time to preparing to run for re-election than was necessary in the past when, so often, money took the place of time.[1] But whatever may be lost in the distraction of the Senator who is running for re-election, from his duties in Washington, is more than made up for by the increased knowledge and authority that the Senate, as a whole, gets from its direct contact with the voters. It is, indeed, true that direct election does not guarantee sense, integrity, industry or independence, but it makes the Senate display its claims to these qualities in public. And, since one of the weaknesses of the Senate's position (and an increasing weakness) is that it so grossly overrepresents the declining rural elements of the population, it is fortunate that this weakness is not compounded by the Senate being the choice of legislatures almost all of which, in their turn, grossly overrepresent the rural areas. In states like New York, like Illinois, like Massachusetts it is doubtful if the Democratic party would, in normal circumstances, ever elect a Senator through the legislature, as they hardly ever carry the state legislatures against the entrenched rural pocket boroughs. The

[1] Professor Haynes has suggested that direct election has contributed to Senators neglecting their duties in Washington in order to 'mend their fences' at home. 'This has become so much a matter of course that one of the leading Progressives intimated that any Senators "who are engaged in campaigns ought to be excused."' George H. Haynes, *The Senate of the United States* (1938), vol. I, p. 350.

weight of the Senate would almost certainly be reduced were it even more unrepresentative than it is.

There *is* one serious drawback to the direct election of Senators, the crushing burden of minor jobs it imposes on the Senators from the big states, but whether an accumulation of petty jobs is better or worse than the devotion to a few, big, identifiable interests which, in turn, had even more temptation than they have now to attempt to control state politics so as to control the election (and activities) of Senators, is a matter of opinion. But the fact that the Senate continues to dominate the House, that when, as happens often enough, each House legislates on the same subject in a slightly different form, it is at least as often the House that gives way when its representatives meet the Senate's representatives in conference, suggests that no real harm has been done to the prestige of the Senate in the country. And it is doubtful whether the old, 'statesmanlike', indirectly elected Senate could have held its own, today, with the House in such contests. It is the strength that, Antaeus-like, the Senate gets from its necessary return to the soil where the voters live, that enables it to defy the political laws of gravity and preserve, almost intact, the prerogatives that it won in very different days.

The House may and does resent this, but it is in part (or political tradition is in part) responsible for the weakness of the House, by its insistence on the 'locality rule'. For tradition here represents a deep and, probably, ineradicable American feeling that the representative ought to represent in a double sense, express the views and defend the interests of a state and district, which makes it unlikely that one important and desirable change will be brought about, however powerful the arguments for it.

The Constitution provides that Senators and Representatives shall be residents of the states they represent. As far as the Senate is concerned, the theory that a Senator is a kind of ambassador representing a sovereign body politic gave, and perhaps still gives some plausibility to the view that he must be a citizen of that body and a resident within its jurisdiction. True, since the replacement of the state legislature by the voters as the electing body, the ambassadorial status has become less important and with the increasing social and economic integration of the states the fiction of state sovereignty has become less plausible. But the Constitution is, on this point, clear, and there is no doubt of the intention of the framers. The case against restricting membership of the Senate to residents of the states they represent is not as strong as that against the gloss on the Constitution which limits membership in the House to residents of the congressional districts they represent. This, although mere custom, has acquired over the generations practically the force of constitutional law. A candidate may, very rarely, be allowed, in urban areas, to run in a district next to that of his residence and, in special circumstances, the reality of the alleged residence may not be too closely questioned.[1] Cases have been known of politicians successfully changing their states or districts, but they are not common and it is, in general, true that a politician seeking a congressional career must do so in the district and state that he is resident in.

The consequences are serious and almost uniformly bad. A large number of seats in the House of Representatives are 'safe', that is never return anything but, in one case, Republicans, in the other case, Democrats. Safe seats are, of course, common enough in Britain, France, Canada, but a parliamentary aspirant in these countries is not debarred from trying elsewhere should he have the misfortune to live in a district safely dedicated to the immortal principles of the other side. In the United States, a Democrat in a Republican district, a Republican in a Democratic district cannot enter Congress at all. He must change either his party or his residence. So the locality rule reinforces the strength of the one-party system by tempting the ambitious to join the locally dominant party. A young man cannot acquire merit by making a gallant

---

[1] Thus there were grumbles that Franklin D. Roosevelt, Jr., was only in a very recent sense a resident of the twentieth New York district when he succeeded the late Sol Bloom in a by-election. But New York or, at any rate, Manhattan districts, are arbitrary agglomerations of city blocks and a rigorous insistence on residence in these artificial entities would carry the rule over the border of absurdity. Sol Bloom had been a bona fide resident of the nineteenth, later twentieth district. But even he had to cater to local pressures. Always a snappy dresser, he wore a Borsalino hat. A party worker picked up the hat. 'His hand trembled as he pointed to the manufacturer's label. . . . "I don't know where Borsalino is, but it's not in the U.S.A., and you've got to think about the labor vote. This label might ruin you".' *The Autobiography of Sol Bloom* (1948), p. 201.

fight as a Democrat, in Vermont and be later rewarded by being allowed to fight a more hopeful district in Massachusetts or New York.

Then the locality rule, by limiting the opportunities of a candidate to one district, makes a congressional career, in an unsafe district, unduly hazardous. For if a successful candidate loses his seat in a tidal wave for the other side, he cannot be brought in, however talented he may be, for another seat and, by losing his seat, he loses his congressional seniority.[1] The locality rule adds to the unattractiveness of a career in the House of Representatives and is a powerful force in ensuring that the House will not be able to claim that it contains the greater and better part of the political personnel of national politics. The Representatives are simply those politicians of the dominant party in each district who have got the party nomination. As such, they cannot have and do not have the prestige of the members of the House of Commons in Britain or Canada where it is fairly safe to assume that most effective politicians will be found in these chambers, or can get there if they really want to. It is, perhaps, a sufficient commentary on the system that Franklin Delano Roosevelt, Sr., could never have become a member of the House of Representatives from his ancestral home and legal residence, although he was twice elected Governor of New York and four times President of the United States.[2] Other examples could be given. Thus Mr. John Foster Dulles, appointed to serve part of a senatorial term but defeated at the next election, could not be found a seat in the United States Senate, although he was one of the two or three chief spokesmen of the Republican party on foreign affairs.

Whole classes, with legitimate political ambitions, may be debarred from gratifying them by the locality rule. Thus there was only one straight Republican Representative in the 83rd Congress from Manhattan, yet there are a great many capable Republicans who might wish to serve in Congress, resident on that opulent island. And as long as this is so, it will be idle for the House of Representatives (or even for the Senate) to assume that

[1] For the 'seniority rule', see p. 319.
[2] He was elected to the New York Senate, but that was in rather exceptional circumstances.

their majorities represent the American people; they represent an artificially restricted exercise of the voting rights of the American people and must pay the price in a less than wholehearted admiration and allegiance given them.

The contrast with other democratic countries makes the point clearer. The parliamentary careers of Gladstone, Clemenceau, Mackenzie King, Churchill would have been impossible under the operation of the American locality rule and no one knows how much frustrated political talent has been buried in the United States or confined to law or business because of it. It was a series of accidents that brought back into active national politics, former Representative Abraham Lincoln of Illinois and party catastrophes, like those which overwhelmed the Democrats between 1854 and 1868, or the Republicans between 1930 and 1938 may have ended many careers of great promise. Congress as a whole, and the House of Representatives in particular, cannot compete with the President as long as their membership is so arbitrarily limited by the geographical exclusiveness of the Constitution and by this gloss upon it.[1] A result almost as serious as the necessary diminution of the prestige of the House of Representatives and of the Senate, is the difficulty that the locality rule puts in the way of a Representative, or even of a Senator, who wishes to resist a local pressure group in defence of the national programme of his party or of the national interest. For his party and the nation are, in such cases, remote and unhelpful abstractions. The concrete pressure group is a near-by reality which can punish and reward. The national party can, indeed, reward if it is in power, but not by finding another seat in Congress, only by taking the public-spirited politician out of congressional politics, giving him a federal, appointive office and so further weakening congressional personnel. The locality rule, that is to say, further weakens Congress as a body framing a national

[1] Bagehot pointed out nearly ninety years ago, how much the Conservative representation of the county seats was made ineffective in the House of Commons by the rural dislike of what were about to be called 'carpet-baggers'. The disappearance of the old, sharp division between county and borough seats has made this bias less important and less apparent. Mr. Attlee, for long, lived in a constituency which was represented by his predecessor and successor as Prime Minister, who is now Sir Winston Churchill.

policy, further reduces it to being almost a mere field of force in which pressure groups, national or local, are at work to produce a result that may not be to the general interest of the United States, or of either party, or even of most of the pressure groups themselves.[1]

If the American people resented the limitation on their right to vote for whom they chose, resented the restriction of their choice to the best of the local talent (which may not be very good), Congress might become a more important body. After all, 'the locality rule' as applied to the House is mere custom, not formal law. But the fact that the custom has the force of law shows that the American people do not want a national governing personnel; they want local representation by local men. They get it and are willing to pay the price, a national legislature that very imperfectly represents the American people. And, since this is well-known, Congress pays the price in having all its efforts to 'sell' itself as the embodiment of the will of the 'People of the United States' fail as, in the circumstances, they must do.[2]

Yet the House of Representatives is, it must again be emphasized, representative in the American sense; the Congressman represents first of all (sometimes not always, all of the time) Buncombe

[1] The old distinction between the Member of Congress who could seldom afford to defy local pressures in favour of the party programme and the British Member of Parliament who had much more to gain from supporting the party than from currying local favour, is not so clear as it was. For with the increasing intrusion of the government into economic affairs, M.P.s tend, more and more, to act outside party lines, as representatives of dominant local interests, whether they be Lancashire cotton interests threatened by Japanese competition or farmers outraged at the falling price of eggs. But the party leaders in Britain still have powers of reward and punishment unknown to the party leaders of the United States.

[2] During the late war, intelligent American soldiers were astonished at the 'undemocratic' practice of electing non-residents to the House of Commons. Equally intelligent British soldiers were astonished at voters being debarred from voting for candidates from any part of the country. To the Americans 'democratic' meant egalitarianism; a seat in Congress was a piece of local patronage that should go to a local boy. To the British, it would have been tyrannous, indeed, to restrict the voters of Woodford even to the most talented local resident and debar them from voting for the then Mr. Churchill because he lived in Kent, not in Essex.

County. He has only to please his own electors. Thanks to the locality rule, he is not tempted to please electors in other districts who cannot, in any circumstances, do him any good as a Congressman and he has only to fear the competition of rivals, inside and outside his party, in his own district. He has them and the district's voters in mind and need have nothing else in mind and, if he does not have them in mind, his congressional career is over. A Congressman understands perfectly the answer of the Irish M.P. in the old days who, when asked had he seen what *The Times* said of him, said he wanted to know what the *Skibbereen Eagle* would say of him. And forgetfulness of this fact makes many criticisms of Congress not so much unjust as irrelevant. Representatives 'represent, in varying degrees, almost every interest in their district once they are elected. . . . All this makes them peculiarly insensitive to any *national* opinion about them. The nation cannot vote for them, and they need not consider what it thinks of them personally, unless they have an eye to the presidency. But it makes them keenly sensitive to local opinion. . . . That is why, to many a stranger, American national politics and speeches seem full of initiatives doomed to failure, proposals that are demonstrably half-baked and parochial notions and conceits. The stranger must be aware. The overwhelming majority of American representatives are fully aware of all that. But they are representative. They do represent. If the Congress or assembly crushingly vote them down, they do not turn a hair. Why should they? Words are cheap; and their words are not generally their thoughts. They are only the thoughts of some electors. The delegates are only doing their duty "for the record" by having them recorded. In an age that has seen representative government overturned and spat on, and august legislatures turned into rubber stamps, there is much more to say than has been said for the American political system. It produces representatives who really represent.'[1] A Senator, at any rate a Senator from a populous state, can afford to take a wider view. He is elected for six years, from a large constituency. The fact that he *has* been elected normally proves political views and capacities wider than those of the average Representatives, but even a Senator with great personal prestige cannot afford to disregard all or most of the pres-

[1] Graham Hutton, *Midwest at Noon* (1946), p. 287.

sure groups and sectional interests in his state, no matter how good may be the reasons, from a national point of view, for doing just that.[1]

It is a grievance and a real grievance of Congress that it usually has a bad press and a slightly scornful public. 'Senator Sorghum' and 'Senator Claghorn' are only some of the stereotypes that reflect the conviction of the press and the entertainment industry that Congress is always good for a laugh. Errors of a Representative or a Senator, or a group of them, are eagerly pounced on and exploited. That most members in each house are honest, hard-working and reasonably capable, is a truth not effectively insisted on.[2] Representatives, unlike Senators, are not intrinsically important, even in Washington. Both are open to constant uncharitable suspicion of their actions, their conduct is too generally thought of as represented by the most venal of their colleagues. They are suspected, not only of venality (which is rare), but of legalized greed. Yet most Senators and Representatives could now make a better net income pursuing their normal avocations and many make serious financial sacrifices for their political careers. The American public is touchy about, not for Congress, and often explodes over minor issues with demoralizing effects on its elected spokesmen. 'Most of these indignant outbursts spring from relatively superficial issues. The chorus of ridicule reached its highest point when Congress voted to extend the federal retirement system to its own members. . . . Congress was so alarmed by the public reaction to its "pensions grab"

[1] I have long thought that the Senate ought to erect a monument to the martyr, Senator Edmund Gibson Ross of Kansas who refused, although a Republican, to vote for the conviction of President Andrew Johnson, on the ground that 'I have taken an oath to do impartial justice'. Sound Republicans, in Kansas or elsewhere in 1868, did not want impartial justice and when Ross's vote defeated the impeachment, he was denounced and politically and financially ruined. He was told that 'Kansas repudiates you as it does all perjurers and skunks'. (Dictionary of American Biography (1935), vol. XVI, p. 117. Shortly before Ross died in 1907, the then Governor of Kansas apologized.

[2] I was once present at a party where, among the guests and unknown to some of them, was an ex-Congressman of great ability. He listened to the usual denunciations of Congress and finally announced, that he thought most American voters got better Representatives than they deserved. I agreed with him.

that it hastened to repeal the act.'[1] There lingers in the American mind not merely the memory of less correct days, when there were real 'salary grabs',[2] when a Congressman could save enough of his salary to start a small bank, but when rumours of graft were more current than they are today and an absent-minded Senator could raise a laugh by carelessly replying 'Not guilty', on a roll call. These days are gone but the voters do not necessarily know it.

True the *esprit de corps* of Congress is very great. It reaches its height in the Senate, but it is lively enough in the House. All but the most curmudgeonly members sympathize with their colleagues, no matter of what party, in their reluctance to lose their seats and be forced to 'go back to Pocatello'. Anything, in reason, that can be done to save them from this fate appeals to congressional good nature and although party feeling sometimes runs high, friendships seldom follow strict party lines.[3] The results are credited to the

[1] Merlo J. Pusey, *Big Government* (1945), p. 112. This was a perfectly legitimate, and not extravagant attempt to deal with the problem that rises in all legislative bodies whose members risk their livelihood every time they face an election. It was torpedoed by a wit who called the bill 'Bundles for Congress', after the famous wartime charity, 'Bundles for Britain'.

[2] The great salary grab of 1873 was the work of a 'lame-duck' Congress a large part of whose members had lost their seats in the preceding November and who, retrospectively, raised their salaries. It was the Representatives who were re-elected who had difficulty in explaining this away to their voters at the next election. Among those embarrassed was General James A. Garfield, the future President, who complained that his role had been misunderstood. His friend and mentor, B. A. Hinsdale, gave him rather cold comfort. 'You must remember that times are hard in Ohio and that to our cheesemakers $5,000 is a vast sum. . . . Now the people do not know, and can hardly be made to feel, the embarrassment of the position in which you were placed.' Mary L. Hinsdale, *Garfield-Hinsdale Letters* (1949), p. 222. Voters are hardly more understanding today.

[3] An ingenious Kentucky congressman had been trying in vain to get a post office for his district. As the session was ending this statesman 'arose to a question of personal privilege. This at once arrested the attention of the Speaker, and he requested the gentleman from Kentucky to state his question of privilege. "I rise, Mr. Speaker," said McKenzie, "to a question of the highest privilege, one pertaining to the right of a member of Congress to a seat upon this floor in the next Congress. If I don't get that

kindness of the members of Congress and, in being so kind, they
do not differ from businessmen, professors, doctors, lawyers, all of
whom show much the same spirit, but who do not have to do it in
public, under the critical eyes of the press and the sometimes angry
eyes of the voters. For again, the outside world is not impressed by
the comradeship of Congress and it is surely odd that Congress
should be the only important institution in Washington, indeed, in
the United States, with no press agents, no public relations counsellors, that it, alone, should have to let its deeds speak for themselves.

Congress, especially the House, suffers and knows that it suffers
from the near monopoly of worthwhile publicity enjoyed by the
President. It can only get the headlines, or even the front pages,
by being noisy or scandalous. Few papers, few commentators take
anything like the pains in reporting Congress that they give
automatically to the easier job of reporting the President, or even
to reporting such cabinet officers as the Secretary of State or the
Secretary of Defence. Relations between the President and the
press are not always good, but they are, as a rule, much better than
the relations between Congress and the press. The correspondents
even conduct polls on 'the most useful and most useless members of
Congress' and those praised are less grateful than those mocked are
angry.

'Newspapermen thrust into daily contact with Congressmen
develop a profound dislike for many of them. They see the solons
without benefit of public "front". . . . More important, the correspondents are compelled, by circumstances and by the traditions of
political journalism in the United States, to gild the lily of reality—
reporting chicanery without indignation and clothing the nonsense
of demagogic oratory in the undisturbed language of news dis-
patches. . . . The inability to "let off steam" and "expose" political

---

post-office bill through now, my seat will be imperilled." ' Adlai E.
Stevenson, *Something of Men I Have Known* (1909), p. 50–1. (The author
was Vice-President of the United States from 1893 to 1897. His grandson
was Democratic candidate for President in 1952.) It might be noted that
the seat for which McKenzie sat was impregnably Democratic, so that
from the Republican point of view, McKenzie's defeat would have
meant no party gain.

charlatans intensifies hostility.'[1] Thirteen years and a world war later, it was much the same story. 'Debate in the House is almost indescribable. It is a shamble of low humor, rank partisanship, incredible demagoguery, and wild misinformation spiced with miscellaneous and grotesque irrelevancies.... Speeches frequently have utterly no relation to one another. A Republican rises to heckle the administration on the potato surplus. A Southern Democrat thunders against communism. Another member asks for unanimous consent to "revise and extend my remarks", which is a formal way of saying he wants to insert a lengthy—and usually ghostwritten—harangue into the Congressional Record at a cost to the taxpayer of $72.50 a printed page.'[2] Many hardworking and capable members of Congress feel that these pictures of their public performances are unfair. They are. But the House has largely surrendered the function of being a real debating chamber by the rigidity of its rules and the power it gives to committees, while the Senate, by its refusal to have any rules, puts itself at the mercy of its most loquacious but not necessarily most respectable or respected members, so that the press finds it easier to report the nonsense that is, at any rate, newsworthy, rather than the sense that is so often dull and often said in secret.

Many of the troubles of Congress are simply due to the immense growth of the business of the federal government and so of the business of Congress. As federal power has grown, as the power of government as such has grown, Congress has, like the presidency, found its functions so expanded that its old methods no longer are adequate. 'In volume, scope and complexity the legislative agenda of 1943-4 was obviously a far cry from that of 1790.... It was a far cry even from 1911 when Robert Ramspeck, Democratic whip in the 79th House, came from Georgia to Washington to work in the Capitol Post Office and serve as a congressional secretary. Congress was then in session only nine months out of 24, and the members spent the remainder of their terms at home, practising law or attending to their private business. The mail they received then dealt

[1] Leo C. Rosten, *The Washington Correspondents* (1937), p. 205. By British standards, the gilt is, at times, thinly applied.

[2] Robert S. Allen and William V. Shannon, *The Truman Merry-Go-Round* (1950), pp. 169-70.

largely with free seed, rural routes, Spanish war pensions and occasionally a legislative matter. Members had ample time to attend to
their congressional duties. "It was a pretty nice job that a Member
of Congress had in those days," Representative Ramspeck remin-
isced when he appeared 34 years later before a joint committee
studying the burdens of legislators. "At that time the Government
affected the people directly in only a minor way. . . . It was an
entirely different job from the job we have to do today. It was
primarily a legislative job, as the constitution intended it to be." [1]
The burden varies, of course, a great deal between Senate and
House and between Senator and Senator and Representative and
Representative. It is not certain that a Senator from a remote state
has as great a burden as a Representative from an eastern and
populous district. There are a good many districts with many more
voters than Nevada for instance. But the burden is heaviest for the
Senator from a very populous state and still heavier if that state is
near Washington, for although that may not increase the number
of problems it increases the time (and money)-wasting number of
letters and visitors.

'Senator Lehman receives more mail than any other member
of the United States Senate, largely because of the population
and the diversity of interests of his state. Lehman's mail is
greater than that of Senator Irving Ives, his colleague from the
Empire State, because the bulk of the mail emanates from New
York City, and the bulk of New York City mail goes to Senator
Lehman.'[2] Thus on one day, Senator Lehman received 159 letters

[1] George B. Galloway, *Congress at the Crossroads* (1946), p. 52. The
change was not confined to the United States. A prominent private
member in the British parliaments before the first war once told me that,
within a year of the enactment of the Insurance Act of 1911, his correspondence trebled.

[2] Stephen K. Bailey and Howard D. Samuel, *Congress at Work* (English edition, 1953), p. 99. Senator Lehman maintains four offices, in
addition to the official one provided for him. One is in New York City,
one in the Capitol, one in the Library of Congress, one in the basement
of the Senate Office Building and there also is the official suite. This of
course costs much more than the Senator's salary and the allowance made
for office expenses, even though these are, to some extent, adjusted to the
size of the constituency. Senator Lehman is a rich man, but the 'secret
fund' provided for Senator Nixon (as he then was) was an answer to a

while, on the day chosen, Representative Ayres received eleven and on another sample day, Representative Frank E. Smith of Mississippi received round twenty.[1]

The American voter takes it for granted that his Representative, even his Senator, will be ready to do his chores for him and is quite capable of complaining that members of Congress are not statesmen and, at the same time, so flooding them with business that they cannot find time to be legislators, not to speak of statesmen. Congress recognizes, the public recognizes, the 'consular' character of the members, the fact that they must work, lobby, argue for the voters of Buncombe County as well as speak for it.[2] The great 'office buildings' that house the secretaries and assistants of the Senators and Representatives[3] give a fair idea of the amount of mere consular duty that is expected of the people's spokesmen. No parliamentary assembly provides such lavish office and secretarial facilities, but for many members even these are not adequate. The fact that they exist, possibly makes the voters less scrupulous about taking up the time of the Senator or Representative and a great deal of congressional time and federal money is wasted on making petty enquiries and arranging for petty favours. But although there have been cases of members who avoided most of these jobs and still kept their seats, like one celebrated Massachusetts Representative who was able to indulge his sport of lion hunting in Africa

---

real problem for a poor man who was Senator of one of the three most populous states. Representative Ayres 'estimated that his two-year term would cost him $5,000 more than he received from the government'. Mr. Ayres' chief extra expense was in travel. 'Congressional expenses allow for one round trip per session, not two round-trip plane tickets each week.' Ibid., p. 124.

[1] Ibid., pp. 101, 114, 127.

[2] This congressional habit got its name, so it is asserted, from the candid admission of Felix Walker, who justified a long and tedious speech by saying 'that come what might he was bound to make a speech for Buncombe'. Mitford A. Mathews, *A Dictionary of Americanisms*, vol. I, p. 219. Buncombe County was part of the orator's North Carolina district.

[3] The Senate Office building is joined to the basement of the Capitol by a toy underground railway, presumably justified on the ground that Senators are expected to be old men, incapable of movement. This railway is the delight of visiting children of all ages. I do not think that I have ever seen a Senator use it.

without alienating his voters, few politicians can risk such indifference to the rules of the game. Members of both houses have to work hard for their voters; if they don't, they don't remain members. But their voters, alas, are not adequately grateful and Congress does not get from the public either the respect or gratitude that it thinks, not altogether wrongly, it deserves.[1]

But although much of the burden imposed on Congress cannot be lifted except by abdication, some burdens are willingly accepted and, by the waste of manpower and time that they impose, force abdication in important fields. Thus the proliferation of often overlapping investigation committees, however useful they may be in showing the Democratic rascals up and keeping them out, keeps many Congressmen from doing their current job of legislating and watching the present administration. Congress, for example, keeps a detailed control over the Post Office, thus ensuring that it will remain in politics and 'in the red'. This may be what the people want, as Senator Carlson of Kansas suggests, but it both makes it impossible to run the Post Office with anything like business efficiency, and wastes what is, in theory, valuable congressional time on petty business and on matters of post office financial policy that Congress is peculiarly unfitted to deal with.

Another example is the way in which Congress clings to its role as the city council of Washington (the District of Columbia). The inhabitants of that now large city are forced to endure taxation without representation. They are forced to approach their rulers in Congress unofficially[2] and Congress wastes its very expensive time

---

[1] Making an illegal profit out of their allowances for secretarial assistance is the financial temptation which, it appears, most frequently assails the Representatives. A series of members of the House of Representatives have gone to the penitentiary for taking a 'kick-back' from the salaries of their clerical staff. Perfectly legal, but sometimes frowned on, is the habit of putting a wife or other kin on the pay-roll. But a recent President of the United States did so when he was a Senator, with no consequent loss in public esteem, and Senator Sparkman, Democratic candidate for Vice-President in 1952, did not suffer much, if at all, from the fact that he employed his wife in his office.

[2] Even in this century, there have been odd stories of the forms these approaches have sometimes taken.

on trifles. 'Hours have been consumed by the nation's legislators in discussing such matters as how to kill Washington's starlings, which are growing more and more pestiferous. Favourite roost: the Treasury. The starlings' chief supporters: professional car washers and Senator Taft, who maintains they eat Japanese beetles. . . . The last anti-starling bill cleared the House in 1949; a Senate committee reported the bill out. But Mr. Taft refused to give unanimous consent to its consideration because it provided no alternative method for combating beetles. There the matter rests. The starlings still roost.'[1]

There are, it is said, serious reasons from the point of view of supporters of 'white supremacy' against giving the inhabitants, one can hardly call them citizens, of Washington, home rule. A large part of the population is Negro and the thought of their electing, though the risk is remote, a Negro Mayor, justifies, on this view, the denial of normal political rights to the inhabitants of the city that houses the Declaration of Independence.[2]

Congress will never again find its burden light. But it will not be able to do its real business, or resist executive encroachment, as long as it refuses to divest itself of what Burke called 'a confused and scuffling bustle of local agency'.[3]

It is inevitable that in the American system, 'lobbies' and 'pressure groups' should play a great role. They play an important role in all governmental systems. Courts, whether monarchical or dictatorial, know them as do parliamentary governments. Trade union members, farmer members, business members are all known to the British House of Commons.[4] But the separation of powers and the business methods of Congress make them especially note-worthy in the American system. In Britain (and in Canada) the efforts of the lobbyist and the pressure group are directed first of all, and often all of the time, at the Cabinet. It can deliver the goods if

[1] *Fortune*, February 1952, p. 83.

[2] The seniority rule has, in recent times, promoted to the chairmanship of the congressional committees that control the District, members from the South very reluctant to give the Negro minority any rights that might create dangerous precedents.

[3] Quoted by Lindsay Rogers, *The American Senate* (1926), p. 102.

[4] Bagehot noted that there were supposed to be round two hundred 'railway members' in the House of Commons of his time.

it wants to. It may be worthwhile beating up support among the supporters of the ruling party, but as a rule power is centralized. It is more profitable to haunt Whitehall than Westminster. But in the United States, although there are many things that the executive departments can do off their own bat, there are many that can only be done by and through Congress. The effort of the individual or the group, then, may have to be divided; divided between the executive departments and Congress and, in the latter case, what is really meant is the committees of Congress.

Because nearly all the real business of Congress is done by the Committees and because the committee method of doing business is by 'hearings', the lobbyist or the pressure group approaches the members of the committees, privately or publicly. The lobbyist is more likely to use the private approach, the pressure group the public. For the lobbyist is an expert in political public relations. He is no blind partisan. He is a hired man of a group or a free lance putting his expertise at the disposal of any individual or group willing to pay for it.

It is important to distinguish between the 'mere' lobbyist and the representative of the pressure group. It is not a question of ethical superiority on either side. The mere lobbyist may be as honest as a good corporation lawyer, the spokesman for the pressure group may not only be honestly unscrupulous in the real or supposed interests of his group, but put his own pride or pocket before those of the group. But the pressure group leader has to be a practising politician, for his power and utility is a function of his representative character. He must be able to promise the support or threaten the opposition of the group and, for that reason, he must spend a great deal of his time in keeping control of his own nominal employers. 'All the chiefs of important pressure groups are as obviously intent upon getting members—and the support of members—as any politicians are on getting votes. In neither case is the process necessarily evil. It is a pretty poor Congressman who cannot convince himself that the best interests of the Republic depend on his re-election. Such calm self-confidence in the service of their constituents is not denied to farm or labor leaders or the executive secretaries of the organizations of business and industry. They need it in the electoral processes of organizations, which are generally a good deal less freely democratic than elections are in plain politics.'[1]

The chief charge against the lobbyist is not that he is dishonest, but that he is either superfluous or is, in fact, trading on knowledge and contacts acquired while he was in the service of the government —or in Congress. He *is* often superfluous. Many businessmen, and many persons with more or less legitimate claims on the government, are bewildered when confronted with the labyrinth of official Washington. Often the lobbyist does no more than tell his client what his rights are and where he can put in his claim. He does no more harm or good than a doctor giving a nervous or hypochondriac patient a placebo. Ethically more worthy of criticism, is the using of knowledge acquired in a previous official career. Again, there need be no question of corruption. But it is often convenient to know who is the really effective power in a department; it is often convenient to be known to important committee members in whose good graces executive officials wisely prefer to be. So Washington is full of former Congressmen loath to 'go back to Pocatello' and of former officials, usually classed as lawyers, whose chief asset is not a knowledge of law, but of the *arcana imperii* of the great departments.[2] Yet the standard of the lobbyist of today would seem pedantically scrupulous to the great practitioners of the past and the fact that there has been an improvement is often ignored.

The great age of the pure lobbyist, pure in the scientific sense, lay between the end of the Civil War and the beginning of the twentieth century. Party divisions were purely doctrinal, the ruling groups in both parties thought much the same about the real issues of the day, agreed that the 'business of the United States is business' as President Coolidge was to put it.[3] Power even in the South was

[1] Jonathan Daniels, *Frontier on the Potomac* (1946), p. 150.

[2] It is illegal to appear before a Court in cases in which the department concerned was the lawyer's employer until a certain number of years have elapsed. But this law can and is evaded in the spirit if not the letter.

[3] Dr. Claude Fuess points out that Coolidge was misunderstood, that he went on to say 'only those who do not understand our people . . . believe that our national life is entirely absorbed by material wants'. Claude M. Fuess, *Calvin Coolidge* (1940), p. 358. But the public which remembered only the first epigrammatic statement, expressed its own

passing to men who saw in the new industrial civilization a source of power and profit. 'Old Southern commonwealths that had once been the bailiwicks of planter statesmen, with a peculiar institution to serve, were now found to be organized in the service of a new set of interests.'[1] In the West, there were revolts but no revolution. The Democratic officers had more difficulty in keeping their troops in hand than had the Republicans but, basically, East and West, North and South, the parties avoided interfering with the new economic order.

At the same time, the eclipse of the presidency put far more power into the hands of important congressmen than had been usual in other epochs in American history and, lastly, the almost equal balance of power between the parties caused a series of political deadlocks, ensured that leaders of both parties had great power and necessitated the creation of an effective but necessarily secret governmental system.[2] It was a world that called for the services of the lobbyist, the honest broker (for a fee) who could oil the wheels of the cumbrous machine and see that the sellers and buyers did not waste time in laborious search for each other. The most famous of the lobbyists, 'Uncle Sam' Ward, the 'King of the Lobby',[3] described his functions in not totally disingenuous terms. 'This business of lobbying, as it is called . . . is as precarious as fishing in the Hebrides. . . . I am not at all ashamed—I do not say I am proud—of the occupation. It is a very useful one. In England it is a separate branch of the legal profession. There they have parliamentary lawyers who do no other business.'[4] 'Uncle Sam' did describe methods that, it is believed, are not customary at the English Parliamentary Bar. 'Talleyrand says that diplomacy is helped by good dinners. At good dinners people do not talk shop,

---

view if not Coolidge's. The politicians of the era between 1865 and 1900 had no doubts.

[1] C. Vann Woodward, *Reunion and Reaction* (1951), p. 40.

[2] Between 1872 and 1888, there were only two years in which the presidency and both houses were controlled by the same party.

[3] Although he had married an Astor and was the brother of Julia Ward Howe, the author of 'The Battle Hymn of the Republic', Sam Ward had no business ability of the humdrum kind and had no crusading fervour.

[4] Maud Howe Elliott, *Uncle Sam Ward and His Circle* (1938), p. 547.

but they give people a right, perhaps, to ask a gentleman a civil question and to get a civil answer. Sometimes a railroad man wants information. Sometimes a patentee wants his patent renewed; that is a pretty hard fight. Then, a broker wants to know what the Treasury is going to do about a certain measure; a banker is anxious about the financial movement in Congress, or a merchant about the tariff. All these things we do constantly, and we do not make any charge for them. We keep up a certain circle of friends, and once in a while an opportunity comes of getting something that is of real service, and for which compensation is due and proper.'[1]

The services rendered, an acute observer of the contemporary political scene has noted, are not only those rendered to employers of the lobbyist. He, at times, renders a service to the legislators, under pressure from groups no more edifying than those the lobbyists represent (they may have their lobbyists too). And, the comparison is not too far-fetched, a competent lobbyist may render to a legislative body some of the services a good lawyer renders to a court. 'The legislators know that the lobbyist is a useful appendage, as important in his own way as the press, and better informed in his own particular field. Many a lobbyist, because of his special know-ledge, has saved a legislator from looking foolish.'[2] It is not only that the lobbyist is sometimes useful, but that, in federal politics, his methods are now less crude. 'In former times, the ways which men used to corrupt public officials were both crude and direct. The lobbyist at strategic moments would equip himself with a little

[1] Ibid., p. 548. This was the Washington of Mark Twain's novel, *The Gilded Age*, of Henry Adams's novel, *Democracy*. It was believed that the lobbyists, or some of them, were willing to go to great lengths to get their principals in a generous mood. The voter, had he reflected, might have described the formal political campaigns in the terms of Belloc's epigram.

> The accursed power which stands on Privilege
>   (And goes with Women, and Champagne and Bridge)
> Broke—and Democracy resumed her reign:
>   (Which goes with Bridge, and Women and Champagne).
>
> Epigram XX 'On a General Election' from
> *Sonnets and Verse* by Hilaire Belloc, Duckworth & Co.

Of course in that era it would be necessary to read poker for bridge.

[2] Warren Moscow, *Politics in the Empire State* (1948), p. 200.

black bag stuffed with bank notes. These would be slipped under the table or given to public officials at surreptitious meetings.'[1] ... It is not quite so certain that lobbyists of the old school do not practise their arts in state capitals, but in Washington today, the ethical and prudential standard is higher than in the age of General Grant, or even of later epochs.[2]

Naturally, the lobby was not and is not equally active all the time. It may be wise for the spokesmen for a given interest to let sleeping dogs lie. In the great days of Republican dominance, a tariff revision (which, of course, was always upward) did not need much lobbying pressure. The party leaders knew what they wanted and had, despite occasional revolts, the power to get it.[3] It was different when it was a question of reducing the tariff. Aldrich could be *syndic*, as the French put it, for the great interests for whom the high tariff was a positive benefit, if not an absolute necessity. But there were few powerful interests equally and visibly benefited by a reduction of the tariff; its beneficiaries (on low

[1] Paul H. Douglas, *Ethics in Government* (1952), pp. 43–4. Senator Douglas attributes the decline in these crude methods, in part, to the vigilance of columnists like Drew Pearson and Robert S. Allen.

[2] We have testimony to the relative purity of Washington from Representative Eugene D. O'Sullivan of Nebraska who declared, in 1950, that 'the practice of having legislators and others embraced in the toils of the harlots is still in vogue at the seat of many state governments but has been practically abandoned in Washington, D.C.' Quoted from V.O. Key, Jr., *Politics, Parties, and Pressure Groups* (Third edition, 1952), p. 163. 'Alfalfa Bill' Murray, the vigilant Governor of Oklahoma, wished to have the members of the legislature of that state locked up in dormitories at night to save them from the temptations of Oklahoma City.

[3] Thus the 'progressive' revolt did not prevent the passage of the Payne-Aldrich tariff of 1909. As an anonymous and admiring poet put it.

> So wind 'em up and let 'em run,
> Fakirs and false alarms;
> Slow death is what they would have done
> To mills and mines and farms!
> And, Boy; remember drool is cheap
> By babes in the tariff woods;
> So let 'em drool their samples,
> For Aldrich has the goods.

Nathaniel Wright Stephenson, *Nelson W. Aldrich* (1930), p. 361.

tariff or free trade theory) were the whole people of the United States, the whole American economy. It was in face of this problem that Woodrow Wilson, trying to push through the Underwood tariff in 1913, made his famous direct appeal to the people.

'There is every evidence that money without limit is being spent to sustain this [high tariff] lobby and to create an appearance of a pressure of opinion antagonistic to some of the chief items of the Tariff bill. It is of serious interest to the country that the people at large should have no lobby and be voiceless in these matters, while great bodies of astute men seek to create an artificial opinion and to overcome the interests of the public for their private profit.'[1]

Wilson scared off that particular lobby and the tariff of 1913 went through rapidly, and with less suspicion of being rigged to suit special interests, than any tariff since the Civil War. But both lobbies and lobbyists remained, for they performed a useful function in the disjointed governmental system of Washington.

A more respected and equally useful function is performed by the pressure groups and by their agents. A pressure group may represent a permanent economic or social interest, or the sponsors or opponents of a particular piece of legislation or administrative policy. They may want to protect migratory birds, or the Indians, or national monuments like Mount Vernon, to ban lascivious films or get federal aid for schools. Every important church, every important 'movement' is a pressure group and it has its agents and offices in Washington.

They flood the Capitol (and the National Press Club) with literature; they seek for and often find means of getting free publicity; they give teas and cocktail parties.[2] Among these pressure groups may be counted the foreign embassies, but their aim is to induce general amiability, rather than to bring pressure on Congress for specific proposals. But the pressure groups' main business is

---

[1] *The Public Papers of Woodrow Wilson: The New Democracy* (1926), vol. I, p. 36.

[2] Patriotic drys often attribute the frequent betrayals of America which they deplore, to the 'Demon Rum' i.e. martinis. The Washington consumption of alcohol is the highest per head in the United States by a good deal.

with Congress. They have two weapons; the threat, sometimes formidable, sometimes not, that their millions of (possibly mythical) members will vote against the errant Representatives or Senators who are for (or against) a certain measure. But not only do mere threats of this kind cancel out; members of Congress have acquired a good deal of sceptical skill in dealing with the claims of pressure groups. They can see the big corporation hiding behind the small business, the massive public indifference of Catholics or Methodists, lying behind the peremptory demands of their official spokesmen.

More effective, in most cases, is an educational campaign directed at the voters through congressional hearings, or even directed at the committees, for many members have open minds on the projects before them and, other things being equal, would rather vote wisely and well than not.[1]

If it is desirable that legislation should represent more than the views of bureaucrats and of politicians, the pressure groups perform a very useful function. For they can send in well-briefed members, or their permanent officials, confident that, if they represent any serious body of opinion, they will get a respectful hearing. This is very different from the interview with the Minister, perhaps headed by a few tame M.P.s, that is the English equivalent. Of course, there are royal commissions and parliamentary committees, but they are not frequent and their reports do not always lead to action. Congressional committees are permanent commissions and they are always taking evidence. Rare indeed are the cases in the United States when an important interest is neglected or not given its day in court—and in public.

And the British Minister, negotiating with the miners or the farmers or the railway workers, is forced less often to remember that there is a general public, than is the American legislator. Of course, in Washington as in England, there are some permanent and powerful pressure groups whose views are always listened to and sometimes docilely accepted.

[1] Some committees are packed from the beginning. Thus the agricultural committees of both houses are recruited from the farm states. A consumer's lobby would be wasting its time trying to convert these committee members to the consumer's point of view.

The first of these is what used to be called in England 'the agricultural interest'. The most sacred if not the most important of the pressure groups is that vaguely called 'the farmers'. They are important for several reasons. They are numerous, far more numerous than in Britain. They represent a very important segment of the economy. They are politically stronger than their numbers justify in the House of Representatives and still stronger in the Senate. And, perhaps as weighty as the other reasons for the attention paid to their demands, the farmers are *sacred*.

It was the belief of the founders of the Republic that the farmers were the salt of the earth. If Jefferson's dream of a republic of virtuous husbandmen was beginning to be merely a dream by the time of his death, it remained a potent myth. From the farmers came the men who made America. 'From log cabin to White House' was a well-travelled road. It was profitable for a politician to have a rural background and to continue to have one. More politicians than one described themselves, as a cynic noted, as 'farmers', because 'they had one cow and twenty banks'. But despite the praise and indeed adulation lavished on the farmer, he did not do so well materially as he did spiritually. He was told of his happy lot, but repeatedly refused to accept it. It is an old story.

> *O fortunatos nimium sua si bona norint*
> *Agricolas,*

as Virgil prophetically put it.

Farm discontent became a feature of the American political landscape. Organisations of all kinds sprang up to represent him and to lobby for him. The oldest still active is 'the Grange', the 'Patrons of Husbandry'. This body originally aimed at elevating the farmer intellectually and morally as well as financially. It tried to give the farmer a rural ethos as well as tangible material reward for his public-spirited activities.[1]

The Grange, however, is no longer an effective national lobby.

---

[1] In its concentration on uplift the Grange recalls its contemporary but long-dead 'Knights of Labour'. It is characteristic of the Grange that its national governing body is the 'Assembly of Demeter' presided over by the 'High Priest of Demeter'.

Its lodge buildings are more likely to be found in the diversified farming regions of New England raising dairy cattle, market garden crops, and tourists, than in the basic-crop regions of the Middle West. More important is the Farm Bureau Federation which, basically, represents the grain and cotton areas. It represents, too, the more prosperous and conservative farmers and, in fact though no longer in form, it is in close contact with the state agricultural extension services, an alliance that gives the Farm Bureau the inside track in farm politics in many states. The National Farmers' Union is a more radical though not very radical alliance of the less prosperous farmers, the heir of the old agrarian radicals of the nineteenth century.

All of these groups dabble in politics, but there is not, at the moment in America, an open, united agrarian movement of the type that in the past repeatedly led the embattled farmers into usually fruitless battles for their rights. The early 'Grangers', the Alliance, the farm co-operatives, the Non-Partisan League, represented a different approach to farm politics than that favoured by the farm lobbies of today. The most radical and the most interesting of the organizations that sought to capitalize the discontent of the farmers was the Non-Partisan League. Its centre was in the wheat belt, above all in North Dakota, whose farmers were most exposed to the vicissitudes of the market, had a remarkably homogeneous, mainly Scandinavian-American culture and were the victims of the last great expansion of the arable frontier, just as the expanding market for grain began to sag and then collapse. The title of the League revealed its aim, to circumvent the established party system, and it was helped in this by the impact of the first war on communities that were either neutral in spirit, like the Scandinavians, or for American neutrality if not neutral themselves, as were the Germans. And there were few or no industries to weaken the conviction that the farmer was the salt of the earth, his way of life almost the only human way of life. 'League leaders pointed to agriculture as "the most important industry under the shining sun". Emperors, Kings, Ministers, Presidents, Parliaments, Congresses, great generals, mighty armies with monster guns and forests of bayonets and mountains of shot and shell are down on their knees before the man with the hoe. Yet, he has had but little direct voice in affairs of government that determine his weal or woe. Men who can hardly tell the difference between a cotton boll and a chrysanthemum, are expected to legislate for the most vital industry of all'. . . . The case of the North Dakota farmers was but one instance where 'the farmers had been vainly begging a bunch of windjamming, booze-fighting politicians for legislation to protect them against the flour-mill trust and the grain gamblers.'[1]

But although the League had its moments of success, its experiments in state Socialism broke down and it simply added a variation to the political organization of the Middle West and provided a political springboard for politicians like former Senator Gerald Nye and present Senator William Langer.

More promising was the 'farm bloc' composed of middle western and southern members of Congress, candidly out for what they could get for their interests and their sections. After the first war, the farm bloc had some success if only in upsetting the conservative high command of the Republican party. But all attempts to get Congress to do something substantial for the farmer failed. He could not, in presidential elections, be wooed away from the GOP, and the Republican leaders saw no real reason for doing anything substantial for him, apart from giving him useless tariff protection. With the New Deal, came a different attitude and, before many years were out, it was discovered that what the farmer wanted was high prices for his crops paid in cash; whether they were paid by the consumer as consumer or as taxpayer, became more and more a matter of indifference to the farmers. After being at the 'little end of the horn' for generations, the farmer became, if not the pampered pet of the federal government, at any rate the chief visible beneficiary of federal bounty. His crops were 'supported' by the government which bought them when they fell below a fixed price level. This kept the prices up and, in some cases, priced his farm products out of the market. Great quantities of foodstuffs were stored in federal granaries and on the farms; the little metal store houses, like miniature gasometers, dotted the landscape; and it was the belief that the Republican eightieth Congress was opposed to providing adequate storing facilities and so to getting just prices

[1] Theodore Saloutos and John D. Hicks, *Agricultural Discontent in the Middle West 1900–1939*, p. 160.

for the farmer, that turned some middle western states in favour of Mr. Truman in 1948.

Since that political earthquake, politicians have been more than nervous in dealing with 'the farmers' and the degree to which politicians have been intimidated makes the enactment of a rational farm policy almost impossible. Yet the farmers are no more a block of identical interests than are 'business men' and possibly less than is 'labour'. The various spokesmen for the 'farmers' represent very different economic levels and interests and what suits the Farm Bureau Federation need not and usually does not suit the Farmers' Union and not always even the Grange. 'The Union, as the avowed champion of the poor family farmer, has pitted itself against the Farm Bureau Federation as the alleged champion of the large-scale commercial producer. According to the Union and its sympathizers, the Federation is the ringleader of an alliance composed of itself, the Grange, the National Council of Farmer Co-operatives, the Co-operative Milk Producers' Federation, and other big producers' organizations representing the "top tier" of farmers, processors and distributors.'[1] These farmers have a very different interest from that of the poorer farmers and look on federal policy with a very critical eye if it seems to threaten the present set-up. Thus, we are told, the Farm Bureau regarded with grave suspicion the work of the Farm Security Administration, which was attempting to salvage the marginal farmers, ruined in the depression, and desperately clinging to their often uneconomic farms. 'Even though it has helped with cash and encouragement in thousands of pitiable cases of human misery, it is accused of harboring outright "reds" as well as "pinks" on its ample pay roll. . . . Farmers are the main accusers, especially the American Farm Bureau Federation, which represents the American equivalent of the "landed aristocracy" and the most powerful of the farmer's general pressure groups.'[2]

The interests of farmers vary a great deal and produce opposing patterns of political demand accordingly. A congressional sub-committee touring New England, finds that the farmers of that region have very different interests from the grain farmers of the

---

[1] A. Whitney Griswold, *Farming and Democracy* (1952), p. 191.

[2] W. M. Kiplinger, *Washington is Like That* (1942), p. 228.

Middle West who want a high price for what they sell to New England farmers, grain stuffs, for instance. Dairy farmers have much the same interest, nationally speaking, in all parts of the country. But in state politics, dairy farmers want, and sometimes succeed in getting, legislation that sets up a kind of tariff wall to protect their rights in *their* 'milk shed', not only from Canadian exports, but from exports from Wisconsin. Then, since American farmers are human, they are, to a certain, though not to a crippling extent, embarrassed by the contrast between the legend and the facts. They see themselves as the sole, independent, self-supporting element in the American community. They may have to accept what they think their due from the federal government, but they would rather (especially if they belong to the 'landed aristocracy' of the Farm Bureau) do without open handouts. For the farmers, the 'country's pride', have a pretty clear picture of what a farmer should be—and they don't quite fit into the picture. 'They picture the farmer standing alone and independent on a hilltop watching an unseasonal storm destroy his crop. But when the California farmer sits before his television set, listening to the heavy rain beating on the roof and realizes the government stands ready to help him out, he knows he is neither alone nor independent. Then he feels guilty.'[1] It would be unkind to dismiss this moral malaise as mere humbug. But it would be idle, too, to expect the farmer, at any rate the average farmer, not a member of highly disciplined religious groups like the Mormons or Mennonites, to prefer his lonely mountain top of independence to what he thinks is his due. Frederick the Great said of the scruples that afflicted the Empress Maria Theresia about taking part in the partition of Poland: 'she wept and took.' So does the American farmer.

It is possible, but no more than possible, that the farmer may, politically as well as economically, be pricing himself out of the market. The great urban majority that cannot pay for the foodstuffs whose price it keeps up through the taxes it pays, is becoming restive. The ending of the generations-old ban on uncoloured margarine is possibly significant. State and federal law attempted, by taxation and by prohibiting the addition of colouring matter to the white margarine, to prevent the urban consumer from being

[1] Orr Kelly in *The San Francisco Chronicle*, 10 November 1953.

cheated—and from being tempted to give up butter.[1] Fashions and fads in food, the terror of calories that affects the American woman, the decline of the hard manual labour that provoked the appetites of the men, changes in world production, all have upset the American farm pattern and law and lobbies, in the long run, must be adjusted to the facts. But it may be quite a long run, at any rate as long as the American people believe with the 'Country Life Commission' appointed by Theodore Roosevelt, that one aim, perhaps the main aim of American policy, should be 'to preserve a race of men in the open country that, in the future as in the past, will be the stay and strength of the nation in time of war, and its guiding and controlling spirit in time of peace'.[2]

The difficulties of a pressure group are illustrated by the action of 'labour'. In few districts is 'labour' in a condition to lay down the law to the politicians. It must deal with them. They have their organization, their obedient voters and a clientele, either actually or potentially, wider than has 'labour' (or, indeed, than any other group). It is still harder to control a state. The miners in West Virginia are the biggest voting block, but they are not in a position totally to disregard the regular political set-up or simply to take it over. The automobile workers are the biggest voting block in Michigan, but neither in the state nor in Detroit, are they above the need of allies.

The labour difficulty is best illustrated in the campaign in which 'political action', the backing of a candidate in an important election, was most effectively dramatized. In 1950, labour was determined to defeat the chief author of the Taft-Hartley Act, Robert Taft, who was running for re-election as Senator from Ohio. Yet labour could not impose a candidate on the divided Democratic party of the State. It had to take what it could get, that is the State Auditor, 'Jumping Joe' Ferguson, instead of the candidate it favoured, Murray Lincoln, who could not hope to get the Democratic

---

[1] Grocers, selling white margarine, thoughtfully added a little bag of yellow colouring matter which, when kneaded into the margarine, produced the desired colour effect. This kneading was one of the regular chores of American husbands and even of house guests. It will be soon as lost an art as home brewing became after the repeal of prohibition.

[2] Griswold, op. cit., p. 147.

nomination. The CIO had not 'captured' the Democratic party; it operated 'as an independent interest group which happened to prefer Ferguson to Taft and therefore agreed to supplement a Democratic campaign'.[1] It expended a great deal of money and, what was possibly more serious, of prestige in an attempt to beat something with nothing, for Senator Taft was one of the ablest and most generally respected of Ohio politicians and his opponent was a run-of-the-mill popular office-holder with his own minor machine based on patronage.[2] Taft won with ease. It is possible, indeed, that the CIO helped Taft, that the high-pressure sales campaign alienated many voters and brought out on Taft's side many normally indifferent voters who thought that 'labour' was showing an excessively vaulting ambition in daring to try to defeat a great man on a class issue.

The CIO did better in Michigan where it became powerful *inside* the Democratic party, accepting the fact that 'while it had sufficient money votes and money to dominate the coalition, it did not have sufficient resources to win a general election'.[3] Not only did the CIO accept this fact, it did not stress its own role inside the Democratic party and thus did not alienate the regular Democratic voters who were afraid (as they had been in Ohio) of labour 'taking over'. And, unlike Ohio, the CIO were rewarded, in 1950 and in 1952, by electing the Governor, E. Mennen Williams, and they were not weakened in the campaign by the fact that the Democratic candidate, although supported by Walter Reuther, head of the Automobile Workers and soon to be head of the CIO, was a member of a very rich soap family and not, by social origin, a dangerous Red.

The two great labour federations have formally, at any rate, a different attitude to politics. The American Federation of Labour almost always claims to be non-partisan, to restrict its intervention in politics to 'rewarding its friends and punishing its enemies'. But taking the Taft-Hartley Act as a threat to the existence of trade unions, it founded 'Labor's League for Political Education' and

[1] Fay Calkins, *The CIO and the Democratic Party* (1952), p. 16.
[2] Mr. Ferguson was later described as 'the only zombie in politics'. This was an exaggeration.
[3] Ibid., p. 128.

educated the voters on the simple issue that all who voted for Taft-Hartley were to be opposed. It claimed great success for its punitive measures; it may have been decisive in a few cases but later experience suggests doubts. A politician would rather have AFL support than not, but he may decide that he needs other support more, even in areas where the AFL is numerically strong.

The CIO has been fairly openly in politics since its foundation. It owes a great deal of its growth not only to favourable legislation like the Wagner Act, but to favourable administration of that law and, possibly, to very tepid administration of the Taft-Hartley Act by the Truman administration. The infant CIO had already created 'Labor's Non-Partisan League', but a CIO historian attributed the troubles of that organization to 'circumstance and the ego of a single individual [John L. Lewis]'.[1] The fourth election of FDR, the defeat of some prominent labour-baiters (which the Political Action Committee, the PAC, chalked up to its own score on insufficient evidence), probably deceived many CIO leaders as to the amount of political strength they could 'deliver'. Yet not only did they suffer humiliating defeat in Ohio in 1950, but General Eisenhower was able to ignore the hostility of official labour and yet win, although, both AFL and CIO hostility may have defeated and, probably in some cases did defeat, Republican candidates for House and Senate.[2] Labour, that is to say, is a very powerful pressure group, but it is a pressure group like any other. It is not 'the people' as British labour, with some justification, assumes that it is.

It is, indeed, American business that assumes that it represents the people. Their true will, in the Hegelian sense, is represented by the custodians of the 'free enterprise system' even if the mass of the

[1] Joseph Gaer, *The First Round: the Story of the CIO Political Action Committee* (1944), p. 53.

[2] I formed the impression, both in 1948 and in 1952, that 'labour' in the United States shows a good deal less political zeal than 'labour' does in Britain, that even union officers are content to leave the hard work to young non-labour zealots—or to the old politicians. The 'door-bell ringing' campaigns that I have seen were not, by the standards of British canvassing, well run or, if they were, they did not owe this to labour. I also noticed that most American small houses don't have door-bells to ring.

voters don't know it. It is true that for the great part of modern American history, from the end of the Civil War to 1932, the American businessman not only regarded himself, but was regarded by the mass of the Americans, as *the* representative man whose judgement was to be respected and whose leadership, normally, was to be accepted.[1] The leadership of both parties, especially in the Senate, was the most effective of lobbies for business and if the Republican party was normally *the* party of business, the Democratic party was only, intermittently and unwillingly, the party of anti-business. The increasing correlation between class lines and party lines has wedded business even more securely to the Republicans and brought about a separation, if not quite a divorce, between business and the Democratic party in most sections of the nation.

It is only since 1932, or more accurately, since the great depression that produced the political revolution of 1932, that 'Business' has been on the defensive. And it has been more on the defensive than it need have been and it has often cried out before it was hurt and kept on crying out, after it was obvious that it had not been hurt. The New Deal was no violent revolution and business suffered little. Had the political leadership of business been more adroit, had there been less reliance on the law, even the hurts to the *amour propre* of the business world might have been lessened.[2]

But business had to be in politics, under the New Deal, as it had to be in politics under the old deal. For some politicians wanted business in politics since it raised their price. But it would be absurd to assert that business only went into politics to 'protect itself'. The Southern Pacific in California,[3] the Boston and Maine

[1] The great English journalist, G. W. Stevens, covering the presidential campaign of 1896 for the infant *Daily Mail*, was astonished by the deference, even the reverence with which 'business' and 'businessmen' were regarded. Even as long ago as 1896, he had not 'found such faith in Israel', i.e. in England.

[2] In the early days of the New Deal, I asked an important Washington journalist, no dangerous radical, why business was so sulky. He replied that business resented having to come to Washington to ask for favours, even though it knew it would get them. It wanted the government to send emissaries to Wall Street and La Salle Street to offer the favours.

[3] The old railroad lobby in California has long been dead in its classical form (although no Californian administration would completely ignore

in New Hampshire did more than 'protect themselves'. But they had to protect themselves all the same. One simple device of the financially ambitious politician was the 'strike bill'. This was a bill, plausibly designed to appeal to the masses and threatening the financial interests of the corporations; mainly railroads, in the earlier epochs; public utilities, especially power companies, later on. The sponsor of the bill conveyed to the threatened interests that the bill could be quietly killed or emasculated for a consideration. It was a fairly easy method of making a living in politics. 'The misdeeds of the utilities make them suspect and fair game for those who would take advantage of the latent public prejudice against them.'[1] These tactics are far more common at state capitals than at Washington, and the chief national importance of these lobbies, and these open-minded politicians, is that in the course of controlling state politics or protecting great interests against legislative rapacity, the 'interests' acquire political power that can be used in Washington. Thus the late John Henry Roraback was not merely Republican boss of Connecticut and representative of the power interests in that state, but a very important national figure in the Republican organization and it was as a defender of the interests of the Commonwealth and Southern against the Tennessee Valley Authority, that the late Wendell Willkie first became a public figure.

But in addition to protecting itself or getting favours from the states or the federal government, 'business' has general needs, or thinks it has. It wants federal legislation, federal administration to weaken the labour unions. It wants taxation to encourage capital investment which means it is against high corporation taxes and in

---

the views of the Southern Pacific, any more than a Pennsylvania administration would ignore the views of the 'Pennsy', the Pennsylvania Railroad). But there is, or was, a lobby in California headed by a highly independent lobbyist, Arthur H. ('Artie') Samish, whose main power came from his control of the liquor businesses of the State. He has recently been convicted of income tax frauds. The name of his successor is not yet known.

[1] V. O. Key, Jr., *Southern Politics* (1949), p. 475. Professor Key suggests that for an honest public servant, it is often better to deal with the heads of the power companies than with their lawyers. The heads of the companies are, sometimes, ready to see that the public has a real case, while their legal talent is concerned to protect the company at nearly any cost.

favour of something very like a federal sales tax, as like it as is possible to be without being politically impossible to push through. It is, as a whole, in favour of low government expenditure, but, in many concrete instances, it wants the government to spend money where it will do some powerful segment of business good. And, of course, business, once it gets away from generalities, is often as divided as any other pressure group. Thus, although, in general, 'business' may be in favour of the diminution of direct taxes, the substitutes may be not only politically harmful, but affect or be thought to affect, important segments of business adversely.[1]

Just as there is a cleavage between the big farmers and the small farmers, there is a cleavage between big business and small business. Thus the Eisenhower administration found that it was one thing to promise an end to easy money, during the campaign, but quite another thing to refuse it to numerous small businessmen when in office, businessmen whose first reaction was to go to their Congressman. So the rigid purism of the administration's financial policy had quickly to be abandoned, no doubt for general economic reasons, but those reasons were seen more clearly when they took a political form.

Nevertheless, there are general business interests and there are in consequence organized business pressure groups. Sometimes these confine their efforts to concrete problems where they may pick up allies not normally bedfellows of 'business'. The operators of coal mines have the same interest as have the miners in opposing the St. Lawrence Seaway which, they both fear, will cut down the demand for coal. So have the operators and employees of coal-carrying railways. They can all work together. The employers and

---

[1] Thus the retail storekeepers of New Jersey were the main power behind the campaign to repeal the sales tax in New Jersey. They were so successful that they shook even Mayor Hague's control of the Democratic party in the state. This campaign did not, as was supposed, cost a great deal of money. It was a popular issue and 'a great amount of noise can be produced by a very little money'. David Dayton McKean, *Pressures on the Legislature of New Jersey* (1938), p. 185. It is worth noting, however, that it was by their success in intimidating candidates in the *primaries*, that the enemies of the sales tax won. Under the old convention system, Governor Hoffman and Mayor Hague might have been able to hold their legislators in line.

employees in the New England textile industry have the same interest in getting the federal minimum wage raised to lessen the 'differential' that favours their Southern competitors.

But business is business. Its two chief representative general lobbies are the National Association of Manufacturers and the United States Chamber of Commerce. Each has its own characteristics. The NAM is, in a sense, like the AFL. It is old, conservative, given to interpreting its own interests narrowly and the nation's interests in terms of its own. The Chamber of Commerce is a more modern-minded body. It knows more of the world in which the United States, and even American business has to live. It understands better than does the NAM, that Hanna and Aldrich are dead and it is less afraid of the new forces in American life which it may have to fight but can no longer hope to suppress. And Congress listens with respect to both bodies, as it listens to the rulers of the gigantic corporations like General Motors and General Electric which do not need the national organizations at all. Their views would not be disregarded if there was not a lobbyist or a pressure group in all of Washington.

A pressure group for which every Senator and Representative is the automatic lobbyist, is what used to be called 'the pork barrel'. The pork barrel is or was the trade name for expenditure on 'improvements' paid for by federal money spent locally. A failure to agree how much money should be so spent, and where, was one of the causes of the break-up of the Democratic party and of the Civil War. No politicians, North and South, have ever again taken such risks. In the olds days, the pork barrel was a simple bit of mutual backscratching. There *were* desirable and necessary improvements; but they were not evenly scattered over the land. So in order to get some desirable and, nationally-speaking, useful improvement, in Pelissippia, it was necessary to support some preposterous improvement in Winnemac. The next stage came when one useless improvement was bargained for against another, when navigation works on an empty river were made possible by harbour works in an empty port. Presidents and economists protested in vain. Reformers proposed that the President be allowed to veto items in appropriation bills, so as to permit him to exercise some discrimination in the national interest, but in vain. The pork fattened too many voters to be condemned in any fit of rigorism. Some politicians' whole career was a single-minded search for edible pork for district or state. Post offices were built, lavishly, with money that might have improved the service. Customs houses collected more votes than revenues. And 'rivers and harbours' were improved, generation after generation.

With the coming of the New Deal, the pork barrel became nearly obsolete. For necessary social expenditures were undertaken on a scale that would have startled the old pork barrel philosophers. Of course, many of the New Deal expenditures had no or little political aspect (except as far as they made the administration nationally popular and that reflected credit and popularity on Democratic Senators and Representatives). Some great New Deal enterprises were ostentatiously un-political, like the TVA.[1] The vast expenditures of the war provided opportunities for congressional pressure to ensure that war plants were put in districts that needed them. And since the end of the war, the location of industry, affected by the policy of such lending bodies as the Reconstruction Finance Corporation, has not been immune to general political considerations. Thus a steel mill has been located in New England that, it is fairly safe to guess, would not have been put there but for political pressure.[2] And a Senator who found that to save a miserable $12,000,000, an important improvement in his state had been postponed, proposed to take the money out of the foreign aid programme, none of whose beneficiaries voted in South Dakota.

The pork barrel has had another result; it has brought a section of the Army into politics and has kept and is keeping it there. One

[1] A Democratic Congressman remarked to me that the triumvirs of the TVA carried their non-political attitude to extremes, as when they put the headquarters of the TVA in the incorrigibly Republican city of Knoxville, instead of in the more central, more convenient—and Democratic—city of Chattanooga.

[2] The old type of pressure is not obsolete. Thus the current programme of naval construction distributes the orders between Virginia, Massachusetts and New Jersey. All three states have shipyards, but all three states also have Senators whom it is politically desirable to conciliate—and support. But it would only be true 'pork' if it had proved necessary to build the yards to build the ships.

consequence of the absence of a regular, respected and competent bureaucracy was to give to the administration of the armed forces, in democratic America, a peculiarly militaristic character. For the posts in the War Department and in the Navy Department that, in other countries, were held by civilian officials of high rank, were held in Washington by serving officers doing a turn in the departments, forced by their jobs to be politicians. The fact that no officer could be promoted even to the rank of colonel in the army or of captain in the navy without senatorial confirmation, made serving officers timid and, at the same time, politically minded. And what was a minor matter when the armed forces were small, was another matter when they became huge. For over a century, the officers, trained for the most part in the two great academies, were the nearest approach to a professional civil service that the United States knew and yet, for the reasons given, even they were entangled in politics to a degree that would have been thought extraordinary in Britain.[1] Perhaps the oddest and oldest of these military lobbies is that of the Army Corps of Engineers. For this semi-military body has successfully defeated all attempts to combine its functions with those of civilian agencies doing the same work. Its age, prestige, its ability to make friends and influence people have left to this small *corps d'elite* great civilian tasks. Partly this is due to tradition. The Army Engineers were for long the only adequately trained engineers in the United States. It was natural to leave to them such tasks as taming the Mississippi and the designing of harbour works as well as fortifications and long after, when civilian engineers had failed, to trust to a soldier the greatest of such tasks that the federal government had up to then undertaken, the building of the Panama Canal.[2]

[1] When he was Assistant-Secretary of the Navy, Franklin D. Roosevelt pointed out to a congressional committee, that a Secretary of the Navy had no civilian aids of any rank in the permanent organization of the Department and he contrasted with the British system of high-paid civilian officials the American system where 'the United States Navy Department, could offer its top career civilians only three thousand dollars a year; the next highest six or eight positions paid twenty-four hundred. As a result the Navy lost nine out of ten of its efficient civilian workers'. Frank Friedel, *Franklin D. Roosevelt* (1954), vol. II, p. 32.

[2] The Military Academy at West Point was, in part, an imitation of

Since then, the Department of the Interior, the Department of Agriculture as well as independent agencies like the Tennessee Valley Authority have all entered the field, but the Army Engineers have not left it. The Corps deals directly with Congress and its policies are not by any means necessarily in accord with those of its political superiors, not even with those of the Commander-in-Chief, the President of the United States.[1] Then the very imperfect control of Congress by the President, and by the executive departments imposes, or is thought to impose, on serving officers duties that, were they carried out by civilians, might be described as those of lobbyists. All the defence departments have kept in close touch with the relevant committees of Congress and with Congress and the voters. The officers of the Navy, we are told, 'have accepted the responsibility for seeing to it that the United States authorized and built the kind of navy that naval men believe it should have. Naval officers have, therefore, not found it incompatible with their functions as professional public servants, to take the issue directly to the people and to employ a highly developed technique of "educational" systems of the press and the numerous and influential civilian and patriotic elements of the nation.'[2] But these, in turn, are used not only to encourage Congress to be more generous to the Navy but generous too to all the competing departments in their struggle for a bigger slice of whatever cake Congress provides. For the unification of the defence departments under one Secretary has not abolished, although it may have diminished, the inter-service

<hr>

Rome. He began, in Paris and like it had civilian as well as military aspects. He lived, he spent a good deal of his military service trying to control the Mississippi.

as a member of Frank Smith of Mississippi, by supporting the St. Lawrence Waterway, antagonized the railroads and utility companies, but gained the co-operation of the Corps of Engineers, which favoured the project. Weighing the balance, the Corps of Engineers, which supervised flood-control projects, was the more valuable ally'. Stephen K. Bailey and Howard D. Samuel, *Congress at Work* (1952 English edition), p. 129.

[2] Professor George T. Davis quoted in Lawrence H. Chamberlain, *The President, Congress and Legislation* (1946), p. 243. The Navy Department acted, that is to say like the German Admiralty-inspired Navy League in the period between 1898 and 1914.

and the Navy, the Air Force, the Army have each their own
ters and lobbyists.[1]

of the most powerful lobbies, some think the most powerful
lobby, is that of the Veterans,[2] that is ex-soldiers, sailors, marines.
From the beginning of the United States, veterans were a political
force, wanting land grants, pensions, preferences of various kinds,
but only after the Civil War did they become a great political force,
organized in the 'Grand Army of the Republic'. Their claims for
disability pensions, then for pensions regardless of disability, made
them a very important pressure group and, on the whole, a valuable
ally to the Republican party which was thought, rightly, to be
more sympathetic to the claims of the GAR than were the Democrats, who had so many ex-Confederate soldiers in their ranks who
could only claim meagre state pensions and were not anxious to see
federal bounty lavishly poured out on their former foes. Other
wars, with Indians, with Spaniards and Filipinos, produced other
veteran groups, but it was the first world war, with its millions of
conscripts, that produced the rival to the GAR, a rival and successor
that has bettered the GAR's instruction.

Founded in Paris, in 1919, the preamble of the constitution
of the American Legion, advocated a series of worthy causes
from support for 'God and Country' to consecrating and sancti-
fying 'our comradeship by our devotion to mutual helpfulness'.[3]
Apart from the ambiguous allusion in the last clause, the
founders of the Legion made no reference to what, at once, became
and has ever since been its main business, getting tangible favours
for veterans. True, the other objects of the Legion have not been
forgotten. It has been a vigilant enemy of all kinds of seditious
doctrine and it has taken a very broad view of what constitutes

[1] The Marine Corps has its own lobbyists and usually can count on the
support of its patron and parent, the Navy, in its war with the Army
and Air Force. President Truman showed his characteristic courage, or
rashness, when he expressed an opinion that the welfare of the United
States and of the Marine Corps were not quite identical.

[2] The term 'veteran' was used, in its old meaning, in the Civil War. It
was applied to a soldier who, after serving three years, re-enlisted. It
now applies merely to having served.

[3] Text in David Dayton McKean, *Party and Pressure Politics* (1949),
p. 511.

sedition. It has inspected—and condemned—history text-books that were not sufficiently patriotic and it has, at times, lent a hand when physical force was needed to stamp out incipient treason, or what the Legion thought was treason. This was as it should have been, for one motive of the founders of the Legion was to wean the soldiers, about to be demobilized, away from radicalism. The men who made the Legion had the same fears as the new Communist party in America had hopes. But the judgement of the Legion founders was proved better than that of the Communists. There were to be no Workers' and Soldiers' Councils in America. There were to be, instead, the Legion club rooms, with pool tables, in some cases, where the law permitted, bars, in others where the law did not permit, other facilities of the same kind. These club houses grew until the Legion property was estimated at $200,000,000 and each clubhouse and Legion post was 'a kind of continuous caucus, and men who do not belong to it stand at a great disadvantage in local politics'.[1] It is not, however, partisan as the GAR was. It served and serves the ambitions of Democratic as well as of Republican politicians. And its main task is to get as much as possible for the Legion and the Legion's members and even for veterans who are not members of the Legion. In that it has been phenomenally successful. It has got national and state bonuses; it has got pensions for veterans and for their dependents.[2]

But the endeavours of the Legion have not been confined to getting cash. They have got other benefits for their members. Thus, in the federal civil service and in the civil service of most states, 'veteran's preference' plays a great part. A veteran taking a civil service examination is, if he passes at all, upgraded so as to outrank civilians with much better marks. In the same way, a veteran has far more security in his job than a civilian. Indeed, the existence of veteran's preference is as much of an obstacle to the return of the old, simple spoils system, as national devotion to the principles of civil service. It also produces a neglected rider to the theoretical

[1] Ibid., p. 520.

[2] Success in this last endeavour has made elderly veterans a good buy for young women in the marriage market. They usually survive their husbands and draw pensions as widows. There was one widow of the Revolutionary War alive in 1906 (it ended in 1783): and several widows of the Mexican War alive in 1930 (it ended in 1847).

equality of the sexes in America. For there was no conscription of women in America in the last war and veteran's preference, in effect, reserves a great many jobs for men only.[1]

Then the veteran is free of the Veterans hospitals and in a country where horror of 'socialized medicine' is part of the official credo, many millions of adults have rights to lavish medical care, as veterans, that they and women and children could not hope to have as mere citizens.[2]

The Legion is both a pressure group and a lobby. As a pressure group, it canalizes and directs the political weight of the veterans (now over fifteen millions strong). Such a group, with its emotional unity and power of appeal, and its easily identifiable interests would, in any case, be extremely powerful. Politicians probably do not need much pressure to be induced to look after the veterans and to oppose them has long been recognized as an extreme of rashness. A President, like Roosevelt at the height of his popularity in 1936, could oppose the granting of the 'bonus', but it was passed over his veto, the veterans got the money and Roosevelt did not suffer. On the other hand, Representatives and Senators who did oppose the bonus or other measures favouring the veterans, as a rule paid for it dearly. And the expulsion of the 'Bonus army' from Washington by the army in the summer of 1932 was chalked up against President Hoover.[3]

[1] Of course the pensions and bonuses go, for the most part, to men only. But not only are there widows and other female dependents to get pensions, most male beneficiaries have wives, mothers, daughters. But the woman who is excluded from a job to which she has acquired, she thinks, a right, is not usually consoled by the thought that the salary paid her veteran supplanter is probably going to some other woman.

[2] The location of Veterans hospitals is a political question of some importance, for Congressmen want these in the most healthy, politically speaking, places; officers of the Legion want them where they will do the Legion or the officers most good; and the Veterans Administration would like to put them where they would do the patients most good. Sometimes it is possible to meet these three conditions.

[3] Mr. Hoover thinks that the Bonus Army was a Communist-inspired organization and that the expulsion of the 'veterans' was necessary, but was exploited as part of a general conspiracy. This may be so, but the expulsion would have lent itself less to radical exploitation if it had been

But the Legion is also a lobby, a less inevitable feature of the American scene and, as a lobby, its interests are not necessarily the same as those of the majority of veterans who are not, after all, members, nor, indeed, possibly of the millions of veterans who are members. Thus as a lobby, the Legion can and does further the political ambitions of high officials of the Legion, although these may have no particular connection with the interests of the veterans. Like other lobbies and lobbyists, the Legions has no great interest in simplifying procedure, for it gains a great deal of credit in successfully prosecuting claims, some of which, so critics assert, could be as easily prosecuted by the individuals concerned without any elaborate organization. Indeed, some go so far as to assert that the Veterans Administration could serve the needs of the Veterans better, without any help from the Legion. But the Legion, with its now great property assets, its ramified political connections and its reputation for patriotism is too powerful to be ignored and too dangerous to be thwarted. And it has views, as well as claims. It is still defending America from the radicals, still a vigilant censor of dangerous thoughts.[1] It has its rivals. There are the Veterans of Foreign Wars for example; there is the American Veterans Committee. But the first is too limited in its field of recruiting and the second (which has the novel slogan: 'Citizens First, Veterans Second') makes no financial claims and has a very small membership.[2] The Legion has nothing to fear from these rivals and, as long as it remains as powerful as it is at present, it will succeed in transferring an increasing share of the tax revenue of the country to the pockets of veterans, nearly all of whom, it is again repeated, are males.

Again, it is because Congress spends so much of its time in distributing special favours, that it is regarded with something less

---

carried out in a less flamboyant manner, in fact if it had not been carried out by General Douglas MacArthur.

[1] Censorious types point out that the resolutions passed by the annual Legion conventions are passed on the fourth day when most Legionnaires are dealing with their hangovers and have no time or energy to devote to national and world problems.

[2] Its current President (1954) is Mr. Bill Mauldin, the famous war cartoonist.

than awe, even by the beneficiaries of its bounty. *E pur si muove*; simple steals if not simple handouts are less common; a decent respect for the opinion of mankind is more common. Indeed the great offender in demonstrating an indifference to that opinion, has been the executive department. Despite legislation, an increasingly critical public opinion and a genuine improvement in political morals, a series of recent scandals have shown that the old Adam is not dead and that the appetite for 'a quick buck' and a readiness to 'cut ethical corners rather fine' are still to be found, with very little search, in Washington—and elsewhere.

The late war, of course, made it certain that the government would make many bad hasty bargains (it also ensured that many businessmen would make many bad hasty bargains). Ordinary accounting controls were impossible and all kinds of irregularities, ranging from mere slips in judgement to covert deals to the common profit of the official and the contractor and to the loss of the public occurred, as they were bound to occur. *Born Yesterday* was only a slightly embroidered version of the truth. But equally open to exploitation was the almost equally great job of getting rid of the vast stocks that became surplus with the ending of the war. If all the usual precautions were taken, the stocks would be unsaleable by the time the sales were 'processed'. The law, hastily drafted in the summer of 1944, asked for 'interpretation', for it was a mastérpiece of ambiguity. 'It called on the administrators of surplus disposal to sell the property in the fastest possible time. But it directed them to go slowly and give priorities in the disposal to federal agencies, state and local agencies, educational institutions, veterans, farmers and established merchandizers in that order. . . . It soon became apparent that Congress had created a program with so many purposes that it really had no purpose at all. . . . Congress amended the law three times and investigated the program seven times without improving it.'[1] It was a golden opportunity for the enterprising and it was taken. Money was made simply by studying, carefully, the lists of surplus stores. That was the reward of vigilance. Money was made by knowing what was to be disposed of and when; this information often came from the 'inside'. Money was made by floating companies, on very little capital, to buy government

[1] Blair Bolles, *How to Get Rich in Washington* (1952), pp. 80–1.

surplus which, sometimes, (especially after the outbreak of the Korean war) could be sold back to the government at very handsome profits. The commissions paid to agents for selling government property were often far greater than the value of what they sold or, to put it more accurately, of what the government was paid. Few commodities were not disposed of in this fashion from minor gadgets to ships.[1] There were splendid chances to make a killing, especially if you had the right political connections. They were taken. It was especially insisted on, by the censorious, that men claiming to be 'friends of Mr. Truman' did very well in this way. True, it no more followed that they were friends of Mr. Truman than the assertion that one was a 'friend of Mr. Sweeney', used as a pass word to get into a speakeasy in prohibition days, proved that you *were* a friend of Mr. Sweeney. But when it was shown that some of those who claimed to be friends of Mr. Truman and who had exploited that connection were, at least, acquaintances, grave damage was done to the administration. Especially grave damage was done when it was shown that political pressure got special favours from the Reconstruction Finance Corporation which lent money to very bad risks and, still more, when it was discovered that the Bureau of Internal Revenue was willing to adjust tax claims for important contributions to Democratic party funds. Public toleration snapped. There were palliations. Many of the inculpated employees were not so concerned to collect funds for the party that put them in office, as for themselves. Many of the agents were impostors who preyed on the credulity of businessmen and others, feeding them with confidential information picked up in no more secret spots than the coffee bars of the Pentagon. Some of the peccant officials were standard specimens of spoils system appointees whose record, once revealed, suggested that even if they had been honest, they would still have been totally incompetent. But 'the buck stops here' and the Truman administration had to take the buck, not pass it.[2]

[1] A case involving important politicians, diplomats, businessmen and ships is before the courts at the moment (1954).

[2] Democrats (and others) noted, with amusement, that scandals did not stop the moment the Republicans came into power. The standard charge under the Truman administration, so the legend went, was five

Public irritation was deeper than most politicians believed and there was in that indignation, a smugness that some politicians, themselves above suspicion and vigilant in guarding political morals, found a little irritating. 'The indignation which is shown when these practices begin to creep into government proves that on the whole we expect higher standards in the public service than in private business. We should. But some of the moral indignation and ethical energy which businessmen are developing over the delinquencies of government officials might also be properly applied to raising the moral level of their own operations.'[1]

Congress, although its members were not and are not all above doing a favour for a friend, was less blamed and less to blame for this mess, than was the executive. But Congress was to blame too, for often the laws through whose loopholes so many ingenious gentlemen wriggled out with their plunder were the result of bad drafting, and some of the scandals come from laws so tight that they cannot be administered competently and perhaps can only be administered at all by 'adjustments' for which it is tempting to charge.[2]

But the voters, conscious of how vast is government and not endowed with much simple faith, do expect Congress to keep an eye on the more flagrant forms of theft and are willing to overlook extravagances in language and abuses in methods if assured that their hired men are not asleep on the job. And the best way to show that they are not, as any dog knows, is to make a loud noise. Some of the gestures made by Congress in an attempt to restore its position in the constitutional system are of the character of loud noises. Of such was the ill-fated Bricker amendment to weaken the President's (and the Senate's) control over foreign policy. So, in all probability, was the successful amending of the Constitution to

per cent. 'The five percenters' were a known occupational group. But in one of the first Republican scandals, the agent was ready to take four per cent, thus showing that the Republicans meant what they said when they promised to cut down government expenditure.

[1] Paul H. Douglas, op. cit., pp. 25–6.

[2] 'The executive branch, for its part, complains that Congress frequently usurps *its* functions, in some cases writing laws that leave too little play for administrative judgment . . . or in other instances, through noisy public investigations or quiet pressure applied directly, seeking to control what are essentially administrative decisions.' *Fortune*, February 1952, p. 224.

make of the old tradition that a President should serve for only two terms, not mere tradition *that* (as the event showed) could be defied, but a part of the 'supreme law of the land'. To the member of Congress, anxious about the decline in congressional power and prestige, the success with which Franklin D. Roosevelt defied one of the oldest and most sacred taboos in American constitutional practice, the limitation of a President to two terms in office, was ominous. A tradition dating back to Jefferson and, in popular belief, back to Washington, defied in vain by Theodore Roosevelt,[1] was set at naught by the second Roosevelt. With the resurgence of Republican strength in 1938, a good many Democrats, conscious that the party was less strong than its President, began to dream wistfully of getting 'the Champ' to run again, the more that, under the shadow of that oak, no very sturdy presidential saplings had managed to grow. And the third term traditions began to be described, like so many other old habits, as part of a dead and gone, 'horse and buggy age'.

Yet it is improbable that the tradition could have been so easily overthrown but for the great and increasing emergency of the war. Hitler's triumphs were one of the most powerful forces making for the acceptance of the breach of the tradition and one of the forces making for the attempt to break it. It turned out that hammering on the sacredness of tradition and attempts to scare the voters by threats of an American dictatorship were of little moment compared with what was seen, by millions, as a threat from a German dictatorship. And those Americans who were both frightened of Roosevelt and of Hitler were more frightened of Hitler. Those who were not frightened of Hitler were nearly all against Roosevelt anyway. 'How many, many times did one hear the remark, "Well, I'm really opposed to the idea of a third term for any man but with such a madman loose in Europe, it becomes necessary to keep a trained and experienced man at the helm". Naturally the third term argument cost the President some votes, as it would any man. But, despite all the publicity and hullabaloo given to the issue by the Republicans, not

[1] It was the contention of the partisans of the first Roosevelt that the tradition only barred two *elective* terms, that serving-out the remainder of a President's term did not count.

as many people voted against Franklin Roosevelt on grounds of the third term as might have been expected under the circumstances.'[1] When 1944 came round, there was far less of discussion, far less opposition to a fourth term than there had been to a third. As a senatorial wit is supposed to have put it. 'There's a law against bigamy; there's no law against trigamy.' But the resentment and the fears of 1940 were not dead and Congress proposed and the states accepted an amendment giving to the violated two-term tradition, the force of constitutional law.[2] No doubt, in part, this amendment was a belated revenge on the dead Roosevelt, but no doubt, also, it represented a possibly prudent feeling that, since presidential power was likely to grow, the best and only effective remedy was to secure that it would not be exercised by one man for more than eight years.

Something of the same fear of the encroaching power of the presidency probably lay behind the new law on the presidential succession adopted in 1947. By the law of 1886, after the succession of the Vice-President in the event of a presidential vacancy, provided for in the Constitution and not to be dealt with by mere statute, the succession ran through the cabinet officers in the order of the seniority of their departments, i.e. beginning with the Secretary of State. By the act of 1947, after the Vice-President now come the Speaker of the House of Representatives and the President *pro tempore* of the Senate.[3] This alteration had little to commend it. It was defended and justified by its sponsors (including President Truman) on the ground that it was more democratic, that the Speaker and the presiding officer of the Senate were elected and the Secretary of State and the other cabinet officers merely appointed.

[1] Charles W. Stein, *The Third Term Tradition* (1943), p. 338. Dr. Stein believed that if the Republicans had fought the Roosevelt foreign policy more, and the third-term threat less, they would have done better. His full title was premature. *The Third Term Tradition. Its Rise and Collapse in American Politics.* There was life in the tradition or, at any rate, possibilities of a resurrection as the event showed.

[2] Mr. Truman was specifically exempted. He could have run in 1952 had he chosen.

[3] The Senate elects a President *pro tempore* to take the place of the Vice-President who is President of the Senate *ex officio*. When the Vice-President has succeeded to the presidency, the President *pro tempore* is the normal presiding officer of the Senate.

But neither the Speaker nor the President *pro tempore* are elected to these offices by the American people. They are elected inside the elaborate seniority system of Congress by their colleagues of their own party. That party might not be the party of the deceased President or Vice-President, while the Secretary of State would, at any rate, be the nominee of the leader of the party that had won the presidency. So far there has been no case of a Secretary of State or a Speaker succeeding, but the possibility that a Speaker *might* succeed is a superfluous complication of an already sufficiently complicated process. It can, at best, be justified as a sop to the *amour-propre* of the professional politicians. In no plausible sense of the term is it any more 'democratic' than the system it replaced.

But the presidential succession is not a burning question, nor has it been so far a serious problem. What has often been a serious problem is the possibility that has often become a reality, that the midterm elections will transfer the legislative control from the party that had won the last presidential election to the victors in the midterm elections, thus intensifying the struggle for supremacy between the executive and the legislative branches. It is true that party control in Congress is an ambiguous term, implying, very often, a good deal less than complete harmony between the party leaders in Congress and the national leader of the party, the President. But it is not entirely devoid of meaning and, except in the rarest circumstances, the congressional leaders, with a presidential election approaching, will at any rate make some formal sacrifices for electoral appearances' sake. But the electoral interests of the other party are directly opposed to such harmony; even if there is no real ground of division, one must be found and emphasized. This may mean and has meant that at important crises in American history, there has been an artificially stressed conflict between the Capitol and the White House. Whatever chances Mr. Hoover's programme had of success in the last two years of his term, were lessened by the loss of effective control of Congress to the Democrats.[1] In 1946, the Democrats lost control of both houses.

[1] Mr. Hoover's difficulties were magnified by the fact that, although the Democrats narrowly got control of the House of Representatives, the Republicans kept a very nominal control of the Senate, thus further confusing the issue of responsibility. See p. 322.

Senator Fulbright of Arkansas, feeling that, above all, the United States needed unity in face of the dangerous international situation, proposed that Mr. Truman resign and turn the presidency over to the Republicans. This well-meant suggestion was not adopted[1] and rightly so. For midterm elections are not general elections, but an aggregate of local contests and, more serious, there is no 'leader' of the opposition whom the retiring President could 'send for' to use the English phrase.[2]

The only way to deal with this very real problem is to undertake a much more fundamental reform, to extend the term of the House to four years. There are other good reasons why this should be done. The term of two years is far too short for a new Representative to learn his business. Further he, like nearly all his brethren, has to consider, almost from the moment of election, his chances of re-election, for if the primary campaign be considered, he has barely a year in which to settle down before he has to fight for the nomination and then for election. The two-year term also, increases the bad effects of the seniority rule, giving more peace of mind, leisure—and power—to members for safe seats. The risk of cleavage between the President and Congress would be diminished by a four-year term. A President would not have to pull his punches in his first two years. He could plan for at least three, and not be forced to submit his legislative and administrative achievements for premature assessment. And, lastly, the restriction of elections for the House of Representatives to presidential years, would make of the House a more national and nationally responsible body. It would diminish the temptation that assails both President and Congress to pass the buck and, as the comparatively low poll at midterm elections suggests, it would not deprive the American voter of any privilege that he appears to treasure deeply.

[1] It is understood that this suggestion was ill-received by Mr. Truman who may have thought that Senator Fulbright had been corrupted by the political teaching he received at Pembroke College, Oxford.

[2] Woodrow Wilson, in 1916, had decided, if the Republicans won, to ask his Vice-President to resign, to appoint the President-elect, Secretary of State, then to resign himself, so that there should not be an interregnum of four months at such a critical period of American history. But in the successful presidential candidate, there was an obvious successor such as is not present at mere midterm elections.

There is one weighty objection to this change (apart from the fact that it would need a constitutional amendment). The Senate would be difficult to fit into the reformed system. For it is probably inadvisable to extend the Senate term to eight years and, unless that is done, it is difficult to provide for the partial election of the Senate. And it is undesirable to elect the Senate *en bloc*, for some of the value of that august body comes from its continuing character, from the fact that it is, in part, immune at any given moment from proximate electoral cares.

But is there any real objection to continuing to elect a third of the Senate every two years, even though the House is elected for four years? By such a system, a sample of public opinion would be taken every two years which would not decisively upset the balance of power, since the House would remain unchanged. A Senate differing from the House and the President in party colouring would be a nuisance but not, as is the case with a Congress differing from the President, possibly a national danger.[1]

The classical remedy which appeals to critics of the American system, especially to academic critics, is to attempt to graft onto the constitutional system, some of the characteristics of the English parliamentary system. That the essentials of the British system are compatible with a Federal government exercising authority over a vast area under a written constitution, the experience of Canada and Australia shows.[2]

But there are important variations from English practice both in Canada and Australia and, what is much more important, Canada

---

[1] There is even a case for electing one half of the Senate every three years, in odd-numbered years, thus separating the election of this already anomalous body from the national general elections. But this change is so unlikely to be adopted, that it would be profitless to discuss it.

[2] 'While a Canadian Cabinet differs from the British in the presence of this federalism, it is on the other hand strikingly like the British in the thorough manner in which it accepts the pre-eminence of the prime minister along with the rules of secrecy, unity and collective responsibility.' Alexander Brady, *Democracy in the Dominions* (1947), p. 77. 'Although the Australians embodied little in statutes, about the everyday methods of cabinet rule, they assimilated the solid fabric of British conventions concerning responsible or cabinet government, which ensures what Walter Bagehot described as "a close union and nearly complete fusion of the executive and legislative powers".' Ibid., p. 168.

and Australia deliberately adopted English parliamentary government when its characteristics had been demonstrated in practice (as
they had not been in 1787) and, at the same time, when the characteristics of the system adopted in 1787 had been observed and
rejected.[1]

The form that the adoption of English methods, it is suggested,
should and could take, is an adaptation of the cabinet system to the
congressional system. One suggestion is simple, but not really
important. The President, it is suggested, could make of the leaders
of each house, a kind of legislative council. He would consult with
them, and they and the President could put forward a joint programme. But a wise President does just that and yet does not always
find it easy to agree on a joint programme even when his party
'controls' Congress. And when he and the congressional leaders do
agree, they do not do so for institutional reasons, but for party
or personal reasons. For the President does not choose and cannot
get rid of the congressional leaders. He can, occasionally, when there
is a vacancy, see that X is made leader instead of Y, as FDR did
when he, successfully but narrowly, secured the election of Alben
Barkley over Pat Harrison as Senate floor leader. But that was an
unusual and difficult exercise of power. And Roosevelt's nominee,
in 1943, by his vehement protest against the President's veto of a
tax bill, forced a White House withdrawal. No 'council' would
have increased or diminished the President's power—or Senator
Barkley's. And the failure of FDR, in 1938, to 'purge' the Democratic Senators who had opposed him and who were up for re-
election, made it certain that no President was likely to possess the
power of sanctions which would make his relations with the
congressional leaders any closer and more co-operative than they
were already.[2]

[1] As Professor Creighton has reminded us, it was an argument constantly repeated by Sir John Macdonald, in his campaign for the creation
of a united Canada, that the British parliamentary system was superior to
the American congressional system. It must be remembered that this argument was especially effective during and immediately after the Civil War.

[2] It is true that FDR was able to 'purge' John O'Connor, the rebellious
chairman of the Rules Committee of the House. But O'Connor was a
New York Congressman and the President (or Mr. Farley) was the
leader of the Democratic party in New York.

The suggestions made to bring about a closer relationship between the executive and Congress based on the English parallel have one weakness and that a fatal one. To be effective, they would involve a far more complete recasting of the American system than the mere admission of cabinet officers to the floor of the House and the Senate. They would involve recasting the committee system of each house. They would involve recasting the party system. They would involve the abolition of the locality rule. They might well provoke far more frequent conflicts between the two houses and not notably diminish the risk of conflict between the President and either or both houses of Congress.

In the twentieth century, congressional committees have been, at times, instruments of party control, but when that has been so, it has been because of leadership from the White House. No Congress would be likely to submit to the rule of a Speaker like 'Czar' Reed again. In any case, if the simple legislative and financial problems of sixty years ago could be dealt with by such leadership, the facts of life in the modern world put leadership in the White House or nowhere. Where Congress has been active, its activity has usually been bipartisan. Where committees have been powerful, it is often because of a coalition of Democratic and Republican members. If the English analogy were to be followed, the cabinet officers would be dealing only with the members of the committees who were of their own party (assuming that the cabinet officers really had a party, as not all have). But the seniority rule, in itself, makes party leadership an ambiguous term and a cabinet officer might well find himself dealing publicly (as he must deal privately) with party leaders who felt no particular sense of loyalty or duty to the administration.

Party leaders, safely ensconced in their own districts or states, could and often would ignore the most effective leadership from the floor, the most convincing and popular appeals to the voters, as they can ignore them, in many cases, when they are made to the Congress or to the country by the President. Cabinet officers, as it is, spend a great deal of time before committees; they would probably spend as much as before and have to spend extra time in one or other house. Cabinet officers, already torn between House and Senate, forced to court both, would be worse off than before, for jealousy

between the houses is an ineluctable fact of American political life.
And so is jealousy of the executive. For Congress knows, in its
bones, that it has an increasingly difficult fight in holding its own
against the encroaching power of the executive. Is it at all likely, for
instance, that because either house had official representatives of
the executive to question and to listen to, it would give up its claim
to hear not merely cabinet officers, but under-secretaries, bureau
chiefs, lobbyists of the various departments and agencies? Leadership in Congress is the sole reward that membership in Congress
offers to its members. If they want other types of reward they must
leave Congress. The same kind of egalitarian sentiment that lies
behind the seniority rule, behind the need for organizing the business of Congress by a powerful committee system, would prevent
the right of appearance on the floor of Congress being more than an
occasion for oratory. Work would have to be done, as at present, in
committees, in private, 'on the Hill', in the White House. For the
system has its own logic, and cannot usefully be tinkered with. It
must be changed root and branch and it will not be so changed
until there is so great a pressure of public opinion for change that
possibly more than the means of representation of the executive
before Congress will be called in question.[1]

And it is always well to remember that many Americans,
intelligent, public-spirited, well-informed do not *want* to see too
close a harmony between the executive and the legislative departments. 'We reap the benefits of hostility. Always the legislative and
executive branches are arrayed against each other. Even when the
majority of Congress or the Legislature is of the same political
faith with the President or Governor, and personal relations are of
the most amicable, instinctively official action will be at least
colored by rivalry or by antagonism in some other form, however

[1] One of the few alterations made by the South when it adopted the
'Constitution of the Confederate States of America' was to provide that
'Congress may by law, grant to the principal officer in each of the
Executive Departments a seat upon the floor of either House, with the
privilege of discussing any matter appertaining to his department'.
Article I. Section 6. (2), in Commager, *Documents*, vol. I, p. 378. This per-
mission was never acted on and at no time in the history of the United
States, have the relations between the President and Congress been as
farcically bad as they were in the Confederacy.

mild and gentle. Critics err in thinking this unfortunate, undesirable. On the contrary it is the cardinal merit of our system. We get the good of two points of view. When controversy results, it does no abiding harm. Everything that moves makes friction. Only by the conflict of ideas do we reach wise ends in government. The more of conflict, the better.'[1] This may not be the view of the average American who alternates between denouncing Congress as a fifth wheel on the coach or a rubber stamp. But it is a representative view among members of Congress and until they change their collective mind, the system will not be changed.

And the case for leaving more or less well alone, can be put, and has been put, on higher grounds than that Congress will not willingly undergo the risks of 'the executive embrace'. 'The American constitutional system is just as much the product of our own society and environment as the parliamentary is of another. Certainly our federal government today is no artificial creature. It, too, is rather the result of innumerable, fortuitous day-to-day adjustments over three and a half centuries of governmental experience in the American environment. Such is the complexity of American society, with its conflicts of interests and of sections, that a resort to a prompt settlement of its major issues by the simple majorities implicit in a parliamentary system might prove positively explosive. Conflicts inherent in our society are not to be resolved by a simple shift in the mechanics of government. These very conflicts, indeed, determined the nature of our constitution, and this con-stitution cannot be held responsible for such clashes.'[2]

And the American voter, politician, publicist, professor is far more soaked in the presuppositions of the present system, far more broken into its ways than, perhaps, he realizes. Good political habits —and American habits are, on the whole good (no more can be said of British habits)—are too rare a thing to be thrown away in the world of today. The American people are right not to let the best be the enemy, not only of the good, but even of the slight improve-ments that the system is capable of without changing its basic character.

[1] Robert Luce, *Legislative Problems* (1935), p. 339.
[2] Wilfred E. Binkley, *President and Congress* (1947), p. 295–6.

Chapter Nine

POLITICS AND LAW

THE judicial organization of the United States is the institution which a stranger has the greatest difficulty in understanding. He hears the authority of a judge invoked in the political occurrences of every day, and he naturally concludes that in the United States the judges are important political functionaries; nevertheless, when he examines the nature of the tribunals, they offer at the first glance nothing that is contrary to the usual habits and privileges of those bodies; and the magistrates seem to him to interfere in public affairs only by chance, but by a chance that recurs every day.' But, Tocqueville goes on to say, it is not by chance but by a peculiarity of the American constitutional system. 'Whenever a law that the judge holds to be unconstitutional is invoked in a tribunal of the United States, he may refuse to admit it as a rule; this power is the only one peculiar to the American magistrate, but it gives rise to immense political influence.'[1]

It is indeed 'peculiar to the American magistrate', and the power to invalidate legislation, the wide extension given to this power, is the most peculiar feature of the American Constitution.

Despite the central role of the Supreme Court in the American system, and despite the reverence for the written law bred not only by the written constitution, but by the Court's interpretation of it, there is some room for doubt whether the power of 'judicial review' was, in fact, part of the constitutional plan. The most that a leading

[1] Alexis de Tocqueville, *Democracy in America*, translated by Henry Reeve, edited by Phillips Bradley (1945), vol. I, pp. 98, 101. (First published in 1835.)

authority can say is that 'the general agreement that state courts might declare federal laws contrary to the Constitution invalid and the arrangement for appeal of such cases to the Supreme Court, as well as the suggestion that the judiciary was to have an independent constitutional status in order to protect the fundamental law, were evidences of the belief that federal courts, as guardians of the Constitution, might, when occasion arose, declare both state and federal acts invalid'.[1] It is noteworthy that this unique characteristic of the American Constitution should have an uncertain origin, so that it is still possible to debate the point whether the framers of the Constitution intended to give to the Supreme Court a general reviewing power over Congressional legislation or a general censorial power directed to protecting states and individuals or 'persons' against usurpation of powers by the Congress or the President. It has been dogmatically asserted that this was the intent of the makers of the Constitution and equally firmly argued that judicial control, except in a very narrow sphere, the protection of the rights and duties of the federal courts themselves, is a usurpation when applied to federal legislation. The late Charles Beard had no doubts on the matter and no patience with those who had doubts. 'It is incumbent upon them to show that the American federal system was not designed primarily to commit the established rights of property to the guardianship of a judiciary removed from direct contact with popular electorates. Whether this system is outworn, whether it has unduly exalted property rights, is a legitimate matter for debate; but those who hold the affirmative cannot rest their case on the intent of the eighteenth-century statesmen who framed the Constitution.'[2]

But, in fact, this affirmative view has again been put forward by a living scholar with great learning and a firmness equal in intensity to Beard's. Professor Crosskey has attacked, if not quite the whole doctrine of judicial review, at least judicial review as it has been practised since the Civil War and he has attacked the assumed duty of the Court to keep a watch on its co-ordinate

[1] Charles Grove Haines, *The American Doctrine of Judicial Supremacy*, second edition (1932), p. 147.

[2] Charles A. Beard, *The Supreme Court and the Constitution* (1912; 1938 reprint), p. 126.

partners, the President and the Congress, and the supporting belief
that they especially need watching. 'For there is, after all, no more
reason to expect deliberate infidelity to their Constitutional oath,
on the part of the President and Congress, than there is to expect
such infidelity from the Court. And, in the light of the Court's
record, it cannot very well be said, with any plausibility, that the
Justices, over the years, have shown any very singular capacity to
understand the Constitution correctly. So, except perhaps in the
rare cases—assuming there ever can be any such—in which the
Court can reasonably conclude that some clear provision of the
Constitution has been inadvertently violated by the President or
Congress, the Court, it would seem, ought never to disregard the
acts of these two co-equal departments for unconstitutionality
where its own prerogatives are not immediately concerned. For the
Court cannot decently impute to either of its co-equal fellow
departments a deliberate intention to violate their solemn oaths;
and if there is any room for interpretation, the right to interpret,
where their own powers only are concerned, ought, on the principle of co-equality, to belong to the President and Congress,
equally with the Court.'[1] This doctrine had the support of President
Andrew Jackson, as far as it is a matter of giving each organ the
power to do its own duty as it sees it, but well over a century of
history has not made it part of the living if malformed Constitution under which Americans have long been accustomed to live
and outside of which they might gasp for air like a fish on dry land.

It must be noted that even so vehement a critic of the current doctrines of judicial review as Professor Crosskey, has no doubts that
the federal courts have a duty and a right to control state courts and
legislatures. Indeed, he thinks that Congress and the courts have
been remiss in exercising their rights as against the states for he takes
what in the seventeenth century would have been called a 'high
Prerogative' line about federal power. But many who do not take
the line yet see in the federal judicial control of state courts and
legislatures a necessary and proper instrument of federal government. They agree with Justice Holmes when he said 'I do not think
the United States would come to an end if we lost our power to

[1] William Winslow Crosskey, *Politics and the Constitution in the
History of the United States* (1953), vol. II, p. 1006.

declare an Act of Congress void. I do think the Union would be imperilled if we could not make that declaration as to the laws of the several States.'[1]

But nevertheless, the American system of 'judicial review', whatever its origin and historical justification, is still part of the system and, in recent years, if it has, in operation, disappointed old friends, it has acquired new ones and it is still true, as it was in Tocqueville's time, that American politics is permeated by law to an extent that Europeans find it very difficult fully to understand and that the basis and extent of that control of legislation by the courts which Americans call 'judicial review' is even less understood.

This temper and this system are sometimes easily, too easily, explained in terms of federalism. 'Federalism means legalism—the predominance of the judiciary in the constitution—the prevalence of a spirit of legality among the people.'[2] That the federal structure and the existence of the federal constitution encourage a legal temper in the nation is undoubted; that the spirit of litigation thus bred and the repeated cases of 'conflict of laws' and of disputes as to the type of law bearing on a given situation further encourage a legal way of looking at political questions is undoubted. More than most democratic systems, the American is manned by lawyers.[3]

It is often held, too, that control of the validity of legislation is a *necessary* result of having a federal constitution or even of having a written constitution. Yet this is not certain. 'The example of Switzerland shows that federal government and good government do not invariably require that the power should be completely exercised by the ordinary courts, nor that it should be exercised by lawyers at all.'[4] For it is the special American characteristic that most, though not all questions of the validity of the powers claimed by states, by the federal government or by parts of it, are, if questioned, usually questioned by the forms of private litigation; that what, in

[1] Oliver Wendell Holmes, *Collected Legal Papers* (1920), pp. 295–6. The speech from which the quotation is taken was delivered in 1913.

[2] A. V. Dicey, *Law of the Constitution* p. 175.

[3] 'There were 56,368 lawyers employed as such in the Federal service in 1939. No one has ever counted how many are employed in non-legal posts.' R. N. Spann, 'Civil Servants in Washington', in *Political Studies*, October 1953, p. 235.

[4] K. C. Wheare, *Federal Government* (second edition), p. 66.

other countries, even countries with a written constitution, is dealt with by political sanctions, is, in America, dealt with by the courts, state or federal.

Nor is it now what it may have been in the beginning, a mere matter of setting two laws one beside the other, and giving authority to that which is supreme, the Constitution, over the derivative and inferior mere statute, or state laws or constitutions which are under but not part of the 'supreme law of the land', as the Constitution puts it. This view was put in its classical simplicity by Chief Justice Marshall in the leading case of *Marbury v. Madison*. 'The constitution is either a superior paramount law, unchangeable by ordinary means, or it is on a level with ordinary legislative acts, and, like other acts, is alterable when the legislature shall please to alter it. If the former part of the alternative be true, then a legislative act contrary to the constitution is not law; if the latter part be true then constitutions are absurd attempts, on the part of the people, to limit a power in its own nature illimitable.'[1] Marshall chose his ground well, for he denied the remedy sought against the Secretary of State, Madison, on constitutional procedural grounds, thus not giving the Jeffersonians then in power the provocation of an effective decision against them and, at the same time, he laid up for further use, a weapon that his successors might wield in happier times.

More immediately important was the series of decisions extending federal jurisdiction, positively or negatively, by accepting federal claims to jurisdiction or by denying state claims to jurisdiction, not only as against the United States but as against individuals and corporations as in the *Dartmouth College* case (1819). And despite some restoration to the states of what Marshall's successor, Taney, called 'the police power', the habit of taking state legislation into the federal courts for adjudication of its validity was fully established by the time of the Civil War. Every state statute was mere putative law, subject to appeal.

Not until the very eve of the Civil War, did the Court risk invalidating another federal statute and it did so in the too celebrated case of *Dred Scott v. Sanford* (1857) in the misguided belief that the

[1] 1803. Cited from Henry Steele Commager, *Documents of American History* (fourth edition,), vol. L, p. 193.

bitter controversies over slavery in the territories could be settled by a court decision. All that the decision did was to envenom the conflict, to destroy, as far as the Court could do it, the legal basis of the new Republican party and give that party a bias against the Courts which lasted until the advantages of judicial review were clearly seen by the lawyers of the great business organizations of which the Republican party was now the spokesman and agent.

The new instrument of political control, applied to the states, was not the defence of federal jurisdiction or the constitutional prohibition of the passage of legislation 'impairing the obligation of a contract', or the power of Congress to regulate 'commerce among the states', but the new power, given by the XIVth amendment, passed after the Civil War, which extended to the states the prohibition against depriving 'persons of life, liberty, or property without due process of law'. Such a prohibition had been imposed on the federal government by the Vth amendment, but at this time, the federal government seldom legislated in the domestic field and 'due process' meant procedural regularity, although there were faint signs before the Civil War of a wider interpretation coming into favour.

Under 'due process of law', 'substantive due process', the court in general and the Supreme Court at the end of the chain, could and increasingly did define 'due process' in terms of natural justice, of the principles that were assumed to lie behind any legal system that could claim to provide due process.

Whether this was the secret intent of the drafters of the XIVth amendment, under cover of preserving the new rights of the freed slaves against their late masters, is uncertain and, except as a question of mere history, does not matter in this context. For it may be taken as established that 'due process' became the most important instrument of judicial control of what we now call social legislation and, by that fact, projected the court into the heart of controversies which no legal fiction could make unpolitical. As a learned historian of the general doctrine has put it: 'the phrases "due process of law" and "the equal protection of the law" are the most significant expressions in American constitutional law. Due process of law which formerly referred in England to a method of procedure in criminal trials, was eventually considered as procedure according to ancient customary law, and after 1689 might be changed by parliamentary enactment as well as by judicial decisions. When the term "due process of law" or "the law of the land" was inserted in the American state constitutions it was accepted with the usual English significance. Both in England and in the American states there were occasional broad claims for due process as a guaranty of good government and of principles of justice and reasonableness. But in practice these words were chiefly used as a protection to individuals against summary and arbitrary executive action. With the exception of Coke's extravagant claims they were not regarded as a check on legislative authority.'[1]

The Court itself was, for long, divided, but the majority that saw in the due process clause the weapon with which to save the American way of life grew; and finding a way to bring statutes disliked by some opulent interest or other under the ban of the XIVth amendment, became a great legal industry. Of course, some of the most famous cases involving an unpopular exercise of judicial review were not 'due process' clauses in form, for instance the striking down of the income tax laws in 1894 was done by an appeal to the letter of the main body of the Constitution.[2] But the

[1] Charles Grove Haines, *The American Doctrine of Judicial Supremacy* (second edition, 1932), p. 416. As Professor (now Justice) Frankfurter pointed out, since there was no XIVth amendment in Marshall's time, he used the commerce clause somewhat in the fashion that later judges used the due process guarantee of the XIVth amendment. Felix Frankfurter, *The Commerce Clause under Marshall, Taney, and Waite* (1937), p. 75. 'It has been said that had there been a due process clause against the states in the Constitution in 1819, the doctrine of the College case might never have been announced'. Bruce R. Trimble, *Chief Justice Waite* (1939), p. 233. The 'College case' was the famous case of Dartmouth College in which the Court gave a ruling which makes the legislative reform of chartered American universities extremely difficult.

[2] 'No capitation or other direct tax shall be laid, unless in proportion to the census of enumeration hereinbefore directed to be laid.' Article I, Section (9). Although an income tax had been imposed and collected during the Civil War and the Court was narrowly divided (and, indeed, one Justice was supposed to have changed his mind and so killed the statute) it was not until the adoption of the XVIth Amendment in 1913, that this gap in the federal tax armoury was filled by the only power superior to the Supreme Court, the 'People of the United States' acting as the sovereign behind the Constitution.

spirit of 'due process' can be seen even in decisions based mainly or exclusively on other constitutional prohibitions.[1]

With the coming of the twentieth century, judicial review, as then practised, came under greater and greater attack. It was open to attack on several grounds. It was extremely erratic in its operation, since it depended on the private litigant's sense of grievance to bring a matter before the Court. Even collusive actions to get the law determined were not totally satisfactory, as the Dred Scott case showed. Important statutes might live in the limbo of possible unconstitutionality for years, leaving good and ordinary citizens in doubt as to their rights and duties. As the law then stood, a state court might strike down a state statute as infringing federal rights, while a federal court, including the Supreme Court, would probably have upheld it, but there was no appeal against a state court upholding federal powers, for the fiction (which was once a fact) that the conflict of jurisdiction was simply between the Union and the States, was still upheld.

On the other hand, states' rights were often invoked by eminent lawyers because in certain fields they could not be used effectually or at all. The old arguments for the use of the commerce clause to make commerce truly national, now seemed dangerous, since national commerce was subject to federal control and the Federal Government was both more ambitious and more competent than were most of the states. 'As viewed by Daniel Webster in the argument of *Gibbons v. Ogden* in 1824, the purpose of the commerce clause was to protect as a single entity all that commerce which affected more than one state. . . . "Henceforth", he declared, "the commerce of the states was to be a unit; and the system by which it was to exist and be governed, must necessarily be described in the flag which waved over it, *E Pluribus Unum*". . . . [But] In Webster's time to say that "the commerce of the states was to be a unit" was

---

[1] Thus in the *Schechter* case which killed the NRA (see p. 396), although the excessive delegation of powers to the President was the main ground of disallowance, it was not the only one. 'The legality of the procedure is the point at issue, not the kind of agency. In short, another separation of powers argument turned out, upon analysis, to be a due process argument.' Robert E. Cushman, *The Independent Regulatory Commission* (1941), p. 437.

to say that for the most part such commerce was to go unregulated.'[1] It was not until the federal government began to regulate railways and oppose monopolies that the argument over the commerce clause shifted ground. Federal power was resisted in the name of states' rights by interests threatened by the intrusion of federal jurisdiction into areas in which state jurisdiction was not exercised, or could only be exercised ineffectually. In the main, the Court supported these extensions of federal authority even where the activity was apparently intra-state. 'Whenever the interstate and intrastate transactions of carriers are so related that the government of one involves the control of the other, it is Congress, and not the state, that is entitled to prescribe the final and dominant rule.'[2] But it was very different when 'the attempts under the National Recovery Act to regulate everything from the cutting of trees in the backwoods to the shining of shoes on the street corner represented the most comprehensive effort Congress had ever made to use the commerce clause as a source of power to regulate the economy of the country'.[3] A unanimous Court held in what was frivolously known as 'the case of the sick chicken' that the 'poultry had come to a permanent rest within the state'.[4] No one (except possibly President Roosevelt) much regretted the death of the National Recovery Administration which followed on the Schechter case, but it was another matter when the Court restricted the range of the Commerce clause by invalidating a railroad pensions law over the dissent of Chief Justice Hughes who (consistently with his opinion in the Shreveport case) laid it down that 'the power committed to Congress to govern interstate commerce does not require that its government should be wise, much less that it should be perfect. The power implies a broad discretion and thus permits a wide range even of mistakes'.[5] Coming along with the invalidation of the Agricultural Adjustment Act (*U.S. v. Butler*

[1] Carl Brent Swisher, *The Growth of Constitutional Power in the United States* (1946), pp. 79–80.

[2] Justice Charles Evans Hughes in 'The Shreveport Case' (1914) in Commager, *Documents*, vol. II, p. 275.

[3] Swisher, op. cit., p. 83.

[4] *Schechter, Poultry Corp. v. United States* (1935), in Commager, op. cit., vol. II, p. 642.

[5] *Railroad Retirement Board v. Alton Railroad Co.* (1935), ibid., p. 488.

(1936)) which produced one of the most vigorous dissenting opinions in the history of the Court from Justice (later Chief Justice) Stone, the limitations on the use of the commerce power produced some of the most bitter criticism of the court and gave (and give) an opportunity for some of the most telling criticism of the talmudic distinctions that the Court has been forced to make. One such critic has taken the oddities of legislation and adjudication arising out of employer's liability to illustrate the absurdities to which the law can be reduced. Conundrums like these were solemnly debated and decided. 'Is a section hand tamping cross ties on a line of track used both by interstate and intrastate trains engaged in "interstate transportation" or, in the alternative, in work "so closely related to interstate transportation as to be practically part of it?" ' 'Is a cook cooking for a bridge-maintenance gang on an interstate railroad so engaged? Is a lineman wiping insulators on an electrically operated road of the same kind so engaged? Or a section hand scraping a line of track clear of material dumped upon it to fill a ravine living underneath? Or a laborer drying sand for sanding locomotives used in the movement of interstate trains? Or a towerman starting a pump to fill a water tank for the supplying of locomotives so used?'[1]

Long before the great crisis of 1937, the principle and, still more the practice, of judicial review were under heavy fire. Federal legislation and state legislation alike was vetoed and that over the protests of some of the most eminent members of the Court. Laymen and even lawyers began to note the 'dissents' of some of the justices, Harlan and then Holmes, and those dissents began to influence the teaching of the great law schools and the writings of the great jurisconsults like Thomas Reid Powell. With the accession

[1] William Winslow Crosskey, op. cit., vol. I, p. 24. Professor Crosskey holds that all this hair-splitting is needless because the Constitution gives Congress 'a complete not a fragmentary, power to' regulate Commerce. 'And if the Supreme Court of the United States were only holding this, all the many evils . . . resulting from the supposed incompleteness of this important national power, could be very easily brought to an end. . . . And this being true, it would seem to follow that the Court is in duty bound to take this step and thereby get back, at least in its decisions under the Commerce Clause, to the ancient and sensible document it is solemnly sworn to uphold.' Ibid., vol. I, p. 292. It is my guess that the Court won't.

of Louis Dembitz Brandeis to the Court in 1916, after one of the
most bitter fights over a judicial nomination in the history of the
Senate, it became customary to look to the opinions of the great
twin brethren, Holmes and Brandeis, for the true state of the law.

Even then it was ignored not only that they spent by no
means all their time dissenting, even in defence of civil liberties, but
that they already dissented on different grounds, Brandeis basing
his dissents on an immense accumulation of evidence that
justified a legislature in taking the line it did, Holmes on the simpler
principle that the legislatures and Congress had the right, within
very wide limits, to do as they thought fit. Politicians, as well as
judges, were deemed to be 'reasonable men'.[1]

Thus arose in the minds of the educated public, especially among
the 'liberals' a confusion of mind about the grounds on which
judicial review could be attacked. As the Court struck down social
legislation, by nation or by state, with irritating regularity and as,
in some notorious cases, it failed to strike down legislation or
administrative actions that impinged on the traditional guarantees
of private 'liberty', the dissenting opinions that harked back to older
or looked forward to newer conceptions of judicial authority were
more and more prized as expressing the true spirit of the Constitution or, if that were historically implausible, as some held it was,
the spirit of what the Constitution ought to be. The enemies of the
Court cherished the memories of such righteous judges as Miller
and Harlan, but their real devotion went out to Oliver Wendell
Holmes, Jr., and to his colleague, Louis Brandeis.[2]

[1] Professional critics, of course, could see the difference in the two
attitudes. They were also impressed by the technical virtuosity of
the dissenters and by the mere bludgeoning tactics of some of the
conservatives. It was to McReynolds, the most obdurate defender of the
old order, that the Dean of a famous law school is reported to have
replied, when asked was he the young man who taught his students that
the Justices were fools. 'No, we let them find out for themselves.'

[2] Harlan and Holmes overlapped in time on the bench. Harlan's last
famous dissent was in the Standard Oil case in which he thought the
Court had legislated the true intent of anti-trust legislation out of
existence. The vehemence of his dissent in the actual delivery of it was
increased, so it was said, by the amount of whisky Harlan had consumed
before attacking the judgement of his brethren. But to the radicals and
progressives, Harlan was on the right side, whisky or no whisky.

But although Holmes and Brandeis often dissented (and agreed) in common, they did, in fact, represent two different schools of judicial thought, schools that divide the Supreme Court today. Holmes had little or no belief in the panaceas of the time. Most men were fools and most legislation was foolish, but it was the duty of the Court to answer the fools according to their folly and not to veto the right of the sovereign people to damage itself in pursuit of Utopia.[1] Holmes himself knew how wide of the mark much of his popular reputation was. He had no particular passion for social justice and was indifferent to the new style of sociological argument brought in by Brandeis.[2] It was because Holmes had few, if any, basic judicial principles that he differed so often from his brethren who had, he thought, far too many. What the voter wants was the only 'practical criterion. . . . Personally I bet that the crowd, if it knew more, wouldn't want what it does, but that is immaterial'.[3]

The very fervour with which conservative elements in American life clung to extreme doctrines of judicial review, the importance, almost the omnipotence they attached to it, were a source of danger for the Court and still more for the courts, state and federal, which were busy dealing with scores of contested statutes. The emotional eloquence with which great lawyers like Joseph Choate and George Wharton Pepper addressed a body of nine, usually elderly, professional lawyers, is revealing enough in itself of the super-judicial

[1] Holmes' most publicized dissent, the one the critics of the Court most delighted to honour, contained the famous phrase: 'The Fourteenth Amendment does not enact Mr. Herbert Spencer's *Social Statics*.' (*Lochner v. New York*, 1905.) But Holmes was a great and, indeed, uncritical admirer of Herbert Spencer. 'H. Spencer you English never quite do justice to, or at least those whom I have talked with do not. He is dull. He wrote an ugly, uncharming style, his ideals are those of a lower middle class British Philistine. And yet after all abatements I doubt if any writer of English except Darwin has done so much to affect our whole way of thinking about the universe.' Holmes to Lady Pollock (*The Pollock-Holmes Letters* (English edition), edited by Mark DeWolfe Howe (1942), vol. I, pp. 57-8).

[2] ' "In my epitaph," he humorously remarked to Hughes, "they ought to say, 'Here lies the supple tool of power'." ' Merlo Pusey, *Charles Evans Hughes* (1951), vol. I, p. 287.

[3] *Pollock-Holmes Letters*, vol. I, p. 163. I have amended 'criticism' to 'criterion'.

place given to the Court and to its members. It was difficult for the bar or the bench to escape the influence of the incense so lavishly offered up.[1]

And by the beginning of this century, the recourse to the Courts had become the favourite, almost the only weapon favoured by American conservatives. The Court and the Constitution together, 'one and inseparable', were the sole bulwarks of an American way of life, not, in fact, in any great danger. Probably many lawyers shared the ecstatic reverence of Henry R. Estabrook when he contemplated the Court (then under attack). 'Our great and sacred Constitution . . . serene and inviolable, stretches its beneficent powers over our land—over its lakes and rivers and forests, over every mother's son of us, like the outstretched arm of God. What the People of the United States did in setting up this Constitution was to set up a Supreme Court, the most rational, considerate, discerning, veracious, impersonal power—the most candid, unaffected, conscientious, incorruptible power—a power peculiar and unique in the history of the World. . . . O Marvellous Constitution! Magic Parchment! Transforming word! Maker, Monitor, Guardian of Mankind!'[2]

But the laity were not so enamoured of the 'Magic Parchment'. Trade unions threatened with injunctions (and not saved from 'yellow dog' contracts forbidding workers to join unions), devotees of 'civil rights' who saw that the XIVth amendment had been very effective in protecting the corporations, but practically useless in

[1] Although the gossip of the bar is full of stories reflecting on the competence of judges, the formal reverence they receive in court affects some of them and the most lavish praise of a judge is praise of his function and so of the whole profession. A great judge once commented on this. 'There is nothing within the circle of human emotions, unless it be the pleasure with which a lover praises the real or imaginary charms of his mistress, at all to be compared with the delight experienced by a lawyer in glorifying a court.' Charles Fairman, *Mr. Justice Miller and the Supreme Court 1862–1890* (1939), p. 142. This admiration of the Courts is compatible with severe criticism of specific judges and judgements, but it seldom leads to criticism of the legal approach to the questions debated. Yet I have heard an eminent Oxford logician of the old school say, reflectively, that he had never been able to understand what lawyers meant by reasoning.

[2] Quoted in Ralph Gabriel, *The Course of American Democratic Thought* (1940), p. 402.

protecting the Negro, sponsors of social legislation deemed to impair contracts, state and federal legislators who felt hamstrung, combined to resent the judicial veto as exercised, even if they admitted its usefulness and validity if administered in another fashion. The years before the first world war were full of schemes for limiting judicial review, but with the decline of liberalism that marked the last term of Wilson and the accession of Harding, the sins of the Court were denounced mainly by radicals and lawyers. But as the Court in the years just after the first war began to be more reactionary than it had been before that war, the dangers that the whole system was running, caused by the extravagant use of the judicial veto, were lively in the minds of many non-radical lawyers, and found expression in the dissenting opinions, not only of Holmes and Brandeis, but of Chief Justice Taft (who had been a Republican President), of Chief Justice Hughes (who had been a Republican presidential candidate) and of Justice, later Chief Justice Stone (who had been a Republican Attorney-General).

It was, however, the flood of 'New Deal' legislation that provoked the storm in which the Court, in its old form, nearly foundered. In the first hectic years of the first administration of Franklin D. Roosevelt, not only was much novel legislation passed, but it was passed in haste and was often badly drafted and, in at least one case, was passed although it was widely believed to be unconstitutional.[1] As a result, an unprecedented number of important federal statutes, backed by one of the most powerful administrations in American history, at one of the most socially unstable times in American history were invalidated.[2]

---

[1] I do not share the indignation of many Americans at the passage of the 'Guffey' bill, although its constitutionality was highly doubtful. It was one of the drawbacks of the system, as then interpreted, that it left the final decision to the Court and, by implication, absolved the conscience of Congress and the President. The Court was the 'Keeper of their conscience', but it could not speak until they had done something that brought their action before it.

[2] Three measures with important political pressure behind them were invalidated on one day, *The Frazier-Lemke Act, The National Recovery Act*, the removal of Federal Trade Commissioner, William E. Humphrey by Roosevelt. 'The Chief Justice had raised a question as to whether three such jolts should be inflicted on the Administration in a single day.

Other less doubtful acts were struck down and *not* by a unanimous Court. A permanent majority of the justices seemed to have the power of holding up or undoing a legislative programme supported by unprecedented congressional majorities.

The more than triumphant return of Roosevelt and the Democrats in 1936, brought the controversy to a head. There had been suggestions of constitutional amendments, of legislation making a special, not a bare majority of the Court, alone competent to invalidate a federal statute. But the President kept his own counsel and, working only with a tiny group of lawyers, suddenly produced a bill for the reorganization of the federal judicial system or, as it was immediately named, a bill for 'packing the Supreme Court'.[1] In the bill as it was introduced, there were included a number of useful reforms in the federal judicial system, but all attention was concentrated on what was proposed for the Supreme Court itself. The scheme had the merit of simplicity. All justices who were over seventy and had served ten years were to be given a chance of retiring on full pay. If they did not, justices, up to the number of six, would be appointed to supplement them.[2]

The secrecy in which the scheme had been elaborated, the hiding of the true purport of the bill under a mass of irrelevant and not always accurate information about the state of business in the federal courts, combined to irritate the opposition more than they consolidated the supporters. It is possible that a frank statement of the administration case, that no Justice had been appointed since Roosevelt came into the office, that necessary and proper legislation was being held up by the prejudices of judges whose whole philosophy of life had been repudiated by the people, would have served the President better than this method of indirection. And although the popular phrase 'the nine old men' had great emotive effect, it was, as the event proved, dangerous.[3]

Brandeis had replied that he could see no objection.' Pusey, op. cit., vol. II, p. 742.

[1] See p. 406.

[2] One of the minor ingenuities of this scheme was that something like it had once been suggested by Justice McReynolds.

[3] The great age, if not the venerableness of the members of the Court, was an old grievance. Clinging to their seats, long after they had ceased

In 1937, tactically and practically, one of the weaknesses of the argument by age was that the oldest member, Brandeis, was the Justice most respected by the very forces in the country, and in the Democratic party, that backed the bill. And Brandeis agreed with Hughes and Van Devanter to write a letter refuting, successfully, the suggestion advanced in the Attorney-General's brief that the Court was badly in arrears and the implication that this was in part due to the advanced age of the Justices. The insult to Brandeis and his willingness to support Hughes shook some faithful Democrats. And it was soon evident that, to get the bill through, arguments about the difficulties of litigants would not do. The President had to attack the political role of the Court, its flouting of the wishes of the popular majority which, so recently, had made him President for the second time. He listed the legislation struck down, the problems that remained. And the way to deal with the problems was by getting the Court in a proper frame of mind.[1]

---

to be in fit condition for their work, representing a dead political order whose spirit survived in the Court, if not in Congress or the White House, long-lived justices were stones of offence to many. Thus when 'Ben' Wade noticed that, despite his frailty, Chief Justice Taney was living on and thus preventing Lincoln nominating a Republican successor, he said. 'No man ever prayed as I did that Taney might outlive James Buchanan's term . . . but now I am afraid I have overdone it'. (Quoted in Carl Brent Swisher, *Roger B. Taney* (1935), p. 573.) One of Taney's Democratic colleagues, Nathan Clifford, clung to life in the desperate hope that the Democrats would return to power. His mind had noticeably decayed although he continued to take part in the business of the Court. He felt it a 'sacred trust to use what power he had to keep alive the flickering flame of the faith to which his first and abiding allegiance had been sworn'. Charles Fairman, *Mr. Justice Miller and the Supreme Court* (1939), p. 379. Clifford died four years before the Democrats came back to power. Even the most zealous members of that party who had business before the Court may have thought that Clifford carried party loyalty rather far. Justice Holmes continued to be in full command of his faculties until his ninetieth year, but age overtook even him and it fell to Chief Justice Hughes (with the approval of Brandeis, Holmes' closest friend on the bench), to ask him to resign, which Holmes did with none of the acrimony with which Stephen Field has answered a similar suggestion.

[1] The ending of the speech at the 'Democratic Victory Dinner' on 4 March 1937 ,was, in its way, a masterpiece. 'Here are strikes more far-

The initial mistake in not being candid was compounded by the mistake in limiting the time of witnesses for the bill and leaving much more time for its opponents. As hostile witness after hostile witness testified, the number and weight of the witnesses for the bill and the character of their criticism of the working of judicial review, were easily forgotten. And some of the witnesses did not make the mistake of ignoring the real character of the bill, or the problem, or fall back on mere historical rhetoric. Thus the President of Princeton University, Dr. H. W. Dodds, said:' Realism compels one to recognize that in elaborating the clauses of the Constitution, our courts have entered the field of political questions and have, therefore, often been the objects of political attack. Because the powers of our courts do extend to such broad questions of public policy, the pressure of political interests on them is heavier than obtains in the majority of other constitutional countries. For this reason the greatest vigilance is necessary to protect our finest political tradition, the judicial independence of the Supreme Court.'[1]

It was, indeed, the confused and unsophisticated view that 'the judicial independence of the Supreme Court' was one of America's 'finest political traditions' that helped to kill the bill and some of the least academically interesting witnesses were politically the most representative and important.

But there was another force at work. The 'New Deal', hampered and harassed by the Supreme Court, was not the only experiment in government on which the eyes of the world were turned. Mussolini's armies had conquered Abyssinia; Spain was in the throes of civil war; the power of Hitler grew daily. Was this a time to abandon old safeguards? Was it by any means certain, as was pointedly asked, that a 'conservative' administration need not run across a judicial veto anyway, as it proposed to maintain the *status*

---

reaching than we have ever known, costing millions of dollars—NOW. Here are Spring floods threatening to roll again down our river valleys— NOW. Here is the Dust Bowl beginning to blow again—NOW.' *The Public Papers and Addresses of Franklin D. Roosevelt, 1937 volume* (1941), p. 121. A subsequent 'fireside chat' was equally effective. I remember the irritation of an opposition Senator whose wife was converted by listening to it.

[1] *Reorganization of the Federal Judiciary Hearings*, Part I (1937), p. 618.

quo. For what is the content of the *status quo?* 'The conservatives "don't just pass laws". Indeed, ... Has he [Robert H. Jackson] never heard of laws passed in other lands by very conservative administrations abolishing trade unions, conscripting labor, censoring the press, prohibiting assemblies, outlawing political parties?'[1] And the same note was struck by a volunteer witness before the Senate Committee, Miss Dorothy Thompson, who said. 'You might say I have been a researcher into the mortality of republics'[2] and republics were dead or dying all over the world.

The fate of the bill was probably decided by the action of the Court itself in beginning to validate New Deal legislation like the Wagner Act and thus removing the immediate and pressing necessity for 'doing something about the Court'. We know, now that the reversal of policy had already been settled by the decision of Justice Roberts to go over to the side led by Chief Justice Hughes, a shift in the balance of power in the Court that might not have been so long delayed but for the illness of Justice Stone. It is possible, too, that the unity of the opposition would have been broken if they had been asked to provide a satisfactory amendment to serve as a substitute for the bill.[3]

The Senate Judiciary Committee reported the bill adversely and, within a few months of his greatest victory, Roosevelt was defeated. Or was he? Since it was widely believed that it was the implied threat in the Court bill that caused the change in the temper of the Court, it was easy, though we now know wrong, to give to the President, the spoils if not the honours of war. Roosevelt was soon able to begin to replace retiring Justices and, before he died, every

[1] Walter Lippmann, *The Supreme Court Independent or Controlled?* (1937), p. 56.

[2] *Hearings*, p. 859. I remember the emotion with which this statement was made.

[3] It was the opinion of two shrewd observers at the time, that announced willingness to accept a satisfactory substitute would have divided the opposition. 'Nine chances out of ten the opposition group would have been torn to bits in fratricidal combat if the President had asked them all to agree on one of their numerous amendments. His failure to make such an easy and meaningless gesture appears to have been one of his most serious tactical mistakes.' Joseph Alsop and Turner Catledge, *The 168 Days* (1937), pp. 113-4.

member of the Court save one owed his appointment to Roosevelt and that one, the only surviving Republican, owed to him promotion to the chief justiceship. With the change in membership came a change in doctrine. Most of the legislation of the 'first New Deal' (the not lamented NRA excepted) was re-enacted in forms that the Court upheld.

Thus many had thought that an excessive limitation of federal power under the commerce clause was one of the sins of the old Court and a justification for giving to the federal government, by constitutional amendment, adequate powers to deal with the nearly seamless web of commerce. This proved unnecessary.[1] With the validation of the Wagner Act in 1937, the Court began a reversal of the restrictive tendency 'until the commerce clause is today an ample source of federal legislative authority to deal with a wide range of problems arising out of or having any substantial effect upon interstate commerce.'[2]

The battle between the President and the Court was at best indecisive and (apart from some important but not basic reforms), the question of the role of the Court is left much where it was before, in the custody of the consciences, prudence and learning of the members of the Court. It was by making this plain, by destroying the old and increasingly implausible fiction of the 'Constitution' as a Sinai from which the Court brought down objective, unpolitical and final judgments, that the great debate over the functions of the Court did most good. It was realized, though not quite in the sense that its author meant it to be taken, that the too famous phrase, 'the Constitution is what the judges say

[1] Some suspected this at the time. There is a story of a dinner of eminent legal scholars who fell to discussing what kind of amendment would be needed to give the federal government adequate powers. One diner suggested that 'Congress shall have power to regulate Commerce among the several states', a suggestion well received for a few minutes until it was realized that the Constitution provides exactly that. (Article I, Section 8.) Dr. Crosskey holds that the Constitution means what it says, but even those who are not sure that it means that, are sure it means more than the 'old Court' thought it did.

[2] Vincent M. Barnett, Jr., in The American Political Science Review (1948) 'Ten Years of the Supreme Court', p. 1171. One result was to make Paul v. Virginia (1869) obsolete.

it is', as the politician who was later to be a great Chief Justice had put it, was true.[1]

The truce between the President and Congress on one hand and the Courts on the other has lasted, with a few minor skirmishes, down to the present day. Where it had intervened decisively it has been not against the political departments but when, as in President Truman's seizure of the steel plants, it was denying to the executive alone a power that it might have granted to the President and Congress. As Justice Frankfurter put it. 'We must . . . put on one side consideration of what powers the President would have had . . . if the seizure had been only for a short, explicitly temporary period, to be determined automatically unless Congressional approval were given.'[2]

There have been complaints, indeed, that the Court has not insisted enough on its positive duties, that it has allowed the states to interfere with the free movement of commerce under the guise of regulation of traffic, that it is not enough to strike down a most obvious attempt to put a tariff on cement coming into Florida, that the vigilance of a John Marshall is still needed. But states have rights, rights to revenue, rights to experiment, especially in fields where Congress could legislate but has not done so. To respect the judgement of the legislator, without necessarily thinking it right, has been the lesson critics have been preaching to the Court for most of this century.

It is in another field that the Court, in recent years, has won most praise and most blame. That is in the field of 'civil rights', the personal guarantees of freedom given by the 'Bill of Rights'.[3] It was natural, as recently as 1938, to oppose to what Professor

[1] Hughes was, in fact, opposing undue extension of judicial review. *Because* 'we are under a Constitution, but the Constitution is what the judges say it is . . . no more insidious assault could be made upon the independence and esteem of the judiciary than to burden it with these questions of administration—questions which lie close to the public impatience, and in regard to which the people are going to insist on having administration by officers directly accountable to them'. Pusey, op. cit., vol. I, p. 204.

[2] C. Herman Pritchett, 'Libertarian Motivations on the Vinson Court', in *The American Political Science Review* (June, 1953), p. 331.

[3] That is the first ten amendments of the Constitution, adopted in 1791.

Beard called the 'sadism of Congress', the sadism of the courts which, said Morris Cohen, 'will far outweigh that of Congress even though esthetically the procedure of the courts is more refined'.[1]

Since then, fear of the 'sadism of Congress' has grown, trust in the vigilance of the Court has grown, too. A series of 'libertarian' decisions have greatly extended the protection of the Constitution, quashed conviction of Negroes based on forced confessions or obtained before all-white juries, greatly extended the political rights of Negroes in the South (even at the cost of making the Court swallow some recently uttered words) and, in the case of the 'flag salute' cases, showing a majority of the Court converted by a solitary dissenter to a very tender regard for the consciences of parents and children.[2] The Court has, of course, been divided on other issues. Some members have given to parts of the Bill of Rights, the defences of personal freedom, a priority over other guarantees such as the protection given to property. They have imported the XIVth Amendment into the Bill of Rights, thus attempting to secure a control over state action comparable to that control which the Bill of Rights gives the Court over federal action. Judicial review, as some critics see it, has come alive in a new and dangerous form, for the Court is substituting its judgement for that of the elected representatives of the people. Justice Frank-

[1] 'Constitutional and Natural Rights in 1789 and Since', reprinted in *The Faith of a Liberal* (1946), p. 186.

[2] The flag salute cases arose from the order of the Minersville, Pennsylvania, school board that all children should salute the flag every day in school. (This is a common American school ritual.) The parents of the Gobitis children were 'Jehovah's Witnesses' and it was against their religious principles to salute the emblem of a Godless state. Lower courts decided for the parents; the Supreme Court, by eight to one, for the school board. But that one was Harlan Stone, soon to be Chief Justice and, in the case of *West Virginia State Board v. Barnette* (1943), the 'Witnesses' won. Great interest was aroused by the cases, both because of the sudden change in the position of the Court and by the fact that the opinion upholding the order of the Minersville school board was written by Justice Frankfurter, the chief disciple of Justice Holmes. We know that Charles Evans Hughes shared Justice Frankfurter's views and regretted the reversal. The point at issue had a curious resemblance to the problem facing Roman administrators like Pliny, the refusal of Christians to make a formal and harmless gesture to state authority.

furter, loyal to the Holmesian doctrine of tolerance even for legislative and judicial aberrations of the states, protested against the
extension of jurisdiction that his colleagues were bringing about.
'This is a court of review, not a tribunal unbounded by rules.
We do not sit like a kadi under a tree dispensing justice according
to considerations of individual expediency.'[1]

But the role of the Court as a defender of the weak, of the
unpopular, of the unorthodox has won it friends it could hardly
have expected to get twenty years ago. For the dangers of repression
by local law, local administration, as well as by local violence are
possibly as great as they were in the period after the first world war
to which most American lawyers look back with shame (as many
looked on with shame, and protest, at the time). And when
'Americanism' can be given so many forms, when heresy is, with
difficulty, distinguished from treason, the need for judicial review
can be put in very persuasive terms. 'It may of course be true that
no court can save a society bent on ruin. But American society is
not bent on ruin. It is a body deeply committed in its majorities to
the principles of the Constitution and both willing and anxious to
form its policy and programs in a constitutional way. Americans
are, however, profoundly troubled by fears—intense and real fears,
raised by unprecedented dangers and by the conduct of perilous
tasks unprecedented in the history of the Government. . . . Ruin
can come to a society not only from the furious resentments of a
crisis. It can be brought about in imperceptible stages by gradually
accepting, one after another, immoral solutions for particular
problems.'[2]

But objections to judicial review, as it was interpreted in the past,
are still powerful and worthy of consideration, even in an age where
the danger from popular intolerance is greater than the danger
from the immunity of great corporations from the legislative will.

There is, for example, the belief that judicial review by equating
'right' with 'constitutional' not only condemns legislation that a
majority of the Court find unconstitutional although each member
may think it, in a general political sense, 'right', but that the more

[1] Quoted in C. Herman Pritchett, *loc. cit.*, p. 322.
[2] Eugene V. Rostow, 'The Democratic Character of Judicial Review',
Harvard Law Review (December 1952), p. 207.

dangerous converse is true, that what the Court holds to be constitutional, or finds itself impotent to deal with, is also 'right', prudent
and just, in a general political sense. The legislator can 'pass the
buck', gratify local pressure groups, temporary gusts of passion,
and rely on the Courts, either to undo the mischief or to give it a
dress of constitutional propriety that will cover up the ugly or
foolish character of the legislation. The Court, on this view, adds
to the difficulty, already great in the American system, of pinning
responsibility on anybody in particular. The task of preaching
moderation, of making the necessary adjustments that enable a
democratic government to function, is passed to the Courts and
passed in the form of a legal action. That means, in turn, that the
basic question cannot be considered in all its ramifications. 'The
interests at stake cannot all be crowded into the rigid forms of a
case in controversy.'[1]

Some think that the fact that the Court does not deal with a
problem until it is faced with it in the tangible form of a legal
controversy is an advantage. 'The pressure of events brings political
problems near enough to other departments of the government,
meanwhile keeping those that do not call for decision remote
enough not to interfere. For the Court it is the traditional duty of
deciding the instant case that serves this purpose. Not until a
problem is immediate and unavoidable is a man at his best to solve
it. This is the reality-principle of Freud taking the place of the
pleasure-principle. The anticipated decision of a problem, when it is
not preparation in general, has a kinship with fantasy-making and
day-dreaming. It is conditioned by what Freud calls the pleasure-
ego. As the problem comes closer, the reality-ego takes over. The
best individual does best under pressure and in a pinch.'[2]

Then it has always been a difficulty for the defenders of judicial
review that the members of the Court often take such different
views of what the Constitution (and so the law) is. The dissenting
opinions of some eminent judges, overruled as they are, may be
more convincing than the official judgement of the Court and that
judgement, itself, may be supported by a bare majority for very

[1] Walter Hamilton, 'The Smouldering Constitutional Crisis', *New
Republic*, 18 January 1943.
[2] Charles P. Curtis, Jr., *Lions Under the Throne* (1947), pp. 66–7.

varying reasons.[1] If the Court is bound to accept a legislative decision unless it is most evident that the legislature has acted unconstitutionally, why should not one supporting voice save the statute? Why should not unanimity be required for condemnation? The law and the Constitution cannot have, in these circumstances, the certainty and so the authority claimed for them. And this view has led to proposals (adopted by some states for their courts) that a special majority be required for judgements of unconstitutionality.

It was also noticed that not only did the judges not always not agree at a given time, on what it was, but it was noted that the Constitution, from time to time, differed in meaning, for the Supreme Court was and is above the rule binding lesser tribunals; *stare decisis* is not for it. The Justices will, as far as possible, follow precedent, including their own precedents, but since there is no legal remedy for their decisions, no sovereign Parliament to undo a mischievous decision like that of the House of Lords in the *Free Church* case, the Supreme Court must be allowed to change its mind. The motto over the front of the court building may be 'Equal Justice Under Law', but it is not quite the same justice all the time; the equality depends to some extent on chronology. Sometimes the Court evades the problem of upsetting its decisions by ingenious distinctions, but sometimes, with a boldness that lesser tribunals may admire without desiring to emulate, it simply admits its past error.[2]

[1] A French student has pointed out a reason why dissents are often better reading than the opinion of the Court. 'Le dissenteur n'est pas limité par la nécessité d'accords et de compromise qu'exige la rédaction de l'opinion de la majorité. Il est libre d'être lui-même, et lui seul. Il exprime sa conviction profonde et s'adresse autant à ses confrères dont il déplore l'incompréhension qu'à l'opinion publique.' Roger Pinto, *Des Juges Qui ne Gouvernent Pas* (1934), p. 37.

[2] Justice Roberts protesting against the overruling of a decision that he himself had written less than ten years before 'produced what was probably the only successful bon mot of his judicial career'. 'The reason for my concern', he said in his dissenting opinion, 'is that the instant decision overruling that announced about nine years ago, tends to bring adjudications of this tribunal into the same class as a restricted railroad ticket, good for this day and train only.' (Quoted in C. Herman Pritchett, *The Roosevelt Court* (1948), p. 46.) And a great student of the role of the

Perhaps the most startling example of the boldness with which the Court disregards *stare decisis* was the overthrow, in 1938, of a precedent of great importance, nearly a century old. For the Supreme Court had held in *Smith v. Tyson* in 1842 that in cases between citizens of different states, the Court would find what was the law of the state whose law (when found) governed the action. This meant that the Supreme Court was finding or inventing (where it found it unsettled) the law of the states and that the law so found might differ substantially from the law found by the courts of the states in deciding cases between their own citizens. This may have been a usurpation but it was a long-settled usurpation.[1]

The usurpers abdicated in 1938 in *Erie Railroad v. Tompkins*. Justice Brandeis, who had become a critic of the doctrine, speaking for the Court repented of its and his errors. 'Notwithstanding the great names which may be cited in favor of the doctrine, and

---

Court has pointed out another result of the freedom of the Court from its own precedents:

'The conspicuous breakdown of the principle of *stare decisis* in the field of constitutional law has weakened both its historical and its logical foundations. For with what consistency can it be argued that the President and Congress are bound by the Court's past interpretations of the Constitution but that the Court itself is not?' Edward S. Corwin, *Court over Constitution* (1938), pp. 77–9. A friend of mine, an eminent teacher of law in one of the most broad-minded and least traditional of law schools, complained to me that it was now impossible to practise law, since a lawyer could no longer advise a client what the law is since the problem was what the law was going to be.

[1] The Court did not give itself a totally free hand. 'In other words, the doctrine goes no further than to permit the Federal courts to disregard those decisions of State courts which have themselves been founded, not upon statute or usage, but upon the abstract principles of general law.' Westel Woodbury Willoughby, *The Constitutional Law of the United States* (second edition, 1927). Professor Willoughby thought *Smith v. Tyson* a bad precedent, but one so firmly established as not to be worth debating. Professor Fairman attributes the error in part to the fact that Joseph Story in addition to being 'a judge, . . . was also a professor in Harvard Law School. . . . He believed that there was one great body of common or general law which prevailed throughout all the states'. Charles Fairman, *American Constitutional Decisions* (1948), p. 164. Story was imposing a version of what was later to be called 'the law of the state of Ames'.

notwithstanding the frequency with which the doctrine has been reiterated, there stands, as a perpetual protest against its repetition, the Constitution of the United States.'[1] For a century, that is, the guardian of the Constitution had been asleep at the switch.[2] Yet unless the Court is to abandon completely its control over federal legislation, even over state legislation, it cannot tie its hands. For life marches on. New techniques of production (even of production of evidence), new techniques of conspiracy, new problems arising out of the greater and greater integration of the economy have to be dealt with and it may be quite irrelevant and totally harmful to be bound by what Marshall or Taney said before the coming of the telegraph, not to speak of the atom bomb.

Other criticisms of the Court have, for the moment, less validity than they had twenty years ago. The respect for the judgement of legislators that was then preached is now practised, perhaps excessively practised. The traditional profession of extreme reluctance to strike down state or federal legislation is no longer so much a mere formula as it was.[3] That much of the criticism of the Court has

[1] Fairman, op. cit., pp. 170-1.

[2] Professor Crosskey comments vigorously on this reversal of doctrine. 'Such, then, was the case of *Erie Railroad Company v. Tompkins*. The constitutional and statutory grounds of the decision totally imaginary, and the juridical evils against which the decision was directed really attributable to a cause quite other than the doctrine overruled, the case was a remarkable one, indeed. But its most extraordinary feature still remains unnoted: that the Supreme Court actually made its revolutionary decision, changing, by what certainly was no mere "molecular", but a gigantic "molar motion", the existing rules of substantive law, in untold thousands of cases, pending and prospective, in the national courts, *without the elementary safeguard of hearing argument* on the point of constitutional law to be decided. . . . How many millions of dollars, in money and other property, are now in hands other than they would have been, had the Court's unwarranted decision not been made, it is utterly impossible to say. But it is perfectly safe to say that the total must be enormous.' Crosskey, op. cit., vol. II, p. 916. Professor Crosskey believes that one reason for rushing the decision (the point about the invalidity of the precedent in *Smith v. Tyson* was not raised by either litigant) was the advanced age of two of the Justices and the dying state of another. Next year, it is suggested, the decision might have been different. Ibid., p. 1365.

[3] The words of the Court often recalled the traditional schoolmaster assuring the boy whom he is about to cane that the operation will hurt

died down is due, no doubt, to the moderation with which the Court, in recent years, has exercised its functions. This has not been due, as was feared, to any special docility in the 'Roosevelt Court'. It divided as much as its predecessors, if not along the same lines, and to an unprecedented degree carried on personal as well as legal disputes in public.[1]

Nor even in the field of civil liberties has the Court always lived up to its claim to protect the weak, to administer 'equal justice under law' for it found reasons for tolerating the 'relocation' of the *Nisei*, that is for the deportation and internment of American citizens by birth who happened to be of Japanese origin.[2]

---

the boy less than it will the master. Few boys have ever been found ready to believe this. Such oriental politeness worthy of Ko Ko was not always thought obligatory. 'After 1832 a change appears. In the fifteen years following, a considerable number of cases involving the constitutionality of state statutes appeared in the highest law tribunal of the land and the court felt called upon, in various instances, to annul the statute in question. . . . But there were . . . some really important questions argued before the court-questions which had wide-reaching influence on the activities of the states—and yet the court declared these statutes unconstitutional without any apparent hesitancy and with few expressions of regret because they were forced to take this action. . . . During the period immediately preceding and following the Civil War the court in approaching a question of a constitutional nature assumed an attitude of indifference. Its opinions in constitutional cases are short usually, and but little or no space is wasted in softening its decisions, the court simply making some blunt statement that the statute is invalid.' Blaine Free Moore, *The Supreme Court and Unconstitutional Legislation* (1913), pp. 66–7.

[1] A famous cartoon by Fitzpatrick of *The St. Louis Post-Dispatch* showed one robed judge in the library aiming a sling-shot at a colleague. The scandal caused by these disputes was itself proof of how great the prestige of the Court was and is. Such personal disputes were not new, (McReynolds was so bitter an anti-Semite that he refused to meet Brandeis socially), but they were not public.

[2] This action was described by Professor Rostow as 'the greatest mistake of the war'. The plea of military necessity ('the tyrant's plea' of tradition), was especially difficult to swallow, since the Japanese of Hawaii Territory, more numerous, more concentrated, more formidable, were not 'relocated'. The opinion of a victim may be quoted. 'Somehow the feeling that I, an American citizen, with thousands of other Japanese Americans, was being denied every right as set forth in the United States

It is possible that another tradition, that of Britain or of Canada, for instance, might have provided in the United States, effective protection of minorities and an effective political education. But we have to take what history has given us in the United States, and much although not all of the education in the field of private liberties has been given by the Courts (and of course by the Bar).

It may be that the principles of the Bill of Rights, the basic doctrines of the Revolution would in any case have survived in a country more legally-minded than law-abiding, among a people not averse to violence and, never more than today, tempted to equate 'Americanism' with righteousness and ready to spread righteousness by legal and illegal action. But in the present temper of the American people or of many among them, it is worth while pondering the words of Justice Cardozo. 'Great maxims, if they may be violated with impunity, are honored often with lip service, which passes easily into irreverence. The restraining power of the judiciary does not manifest its chief worth in the few cases in which the legislature has gone beyond the limits of discretion. Rather we shall find its chief worth in making vocal and audible the ideals that might otherwise be silenced, in giving them continuity of *life and expression*, in guiding and directing choice within the limits where choice ranges.'[1]

It is because this function is understood (if only confusedly) by the average American, that the Supreme Court, as an educator, has kept the prestige which it was in danger of losing in its days as a super-legislature. No one can have seen the pilgrims who fill the ornate Court room during public sessions, under the bas-reliefs of great law-givers like Napoleon, without being struck by this historical reverence which is something won, not simply conferred. And the audience does answer the prayer of the usher, 'God save the United States and this honourable Court'.

Constitution to prove my loyalty to this country and innocence of any guilt as a dangerous member of society was very difficult to subdue.'
Quoted in Alexander H. L. Leighton, *The Governing of Men* (1945), p. 23.
[1] Benjamin N. Cardozo, *The Nature of the Judicial Process*, p. 118.

Appendix

CONSTITUTION OF THE UNITED STATES
OF AMERICA

────────

(Italics and notes are the author's)

WE THE PEOPLE of the United States, in order to form a more
perfect union, establish justice, insure domestic tranquility,
provide for the common defence, promote the general welfare,
and secure the blessings of liberty to ourselves and our posterity,
do ordain and establish this Constitution for the United States of
America.[1]

ARTICLE I

Section 1.—All legislative powers herein granted shall be vested
in a Congress of the United States, which shall consist of a Senate
and House of Representatives.

Section 2.—*The House of Representatives shall be composed of members chosen every second year* by the people of the several States, and
the *electors in each State shall have the qualifications requisite for electors
of the most numerous branch of the State legislature.*

No person shall be a Representative who shall not have attained
to the age of twenty-five years, and been seven years a citizen of the
United States, and *who shall not, when elected, be an inhabitant of that
State in which he shall be chosen.*

Representatives and direct taxes *shall be apportioned among the
several States* which may be included within this Union, *according to
their respective numbers, which shall be determined by adding to the whole*

[1] Drafted in 1787, went into effect in 1789.

416

number of free persons, including those bound to service for a term of years, and excluding Indians not taxed, *three-fifths of all other persons*.[1] *The actual enumeration shall be made* within three years after the first meeting of the Congress of the United States, and *within every subsequent term of ten years*, in such manner as they shall by law direct. The number of Representatives shall not exceed one for every thirty thousand, *but each State shall have at least one Representive; and* until such enumeration shall be made, the State of New Hampshire shall be entitled to choose three, Massachusetts eight, Rhode Island and Providence Plantation one, Connecticut five, New York six, New Jersey four, Pennsylvania eight, Delaware one, Maryland six, Virginia ten, North Carolina five, South Carolina five, and Georgia three.

When vacancies happen in the Representation from any State, the executive authority thereof shall isue writs of election to fill such vacancies.

The House of Representatives shall choose their Speaker and other officers; and *shall have the sole power of impeachment*.

Section 3.—The Senate of the United States shall be composed of two Senators from each State, chosen by the legislature thereof, for six years; and each Senator shall have one vote.[2]

Immediately after they shall be assembled in consequence of the first election, *they shall be divided as equally as may be into three classes*. The seats of the Senators of the first class shall be vacated at the expiration of the second year, of the second class at the expiration of the fourth year, and of the third class at the expiration of the sixth year, so that *one-third may be chosen every second year*; and if vacancies happen by resignation, or otherwise, during the recess of the legislature of any State, the executive thereof may make temporary appointments until the next meeting of the legislature, which shall then fill such vacancies.

No person shall be a Senator who shall not have attained to the age of thirty years, and been nine years a citizen of the United States, and *who shall not, when elected, be an inhabitant of that State for which he shall be chosen*.

[1] 'Three fifths of other persons', i.e. slaves, cf. Amendments XIV, XV and XIX.
[2] Cf. Amendment XVII.

The Vice-President of the United States shall be President of the Senate, but shall have no vote, unless they be equally divided.

The Senate shall choose their other officers, and also a President *pro tempore,* in the absence of the Vice-President, *or when he shall exercise the office of President of the United States.*

The Senate shall have the sole power to try all impeachments. When sitting for that purpose, they shall be on oath or affirmation. *When the President of the United States is tried, the Chief Justice shall preside; and no person shall be convicted without the concurrence of two-thirds of the members present.*

Judgment in cases of impeachment shall not extend further than to removal from office, and disqualification to hold and enjoy any office of honour, trust or profit under the United States; but the party convicted shall nevertheless be liable and subject to indictment, trial, judgment, and punishment, according to law.

Section 4.—The times, places, and manner of holding elections for Senators and Representatives, shall be prescribed in each State by the legislature thereof; but the Congress may at any time by law make or alter such regulations, except as to the places of choosing Senators.

The Congress shall assemble at least once in every year, and such meeting shall be on the first Monday in December, unless they shall by law appoint a different day.[1]

Section 5.—Each house shall be the judge of the elections, returns and qualifications of its own members, and a majority of each shall constitute a quorum to do business; but a smaller number may adjourn from day to day, and may be authorized to compel the attendance of absent members, in such manner, and under such penalties as each house may provide.

Each house may determine the rules of its proceedings, punish its members for disorderly behaviour, and, with the concurrence of two-thirds, expel a member.

Each house shall keep a journal of its proceedings, and from time to time publish the same, excepting such parts as may in their judgement require secrecy; and the yeas and nays of the members of either house on any question shall, at the desire of one-fifth of those present, be entered on the journal.

[1] Cf. Amendment XX.

Neither house, during the session of Congress, shall, without the consent of the other, adjourn for more than three days, nor to any other place than that in which the two houses shall be sitting.

Section 6.—The Senators and Representatives shall receive a compensation for their services, to be ascertained by law, and paid out of the Treasury of the United States. They shall in all cases, except treason, felony, and breach of the peace, be privileged from arrest during their attendance at the session of their respective houses, and in going to and returning from the same; and for any speech or debate in either house, they shall not be questioned in any other place.

No Senator or Representative shall, during the time for which he was elected, be appointed to any civil office under the authority of the United States, which shall have been created, or the emoluments whereof shall have been increased during such time; and no person holding any office under the United States, shall be a member of either house during his continuance in office.

Section 7.—*All bills for raising revenue shall originate in the House of Representatives; but the Senate may propose or concur with amendments as on other bills.*

Every bill which shall have passed the House of Representatives and the Senate, shall, before it becomes a law, be presented to the President of the United States; if he approve he shall sign it, but if not he shall return it, with his objections, to that house in which it shall have originated, who shall enter the objections at large on their journal, and proceed to reconsider it. If after such reconsideration two-thirds of that house shall agree to pass the bill, it shall be sent, together with the objections, to the other House, by which it shall likewise be reconsidered, and if approved by two-thirds of that house, it shall become a law. But in all such cases the votes of both houses shall be determined by yeas and nays, and the names of the persons voting for and against the bill shall be entered on the journal of each house respectively. If any bill shall not be returned by the President within ten days (Sundays excepted) after it shall have been presented to him, the same shall be a law, in like manner as if he had signed it, unless the Congress by their adjournment prevent its return, in which case it shall not be a law.

Every order, resolution, or vote to which the concurrence of the Senate and House of Representatives may be necessary (except on a question of adjournment) shall be presented to the President of the United States; and before the same shall take effect, shall be approved by him, or being disapproved by him, shall be repassed by two-thirds of the Senate and House of Representatives, according to the rules and limitations prescribed in the case of a bill.

Section 8.—The Congress shall have power to lay and collect taxes, duties, imposts and excises, to pay the debts and provide for the common defence and general welfare of the United States; but all duties, imposts and excises shall be uniform throughout the United States;

To borrow money on the credit of the United States;

To regulate commerce with foreign nations, and among the several States, and with the Indian tribes;

To establish a uniform rule of naturalization, and uniform laws on the subject of bankruptcies throughout the United States;

To coin money, regulate the value thereof, and of foreign coin, and fix the standard of weights and measures;

To provide for the punishment of counterfeiting the securities and current coin of the United States;

To establish post-offices and post-roads;

To promote the progress of science and useful arts, by securing for limited times to authors and inventors the exclusive right to their respective writings and discoveries;

To constitute tribunals inferior to the Supreme Court;

To define and punish piracies and felonies committed on the high seas, and offences against the law of nations;

To declare war, grant letters of marque and reprisal, and make rules concerning captures on land and water;

To raise and support armies, but no appropriation of money to that use shall be for a longer term than two years;

To provide and maintain a navy;

To make rules for the government and regulation of the land and naval forces;

To provide for calling forth the militia to execute the laws of the Union, suppress insurrections and repel invasions;

To provide for organizing, arming, and disciplining the militia, and for governing such part of them as may be employed in the service of the United States, reserving to the States respectively, the appointment of the officers, and the authority of training the militia according to the discipline prescribed by Congress;

To exercise exclusive legislations in all cases whatsoever, over such district (not exceeding ten miles square), as may, by cession of particular States, and the acceptance of Congress, become the seat of the government of the United States,[1] and to exercise like authority over all places purchased by the consent of the legislature of the State in which the same shall be, for the erection of forts, magazines, arsenals, dock-yards, and other needful buildings; and

To make all laws which shall be necessary and proper for carrying into execution the foregoing powers, and all other powers vested by this Constitution in the Government of the United States, or in any department or officer thereof.

Section 9.—The migration or importation of such persons as any of the States now existing shall think proper to admit, shall not be prohibited by the Congress prior to the year one thousand eight hundred and eight, but a tax or duty may be imposed on such importation, not exceeding ten dollars for each person.

The privilege of the writ of *habeas corpus* shall not be suspended, unless when in cases of rebellion or invasion the public safety may require it.

No bill of attainder or *ex post facto* law shall be passed.

No capitation, or other direct tax shall be laid, unless in proportion to the census or enumeration hereinbefore directed to be taken.[2]

No tax or duty shall be laid on articles exported from any State.

No preference shall be given by any regulation of commerce or revenue to the ports of one State over those of another; nor shall vessels bound to, or from, one State, be obliged to enter, clear, or pay duties in another.

No money shall be drawn from the Treasury, but in consequence of appropriations made by law; and a regular statement and account of the receipts and expenditures of all public money shall be published from time to time.

No title of nobility shall be granted by the United States; and no person holding any office of profit or trust under them, shall, without the consent of the Congress, accept of any present, emolu-

[1] That is, the District of Columbia in which Washington is situated.
[2] Cf. Amendment XVI.

ment, office, or title, of any kind whatever, from any king, prince, or foreign State.

Section 10.—No State shall enter into any treaty, alliance, or Confederation; grant letters of marque and reprisal; coin money; emit bills of credit; *make any thing but gold and silver coin a tender in payment of debts;* pass any bill of attainder, *ex post facto* law, *or law impairing the obligations of contracts*, or grant any title of nobility.

No State shall, without the consent of the Congress, lay any imposts or duties on imports or exports, except what may be absolutely necessary for executing its inspection laws; and the net produce of all duties and imposts laid by any State on imports or exports, shall be for the use of the Treasury of the United States; and all such laws shall be subject to the revision and control of the Congress.

No State shall, without the consent of Congress, lay any duty of tonnage, keep troops, or ships of war in time of peace, enter into any agreement or compact with another State, or with a foreign power, or engage in war unless actually invaded, or in such imminent danger as will not admit of delay.

Article II

Section 1.—The executive power shall be vested in a President of the United States of America. He shall hold his office during the term of four years, and, together with the Vice-President, chosen for the same term, be elected, as follows:

Each State shall appoint, in such manner as the legislature thereof may direct, a number of electors, equal to the whole number of Senators and Representatives to which the State may be entitled in the Congress; but no Senator or Representative, or person holding an office of trust or profit under the United States, shall be appointed an elector.

The electors shall meet in their respective States, and vote by ballot for two persons, *of whom one at least shall not be an inhabitant of the same State with themselves*. And they shall make a list of all the persons voted for, and of the number of votes for each; which list they shall sign and certify, and transmit sealed to the seat of the government of the United States, directed to the President of the Senate. The President of the Senate shall, in the presence of the Senate and House of Representatives, open all the certificates, and the votes shall then be counted. *The person having the greatest number of votes shall be the President, if such number be a majority of the whole numbers of electors appointed; and if there be more than one who have such majority, and have an equal number of votes, then the House of Representatives shall immediately choose by ballot one of them for President; and if no person have a majority, then from the five highest on the list the said House shall in like manner choose the President. But in choosing the President, the votes shall be taken by States, the representation from each State having one vote; a quorum for this purpose shall consist of a member or members from two-thirds of the States, and a majority of all the States shall be necessary to a choice. In every case, after the choice of the President, the person having the greatest number of votes of the electors shall be the Vice-President. But if there should remain two or more who have equal votes, the Senate shall choose from them by ballot the Vice-President.*[1]

The Congress may determine the time of choosing the electors, and the day on which they shall give their votes; which day shall be the same throughout the United States.

No person except a natural born citizen, or a citizen of the United States, at the time of the adoption of this Constitution, shall be eligible to the office of President; neither shall any person be eligible to that office who shall not have attained to the age of thirty-five years, and been fourteen years a resident within the United States.

In case of the removal of the President from office, or of his death, resignation, or inability to discharge the powers and duties of the said office, the same shall devolve on the Vice-President, and the Congress may by law provide for the case of removal, death, resignation, or inability, both of the President and Vice-President, declaring what officer shall then act as President, and such officer shall act accordingly, until the disability be removed, or a President shall be elected.[2]

The President shall, at stated times, receive for his services, a compensation, which shall neither be increased nor diminished, during the period for which he shall have been elected, and he shall not receive within that period any other emolument from the United States, or any of them.

[1] Cf. Amendments XII and XX.

[2] Since the Act of 1947, the presidential succession runs from Vice-President to Speaker, to President of the Senate *pro tempore*, then through the cabinet officers in order of seniority of their departments. See p. 380.

Before he enter on the execution of his office, he shall take the following oath or affirmation:

'I do solemnly swear (or affirm) that I will faithfully execute the office of President of the United States, and will to the best of my ability, preserve, protect, and defend the Constitution of the United States.'

Section 2.—The President shall be Commander-in-Chief of the army and navy of the United States, and of the militia of the several States, when called into the actual service of the United States; he may require the opinion, in writing, of the principal officer in each of the executive departments, upon any subject relating to the duties of their respective offices, and he shall have power to grant reprieves and pardons for offences against the United States, except in cases of impeachment.

He shall have power, by and with the advice and consent of the Senate, to make treaties, provided two-thirds of the Senators present concur; and he shall nominate, and by and with the advice and consent of the Senate, shall appoint ambassadors, other public ministers and consuls, judges of the Supreme Court, and all other officers of the United States, whose appointments are not herein otherwise provided for, and which shall be established by law; but the Congress may by law vest the appointment of such inferior officers, as they think proper, in the President alone, in the courts of law, or in the heads of departments.

The President shall have power to fill up all vacancies that may happen during the recess of the Senate, by granting commissions which shall expire at the end of their next session.

Section 3.—He shall from time to time give to the Congress information of the state of the Union, and recommend to their consideration such measures as he shall judge necessary and expedient; he may, on extraordinary occasions, convene both houses, or either of them, and in case of disagreement between them, with respect to the time of adjournment, he may adjourn them to such time as he shall think proper; he shall receive ambassadors and other public ministers; *he shall take care that the laws be faithfully executed,* and shall commission all the officers of the United States.

Section 4.— The President, Vice-President, and all civil officers of the United States, shall be removed from office on impeachment for, and conviction of, treason, bribery, or other high crimes and misdemeanours.

Article III

Section 1.—The judicial power of the United States, shall be vested in one Supreme Court, and in such inferior courts as the Congress may from time to time ordain and establish. The judges, both of the supreme and inferior courts, *shall hold their offices during good behaviour,* and shall, at stated times, receive for their services, a compensation, which shall not be diminished during their continuance in office.

Section 2.—The judicial power shall extend to all cases, in law and equity, arising under this Constitution, the laws of the United States, and treaties made, or which shall be made, under their authority; to all cases affecting ambassadors, other public ministers and consuls; to all cases of admiralty and maritime jurisdiction; *to controversies to which the United States shall be a party; to controversies between two or more States; between a State and citizens of another State; between citizens of different States; between citizens of the same State claiming lands under grants of different States, and between a State, or the citizens thereof, and foreign states, citizens or subjects.*[1]

In all cases affecting ambassadors, other public ministers and consuls, and those *in which a State shall be party, the Supreme Court shall have original jurisdiction. In all the other cases before mentioned, the Supreme Court shall have appellate jurisdiction, both as to law and fact, with such exceptions, and under such regulations as the Congress shall make.*

The trial of all crimes, except in cases of impeachment, shall be by jury; and such trial shall be held in the State where the said crimes shall have been committed; but when not committed within any State, the trial shall be at such place or places as the Congress may by law have directed.

*Section 3.—*Treason against the United States shall consist only in levying war against them, or in adhering to their enemies, giving them aid and comfort. No person shall be convicted of treason unless on the testimony of two witnesses to the same overt act, or on confession in open court.

The Congress shall have power to declare the punishment of treason, but no attainder of treason shall work corruption of blood, or forfeiture except during the life of the person attainted.

[1] Cf. Amendment XI.

ARTICLE IV

Section 1.—Full faith and credit shall be given in each State to the public acts, records, and judicial proceedings of every other State. And the Congress may by general laws prescribe the manner in which such acts, records, and proceedings shall be proved, and the effect thereof.

Section 2.—The citizens of each State shall be entitled to all privileges and immunities of citizens in the several States.

A person charged in any State with treason, felony, or other crime, who shall flee from justice, and be found in another State, shall on demand of the executive authority of the State from which he fled, be delivered up, to be removed to the State having jurisdiction of the crime.

No person held to service or labour in one State, under the laws thereof, escaping into another, shall in consequence of any law or regulation therein, be discharged from such service or labour, but shall be delivered up on claim of the party to whom such service or labour may be due.

Section 3.—*New States may be admitted by the Congress into this Union; but no new State shall be formed or erected within the jurisdiction of any other State, nor any State be formed by the junction of two or more States, or parts of States, without the consent of the legislatures of the States concerned as well as of the Congress.*

The Congress shall have power to dispose of and make all needful rules and regulations respecting the territory or other property belonging to the United States; and nothing in this Constitution shall be so construed as to prejudice any claims of the United States, or of any particular State.

Section 4.—*The United States shall guarantee to every State in this Union a Republican form of government,* and shall protect each of them against invasion; and on application of the legislature, or of the executive (when the legislature cannot be convened) against domestic violence.

ARTICLE V

The Congress, whenever two-thirds of both Houses, shall deem it necessary, shall propose amendments to this Constitution, or, on the application of the legislatures of two-thirds of the several States, shall call a convention for proposing amendments, which, in either case, shall be valid to all intents and purposes, as part of this Constitution, when ratified by the legislatures of three-fourths of the several States, or by conventions in three-fourths thereof, as the one or the other mode of ratification may be proposed by the Congress; provided that no amendment which may be made prior to the year one thousand eight hundred and eight shall in any manner affect the first and fourth clauses in the ninth section of the first article; and *that no State, without its consent, shall be deprived of its equal suffrage in the Senate.*

ARTICLE VI

All debts contracted and engagements entered into, before the adoption of this Constitution, shall be as valid against the United States under this Constitution, as under the Confederation.

This Constitution, and the laws of the United States which shall be made in pursuance thereof; and all treaties made, or which shall be made, under the authority of the United States, shall be the supreme law of the land; and the judges in every State shall be bound thereby, any thing in the Constitution or laws of any State to the contrary notwithstanding.

The Senators and Representatives before mentioned, and the members of the several State legislatures, and all executive and judicial officers, both of the United States and of the several States, shall be bound by oath or affirmation, to support this Constitution; *but no religious test shall ever be required as a qualification to any office or public trust under the United States.*

ARTICLE VII

The ratification of the conventions of nine States shall be sufficient for the establishment of this Constitution between the States so ratifying the same.

AMENDMENTS[1]

ARTICLES in addition to and amendment of the Constitution of the United States of America, proposed by Congress, and ratified by the legislatures of the several States, pursuant to the fifth article of the original Constitution.

[1] The date of the adoption of each amendment has been inserted in brackets.

Article I (1791)

Congress shall make no law respecting an establishment of religion, or prohibiting the free exercise thereof; or abridging the freedom of speech, or of the Press; or the right of the people peaceably to assemble, and to petition the government for a redress of grievances.

Article II (1791)

A well-regulated militia being necessary to the security of a free State, *the rights of the people to keep and bear arms shall not be infringed.*

Article III (1791)

No soldier shall, in time of peace, be quartered in any house without the consent of the owner, nor in time of war, but in a manner to be prescribed by law.

Article IV (1791)

The right of the people to be secure in their persons, houses, papers, and effects, against unreasonable searches and seizures, shall not be violated, and no warrants shall issue, but upon probable cause, supported by oath or affirmation, and particularly describing the place to be searched, and the persons or things to be seized.

Article V (1791)

No person shall be held to answer for a capital, or otherwise infamous crime, unless on a presentment or indictment of a grand jury, except in cases arising in the land or naval forces, or in the militia, when in actual service in time of war or public danger; nor shall any person be subject for the same offence to be twice put in jeopardy of life or limb; nor shall be compelled in any criminal case to be a witness against himself, *nor be deprived of life, liberty, or property, without due process of law;* nor shall private property be taken for public use, without just compensation.[1]

[1] Cf. Amendment XIV.

The Bill of Rights

ARTICLE VI (1791)

In all criminal prosecutions the accused shall enjoy the right to a speedy and public trial, by an impartial jury of the State and district wherein the crime shall have been committed, which district shall have been previously ascertained by law, and to be informed of the nature and cause of the accusation; to be confronted with the witnesses against him; to have compulsory process for obtaining witnesses in his favour, and to have the assistance of counsel for his defence.

ARTICLE VII (1791)

In suits at common law, where the value in controversy shall exceed twenty dollars, the right of trial by jury shall be preserved, and no fact tried by a jury shall be otherwise re-examined in any court of the United States, than according to the rules of the common law.

ARTICLE VIII (1791)

Excessive bail shall not be required, nor excessive fines imposed, *nor cruel and unusual punishments inflicted.*

ARTICLE IX (1791)

The enumeration in the Constitution of certain rights shall not be construed to deny or disparage others retained by the people.

ARTICLE X (1791)

The powers not delegated to the United States by the Constitution, nor prohibited by it to the States, are reserved to the States respectively or to the people.

ARTICLE XI (1798)

The judicial power of the United States shall not be construed to extend to any suit or equity, commenced or prosecuted against one of the United States by citizens of another State, or by citizens or subjects of any foreign State.

The Bill of Rights

ARTICLE XII (1804)

The electors shall meet in their respective States, and vote by ballot for President and Vice-President, one of whom, at least, shall not be an inhabitant of the same State with themselves; they shall name in their ballots the person voted for as President, and in distinct ballots the person voted for as Vice-President, and they shall make distinct lists of all persons voted for as President, and of all persons voted for as Vice-President, and of the number of votes for each, which lists they shall sign and certify, and transmit sealed to the seat of the government of the United States, directed to the President of the Senate; the President of the Senate shall, in the presence of the Senate and House of Representatives, open all the certificates and the votes shall then be counted; *the person having the greatest number of votes for President, shall be the President, if such number be a majority of the whole number of electors appointed; and if no person have such majority then from the persons having the highest numbers not exceeding three on the list of those voted for as President, the House of Representatives shall choose immediately by ballot, the President. But in choosing the President, the votes shall be taken by States, the representation from each State having one vote; a quorum for this purpose shall consist of a member or members from two-thirds of the States, and a majority of all the States shall be necessary to a choice. And if the House of Representatives shall not choose a President whenever the right of choice shall devolve upon them,* before the 4th day of March next following, *then the Vice-President shall act as President,* as in the case of the death or other constitutional disability of the President. The person having the greatest number of votes as Vice-President, shall be the Vice-President, if such number be a majority of the whole number of electors appointed, *and if no person have a majority, then from the two highest numbers on the list, the Senate shall choose the Vice-President; a quorum for the purpose shall consist of two-thirds of the whole number of Senators, and a majority of the whole number shall be necessary to a choice. But no person constitutionally ineligible to the office of President shall be eligible to that of Vice-President of the United States.*[1]

[1] Cf. Amendment XX.

ARTICLE XIII (1865)

Section 1.—Neither slavery nor involuntary servitude, except as a punishment for crime whereof the party shall have been duly convicted, shall exist within the United States, or any place subject to their jurisdiction.

Section 2.—Congress shall have power to enforce this article by appropriate legislation.

ARTICLE XIV (1868)

Section 1.—All persons born or naturalized in the United States, and subject to the jurisdiction thereof, are citizens of the United States and of the State wherein they reside. *No State shall make or enforce any law which shall abridge the privileges or immunities of citizens of the United States; nor shall any State deprive any person of life, liberty, or property, without due process of law; nor deny to any person within its jurisdiction the equal protection of the laws.*

Section 2.—*Representatives shall be apportioned among the several States according to their respective numbers, counting the whole number of persons in each State, excluding Indians not taxed. But when the right to vote at any election for the choice of electors for President and Vice-President of the United States, Representatives in Congress,* the executive and judicial officers of a State, or the members of the Legislature thereof, *is denied to any of the male inhabitants of such State, being twenty-one years of age and citizens of the United States, or in any way abridged except for participation in rebellion, or other crime, the basis of representation therein shall be reduced in the proportion which the number of such male citizens shall bear to the whole number of male citizens twenty-one years of age in such State.*[1]

Section 3.—No person shall be a Senator or Representative in Congress, or elector of President and Vice-President, or hold any office, civil or military, under the United States, or under any State, who, having previously taken an oath, as a member of Congress, or as an officer of the United States, or as a member of any State legislature, or as an executive or judicial officer of any State, to support the Constitution of the United States, shall have engaged in insurrection or rebellion against the same, or given aid or comfort to the

[1] Cf. Amendment XIX.

enemies thereof. But Congress may by vote of two-thirds of each house remove such disability.

Section 4.—The validity of the public debt of the United States, authorized by law, including debts incurred for payment of pensions and bounties for services in suppressing insurrection or rebellion, shall not be questioned. But neither the United States nor any States shall assume or pay any debt or obligation incurred in aid of insurrection or rebellion against the United States, or any claim for the loss or emancipation of any slave; but all such debts, obligations, and claims shall be held illegal and void.

Section 5.—*The Congress shall have power to enforce, by appropriate legislation, the provisions of this article.*

ARTICLE XV (1870)

Section 1.—*The right of citizens of the United States to vote shall not be denied or abridged by the United States or by any State on account of race, colour, or previous condition of servitude.*

Sections 2.—*The Congress shall have power to enforce this article by appropriate legislation.*

ARTICLE XVI (1913)

The Congress shall have power to lay and collect taxes on incomes, from whatever source derived, without apportionment among the several States, and without regard to any census or enumeration.

ARTICLE XVII (1913)

The Senate of the United States shall be composed of two Senators from each State, elected by the people thereof for six years; and each Senator shall have one vote. The electors in each State shall have the qualifications requisite for electors of the most numerous branch of the State legislatures.

When vacancies happen in the representation of any State in the Senate, the executive authority of such State shall issue writs of election to fill such vacancies: *Provided,* That the legislature of any State may empower the executive thereof to make temporary appointment until the people fill the vacancies by election as the legislature may direct.

This amendment shall not be so construed as to affect the election or term of any Senator chosen before it becomes valid as part of the Constitution.

ARTICLE XVIII (1918)

Section 1.—After one year from the ratification of this article, *the manufacture, sale, or transportation of intoxicating liquors within, the importation thereof into, or the exportation thereof from, the United States and all territory subject to the jurisdiction thereof, for beverage purposes, is hereby prohibited.*

Section 2.—*The Congress and the several States shall have concurrent power to enforce this article by appropriate legislation.*

Section 3.—This article shall be inoperative unless it shall have been ratified as an amendment to the Constitution by the legislatures of the several States, as provided in the Constitution, within seven years from the date of the submission thereof to the States by the Congress.

ARTICLE XIX (1920)

Section 1.—*The right of citizens of the United States to vote shall not be abridged by the United States or by any state on account of sex.*

Section 2.—*Congress shall have power to enforce this article by appropriate legislation.*

ARTICLE XX (1933)

Section 1.—*The terms of President and Vice-President shall end at noon of the 20th day of January and the terms of Senators and Representatives at noon on the 3rd day of January,* of the years in which such terms would have ended if this article had not been ratified; and the terms of their successors shall then begin.

Section 2.—The Congress shall assemble at least once in every year, *and such meeting shall begin at noon on the 3rd day of January* unless they shall by law appoint a different day.

Section 3.—If, at the time fixed for the beginning of the term of the President, the President-elect shall have died, the Vice-President-elect shall become President. If a President shall not have been chosen before the time fixed for the beginning of his term or if the President-elect shall have failed to qualify, then the Vice-President-elect shall act as President until a President shall have qualified; and the Congress may by law provide for the case wherein neither a President-elect nor a Vice-President-elect shall have qualified, declaring who shall then act as President, or the manner in which one who is to act shall be selected, and such person shall act accordingly until a President or Vice-President shall have qualified.

Section 4.—The Congress may by law provide for the case of the death of any of the persons from whom the House of Representatives may choose a President whenever the right of choice shall have devolved upon them, and for the case of the death of any of the persons from whom the Senate may choose a Vice-President whenever the right of choice shall have devolved upon them.

Section 5.—Sections 1 and 2 shall take effect on the 15th day of October following the ratification of this article, [i.e. October 15, 1933].

Section 6.—This article shall be inoperative unless it shall have been ratified as an amendment to the Constitution by the Legislatures of three-fourths of the several States within seven years from the date of its submission.

ARTICLE XXI (1933)

Section 1.—The eighteenth article of amendment to the Constitution of the United States is hereby repealed.

Section 2.—The transportation or importation into any State, Territory, or possession of the United States for delivery or use therein of intoxicating liquors, *in violation of the laws thereof*, is hereby prohibited.

Section 3.—This article shall be inoperative unless it shall have been ratified as an amendment to the Constitution *by conventions in the several States*, as provided in the Constitution, within seven years from the date of the submission hereof to the States by Congress.

Article XXII (1951)

No person shall be elected to the office of the President more than twice, and no person who has held the office of President, or acted as President, for more than two years of a term to which some other person was elected President shall be elected to the office of President more than once. But this article shall not apply to any person holding the office of President when this article was proposed by the Congress, and shall not prevent any person who may be holding the office of President or acting as President during the term within which this Article becomes operative from holding the office of President or acting as President during the remainder of such term.[1]

[1] The second part of this amendment was drafted to avoid the charge that the rules were being altered to Mr. Truman's disadvantage while he was still in office. He did not avail himself of the chance to run in 1952 and no one, in the future, can hope for three or even for two terms plus a part of another.

BIBLIOGRAPHY

ADAMS, HENRY, *The Education of Henry Adams* (New York: Houghton Mifflin, 1935).

ADLER, POLLY, *A House Is Not a Home* (New York: Rinehart, 1953).

AGAR, HERBERT, *Price of Union* (New York: Houghton Mifflin, 1950).

ALLEN, R. S. (editor), *Our Fair City* (New York: Vanguard, 1947).

———— (editor), *Our Sovereign State* (New York: Vanguard, 1949).

———— and SHANNON, W. V., *The Truman Merry-go-round* (New York: Vanguard, 1950).

ALSOP, J., and CATLEDGE, T., *The 168 Days* (New York: Doubleday, 1938).

ANDERSON, DEWEY, and DAVIDSON, P. E., *Ballots and the Democratic Class Struggle* (Stanford: Stanford University Press, 1943).

BAILEY, S. K., and SAMUEL, H. D., *Congress at Work* (New York: Henry Holt, 1952).

BAILEY, T. A., *The Man in the Street* (New York: Macmillan, 1948).

BANTA, R. E., *The Ohio* (New York: Rinehart, 1949).

BEAN, L. M., *How To Predict Elections* (New York: Alfred A. Knopf, 1948).

BEAN, WALTON, *Boss Ruef's San Francisco* (Berkeley: University of California Press, 1952).

BEARD, C. A., *The Supreme Court and the Constitution* (New York: Barnes & Noble, 1938).

BELLOC, H., *Sonnets and Verse* (New York: Sheed & Ward, 1945).

BESTOR, A. E., *Backwoods Utopias* (Philadelphia: University of Pennsylvania Press, 1950)

BINKLEY, W. E., *American Political Parties* (New York: Alfred A. Knopf, 1943).

———— *President and Congress* (New York: Alfred A. Knopf, 1947).

BLAKE, N. M., *William Mahone of Virginia* (Richmond: Garret & Massie, 1935).

BLOOM, SOL, *Autobiography* (New York: George P. Putnam, 1948).

BOLLES, BLAIR, *How to Get Rich in Washington* (New York: W. W. Norton, 1952).

BRANT, I., *James Madison, Father of the Constitution* (New York: Bobbs-Merrill, 1950).

BRISSENDEN, F., *The I.W.W.* (New York: Columbia University Press, 1920).

BUCK, PAUL H., *Roads to Reunion* (New York: Little, Brown, 1937).

CALKINS, FAY, *The CIO and the Democratic Party* (Chicago: University of Chicago Press, 1952).

CARDOZO, B. J., *The Nature of the Judicial Process* (New Haven: Yale University Press, 1925).

CARMAN, H. J., and LUTHIN, R. H., *Lincoln and the Patronage* (New York: Columbia University Press, 1943).

CATER, H. D., *Henry Adams and His Friends* (New York: Houghton Mifflin, 1947)

CAYTON, H. R., and DRAKE, ST. CLAIRE, *Black Metropolis* (New York: Harcourt, Brace, 1945).

CHAMBERLAIN, L. H., *President, Congress, and Legislation* (New York: Columbia University Press, 1946).

CHAMBERS, WHITTAKER, *Witness* (New York: Random House, 1952).

CHUGERMAN, S., *Lester F. Ward* (Durham: Duke University Press, 1939).

COCHRAN, T. C., *New York in the Confederation* (Philadelphia: University of Pennsylvania Press, 1932).

COLEMAN, McALISTER, *Eugene V. Debs* (New York: Greenberg, 1930).

COOKE, ALISTAIR, *A Generation on Trial* (New York: Alfred A. Knopf, 1950).

CORWIN, E. S., *The Constitution* (Princeton: Princeton University Press, 1947).

—— *Court Over Constitution* (Princeton: Princeton University Press, 1950).

—— *The President* (New York: New York University Press, 1948).

—— *Total War and the Constitution* (New York: Alfred A. Knopf, 1947).

COULTER, E. M., *A History of the South,* Vol. III (Baton Rouge: Louisiana State University Press, 1950).

COX, J. M., *Journey Through My Years* (New York: Simon & Schuster, 1946).

CRESSON, W. P., *James Monroe* (Chapel Hill: University of North Carolina Press, 1946).

CROLY, H., *Marcus Alonzo Hanna* (New York: Macmillan, 1912).

CROSSKEY, W. W., *Politics and the Constitution* (Chicago: University of Chicago Press, 1953).

CURTIS, CHARLES P., *Lions Under the Throne* (New York: Houghton Mifflin, 1945).

CUSHMAN, R. E., *The Independent Regulatory Commission* (New York: Oxford University Press, 1941).

DANGERFIELD, R. J., *In Defense of the Senate* (Norman: University of Oklahoma, 1933).

DANIELS, J., *Frontier on the Potomac* (New York: Macmillan, 1947).

DAVENPORT, WALTER, *Power and Glory* (New York: George P. Putnam, 1931).

DENNISON, E. E., *The Senate Foreign Relations Committee* (Stanford: Stanford University Press, 1942).

DONALD, DAVID, *Lincoln's Herndon* (New York: Alfred A. Knopf, 1948).

DOUGLAS, PAUL H., *Ethics in Government* (Cambridge: Harvard University Press, 1953).

EBERLING, E. J., *Congressional Investigations* (New York: Columbia University Press, 1928).

ELLIOTT, M. H., *Uncle Sam Ward* (New York: Macmillan, 1938).

EWING, C. A. M., *Presidential Elections* (Norman: University of Oklahoma, 1940).

FAIRMAN, CHARLES, *American Constitutional Decisions* (New York: Henry Holt, 1950).

—— *Mr. Justice Miller and the Supreme Court* (Cambridge: Harvard University Press, 1939).

FARLEY, JAMES A., *Behind the Ballots* (New York: Harcourt, Brace, 1938).

—— *Jim Farley's Story* (New York: McGraw-Hill, 1948).

FLYNN, E. J., *You're the Boss* (New York: Viking Press, 1947).

FLYNN, J. T., *Meet Your Congress* (New York: Doubleday, 1944).

FOSTER, W. Z., *From Bryan to Stalin* (London: Lawrence and Wishart, 1937).

FOX, D. R., *Decline of Aristocracy in the Politics of New York* (New York: Columbia University Press, 1919).

FRANKFURTER, FELIX, *The Commerce Clause* (Chapel Hill: University of North Carolina, 1937).

FREEMAN, JOSEPH, *An American Testament* (New York: Farrar & Rinehart, 1936).

FREIDAL, FRANK, *Franklin D. Roosevelt* (New York: Little, Brown, 1952).

GABRIEL, RALPH, *The Course of American Democratic Thought* (New York: Ronald Press, 1940).

GAER, JOSEPH, *The First Round* (New York: Duell, Sloan & Pearce, 1944).

GALLOWAY, G. B., *Congress at the Crossroads* (New York: Thomas Y. Crowell, 1946).

GARFIELD, JAMES ABRAM, and HINSDALE, B. A., *Garfield-Hinsdale Letters* (Ann Arbor: University of Michigan Press, 1949).

GELLERMANN, W., *Martin Dies* (New York: John Day, 1944).

GITLOW, BENJAMIN, *The Whole of Their Lives* (New York: Charles Scribner's Sons, 1948).

GODSHALL, W. L., *Principles and Functions of Government* (New York: Macmillan, 1948).

GOSNELL, H. F., *Boss Platt* (Chicago: University of Chicago Press, 1924).

GRIFFITH, E. S., *The American System of Government* (London: Methuen, 1954).

———— *Congress* (New York: New York University Press, 1952).

GRISWOLD, A. W., *Farming and Democracy* (New Haven: Yale University Press, 1952).

GRUENING, ERNEST (editor), *These United States* (first series) (New York: Boni & Liveright, 1923).

HAINES, C. G., *American Doctrine of Judicial Supremacy* (Second edition, Berkeley: University of California Press, 1932).

HARRISON, C. H., *Stormy Years* (New York: Bobbs-Merrill, 1935).

HASBROUCK, P. D., *Party Government in the House of Representatives* (New York: Macmillan, 1927).

HAYNES, F. E., *Social Politics in the United States* (New York: Houghton Mifflin, 1924).

HAYNES, G. H., *The Senate of the United States* (New York: Houghton Mifflin, 1938).

HAYWOOD, WILLIAM DUDLEY, *Bill Haywood's Book* (London: Lawrence and Wishart, 1929).

HEARD, A., *A Two-party South* (Chapel Hill: University of North Carolina, 1952).

HICKS, J. D., *The Populist Revolt* (Minneapolis: University of Minnesota Press, 1931).

HOLT, W. S., *Treaties Defeated by the Senate* (Baltimore: Johns Hopkins Press, 1934).

HOOVER, HERBERT, *Memoirs*, Vol. III (New York: Macmillan, 1952).

HOWE, M. D. W., (editor), *Holmes-Pollock Letters,* Vol. I (Cambridge: Harvard University Press, 1941).

HUGHES, RUPERT E., *Attorney for the People* (New York: Houghton Mifflin, 1940).

HUTTON, GRAHAM, *Midwest at Noon* (Chicago: University of Chicago Press, 1946).

ISELEY, J. A., *Horace Greeley* (Princeton: Princeton University Press, 1947).

JAMES, HENRY, *Richard Olney* (New York: Houghton Mifflin, 1923).

JAMESON, J. F., *The American Revolution* (Princeton: Princeton University Press, 1950).

JOHNSON, WALTER, *William Allen White's America* (New York: Henry Holt, 1947).

JOHNSON, W. F., *George Harvey* (New York: Houghton Mifflin, 1929).

KANE, H. T., *Louisiana Hayride* (New York: William Morrow, 1941).

KEFAUVER, ESTES, *Crime in America* (New York: Doubleday, 1951).

———— and LEVIN, J., *A Twentieth-century Congress* (New York: Duell, Sloan & Pearce, 1947).

KELLY, A. H., and HARBISON, W. A., *The American Constitution* (New York: W. W. Norton, 1948).

KENNEDY, JOSEPH P., *I'm for Roosevelt* (New York: Reynal & Hitchcock, 1936) .

KENT, F. R., *The Great Game of Politics* (New York: Doubleday, 1930) .

KEY, V. O., *Politics, Parties, and Pressure Groups* (New York: Thomas Y. Crowell, 1947) .

—— and HEARD, A., *Southern Politics* (New York: Alfred A. Knopf, 1949).

KIPLINGER, W. M., *Washington Is Like That* (New York: Harper & Brothers, 1942) .

LAIT, JACK, and MORTIMER, LEE, *New York Confidential* (New York: Ziff-Davis, 1948) .

LEWINSON, PAUL, *Race, Class and Party* (New York: Oxford University Press, 1932) .

LINDSAY, VACHEL, *Collected Poems* (New York: Macmillan, 1925) .

LINK, A. S., *Woodrow Wilson*, Vol. I (Princeton: Princeton University Press, 1947) .

—— *Woodrow Wilson and the Progressive Era* (New York: Harper & Brothers, 1954) .

LIPPMANN, WALTER, *Supreme Court* (New York: Harper & Brothers, 1937).

LUBELL, S., *Future of American Politics* (New York: Harper & Brothers, 1952) .

MACKAY, K. C., *The Progressive Movement of 1924* (New York: Columbia University Press, 1947) .

MACKAYE, MILTON, *Tinbox Parade* (New York: Robert McBride, 1934) .

McKEAN, D. D., *Pressures on the Legislature of New Jersey* (New York: Columbia University Press, 1938) .

McKENNEY, RUTH, *Industrial Valley* (New York: Harcourt, Brace, 1939) .

MATHEWS, M. M., *A Dictionary of Americanisms on Historical Principles* (Chicago: University of Chicago Press, 1951).

MERRIAM, C. E., *Chicago* (New York: Macmillan, 1929) .

MOON, H. L., *Balance of Power* (New York: Doubleday, 1948) .

MOSCOW, WARREN, *Politics in the Empire State* (New York: Alfred A. Knopf, 1948) .

MOWRY, G. S., *Theodore Roosevelt and the Progressive Movement* (Madison: University of Wisconsin Press, 1946) .

MUZZEY, D. A., *James G. Blaine* (New York: Dodd, Mead, 1934) .

MYRDAL, GUNNAR, *An American Dilemma* (New York: Harper & Brothers, 1944) .

NEVINS, A., *Abram Hewitt* (New York: Harper & Brothers, 1935) .

—— *Emergence of Lincoln* (New York: Charles Scribner's Sons, 1950) .

NICHOLS, R. F., *Disruption of American Democracy* (New York: Macmillan, 1948) .

ODUM, H. W., *Race and Rumors of Race* (Chapel Hill: University of North Carolina Press, 1943) .

—— *Southern Regions* (Chapel Hill: University of North Carolina Press, 1937) .

OGDEN, A. R., *The Dies Committee* (Washington, D. C.: Catholic University of America Press, 1943) .

OGG, F. A., and RAY, P. ORMAN, *Essentials of American Government* (New York: Appleton-Century-Crofts, 1952) .

ONEAL, J., and WARNER, S. A., *American Communism* (New York: E. P. Dutton, 1947) .

OTTLEY, ROI, *New World A-Coming* (New York: Houghton Mifflin, 1943) .

PAULEY, K. B., *Bricker of Ohio* (New York: George P. Putnam, 1944) .

PEARSON, C. C., *Readjuster Movement in Virginia* (New Haven: Yale University Press, 1917) .

PEEL, R. V., *The Political Clubs of New York City* (New York: G. P. Putnam, 1935).

PERKINS, FRANCES, *The Roosevelt I Knew* (New York: Viking Press, 1946).

PERLMAN, S., and TAFT, P., *Labor Movements (History of Labor in the United States*, Vol. IV) (New York: Macmillan, 1935).

POLLARD, J. E., *The Presidents and the Press* (New York: Macmillan, 1947).

PRINGLE, H. F., *The Life and Times of William Howard Taft* (New York: Farrar & Rinehart, 1939).

PRITCHETT, C. H., *The Roosevelt Court* (New York: Macmillan, 1948).

PUSEY, MERLO, *Big Government* (New York: Harper & Brothers, 1945).

—— *Charles Evans Hughes* (New York: Macmillan, 1951).

REYNOLDS, G. M., *Machine Politics in New Orleans* (New York: Columbia University Press, 1936).

RICHARDSON, L. B., *W. E. Chandler, Republican* (New York: Dodd, Mead, 1940).

RIDDICK, FLOYD M., *The United States Congress* (Manassas: National Capitol, 1949).

ROBINSON, W. A., *Thomas B. Reed* (New York: Dodd, Mead, 1930).

RODELL, FRED, *Fifty-five Men* (Harrisburg: The Telegraph Press, 1936).

ROSTEN, LEO C., *The Washington Correspondents* (New York: Harcourt, Brace, 1937).

SAIT, E. M., *American Parties and Elections* (New York: Appleton-Century, 1942).

—— *American Politics* (H. R. Penniman, editor, fifth edition) (New York: Appleton-Century-Crofts, 1952).

SALOUTOS, T. and HICKS, J. D., *Agrarian Discontent in the Middle West* (Madison: Wisconsin University Press, 1951).

SALTER, T., *The American Politician* (Chapel Hill: University of North Carolina Press, 1938).

SANDBURG, CARL, *Always the Young Strangers* (New York: Harcourt, Brace, 1953).

SHELDON, W. D., *Populism in the Old Dominion* (Princeton: Princeton University Press, 1936).

SIMKINS, F. B., *Tillman Movement in South Carolina* (Durham: Duke University Press, 1926).

SMITH, E. C., and ZURCHER, A. J., *New Dictionary of American Politics* (New York: Barnes & Noble, 1949).

STEFFENS, LINCOLN, *Autobiography* (New York: Harcourt, Brace, 1931).

STEIN, C. W., *Third-term Tradition* (New York: Columbia University Press, 1943).

STEPHENSON, N. W., *Nelson W. Aldrich* (New York: Charles Scribner's Sons, 1930).

STOKES, T. L., *Chip Off My Shoulder* (Princeton: Princeton University Press, 1940).

SULLIVAN, MARK, *Our Times*, Vol. III (New York: Charles Scribner's Sons, 1930).

SWISHER, C. B., *Growth of Constitutional Power in the United States* (Chicago: University of Chicago Press, 1946).

—— *Roger B. Taney* (New York: Macmillan, 1935).

TAYLOR, P. S., *An American-Mexican Frontier* (Chapel Hill: University of North Carolina Press, 1934).

THOMAS, B. P., *Lincoln* (New York: Alfred A. Knopf, 1952).

TRENHOLME, L. I., *The Ratification of the Federal Constitution in North Carolina* (New York: Columbia University Press, 1932).

TRIMBLE, B. R., *Chief Justice Waite* (Princeton: Princeton University Press, 1938).

Turkus, B. B., *Murder Inc.* (New York: Farrar, Straus & Young, 1951).

Vandenberg, Arthur H., Jr., and Morris, J. A., (editors), *Private Papers of Senator Vandenberg* (New York: Houghton Mifflin, 1953).

Warner, W. L., and Lunt, P. S., *Status System of a Modern Community* (New Haven: Yale University Press, 1942).

Wehle, L. B., *Hidden Threads of History* (New York: Macmillan, 1953).

White, L. D., *The Federalists* (New York: Macmillan, 1948).

Williams, M., *Shadow of the Pope* (New York: McGraw-Hill, 1932).

Willoughby, W. W., *Constitutional Law of the United States* (New York: Baker Voorhis, 1910).

Woodward, C. V., *Reunion and Reaction* (New York: Alfred A. Knopf, 1951).

Yoshpe, H. B., *Disposition of Loyalist Estates in the Southern District of the State of New York* (New York: Columbia University Press, 1939).

INDEX